Linking Enterprise Data

David Wood

Editor

Linking Enterprise Data

 Springer

Editor
David Wood
3 Round Stones LLC
22408 Fredericksburg Virginia
USA
david@3roundstones.com

ISBN 978-1-4419-7664-2   e-ISBN 978-1-4419-7665-9
DOI 10.1007/978-1-4419-7665-9
Springer New York Dordrecht Heidelberg London

Printed on acid-free paper

Springer is part of Springer Science+Business Media (www.springer.com)

"All problems in computer science can be solved by another layer of indirection, but that will usually create another problem."
David John Wheeler (1927 - 2004)

Preface

Linking Enterprise Data is a new concept, based on an idea more than twenty years old. Tim Berners-Lee's original proposal for the World Wide Web in March 1989 was based on a system of linked information systems. The early Web was intended to interlink information from various systems to solve organizational problems, such as the high turnover of people and the restriction of information to data silos. The hope was to create a distributed information system that would allow "a pool of information to develop which could grow and evolve with the organisation and the projects it describes."

The Web has grown into the world's largest information system. By 2000, Web architecture had been dissected and described by Roy Fielding. Representational State Transfer (REST) was Roy's answer to why the Web worked so well. In a world plagued by software problems, machine crashes, and network outages, the Web never fails. The Web is robust and resilient to change. The Web survives changing machinery, operating system updates, changes in the way we structure index and find information. No other software system provides the features and functions of World Wide Web.

Linked Data techniques have become interesting to organizations of every shape and size. The Linked Open Data (LOD) project began as a community effort of the World Wide Web Consortium's Semantic Web Education and Outreach Group. The project has begun to turn the document-oriented Web into a database of global proportions. The ability of the modern Web to deal with both documents and data have shaped a general solution for information dissemination and integration. The time for linking enterprise data has come.

This book records some of the earliest production applications of linking enterprise data. Parts of it serve as a roadmap for those seeking to replicate their successes. Part I of this book attempts to answer the question why enterprise data should be linked. The chapters in Part I provide valuable guidance to those writing business cases, for those needing to justify internal development efforts, or for those writing requests for proposals to external vendors. Dean Allemang discusses why enterprises must adopt Web techniques for data integration and provides such techniques fit into enterprise systems. Dean makes a strong case that enterprises must change the way they approach information technology systems. Indeed, since information systems have such a profound impact on the operational aspects of a business, he makes the case that enterprises need to change the way they approach their operations.

Edward Curry, Andre Freitas, and Sean O'Riain discuss the role of community-based data curation. Enterprises have become more distributed, less centrally managed and less integrated in their systems. The lessons Ed and his colleagues have captured from real-world attempts to curate distributed data for the purposes of ensuring data quality will apply to many enterprises. They provide some important best practices extracted from early adopters of Linked Data techniques.

Part II is short, but critically important. Part II provides material assistance for business managers seeking to propose Linked Data projects. Bernadette Hyland discusses the characteristics of enterprises ready to take on Linked Data projects and provides useful fodder for business cases. Her simple guidelines for getting a Linked Data project started have generally been lacking in the public discussion to date. Kristen Harris' real-world experiences creating and managing the swoRDFish project at Sun Microsystems demonstrated the potential of linked enterprise data to integrate disparate systems in large enterprises. She provides guidance for the navigation of corporate management to approve and support projects with far-reaching infrastructural ramifications.

The techniques of Linked Data can be subtle and technical, although not out of reach for those with traditional enterprise skills. Part III provides three explanatory chapters that address different technical aspects of linking data. Alexandre Passant, Philippe Laublet, John G. Breslin and Stefan Decker present ways to integrate enterprise social networking solutions such as wikis and blogs. Initial enterprise adoption of new technologies can sometimes create new problems. Alexandre and his co-authors offer both insight and solutions to the integration of Web 2.0 and Web 3.0 techniques.

Roberto Garcia and Rosa Gil demonstrate how the translation of existing data sources may be brought to the Web of data. Reza B'Far and I offer technical approaches to enterprise problems of scale. Reza addresses logical reasoning techniques for enterprise-scale data and I present ways to ensure the long-term viability of Linked Data identifiers.

Part IV provides five success stories from the front line of enterprise adoption. Each story highlights a different aspect of Linked Data in an enterprise context. Thomas Baker and Johannes Keizer address standards for highly distributed operations developed for the Food and Agriculture Organization of the United Nations. Steve Harris, Tom Ilube and Mischa Tuffield show how Linked Data techniques are used as the basis for their Web-scale company, Garlik. Constantine Hondros of publisher Wolters Kluwer illustrates and presents several approaches for solving integration problems of textual content. Chimezie Ogbuji develops a new enterprise system using a Linked Data approach and Yves Raimond, Tom Scott, Silver Oliver, Patrick Sinclair and Michael Smethurst of the British Broadcasting Corporation present their innovative corporate treatment of the Web itself as their content management system.

We have been able to draw some tentative conclusions regarding success criteria for Linked Data projects in an enterprise. First and foremost may be from Jeff Pollock of Oracle Corporation when he said, "If information systems are to keep up with business, we need to change more than technology - we need to change how people deal with technology." Linked Data techniques offer us a means to do just that; we can radically change the interfaces to our existing systems while we build upon them. We can wrap and expose our silos in order to layer a Web-like distributed system over them.

Secondly, the lessons of the Web clearly apply to enterprises. The Web works for some very good, and very explainable, reasons. Those reasons transcend Representational State Transfer (REST), the architectural principles that underlay the idealized Web, and add the techniques of the Semantic Web, especially that subset being used by the Linked Data community. Individual technologies, though, are clearly less important than techniques that have proven their worth. Technologies continue to evolve; good techniques are more resilient and worth building upon.

Note how different the organizations in the success stories are from one another! A broadcasting company, a publishing company, a healthcare provider, a data security firm, an international policy organization. Other chapters referenced other types of organizations, including a utility company and library organizations. If Linked Data techniques work for all of them, those techniques are very likely to apply to others.

All of our success stories have some interesting commonalities: At least one expert in Semantic Web techniques was used by each organization. Each attacked a significant business problem instead of relying on the technologies to "sell themselves". Each leveraged significant existing investments, especially those with captured or implied semantics. Every success relied upon universal addressing of resources via the Web's Uniform Resource Indicator (URI) scheme.

There were also some major differences between the success stories. Those differences define tools and techniques that are more situationally dependent. The most noteworthy is that very different degrees of data modeling were employed. Complete, top-down data modeling is expensive, difficult and should be undertaken only where it provides value. Specific technologies to describe data (OWL, SKOS, RDF serialization formats) varied widely, as did the use of the SPARQL query language.

Trust may be a larger issue in intra-business data than it is on the general Web if business decisions are being made based on the information. Issues of trust in large organizations may be facilitated by social considerations, e.g. via signing of work, taking credit for additions or edits, tying comments to logins. Many of today's enterprises are large and distributed enough to make use of Web techniques for building and maintaining trust socially over a technical framework.

The four parts of this book are presented hierarchically, like most books in the last 2300 years of Western tradition. The material in this book should not be thought of as a hierarchy, but rather like a graph, like the Web itself. All of the chapters in this book contain nuggets of information useful to enterprise professionals looking to apply Linked Data techniques. The opening chapters do address technology and success stories as well as laying and conceptual foundation. The technique chapters reference success stories of their own. The chapters addressing success stories are chock full of lessons learned in relation to management, approach and style. It is no more possible to fit these chapters into a strict hierarchy than it is to do so with content on the Web. Readers are encouraged to troll the index and review the notes at the beginning of each Part to find the information most relevant to themselves.

The enterprise application of Web architecture to business problems is in its infancy. We hope that this book can be used to assist those managers, data professionals and developers at the forefront of solving today's formidable enterprise data challenges.

Observant readers may notice that any given chapter may use either American and British spelling. The use of mixed spelling systems represents the international nature of the contributing authors and, indeed, the international range of Linked Data research and deployment. We consider such diversity to be a feature, not a bug.

Nigam Shah of the National Center for Biomedical Ontology provided reviews and commentary on this book's contents, as did most of the individual chapter authors. Ivan Herman of the W3C and Eric Miller and Uche Ogbuji of Zepheira provided introductions to prospective authors and suggested content. Our editors at Springer, Susan Lagerstrom-Fife and Jennifer Maurer helped to make the creation of this book much easier than it could have been. Thank you to all.

Fredericksburg, Virginia, USA,   *David Wood*
                                                                                         June 2010

Contents

Part II Approval and Support of Linked Data Projects

Preparing for a Linked Data Enterprise   51
Bernadette Hyland

Selling and Building Linked Data: Drive Value and Gain Momentum   65
Kristen Harris

List of Contributors

Dean Allemang
TopQuadrant, Inc., 330 John Carlyle Street, Suite 180, Alexandria, VA 22314-5760, USA, e-mail: dallemang@topquadrant.com

Thomas Baker
Washington DC, USA, e-mail: tbaker@tbaker.de

Reza B'Far
Oracle Corporation, 500 Oracle Parkway, Redwood Shores, CA 94065, USA, e-mail: reza.bfar@oracle.com

John G. Breslin
Digital Enterprise Research Institute, National University of Ireland, Galway, IDA Business Park, Lower Dangan, Galway, Ireland, e-mail: john.breslin@deri.org and Department of Electronic Engineering, National University of Ireland, Galway, Galway, Ireland, e-mail: john.breslin@nuigalway.ie

Edward Curry
Digital Enterprise Research Institute, National University of Ireland, Galway, IDA Business Park, Lower Dangan, Galway, Ireland, e-mail: ed.curry@deri.org

Stefan Decker
Digital Enterprise Research Institute, National University of Ireland, Galway, IDA Business Park, Lower Dangan, Galway, Ireland, e-mail: stefan.decker@deri.org

Andre Freitas
Digital Enterprise Research Institute, National University of Ireland, Galway, IDA Business Park, Lower Dangan, Galway, Ireland, e-mail: andre.freitas@deri.org

Roberto Garcia
Universitat de Lleida. Jaume II, 69. 25001 Lleida, Spain, e-mail:

`rgarcia@diei.udl.cat`

Rosa Gil
Universitat de Lleida. Jaume II, 69. 25001 Lleida, Spain, e-mail:
`rgil@diei.udl.cat`

Kristen Harris
Oracle Corporation, 500 Oracle Parkway, Redwood Shores, CA 94065, USA,
e-mail: `kristen.harris@oracle.com`

Steve Harris
Garlik Ltd, 1-3 Halford Road, London TW10 6AW, United Kingdom, e-mail:
`steve.harris@garlik.com`

Constantine Hondros
Wolters Kluwer, Zuidpoolsingel 2, 2408 ZE Alphen aan den Rijn, The Netherlands,
e-mail: `Constantine.Hondros@wolterskluwer.com`

Bernadette Hyland
3 Round Stones Inc., Fredericksburg, VA 22408, USA, e-mail:
`bernadette.hyland@3roundstones.com`

Tom Ilube
Garlik Ltd, 1-3 Halford Road, London TW10 6AW, United Kingdom, e-mail:
`tom.ilube@garlik.com`

Johannes Keizer
FAO, Viale delle Terme di Caracalla, 00153 Rome, Italy, e-mail:
`Johannes.Keizer@fao.org`

Philippe Laublet
STIH (Sens - Texte - Informatique - Histoire), Universit Paris-Sorbonne, 28 rue Serpente, 75006 Paris, France, e-mail: `philippelaublet@paris-sorbonne.`
`fr`

Chimezie Ogbuji
Cleveland Clinic, 9500 Euclid Ave. Cleveland OH 44195, USA, e-mail:
`ogbujic@ccf.org`

Silver Oliver
British Broadcasting Corporation, Broadcasting House, Portland Place, London,
United Kingdom, e-mail: `silver.oliver@@bbc.co.uk`

Sean O'Riain
Digital Enterprise Research Institute, National University of Ireland,
Galway, IDA Business Park, Lower Dangan, Galway, Ireland, e-mail:
`sean.oriain@deri.org`

Alexandre Passant
Digital Enterprise Research Institute, National University of Ireland,
Galway, IDA Business Park, Lower Dangan, Galway, Ireland, e-mail:

`alexandre.passant@deri.org`

Yves Raimond
British Broadcasting Corporation, Broadcasting House, Portland Place, London,
United Kingdom, e-mail: `yves.raimond@@bbc.co.uk`

Tom Scott
British Broadcasting Corporation, Broadcasting House, Portland Place, London,
United Kingdom, e-mail: `tom.scott@@bbc.co.uk`

Patrick Sinclair
British Broadcasting Corporation, Broadcasting House, Portland Place, London,
United Kingdom, e-mail: `patrick.sinclair@@bbc.co.uk`

Michael Smethurst
British Broadcasting Corporation, Broadcasting House, Portland Place, London,
United Kingdom, e-mail: `michael.smethurst@@bbc.co.uk`

Mischa Tuffield
Garlik Ltd, 1-3 Halford Road, London TW10 6AW, United Kingdom, e-mail:
`mischa.tuffield@garlik.com`

David Wood
3 Round Stones Inc., Fredericksburg, VA 22408, USA, e-mail:
`david.wood@3roundstones.com`

Acronyms

API   Application Programmer Interface: An abstraction implemented in software that defines how others should make use of a software package such as a library or other reusable program.

BPEL   Web Services Business Process Execution Language: An executable software language for defining interactions with Web Services. A standard of the Organization for the Advancement of Structured Information Standards (OASIS).

BPMS   Business Process Management System or Suite: Enterprise software purporting to assist a business to align with its customers' needs. BPMS systems may be composed of a rules engine to encode business processes, analytics, content management and collaboration tools.

BI   Business Intelligence: Enterprise software approaches to finding and analyzing critical information in information silos, especially information related to important business functions such as sales figures.

D2RQ   Database to RDF Queueing: A mechanism to query information in traditional management systems such as relational databases via the SPARQL query language. D2RQ may refer to the language definition or the Open Source Software project.

DAG   Directed Acyclic Graph: A directed graph (like RDF) with the additional restriction that no loops or cycles are permitted. A cycle is a path from a given node that would allow one to find their way back to the starting node.

DC   Dublin Core Element Set: A vocabulary of fifteen properties for use in resource descriptions, such as may be found in a library card catalog (author, publisher, etc). The most commonly used vocabulary for Semantic Web applications.

DCMI   Dublin Core Metadata Initiative: An open international organization engaged in the development of interoperable metadata standards, including the Dublin Core Element Set.

DNS   Domain Name System: The Internet's mechanism for mapping between a
       human-readable host name (e.g. www.example.com) and an Internet Pro-
       tocol (IP) Address (e.g. 203.20.51.10).
DOI   Digital Object Identifier. A persistent identifier scheme used mostly in the
       publishing market. Compare with PURLs.
DTD   Document Type Definition: A type of schema for defining a markup lan-
       guage, such as in XML or HTML (or their predecessor SGML).
EDGAR The Electronic Data-Gathering, Analysis, and Retrieval system of the
       the U.S. Securities and Exchange Commission: An online service provid-
       ing access to filings by public corporations, such as company registration,
       sales figures or annual reports.
ERP   Enterprise Resource Planning (system): An integrated suite of software
       products that serve many or all enterprise departments.
FLOSS Free/Libre/Open Source Software. A generic and internationalized term
       for software released under an Open Source license.
FOAF   Friend of a Friend: A Semantic Web vocabulary describing people and
       their relationships for use in resource descriptions.
GRDDL Gleaning Resource Descriptions from Dialects of Languages: A mecha-
       nism for extracting Semantic Web data in RDF from XML formats using
       transformations identified by URIs and typically expressed in XSLT.
HTML   Hypertext Markup Language: The predominant markup language for hy-
       pertext pages on the Web. HTML defines the structure of Web pages. A
       family of W3C standards.
HTTP   Hypertext Transfer Protocol: The standard transmission protocol used on
       the World Wide Web to transfer hypertext requests and information be-
       tween Web servers and Web clients (such as browsers). An IETF standard.
IETF   Internet Engineering Task Force: An open international community con-
       cerned with the evolution of Internet architecture and the operation of the
       Internet. Defines standards such as HTTP and DNS.
ISO   International Standards Organization: A network of the national standards
       institutes of 162 countries that cooperate to define international standards.
       Defines many standards including in the context of this book formats for
       dates and currency.
LED   Linking Enterprise Data: The use of tools and techniques of the Semantic
       Web to connect, expose and use data from enterprise systems.
LOD   Linked Open Data: An open community project to interlink data on the
       Semantic Web using URIs and RDF.
LSID   Life Sciences Identifier. A persistent identifier scheme for the life sci-
       ences, mostly overtaken by PURLs.
MDM   Master Data Management: A set of processes and tools that attempts to
       consistently define and manage an enterprise's non-transactional data en-
       tities.
N3   Notation 3: An RDF syntax intended to be readable by humans.
ODP   Open Directory Project, a community effort to collect, tag and organize
       information on the World Wide Web.

OLAP   Online Analytical Processing: An approach to answering multi-dimensional analytical queries using specialized databases. OLAP is considered part of BI.

OWL   Web Ontology Language: A family of knowledge representation and vocabulary description languages for authoring ontologies, based on RDF and standardized by the W3C. Standardized variants include OWL Full, OWL DL (for "description logic") and OWL Lite.

PICS   Platform for Internet Content Selection: An older W3C standard for associating metadata with Web resources. PICS has been superseded by the Protocol for Web Description Resources (POWDER) that is based on RDF.

PURL   Persistent Uniform Resource Locator: A persistent identifier for Web-based information resources that is protected from change with time. PURLs are URLs and generally use HTTP redirection to resolve a persistent address to a currently valid one.

RDF   Resource Description Framework: An international standard for data interchange on the Web. A W3C standard.

RDFa   Resource Description Framework Attributes: An RDF syntax encoded in HTML documents. A W3C standard.

RDFS   Resource Description Framework Schema: The simplest RDF vocabulary description language that provides much less descriptive capability than SKOS or OWL. A W3C standard.

RDF/XML   Resource Description Framework eXtensible Markup Language serialization format: An RDF syntax encoded in XML. A W3C standard.

RELAX NG   Regular Language Description for XML, Next Generation: A simple schema language for XML. An ISO standard.

REST   Representational State Transfer: An architectural style for information systems used to greater or lessor degree on the Web and explains some of the Web's key features, such as extreme scalability and robustness to change.

RFC   Request for Comments: A document submitted to the IETF. Internet standards started as RFCs and are often referenced by their RFC numbers.

SKOS   Simple Knowledge Organisation System: A vocabulary description language for RDF designed for representing traditional knowledge organization systems such as enterprise taxonomies in RDF. A W3C standard.

SOA   Service Oriented Architecture: A set of architectural design guidelines used to expose services, often as Web Services.

SOAP   Simple Object Access Protocol: A protocol over HTTP for exchanging structured information in XML to and from Web Services.

SPARQL   SPARQL Protocol and RDF Query Language: A query language for RDF data on the Semantic Web; analogous to the Structured Query Language (SQL) for relational databases. A W3C standard.

TAG   The Technical Architecture Group of the World Wide Web Consortium.

UDEF   Universal Data Element Framework: A mechanism for building controlled vocabularies describing enterprise data. A project of The Open Group, a standards body.

UPDM   The Unified Profile for DoDAF/MODAF: A modeling standard that supports the USA Department of Defense Architecture Framework (DoDAF) and the UK Ministry of Defence Architecture Framework (MODAF).

URI   Uniform Resource Indicator: A global identifier for the Web standardized by joint action of the W3C and IETF. A URI may or may not be resolvable on the Web (see URL).

URL   Uniform Resource Locator: A global identifier for Web resources standardized by joint action of the W3C and IETF. A URL is resolvable on the Web and is commonly called a "Web address".

UUID   Universally Unique Identifier: A large hexadecimal number that may be calculated by anyone without significant central coordination and used to uniquely identify a resource. A standard of the Open Software Foundation.

W3C   World Wide Web Consortium: An international community that develops standards for the World Wide Web. Defines standards such as HTML, XML and RDF.

WFMS   Workflow Management System: Information systems that define and manage the execution of workflows through the use of a workflow engine.

XBRL   Extensible Business Reporting Language: A mechanism for exchanging business information in XML. A standard of XBRL International.

XHTML   Extensible Hypertext Markup Language: A family of versions of HTML based on XML and standardized by the W3C.

XLINK   XML Linking Language: An extension to XML that provides hyperlinks for XML documents. A W3C standard.

XML   Extensible Markup Language: A specification for creating structured textual computer documents. Many thousands of XML formats exist, including XHTML. A family of standards from the W3C.

XSD   XML Schema: Limitations on the content of an XML document that defines what structural elements are allowed.

XSLT   Extensible Stylesheet Language Transformations: Declarative programs to transform one XML document into another XML document.

According to studies by Robert Steele at the UC Berkeley School of Information Management and Systems[1] and Roger E. Bohn and James E. Short of the Global Information Industry Center at the University of California, San Diego[2], the amount of digital information being produced has been growing exponentially for the past two decades. Enterprise information systems have become stressed and have surpassed the point where they are able to scale effectively. Information critical to business success has thus become harder to find, integrate and use. How can industry regain control over business critical information? We know of only one proven approach: The application of Web architecture to the integration of enterprise systems.

Chapters in this part provide a discussion of the information flood and guidance on how to handle it. Dean Allemang tells us that enterprise technology simply must change. He introduces the concept of the Linked Data enterprise and discusses the foundational approaches that define it. Ed Curry, Andre Freitas and Sean O'Riáin provide us with a guide for some necessary social changes within enterprises, specifically in relation to curation of information.

Both chapters provide examples of Linked Data techniques being applied now. The use cases given in these chapters supplement the success stories of Part IV and help to broaden our understanding of where and why Linked Data techniques apply.

---

[1] Robert David Steele, Information Operations: Putting the "I" Back into DIME, DIANE Publishing, 2006

[2] http://hmi.ucsd.edu/pdf/HMI_2009_ConsumerReport_Dec9_2009.pdf

Semantic Web and the Linked Data Enterprise

Dean Allemang

Abstract Enterprise agility is more important now than ever. An agile enterprise needs to involve a wide variety of stakeholders in its information gathering and management efforts. This results in a number of disconnected data silos. A number of technologies have been applied to this problem, but none have been fully successful in resolving the fundamental enterprise-level issues. The World Wide Web is the only technology that has been proven to be able to scale to an appropriate size to resolve the fundamental enterprise issues. This paper describes the *Linked Data enterprise*, in which Semantic Web technology is used to address the fundamental issues that prevent enterprises from achieving the agility they require.

1 Social Data in the Enterprise

Agility is the name of the game in modern business. While it has always been true that the ability to bring a product to market more quickly than a competitor provides a clear advantage, today's world expects unprecedented high volume of novel products, relying upon complex supply chains, delivered through elaborate distribution channels. These products are delivered to an ever-changing international market, in which regulations somewhere in the world change on a regular basis. New product categories have become the rule rather than the exception. Delicate economic times result in corporate mergers, with a concomitant challenge to make the whole more viable than the sum of the parts. It is no wonder that agility, or the ability for an organization to cope with organizational change, has become the key competitive edge in today's business economy.

At the same time, information has become central to the execution of any business model. Supply chains run on accurate and timely information about availability

Dean Allemang
TopQuadrant Inc., 330 John Carlyle Street, Suite 180, Alexandria, VA 22314-5760, USA e-mail: dallemang@topquadrant.com

D. Wood (ed.), *Linking Enterprise Data*, DOI 10.1007/978-1-4419-7665-9_1,
© Springer Science+Business Media, LLC 2010

and stock. Business development, marketing and sales are all information intensive activities. For many industries, information forms a large part of the business itself. Pharmaceutical research consists to a large extent of information management, ranging from bioinformatics to the statistics of clinical trials. Finance instruments are largely information-based. Publishing has always been an information-based industry, but with the ascendance of electronic media over hardcopy, the business of publishing is even more one of information management. Agility in business often means agility in information systems.

A few decades ago, this would seem to be good news. Software was the most flexible, agile part of any business. Unlike hardware systems, it was easy to change a software system to adapt to new business models or new production processes. But the information load on business has taken its toll; this is no longer the case. It typically takes several months to a year to bring a new data backed system online. With new products coming out every few months, the ability to build the software system to manage a product has become a severe bottleneck.

In 2008, industry leaders in informatics met at the Claremont resort in Berkeley for the 7th conference to evaluate the state of database research and its impact on industry. This is a well-established, three decade old industry that is well entrenched in just about every other industry. The resulting report identifies a number of challenges to enterprise information management, including distribution and volatility. The report even goes so far as to point out that relational database technology, which has been such a mainstay of corporate information management, will require an overhaul to be up to the task.

When relational databases took a central place in information management, it was possible to think of the database as a place where one would go to find all information about the business. The database was a destination, where questions could be answered. Even the name of one of the major database vendors echoes the metaphor of the Oracle of Delphi, who sat high upon a mountain, and to whom Kings and Heroes, CEOs and Entrepreneurs, would make a pilgrimage, seeking answers to important questions.

In today's distributed information landscape, this metaphor no longer holds. We expect information to come to us; to be available on our desktops, on our phones, to travel with us over land and in the air. The Web has made us grow accustomed to having a wide variety of sources at our fingertips. Search engines like Google and Yahoo! let us pick and choose from information sources, each vying for our eyeballs. The days of a single, definitive information destination are over. We expect a web of interconnected information.

The structure of that information is no longer static, no longer under the control of a single information architect. Valuable enterprise assets live on desktops, as spreadsheets, presentations or documents. It has become more and more difficult for an enterprise to even know what information assets it holds, giving rise to a different viewpoint on enterprise information, that goes by the name of Enterprise Architecture.

Enterprise Architecture refers to a description of all the data owned by an enterprise; what role it plays in business process, who owns it, how it is maintained and managed. An Enterprise Architecture view (as opposed, for example, to an Information Architecture view) recognizes the fact that there are many competing, complementary, and contradictory information sources in an enterprise, and that these sources can be mapped and managed. Enterprise Architecture is particularly important for an agile enterprise, comprised of merged or acquired subsidiaries, with new product divisions that have grown up quickly in response to a new market opportunity. Above all, Enterprise Architecture recognizes that the information assets of an enterprise are always in flux, and that this flux is the steady state.

1.1 Causes

Why is it so difficult for an enterprise to manage information in an agile way? How can it be, that an organization doesn't know what it knows? One cause is a tendency toward information silos. Information workers (and that includes just about everyone in an enterprise) have to focus on solving their business problems first, and will create information artifacts that assist them to this end. It is often impractical to involve a centralized IT manager in small-scale efforts (or even medium-scale ones). The tremendous popularity of spreadsheets attests to this trend; they provide power into the hands of the information workers themselves, allowing them to organize information in a way that helps them with their own particular task.

Seen from an enterprise point of view, these spreadsheets and other small information solutions are a problem – there is no way to make sure that they are consistent, or to take advantage, at an enterprise scale, of information that is found in them. At best, they represent valuable information assets that are not being used to complete potential. At worst, they are points of resistance to bringing in new, more comprehensive systems.

Another reason why the enterprise doesn't know what it knows is that it just knows too much. One enterprise reported a backlog of over two million technical documents, with over 50 new documents a day being produced. Finding relevant information in such a corpus was a daunting task, growing with each passing day.

This situation results in the following barriers to allowing an enterprise to take full advantage of the data it has:

1. **Commitment to legacy data**. At all levels of the enterprise, data has been organized in a particular way for a particular purpose. Even as the needs of the enterprise outgrow this data organization, it is difficult to let go. Workers have familiarity with the information structure; they know where they can go to answer everyday questions. The difficulty with which new information can be found from old structures stymies innovation, encouraging a (non-agile) status quo.

2. **Commitment to legacy work process**. Going hand-in-hand with the legacy data is legacy work process. Innovation is difficult, and the enterprise has to keep making money, even in an outdated mode. Legacy work processes make

other, non-functional, demands on data infrastructure. Enterprises are accustomed to having top-down control of corporate data. This tendency can be so strong that some enterprises will simply ignore the existence of desktop data (i.e., spreadsheets) to maintain the fiction that enterprise data is organized from the top down. There are strong drivers for maintaining top-down control, ranging from data quality (with a central curator who controls what goes into the database), to issues of privacy and security for corporate data.

3. **Massive size of the indexing problem.** In document-centric situations, the massive volume of documents presents a daunting challenge to any attempt at indexing. Incentive structures that focus on document creation, but not document indexing, result in a large, undifferentiated document corpus. The size of the backlog makes it difficult to get a start.

1.2 Technology Solutions

A number of technology solutions are available today to address many of these problems. Many of them have had some measure of success, but the persistence of the problem suggests that they have not solved the core issues. But we can learn from the successes and shortcomings of each of these approaches.

1.2.1 Data Warehousing

Data Warehousing refers to a collection of technological approaches in which multiple data sets are combined into a single repository, over which certain kinds of federated queries can be made. For the most part, the solutions are based on relational database technology, with some additional layer for federation. In general the approach copies the data from the original data sources into the warehouse, which indexes it for certain uses.

The idea of data warehousing is simple, and this simplicity is a virtue. It is easy to understand how the warehouse related to the original data sources (though the technical details can be quite complex, especially when using aggregation technology like OLAP). The process of creating and querying a data warehouse is well-understood.

Nevertheless, it seems that it is quite easy to find industry veterans with nothing good to say about data warehousing. What is their main complaint? It stems from that process itself.

A typical data warehousing project begins by identifying a set of data sources of interest, and some questions that can be answered by some federation of those sources. Well-defined methodology is used to create a warehouse structure, according to the particular technology being used. Data is transferred from the sources, and loaded into the warehouse, which then responds to the queries.

The usual complaint is two-fold. First, that this process takes too long – it can take several months to design and create a good data warehouse, setting it up to respond to queries. But the second part of the complaint is the killer; once knowledge workers have answers to the questions they wanted to ask at the start of the project, they realize that there are more, follow-up questions to ask of the federation. Questions that use the same data sources, but in different ways. They try to pose these questions to the warehouse, only to be told, in the best case, that the warehouse is not optimized for such questions, and performance will be unacceptably slow, or, in the worst case, that the question cannot be formulated at all. In both cases, a redesign of the warehouse is warranted. The resulting time frame produces considerable frustration for the knowledge workers.

Is this the only way the story can end? Certainly not – there are any number of success stories for data warehousing. But this story does highlight the fact that the Achilles heel of data warehousing lies right at the main pain point of this chapter – it is not conducive to organization of information in the agile enterprise.

1.2.2 Master Data Management

Master Data Management (MDM) refers more to an approach than a technology. Its name harks back to the time when a company could have a Master Data Record – the record that describes what is needed to run the business. Master Data Management responds to the idea that these halcyon days are gone, and that a single master data record is not sufficient for a modern enterprise. But it still works from the intuition that if you could define the data management needs for the enterprise, you could use this definition to drive the development of data sources throughout the enterprise, guaranteeing their consistency and interoperability.

MDM is a relatively new approach, born in part from disillusionment with data warehousing. If we could decide what our business needs are in advance of building any data solution (warehouse or primary source), we could take a holistic approach to enterprise data.

The problem with MDM is the very notion of Master Data. It implicitly assumes that there is a business reality that can be modeled, even if the current state of the model may be insufficient. In the agile enterprise, the reality is that the business is in constant flux, and this flux is the only steady state. The very notion of Master Data is questionable.

1.2.3 Metadata Repositories

A metadata repository is a particular technological approach to enterprise data management, in which a common metadata model is defined in response to some business needs. The metadata is used as a sort of interlingua between data sources. Metadata repository systems typically include mapping tools from legacy data sources (typically, relational databases) to the metadata repository. This helps the organization maintain consistency and interoperability between its data sources.

It is called a 'repository' because it is intended to be flexible in nature, and to be incremental in scope. That is, it is possible to add new metadata structures to the repository and extend the existing mappings. This makes metadata repositories at least temperamentally aligned with the needs of the agile information enterprise, in that they are extensible and can respond to changes in business needs. Most metadata repositories, however, are based on proprietary technology, and do not interoperate well with one another. But successful systems have been built using this approach.

1.2.4 Controlled Vocabularies

The idea of a controlled vocabulary is older than modern computing. A *vocabulary* is set of terms that will be used by an organization to refer to elements of its business. The idea of a *controlled* vocabulary is that this set of terms will be selected and managed by some individual or group in the organization. The controlled vocabulary represents an organization-wide policy about which terms to use to refer to certain things, and their normalization (e.g., spelling, numbering, etc.). Examples of controlled vocabularies go back over a hundred years. Library classification systems are one example of controlled vocabularies; a set of classes is defined by a central organization (e.g., the Library of Congress). A particular work is associated with one or more classes. It is not uncommon for the terms in the controlled vocabulary to be given code numbers (class numbers in the case of the Library of Congress) in lieu of (or in addition to) mnemonic names. Because of the ubiquity of this practice, terms in controlled vocabularies of this sort are often called *codes*. The controlled vocabularies themselves are sometimes called *taxonomies, hierarchies, classification schemes, thesauri* or sometimes even *ontologies*. In these various forms, controlled vocabularies have enjoyed considerable success, on both small and large scale, in managing communication within and between organizations. Much of the following discussion can be seen as an attempt to understand the source of this success, and to utilize that understanding to repeat and enhance that success.

1.2.5 Natural Language Processing

For large sets of unstructured data, it is attractive to have the computer process the text automatically, and determine something about its content. The simplest form of Natural Language Processing as applied to enterprise data is called *concept extraction*; a machine reads a document and determines what concepts are mentioned in the document. Concepts identified in this manner can be used as keywords while searching for the document. Concept extraction becomes more effective if the language processing is informed about background concepts in the domain, so that it can determine, for instance, that a document about *epilepsy* is related to the concept *neurological disorder*. A thesaurus can be a useful source of this sort of background information.

More complex natural language processing approaches attempt to extract information about relations between concepts from the document. For instance, concept extraction could determine that a news story that said, "Microsoft acquired Yahoo! for an undisclosed sum" was about two particular companies. More sophisticated natural language systems could determine that after the story was complete, Yahoo! was a part of Microsoft.

Natural language processing systems as applied to document search have enjoyed only limited success. On the one hand, they have to compete with statistical methods for indexing documents such as those made popular by Google (which can process a very large volume of documents), while on the other hand they have to compete with domain experts (who can process documents with expert accuracy). Rather than finding a sweet spot between these extremes, natural language processing solutions of this sort have not dominated the enterprise information integration arena.

1.3 Localization and Globalization

All of the technical approaches outlined above have enjoyed a limited degree of success in addressing enterprise data integration issues. But each of them has some shortcomings that result in the general problem remaining unsolved – it is still difficult for an enterprise to know what it knows. This is a result of a fundamental tension in enterprise management – between a global view of the data and a local one.

On the one hand, the value of an enterprise-global view of information is clear. If only everyone in the enterprise would simply agree on how to represent its information, then integration would be easy. Each application and work flow would relate to this centralized representation of data in the way it needs to, but exchange of information would also be easy, since everyone represents their data in the same way. It is this intuition that drives ideas like Master Data Management and, to some extent, controlled vocabularies.

On the other hand, small groups and even individuals in an organization have a need to control their own work. They need to organize information, often on a small or medium scale, in a way that is responsive to the needs of their own work flow. They resist any requirement that these small information systems be integrated with global ones. They are right to resist such a requirement from the point of view of expediency; for example, they need to be able to respond to business needs more quickly than an integrated information structure would allow. They are also right from the point of view of specificity; they know their own data requirements better than an enterprise-wide IT department. It is this intuition that causes the widespread use of spreadsheets to manage certain enterprise data. This tension is responsible in large part for the baroque situation that is common in large organizations, in which large amounts of enterprise data is found in spreadsheets on desktops, a number of enterprise-wide efforts for data integration compete for dominance, and the overall business lurches along, managing somehow to get enough data together to satisfy everyday business needs. Each new data warehouse or integration project results in yet another database whose integrity with the enterprise has to be maintained.

2 The Linked Data Enterprise

If each effort to merge data sources simply results in another data silo to be integrated, then surely we must simply despair that no systematic, sustainable enterprise- level integration can ever be achieved. But such despair is premature – experiences from the World Wide Web suggest that there is a way for an enterprise to build a sustainable enterprise information architecture. The idea is to turn the organization into a *linked data enterprise.*

The World Wide Web is the largest information source in history – and it grew to be that size using methods that seem quite unconventional from the point of view of enterprise information. Early contributions that made up the Web were done entirely voluntarily, made by people for whom the value of sharing data outweighed the cost of making it available. Wikipedia is a clear example of what can be accomplished by large groups of experts in various fields. People are motivated to share information, and this motivation can be tapped to produce great results. What is the parallel in the enterprise? How can we tap the potential of groups of experts, to create an enterprise in which large-scale information is shared? The key to this is the linked data enterprise.

A linked data enterprise is an organization in which the act of information creation is intimately coupled with the act of information sharing. By analogy to a learning organization, in which learning from an activity is as important as the activity itself, and documentation of a system is as important as the construction of the system, in the linked data enterprise, sharing data is as important as producing it.

In a linked data enterprise, individuals and groups continue to produce and consume information in ways that are specific to their own business needs, but they produce it in a way that can be connected to other aspects of the enterprise. When the time comes for information to be shared, the investment required to connect it is minimal, and reduces the barriers to information exchange. In the linked data enterprise, the motto of information production is *distributed but connectable.*

In any enterprise, knowledge workers who are expert in some field produce high-quality information that is of immediate value in their own business line, but that also has value throughout the enterprise. In the linked data enterprise, these experts respond as the 30,000 major Wikipedia contributors do to the idea that their information can be re-used. They put in the extra effort to make their data accessible, sharable, and comprehensible beyond the situation for which it was originally created. At first blush, it might seem that knowledge workers don't have the time or the incentive to put in this effort. But as a generation who grew up using Wikipedia enters the work force, more and more knowledge workers are bringing the awareness that they can't afford not to put in this effort. A minute's effort sharing information results in hours saved by tapping the expertise of colleagues. In the linked data enterprise, information silos are no longer the bane of the enterprise architect's existence. Data warehouses no longer become monolithic structures oblivious to the changing needs of the enterprise, but rather participants in an enterprise-wide data network.

The technologies that have been applied to enterprise data integration listed above – Data Warehousing, Master Data Management, Metadata registries, Controlled Vocabularies and Natural Language Processing – are not seen as competing, failed technologies, but rather as tools with which to build the infrastructure for the linked data enterprise.

In the following we will see how these technologies, seen in a slightly different light from their conventional uses, can enable the smooth flow of information in the enterprise. Each of them has their role to play, but the main transformation that has to occur to create the linked data enterprise is that it has to be as easy to share information as it is to create it. Toward this end, the role of controlled vocabularies is key. Controlled vocabularies are quite versatile, and their use is already widespread in a wide range of situations. Used in appropriate ways, they can be the cornerstone of the linked data enterprise.

2.1 Controlled Vocabularies

Controlled vocabularies play a key role in creating and maintaining the linked data enterprise; or more properly put, they can play several key roles. The basic utility of a controlled vocabulary is to provide references for two or more data sources, so that it is possible to understand when they are referring to the same thing. So far, so good. But what sort of 'thing' could a data source refer to, and what ramifications does this have when building or using a vocabulary?

There are two common ways to use a controlled vocabulary to provide a common reference for data – we will refer to these as *schema-style* and *tagging-style*.

Schema-style vocabularies give common reference names for aspects of data schema. They tell us how we can describe our data. Terms in schema-style vocabularies correspond to tag names in XML or to table names and column names in a spreadsheet or a relational database. Schema-style controlled vocabularies are often called 'metadata standards', because their terms are used to describe other data (hence 'metadata'). A well-known example of a metadata standard is The Universal Data Element Framework (UDEF), which provides codes for column names and table names for databases.

Tagging-style vocabularies provide terms to describe data elements themselves. A particular record (which often corresponds to a document or a Web page, but can refer to anything in the data space; a person of interest, a lead, a contract, etc.) is associated with one or more terms from the vocabulary. Tagging-style vocabularies are often used in search applications, providing unambiguous references to document topics.

One way to understand the distinction between tagging-style and schema-style vocabularies is to think how they would apply to a spreadsheet. A schema-style vocabulary provides words that can be used in the *columns* of a spreadsheet, while a tagging-style vocabulary provides words that can be used as the *contents* of a spreadsheet cell.

2.1.1 Tagging-style vocabularies

A Tagging vocabulary provides a set of keywords that can be used to describe the contents of a document or data record. The terms in the vocabulary are often called *Concepts* or *Categories*. It is common practice to associate with each term in the vocabulary a meaningless reference number to uniquely identify it (since two terms could have similar or identical common names). For this reason, the terms in a tagging vocabulary are often called *Codes*, referring to the code number that identifies them.

The normal workflow for using a tagging vocabulary goes as follows:

1. A new entity is submitted to the tagging system. For example, a new book comes into a library, or a new customer prospect is brought to the attention of a sales force.
2. One or more codes (or concepts, or categories) are assigned to the new entity. This process can be manual, e.g., by having a librarian make an educated decision, or automatically, by searching the data about a new prospect for certain patterns.
3. When someone searches the corpus for some entity, they enter as all or part of their search a keyword associated with the code.
4. A search system uses this code to filter the search results, displaying only results that were associated with the requested concept (or related ones)
5. Search exploration is facilitated by the vocabulary, allowing the searcher to examine broader, narrower, or related terms, or using this information to disambiguate terms.

The social aspects of this process can range from highly collaborative to highly controlled. Collaborative websites like Flickr and del.icio.us follow this pattern, but step 2 is done by crowdsourcing. Any participant in the network can associate a concept with a photo or a Web site. Systems of this sort are often called *folksonomies*, since the vocabulary is built and maintained by the common folk. In contrast to controlled vocabularies, terms in folksonomies are created dynamically on an as-needed basis. When terms are associated with items in this dynamic way, the process is often referred to as *tagging*, and the terms as *tags*. Unlike terms in a controlled vocabulary, tags provide no guarantee that two people will use the same tag in the same way. The collaborative, social nature of tagging systems is a strength of this approach. They grow to large scale quite easily by recruiting labor from a large user base. But they suffer from the drawback that there are no controls in place; the lack of explicit, public expression of the meaning of tags inhibits their performance in detailed information sharing situations. In particular, the filtering in step 4 is based on a tag given in step 3. But since the searching user may not understand the term in the same way as the tagging user, the number of incorrect matches will be very high. On the Web, the error rate might be acceptable, but for enterprise search, this approach does little to resolve the information segregation issues in the enterprise.

Another example from the Web is the Open Directory Project (ODP)[4]. Similar to the tagging systems of Flickr and del.icio.us, the ODP is made up of a set of categories that are edited and created by harnessing the social power of the Web. The tagging operation, in which web pages are placed into ODP categories, is done by a large group of people, but not in an uncontrolled manner. ODP has a strict process by which category *editors* are selected. These editors then do the assignments of pages to the categories.

Another common approach to controlled vocabularies is the one taken by international standards bodies, which create vocabularies for particular industries. The West Key Numbering System [8] is a venerable example, in which legal briefs in US case law are annotated with codes ("key numbers") indicating the specific branch of legal practice a particular case deals with. Law professionals in the United States receive training on how to use the West Key Numbering System to locate appropriate materials for their own research. Another example is the AGROVOC [1], maintained by the Food and Agriculture Organization of the United Nations. The AGROVOC provides topics for publications about food and agriculture, and allows sharing of information across agencies who want to find information pertaining to food and agriculture around the world.

In these cases, the vocabulary is built and maintained by a group of curators, who made decisions about how the category system is structured. It is the job of these curators to express, as unambiguously as possible, how a particular term should be used, and how it differs from other related terms. Practitioners are encouraged to learn the system, so that they can associate items with the system, and so that they can use it to find items when they are searching. Standard vocabularies of this sort are not themselves built by a collaborative method, but they do support collaborative organization of data; practitioners who create data use standard vocabularies to communicate with as yet undetermined search users, to tell them what a particular document is about.

Most enterprises who use controlled vocabularies do something similar to the standards organizations, but on a smaller scale. They create an organizational vocabulary in a controlled way. The purpose of the vocabulary is to assist associates or customers to locate materials that are relevant to them. A small group of taxonomists maintain the vocabulary, and information producers are encouraged to use it when creating documents. Search applications make use of the vocabularies as well to filter search results. Sometimes, organizational vocabularies can be quite small, used by only a dozen associates, maintained by only one or two. But they still serve the purpose of allowing the group to write down an agreement on how to use certain terms.

Table 1 Sample data from the US Exhibit 300. The values in the "Service Group" and "Line of Business" columns are taken from the Federal Enterprise Architecture Reference Model.

ID	Bureau	Service Group	Line Of Business	Spending
0049	Department of Defense	Services for Citizens	Health	210.516
0155	Department of the Navy	Services for Citizens	Defense and National Security	56.537
0186	Department of the Navy	Service Types and Components	Supply Chain Management	218.214
0314	Department of the Army	Service Types and Components	Financial Management	133.030
0342	Department of the Navy	Services for Citizens	Defense and National Security	127.686
0392	Department of the Air Force	Management of Government Resources	Information and Technology Management	279.969

Table 1 shows an example of the use of a controlled vocabulary in structured data. The sample comes from a form called Exhibit 300, used by the Federal Government to manage certain project budgets. The data in this table gives a project identifier, the name of the agency for which the project was funded, and its total cost. The table also shows the service group name and the line of business name that the project is related to. The terms in these columns come from the Federal Enterprise Architecture Reference Model, a controlled list of lines of business and service groups that is maintained by the US Government. Only values from these lists are allowed as entries in these columns of the Exhibit 300; any other value in this column would constitute a data validation error. By using these controlled values, it is possible, for example, for an auditor to find projects that pertain to a particular line of business, and determine whether the spending is appropriate.

The Federal Enterprise Architecture Reference Model provides a controlled reference for the Exhibit 300s. But it is also used in a number of other forms. It thereby provides a cross-reference between these different information sources; when one source mentions the line of business, "Health" and another one does too, it is clear that they are both talking about the same thing, and furthermore, it is possible to look up what that same thing is.

2.1.2 Schema-style vocabularies

Schema-style vocabularies look superficially similar to Tagging vocabularies, in that they are made up of a number of terms, which are sometimes indicated by numeric codes. But their use is quite different from that of tagging codes; a schema code is not used to describe a particular data entity. Instead, it is used to rationalize the names used in the schema for the data. In particular, schema-style vocabularies provide references for the column headers in a table.

The simplest, most localized schema vocabulary is a data dictionary, which indicates, for a particular database, the intended meaning of a table or column name. If someone wants to understand what a particular record means, they can look up the meaning of each data field in the data dictionary. The scope of the dictionary is local to a particular database, but the audience is potentially any user of that database. The interpretation of any presentation of the data is given by the data dictionary.

If we want two databases to interoperate, one approach is to share some aspects of the data dictionary. This is the approach taken by UDEF. UDEF provides a standard vocabulary that can be used to normalize a database structure by mapping its tables and columns to UDEF terms.

The workflow for a schema-style vocabulary goes as follows:

1. The designer of a database defines tables and columns for a database according to domain requirements
2. The database designer determines a code in the controlled vocabulary that corresponds to the table or column name
3. If two or more databases have been aligned in this manner, integrating them can be done simply by identifying columns from both databases that refer to the same key item in the standard vocabulary.

Table 2 shows an example of this process using UDEF. The names in the table ("Created" and "Expiration") are domain-specific, and might not even convey the fact that these things are dates. But by mapping them to UDEF keys, not only do we know that these are dates, we also know something about the dates. In particular, that the "Expiration" date is actually referring to copyright, which was not obvious from the name given to the column.

When this data is merged with another data source, it is possible to align the correct date fields by using the UDEF standard to determine which fields should be merged.

Table 2 Sample data using two notions of date. The "Created" column is associated with UDEF code 11.6 ("Creation date"); the Expiration column is associate with UDEF code 3.6.6, ("Copyright Expiration Date")

Document ID	Topic	Created	Expiration
A 845	Budget	Nov 27, 2009	June 10, 2011
CZ 23	Personnel	Aug 23, 2008	June 10, 2011
A 465	Personnel	Jan 1, 2001	Aug 14, 2012
B 54	Marketing	Dec 12, 2009	July 6, 2015

Both styles of controlled vocabulary contribute to the reusability and ease of integration of enterprise data, but they do it in very different ways. Schema-style vocabularies are primarily used by data modelers, to describe how their databases are organized. This definition can be used to align data so that like can be compared with like. Tagging-style vocabularies are used by the data producers themselves to describe domain entities. This alignment can be used to organize and improve search.

Fig. 1 shows how these various forms of vocabularies relate. Folksonomies and the Open Directory Project are both social networking systems, where the vocabulary and associations of documents to the vocabularies are done in a crowdsourced, social way. Data dictionaries, organization-specific vocabularies, metadata standards and standard vocabularies all have published semantics; you can look up what a term means, and even enforce (to some extent) appropriate usage. General categories are shown in the figure in bold, while examples are given in italic. Both schema-style (metadata standards and data dictionaries) and tagging-style (folksonomies, standard vocabularies, ODP) vocabularies are shown.

All of these vocabulary approaches make headway into various issues around sharing data, but none of them is sufficient for creating a linked data enterprise. We'll see in the next section how to make use of these information sharing structures to enable linking data in the enterprise.

2.1.3 Linked Enterprise Vocabularies

Between the two styles of controlled vocabularies, Schema-style and Tagging-style, we have a powerful set of tools for setting up a linked data enterprise. But there is

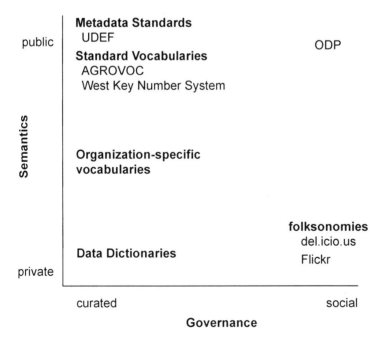

Fig. 1 Various types of vocabularies plotted in terms of governance (social vs. curated) and semantics (public vs. private).

still something missing. The vocabularies provide a way for the organization to express its agreements about how data should be described and represented, but they do not help us come to those agreements. Even in enterprises with very advanced utilization of controlled vocabularies, there is still a tension. Will there be a single vocabulary that guides the whole enterprise, or will there be several competing vocabularies? The main tension of global vs. local vocabulary description still tears the enterprise data management apart.

There is a third way – in which several vocabularies co-exist in a collaborative setting. This places hefty requirements on the vocabularies, regardless of their style.

The basic architecture of linked enterprise vocabularies is shown in Fig. 2. Several vocabularies (triangles) co-exist in the linked data space. Some vocabularies are large and are referenced by many data sets, others are small and relatively private. Any particular data source (drums) can reference (slender arrows) one or more of these vocabularies – either as content (tagging-style) or as metadata (schema-style). Furthermore, any two vocabularies can be mapped to one another (boxes with arrows).

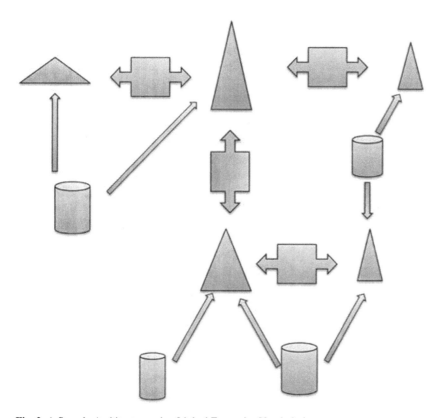

Fig. 2 A Sample Architecture using Linked Enterprise Vocabularies

In contrast to a master data architecture, in which there is a single, enterprise-wide vocabulary that all data sources refer to, this architecture seems chaotic and unmanageable. Redundancies abound, multiple sources have to be maintained in parallel, and the possibility of having competing fiefdoms vying for dominance. These are real drawbacks of any information network that allows for social growth – it is decentralized and, to a large extent, out of control.

But such an architecture has considerable virtues. It resolves the global vs. local issue that is endemic to organizational data management; it allows for the co-existence of multiple vocabularies, each serving its own group of stakeholders. It recognizes that diversity of information sources is the steady state of an agile business. In contrast to approaches like data warehousing, its value is incremental; if two information sources happen to refer to the same vocabulary, then some degree of integration is possible – it isn't necessary to completely re-engineer the whole structure of a dataset in order to get some interoperability.

These virtues allow the linked enterprise vocabulary to support a social network of information workers. By allowing multiple vocabularies to co-exist, it encourages small groups to create and maintain vocabularies, while maintaining connection with the whole enterprise. Its incremental nature allows it to grow as the enterprise grows – small changes in information organization result in partial improvement in information integration. This allows for gradual growth, with incentives at every stage for gradual migration of information sources.

2.2 Prerequisites for Linked Data Vocabularies

The idea of a linked data vocabulary is a simple one – allow several vocabularies to co-exist, in an interoperable way, and let each data source refer to them. Needless to say, the construction and maintenance of such an architecture does not come for free. Most organizations will have to make some change to work practice and technology to achieve it. That's the bad news. The good news is that the changes can be done incrementally; that is, value can be gained by making small changes to how work is accomplished.

There are a few simple technical prerequisites that have to be satisfied to support a linked data enterprise vocabulary:

1. **Terms in vocabularies have to be referenceable.** This simply means that there has to be a way for a data source to make reference to a term in a vocabulary. One common practice in standard published vocabularies to solve this issue is to provide code numbers; the West Key Numbering System and UDEF are prime examples. Any term in one of these vocabularies can be referenced by its code numbers. The system for creating these code numbers can be quite elaborate. Another possibility is to provide URIs for the terms; this is the approach taken by the AGROVOC. For a local vocabulary, any of these approaches can be taken.

2. **References have to be unambiguous.** That is to say, they have to be semantic in the sense defined in [5]. This seems like a simple requirement, but can be the biggest sticking point in creating an enterprise data system. References in relational data bases fall short on this criterion, since primary keys are repeated from one table to the next; they are unambiguous only in the specific context of that database. Vocabularies created by stand-alone vocabulary management tools can have rich structure, but they don't make any guarantees about ambiguity of reference.

3. **Terms have to be mappable.** Once it is possible to have unambiguous references to terms in vocabularies, it becomes possible to make independent statements about how terms relate to one another. In a technical sense, a mapping between one vocabulary and another is simply a dataset that refers to both of them. In many cases, this is all that is necessary; a mapping dataset could list synonyms from one vocabulary to another.

This checklist may seem short, but even so, many systems fail to satisfy all three of these conditions simultaneously. Public vocabularies like UDEF and AGROVOC have unambiguous references, but these public vocabularies make up only part of the story in an enterprise setting. Relational databases are referenceable, but rarely unambiguous. Private vocabularies maintained in spreadsheets have high utility in their own locales, but are not unambiguously referenceable from outside.

It is only recently that a vocabulary standard has been developed that satisfies these goals. For example, vocabulary standards like Z39.19 [3] give advice about how to build and maintain vocabularies, but not about how to represent them for a computer or to exchange them over the Web. The W3C has recently ratified the Simple Knowledge Organization System (SKOS) [6]. SKOS uses URIs to unambiguously reference terms in a vocabulary, and provides a mapping vocabulary (with notions like exact match, close match, broader and narrower match) to provide guidance for how to express the mapping relationships between vocabularies.

Perhaps more important than the technological prerequisites for a linked enterprise vocabulary are the work practice prerequisites. Most enterprises already have a number of competing vocabularies, either at the enterprise level (through formal, supported vocabulary projects) or at the small, individual level (spreadsheets). Their vocabularies are distributed alright, but not connectible! How can one progress from this state to become a linked data enterprise?

There isn't a clear recipe for making the transformation, but some general guidelines are possible. The first transformation is a change of mindset; it is common to think of a vocabulary as the correct way to use a particular term. After all, isn't that why we created the vocabulary in the first place? In the linked data enterprise, a vocabulary is just one member in a consortium of vocabularies; it can be referenced, but does not have authority to prescribe usage. The producers and users of a local vocabulary have to remain open to the fact that other groups will use terms in a different way – perhaps using the same terms differently, or different terms for the same thing.

The other transformation that has to take place is the adoption of the idea of unambiguous reference. Small vocabularies, in particular spreadsheets, satisfy neither goal; they are not easily referenced from outside, and there is no guarantee that the references will be unambiguous. In order to re-tool as spreadsheet for a linked data enterprise, one has to make the terms in the vocabulary unambiguous (on the enterprise scale). The easiest way to do this is to provide an identifier for the local vocabulary itself that is unique throughout the enterprise, then reference each term using that identifier as a namespace.

Fortunately, this transformation can actually simplify the change of mindset as well; having an unambiguous reference actually reduces the impression that any particular vocabulary has central authority. Two vocabularies might not agree on what the word "customer" means; but the linked data vocabulary makes it clear that there are two senses of the word "customer", it is easier to agree to disagree; there are two notions of "customer", and each is unambiguously referenced.

3 Examples

More and more enterprises are making the move to becoming linked data enterprises. One of the virtues of the linked data enterprise is that the change can be gradual, and doesn't have to happen all in one go. But the progress and the intentions are clear. We will examine two examples of organizations that have made the commitment.

3.1 Publishing

The publishing industry is at an important turning point – the advent of wide-spread availability of electronic information has made the production of hard copy works less attractive than it has been in the past. More and more works are being created and disseminated electronically. The publishing industry had, until the end of the 20th century, relied on the relative intensity of the printing process for its revenue model. That part has changed.

So what value can a publisher bring to the work that it disseminates? One value that a publisher can add is better organization to the material that they publish. This sort of added value has been part of the publishing industry for decades, but it is now coming to the forefront, as the importance of information organization becomes clearer.

Publishing is an industry that already understands the need for and use of tagging vocabularies. They use large-scale standard vocabularies (like the Library of Congress Category Index), as well as more specific ones. The problem for them is does not lie in finding a way to get value from a vocabulary, but rather how to deal with a proliferation of too many vocabularies. Publishers with offerings in specialized topics know that detailed vocabularies can help their readers find the documents they need, increasing sales volume.

But as publishers grow their business, branching into new topics, they either have to expand current vocabularies, or acquire new ones. The new vocabularies have typically not been built with the linked data enterprise in mind; so while a certain level of unambiguity has been enforced within each vocabulary, there has been no effort to avoid conflicts between vocabularies.

One such publisher is using SKOS to reconcile all these vocabularies. Each term in a SKOS vocabulary is given a URI, using the Web's notion of reference and uniqueness to satisfy the first two conditions. In the first instance, they aren't linking the vocabularies at all – simply creating unambiguous references for all the terms. Even this simple transformation is a big win for them; it allows them a straightforward way to talk about the various vocabularies, and to detect overlaps where business opportunities could be found.

Future plans involve using the SKOS linking vocabulary to evolve this system into a linked data vocabulary, allowing each group who maintains the vocabulary to extend it in a way that makes sense for their own business needs, while allowing the organization to keep control of the whole merged vocabulary.

3.2 Government

The year 2010 marked a watershed in linked open government data, with the publication of information on websites like data.gov and data.gov.uk. While these developments are interesting from the point of view of linked open data, there are other, lower-profile efforts that are more relevant from the point of view of enterprise data.

A government agency is similar to many other enterprises in its information needs; it consumes information, provides information, and has the same information silo issues as other enterprises.

One European government agency is using schema-style controlled vocabularies to create a linked data enterprise. The underlying technology is strongly based on XML, since that is how the current infrastructure works.

The basic problem is that a government agency deals in a large number of small official documents, ranging from civil documents like birth certificates, marriage licenses, driving licenses and so forth, to criminal proceedings like warrants for arrest, formal levying of criminal charges, and judicial decisions. There is considerable overlap in the topics of these documents; a driving license and a marriage license both refer to people. Eye color and gender are relevant for a driving license, but not for a marriage license. Name and place of birth are relevant for both. If all of the XML forms for these documents are developed independently, then interoperability between them will be very difficult.

It is possible to set up an XML infrastructure that satisfies the conditions, but it is necessary to make unambiguous references to the XML tags and to use those tags in a consistent way. The agency accomplishes this by bringing in a linked data vocabulary (all schema-style) that describes shared understanding of entities and properties. The vocabulary has a notion for person, and associated properties for eye color, name and gender. The XML message schemas are generated based on this controlled vocabulary.

But the situation isn't quite that simple. Legislation changes. New forms have to retain consistency (as much as possible) with previous forms. Different offices have different requirements about what should be included in a form. A master data approach, in which all the schema information is held in a central metadata model, only takes us so far; there is still a need for individual variation in the metadata vocabulary. The agency has defined a process by which new metadata models are built by reference to an original, forming a linked data vocabulary. The resulting linked data enterprise balances the local needs of the offices, the agility requirements of changing legislation, and the global need of the agency to have an integrated view of its data.

The system has been deployed in the agency, and its use is spreading to other agencies and governments.

4 Conclusions

Enterprises today have to be more agile than ever before, and this agility requires a new way of working. A way that allows involvement of a wide variety of information workers without a long turn-around time to develop a new system whenever new information comes to light. But as multiple stakeholders bring their work processes together, the need for information integration becomes a bottleneck. The agile enterprise needs to become the integrated information enterprise.

Technological solutions to this problem have made some headway, allowing information to be merged or warehoused, satisfying the global needs of the enterprise. But these solutions have not succeeded in including the full scope of enterprise stakeholders in the data sharing effort. Until this is achieved, the enterprise will continue to have silos of disconnected information.

Controlled vocabularies provide a key to how this situation can be resolved. Used poorly, they will be rejected as just another meaningless set of rules to follow. Used correctly, a controlled vocabulary can mediate communication between parties. They provide touchpoints for common reference for data description. In this way, they can help forge a linked data enterprise, in which information with sharing in mind.

The idea of a linked data enterprise is an ideal, but many enterprises are making a large part of it a reality. They build datasets with reuse in mind, allowing a wide variety of knowledge workers to contribute to their overall data assets.

References

1. AGROVOC, http://www.fao.org/agrovoc/

2. Allemang, Dean and Hendler, James. Semantic Web for the Working Ontologist, Morgan-Kaufmann/Elsevier, 2008.
3. Guidelines for the Construction, Format, and Management of Mono-lingual Controlled Vocabularies, NISO Z39.19.
4. Open Directory Project, http://www.dmoz.org/about.html
5. Siegel, David. Pull The Power of the Semantic Web to Transform Your Business, Penguin Group, 2009.
6. Simple Knowledge Organization System (SKOS), http://www.w3.org/2004/02/skos/
7. Universal Data Element Framework (UDEF), http://www.udef.com/
8. West Key Numbering System, http://west.thomson.com/westlaw/advantage/keynumbers/

The Role of Community-Driven Data Curation for Enterprises

Edward Curry, Andre Freitas, and Sean O'Riáin

Abstract With increased utilization of data within their operational and strategic processes, enterprises need to ensure data quality and accuracy. Data curation is a process that can ensure the quality of data and its fitness for use. Traditional approaches to curation are struggling with increased data volumes, and near real-time demands for curated data. In response, curation teams have turned to community crowd-sourcing and semi-automated metadata tools for assistance. This chapter provides an overview of data curation, discusses the business motivations for curating data and investigates the role of community-based data curation, focusing on internal communities and pre-competitive data collaborations. The chapter is supported by case studies from Wikipedia, The New York Times, Thomson Reuters, Protein Data Bank and ChemSpider upon which best practices for both social and technical aspects of community-driven data curation are described.

1 Introduction

Using data and quantitative analysis to support decision making is a growing trend within the business environment with many companies reaping significant benefits [1]. However, one of the major pitfalls in data driven decision making is poor quality data. In its December '09 issue The Economist highlighted the problems

Edward Curry
Digital Enterprise Research Institute, National University of Ireland, Galway, Ireland, e-mail: ed.curry@deri.org

Andre Freitas
Digital Enterprise Research Institute, National University of Ireland, Galway, Ireland, e-mail: andre.freitas@deri.org

Sean O'Riáin
Digital Enterprise Research Institute, National University of Ireland, Galway, Ireland, e-mail: sean.oriain@deri.org

D. Wood (ed.), *Linking Enterprise Data*, DOI 10.1007/978-1-4419-7665-9_2,
© Springer Science+Business Media, LLC 2010

some banks have with data quality. "The same types of asset are often defined differently in different programs. Numbers do not always add up. Managers from different departments do not trust each other's figures". One bank official noted "some figures were not worth the pixels they were made of", highlighting inaccurate figures make it very difficult to manage operational concerns such as investments exposure and risk.

Making decision based on incomplete, inaccurate, or wrong information can have disastrous consequences. Decision making knowledge workers need to have access to the right information and need to have confidence in that information. Data curation can be a vital tool to ensure knowledge workers have access to accurate, high-quality, and trusted information that can be reliably tracked to the original source, in order to ensure its credibility.

This chapter discusses the business motivations for curating data and investigates the role of community-based data curation, especially pre-competitive collaborations. The chapter provides an overview of data curation supported by case studies from Wikipedia, The New York Times, Thomson Reuters, PDB and ChemSpider along with best practices for both social and technical aspects of data curation.

2 The Business Need for Curated Data

The increased utilization of data, with a wide range of key business activities (including business intelligence, customer relationship management and supply chain management) has created a data intensive landscape and caused a drastic increase in the sophistication of enterprise data infrastructures. One of the key principles of data analytics is that the quality of the analysis is dependent on the quality of the information analyzed. However, within operational enterprise systems, there is a large variance in the quality of information. Gartner recently estimated that more than 25 percent of critical data in the world's top companies is flawed[1]. Uncertainty over the validity of data or ambiguity in its interpretation can have a significant effect on business operations, especially when it comes to the decision making process. When making decisions or interpreting business intelligence reports or dashboards, business executives must be able to assess the quality of the data they are using.

Perception of data quality is highly dependent on the fitness for use [2]; being relative to the specific task that a user has at hand. Data quality is usually described by a series of quality dimensions which represent a set of desirable characteristics for an information resource (see [3] for a survey of the main data quality frameworks). The following data quality dimensions are highly relevant within the context of enterprise data and business users:

- **Discoverability & Accessibility:** Addresses if users can find the data and then access it in a simple manner. It is important to facilitate users in their search for

---

[1] Gartner, Inc press release. "'Dirty Data' is a Business Problem, Not an IT Problem, says Gartner," March 2, 2007

information. Data curation can streamline the users search for data by storing and classifying it in an appropriate and consistent manner.

- **Completeness:** Is all the requisite information available? Does it need to be cleansed for errors and duplications? Are there any omissions (values and whole records) from the data? In some cases, missing data is irrelevant, but when the information that is missing is critical to a specific business process, completeness becomes an issue. Data curation can be used to conduct data audits and develop data-retention criteria to improve the completeness of and remove duplications from enterprise data. Curation can also be used to provide the wider context of data by linking/connecting related datasets.
- **Interpretation:** Is the meaning of data ambiguous? Reaching a common interpretation of information is a challenging task. Humans can have different underlying assumption that can significantly affect the way they interpret data. While no technology is capable of eliminating misinterpretations, data curation can ensure that any assumptions made during information collection (and calculations) are made explicit, to minimize misunderstandings.
- **Accuracy:** Is the data correct? Unreliable data has drastically reduced usefulness for the enterprise. Data curation can be used to ensure that data correctly represent the "real-world" values it models.
- **Consistency:** Does the data contradict itself? Are values uniform across datasets? Inconsistent data can introduce significant difficulty for organizations attempting to reconcile between different systems and applications. Data curation can be used to ensure that data is created and maintained to ensure it uses standardized definitions, calculations, terms, and identifiers in a consistent manner.
- **Provenance & Reputation:** Is the data legitimate? Where did the data come from? Can it be reliably tracked back to the original source? Is the source of the data highly regarded? Data provenance can be used to assess the trustworthiness and quality behind data production and delivery. When judging the quality of data the reputation of the data sources and/or data producers (organizations and individuals) can be a critical factor. Data curation activities could be used to both track the source of the data and determine their reputation. Reputation can also include the objectivity of the source/producer. Is the information unbiased, unprejudiced, and impartial? Or does it come from a reputable but partisan source?
- **Timeliness:** Is the information up-to-date? Data curation can be used to determine how up-to-date data is, with respect to the task at hand.

By improving these quality dimensions, data curation can increase the credibility and trust of data that passes through the curation process. However, not all enterprise data should be curated. Data curation is suited to knowledge-centric data rather than transactional operations data. It is important to note that not all knowledge-centric enterprise data should be curated, given the associated effort and cost required it would not make sense to do so. Each organization must identify what data would benefit most from curation, and determine if potential returns would support the required investment.

Data governance is an emerging field that is a convergence of data quality, data management, business process management, and risk management which surrounds the handling of data in an organization. A full discussion of data governance is outside the scope of this chapter, but it is important to know that data curation is a complimentary activity that can form part of an overall data governance strategy for the organization.

3 Data Curation

Digital curation is the process of establishing and maintaining a trusted body of digital information within long term repositories for current and future use by researchers, scientists, historians, and scholars generally. Specifically digital curation is defined as the selection, preservation, maintenance, collection, and archiving of digital assets [4].

Data curation, a subset of digital curation, is the active management and appraisal of data over its life-cycle of interest. In the same manner in which a museum curator ensures the authenticity and organization of a museum's collection, data curation is performed by expert curators responsible for improving the accessibility and quality of data. Data curators (also known as bio curators, scientific curators, or data annotators) are recognized as the "museum cataloguers of the Internet age" [5] who have the responsibility to ensure that data is trustworthy, discoverable, accessible, reusable and fit for its current intended use.

3.1 How to Curate Data

The Digital Curation Centre[2] provides extensive support services on digital curation and preservation to the established 'traditional' curation community outlining initiatives towards curation standards, procedures and tools. For the purposes of this chapter, we will provide a high-level overview of some key questions must be addressed to setup a curation process within an organization.

An obvious starting point is to identify the business use case for creating a curated dataset. Typically a curation effort will have a number of motivations to curate data, including improving accessibility, quality, or tracking provenance. Once clearly established, one can start to define "how" the data will be curated. There is no single correct way to curate data and there are many ways to setup a data curation effort. The major factors that will influence the curation approach include the:

- Quantity of data to be curated (include new and legacy data),
- Rate of change of the data,
- Amount of effort required to curate the data, and the

---

[2] Digital Curation Centre, http://www.dcc.ac.uk/ Last Accessed on 8th June 2010

- Availability of experts.

Once these factors are determined, an estimation of the work required to curate the data can be made. If dealing with an infrequently changing small quantity of data (<1,000 records) with minimal curation effort (minutes per record), curation could be easily undertaken by an individual. However, once the number of records enters the thousands, a curation group/department with a formal process has to be considered. Curation departments can deal with large curation efforts, especially when they utilize software to support the curation process, but there is a limit to their scalability. When curating large quantities of dynamic data (>million records) even the most sophisticated curation department can struggle with the workload. An approach to curate data on this scale is to utilize crowd-sourcing *community-based curation* in conjunction with computer-based curation. One popular crowd-sourcing technique is *sheer curation* that integrates curation activities within the normal workflow of those creating and managing the target data. These curation approaches are not mutually exclusive and can be used in conjunction to curate data. These blended approaches are proving to be successful.

3.1.1 Setting up a Curation Process

- **Identify what data you need to curate:** Will you be curating newly created data and/or legacy data? How is new data created? Do users create the data, or is it imported from an external source? How frequently is new data created/updated? What quantity of data is created? How much legacy data exists? Where does the legacy data reside? Is it stored within a single source, or scattered across multiple sources.
- **Identify who will curate the data:** Curation activities can be carried out by individuals, departments or groups, institutions, communities, etc.
- **Define the curation workflow:** How will curation activities be carried out? The curation process will be heavily influenced by the previous two questions. The two main methods to curate data are a curation group/department or a sheer curation workflow that enlists the support of users.
- **Identity the most appropriate data-in and data-out formats:** What is the best format for the data to be expressed? Is there an agreed standard format within the industry or community? Choosing the right data format for receiving data and publishing curated data is critical; often a curation effort will need to support multiple formats to ensure maximum participation.
- **Identify the artifacts, tools, and processes needed to support the curation process:** A number of artifacts, tools, and processes can support data curation efforts, including workflow support, web-based community collaboration platforms. A number of algorithms exist to automate or semi-automate curation activities [6] such as data cleansing[3], record duplication and classification algorithms [7] that can be used within sheer curation.

---

[3] Detecting and correcting (or removing) inaccurate or corrupt records

4 Community-based Curated Enterprise Data

Data curation can be a time consuming and difficult task. Often the effort required to curate anything but a trivial dataset is beyond the capability and capacity of a single individual. As such, it is often within the interest of individuals to join community efforts to curate the data. By becoming part of a community, participants are able to share the costs, risks and technical challenges, while benefiting from the wisdom of the community and the network effect for their curated dataset. One of the most popular community curated datasets is the Wikipedia online encyclopedia, which will be analyzed as one of the case studies in this chapter.

Many enterprises use community-based approaches to meet their data curation needs, which have proved very successful for knowledge centric data curation. Depending on the requirements of the data, an enterprise can utilize an internal community or participate with an external community to collaboratively curate data.

In order to determine the right model, one must consider a number of issues, such as:

- What the purpose of the community is?
- Who participates within the community?
- Will access to the curated dataset be publicly available? Or restricted?
- Is the curation process open to public participation? Or limited to a selected curation group?
- What is the community governance model?

Once these questions are answered one can start to determine what community model will best suit. Two popular models are *internal corporate communities* and *external pre-competitive communities*.

4.1 Internal Corporate Community

Enterprises have started to tap the potential of their workforce to assist within the data curation process. Internal corporate communities can be utilized to curate competitive enterprise data that will remain internal to the company, although this may not always be the case (e.g. product technical support and marketing data). Internal communities often work in conjunction with a formal curation department and their governance will typically follow the organization's internal governance model.

A typical approach is to create a department that consists of curation experts that can work in conjunction with subject matter experts to curate data, after it has been created, in a post hoc manner. This "traditional" form of data curation has proved to be very successful. However, the post-hoc nature of the approach creates a delay in the availability of curated data. With business relying more on data in their day-to-day operations, there is a need to reduce the time taken to make curated data available. Making the situation even more challenging is the increased quantities of data that need to be curated. Data curation teams have found it difficult to scale the traditional approach and have turned to crowd-sourcing [8] and automated/semi-automated metadata annotation tools to assist the curation process [6].

With the increased use of online collaboration tools and the need to curate larger amounts of data, many enterprises have employed decentralized approaches to data curation by turning to internal communities of users to curate data. Often the curation task can be done as the data is created. *Sheer curation*, or *curation at source*, is an approach to data curation where lightweight curation activities are integrated into the normal workflow of those creating and managing data and other digital assets. The results of the sheer curation process can be made immediately available. Sheer curation activities can be as simple as vetting or "rating" the results of a categorization process performed by a curation algorithm. Sheer curation activities can also be combined with the activities of a post hoc curation department to provide more sophisticated curation activities. These blended approaches to data curation allow more immediate access to curated data while also ensuring the quality control that is only possible with an expert curation team.

4.2 External Pre-competitive Communities

For data that must remain private to an enterprise, for competitive reasons, internal communities are best suited. However, a growing trend is for enterprises to participate within external data curation communities where the data is deemed to be precompetitive [8, 9]. Many organizations, both commercial and non-profit, have come together to build sustainable data curation communities that share costs, risks, and technical challenges between members. These communities leverage a larger user base for crowd-sourcing and provide a distinct advantage to improve the wisdom of the crowds [8].

Pre-competitive collaboration is a well-established technique, with a number of industries realizing the benefits of an open innovation model for collaboration. Notable examples are the Airbus consortium of European aircraft manufacturers, the Sematech consortium of US semiconductor manufacturers, and banks working together to launch Visa and MasterCard.

A typical company will leverage its propriety data for competitive advantage. However, many companies also utilize common data that does not provide any competitive advantage. While this data has little potential for differentiation, the company must still invest in maintaining and curating the data. Often many companies will duplicate this effort in-house, incurring the full-cost of maintaining the dataset. In order to avoid this unnecessary cost, companies can collaborate within pre-competitive initiatives.

Pre-competitive data is information that can be shared without conferring a commercial advantage to a competitor. Pre-competitive curation collaboration activities between organizations can help to overcome decreasing budgets by reducing the costs required to provide and maintain data, while increasing the quantity, quality and access to non-competitive data. Company participation within a pre-competitive community can take the form of a direct monetary contribution, personnel contribution, and/or by donating datasets. The common data curation tasks can be carried out once within the public domain rather than multiple times within the private domains of each company.

Participation within a pre-competitive curation community allows participating companies to focus on value-adding competitive activities such as data analysis and data exploration, the Protein Data Bank and ChemSpider case studies being examples of this. Another example is the Pistoia Alliance, a consortium in the Pharmaceutical industry [4]. The objective of these communities is to move the "competitive onus" from novel data to novel algorithms by shifting the "emphasis from 'proprietary data' to a 'proprietary understanding of data'"[10]. The scope of the community can also extend beyond just data curation tasks to include collaboration for developing common pre-competitive software infrastructures for manipulating and storing the data.

Two popular community models are: *organization consortium* and *open community*. An *organization consortium* is a type of community which operates like a private democratic club where participating organizations collaborate on curation activities. The benefit is being able to share risks, costs and technical challenges while also sharing any potential IP created. Consortiums are usually a closed community where members are invited based on their skill set to provide a contribution to curation activities. The availability of the resulting output data may be publicly available or limited to the consortium members. Consortiums follow a democratic process; however the voting rights of each member may reflect the level of investment they make within the consortium. Within these scenarios larger players may become the leaders of the consortium.

Within an *open community* everyone can participate. The founder(s) of the community defines the desired curation activity and seeks public support from a potential unlimited number of participants who feel they have the skills to provide or contribute to curation activates. Wikipedia, Linux, and Apache are good examples of large open communities where anyone can contribute.

5 Case Study: Wikipedia - The World Largest Open Digital Curation Community

Wikipedia is an open-source encyclopedia, built collaboratively by a large community of web editors. The success of Wikipedia as one of the most important sources of information available today still challenges existing models of content creation. As of March 2010, Wikipedia counted more than 19,000,000 articles, with over 3,200,000 in the English language. Wikipedia covers near 270 languages and counts with more than 157,000 active contributors. Previous investigations showed the evidence that both the accuracy [11] and stylistic formality [12] are equivalent to

---

[4] The Pistoia Alliance http://www.pistoiaalliance.org/ Last Accessed on 8th June 2010

resources developed in expert-based closed communities such as the Columbia and Britannica encyclopedias. Despite the fact that the term 'curation' is not commonly addressed by Wikipedia's contributors, the task of digital curation is the central activity of Wikipedia editors, who have the responsibility for information quality standards.

Wikipedia uses a wiki as its main system for content construction. Wikis were first proposed by Ward Cunningham in 1995 and allow users to edit contents and collaborate on the Web more efficiently. MediaWiki, the wiki platform behind Wikipedia, is already widely used as a collaborative environment inside organizations[5]. Important cases include Intellipedia, a deployment of the MediaWiki platform covering 16 U.S. Intelligence agencies[6], and Wiki Proteins, a collaborative environment for knowledge discovery and annotation [13].

The investigation of the collaboration dynamics behind Wikipedia can highlight important features and good practices which can be applied to different organizations. Our analysis focuses on the curation perspective and covers two important dimensions: *social organization* and *artifacts, tools & processes* for cooperative work coordination. These are key enablers that support the creation of high quality information products in Wikipedia's decentralized environment.

5.1 Social Organization

One important feature behind the Wikipedia initiative is the idea of lowering barriers for new contributors, by allowing any user, without prior registration, to edit its contents. What one would have expected to lead to a chaotic scenario, proved to be, in practice, a highly scalable approach for high quality content creation on the Web. Wikipedia relies on a simple but highly effective way to coordinate its curation process and accounts and roles are in the base of this system.

Wikipedia has four main types of accounts: (a) anonymous users - which are identified by their associated IP address, (b) registered users - users with an account in the Wikipedia website, (c) administrators - registered users with additional permissions in the system and (d) bots - programs that perform repetitive tasks. All users are allowed to edit Wikipedia contents. Administrators, however, have additional permissions in the system.

For the definition of the central roles in the curation process we refer to a subset of the roles identified by Stivilia [14]: *editor, administrator, bureaucrat, steward, arbitrator, mediator* and *bots*. The roles can provide a more clear perspective of the tasks that accounts perform, where the arbitrator and the mediator roles can be performed by bureaucrats and administrators. Bureaucrats and stewards are special

---

[5] MediaWiki Testimonials, http://www.mediawiki.org/wiki/Sites_using_MediaWiki/corporate Last Accessed on 8th June 2010

[6] CIA.gov Featured Article, "Intellipedia Celebrates Third Anniversary with a Successful Challenge", https://www.cia.gov/news-information/featured-story-archive/intellipedia-celebrates-third-anniversary.html Last Accessed on 8th June 2010

types of administrators who can perform additional functions while acting on consensus. For a more detailed description of the accounts and roles types the reader is directed to Stivilia [14].

Wikipedia can provide important insights about the social dynamics of open collaboration on the Web. Kollock concluded that the incentives behind open collaboration are based on the expectation of future reciprocity from the community, the improvement of one's reputation and the sense of efficacy (contributing effectively to a meaningful project) [15]. While Bryant et al. [16] investigated the transformation of roles in the process of becoming a Wikipedian (a Wikipedia editor). By interviewing Wikipedians, the authors observed that, over time, the focus of editors commonly changed from curators of a few articles in topics where they were familiarized to a more global curation perspective, motivating and enforcing the quality assessment of Wikipedia contents as a whole.

5.2 Artifacts, Tools and Processes

Wikipedia makes use of different artifacts, tools and processes to provide editors guidance in the digital curation process. In contrast to other environments where information quality is enforced by the application of restrictive permission mechanisms, Wikipedia provides a minimal and effective infrastructure as described below.

- **Wiki Article Editor (Tool):** A wiki is a website which allows users to easily create, edit and publish contents in web pages through the use of a WYSIWYG or markup text editor.
- **Talk Pages (Tool):** Talk pages represent a public arena for discussions around Wikipedia resources. Talk pages are used with the purpose of discussion lists where each editable resource has an associated Talk page. The work of Viégas et al. [17] provide a detailed analysis of the talk pages role in the coordination of the edition of resource contents. Talk pages serve as a multichannel tool allowing users to request/suggest editing coordination, request for information, reference vandalism, reference Wikipedia guidelines and policies, reference internal Wikipedia resources, write off-topic remarks, make polls, request peer review, define status through information boxes, post images, together with other minor uses.
- **Watchlists (Tool):** Every user can put a Wikipedia resource in a watchlist in order to receive notifications of changes of the state of a specific resource. Watchlists help curators to monitor actively the integrity and quality of the set of resources which they contribute.
- **Permission Mechanisms (Tool):** Users with administrator status have the permission to perform critical actions inside the system such as remove pages, grant administrative permissions for new users.
- **Automated Edition (Tool):** Bots are automated or semi-automated tools that perform repetitive tasks over the Wikipedia contents.

- **Page History and Restore (Tool):** The historical trail of changes of a Wikipedia Resource can be accessed in the page history. Editors with certain administrator status can restore the previous status of a resource.
- **Guidelines, Policies & Templates (Artifact):** Resources including 'The Perfect Article'[7], Featured Articles[8] and Layout[9], define the curation guidelines for editors to assess the quality of an article. In addition, a comprehensive set of policies[10], covering every critical aspect of the editorial process behind Wikipedia, are defined.
- **Dispute Resolution (Process):** Disputes between editors over the contents of an article can lead to different dispute resolution mechanisms.
- **Article Edition, Deletion, Merging, Redirection, Transwiking, Archival (Process):** These processes describe the curation actions over Wikipedia resources.

5.3 DBPedia - Community Curated Linked Open Data

Wikipedia provides document-centric access access to information. DBPedia, on the other hand, provides direct access to data through its comprehensive infrastructure of concept URIs, their definitions and basic types.

As of March 2010, DBPedia counted 3.4 million entities and 1 billion RDF triples. DBPedia inherits the massive volume of curated data available at Wikipedia and indirectly uses its wiki infrastructure as a curation platform. Since DBpedia has a broad scope of entities covering different areas of the human knowledge, it is natural hub for connecting datasets, where external datasets could link to its concepts.

The DBPedia knowledge base is built using the information present in well defined links inside the article and infobox-specific properties. The general properties include a label, an abstract, a link to the Wikipedia Article, links to related DBPedia entities, links to external Web resources, a link to an image of the concept and geo-coordinates. Infobox specific properties are mapped using two types of extractors: generic infobox extraction, which build predicates directly from the pairs of attribute-value present on infoboxes and mapping-based infobox extraction, which uses a manually created ontology (170 classes, 720 properties) built from the 350 most frequent infoboxes templates to map the attribute-value pair to the ontology terms. The reader is referred to [18] for a more detailed discussion about the extraction process behind DBPedia.

The use of a wiki as a collaborative platform for the creation and maintenance of lightweight ontologies is covered by Hepp et al. in [19], which also found that Wikipedia can provide high quality and stable concept identifiers. Hepp also high-

---

[7] http://en.wikipedia.org/wiki/Wikipedia:The_perfect_article Last accessed on 8th June 2010

[8] http://en.wikipedia.org/wiki/Wikipedia:Featured_articles Last accessed on 8th June 2010

[9] http://en.wikipedia.org/wiki/Wikipedia:Layout Last accessed on 8th June 2010

[10] http://en.wikipedia.org/wiki/Wikipedia:List_of_policies Last accessed on 8th June 2010

lights that ontologies work not only as a formal representation of a specific domain but also as a community contract over this representation. By having a larger community of contributors, the collaboratively created ontology is more likely to express this social agreement. One additional positive point is the fact that, by being a widespread and popular technology, wikis can lower the entry barriers for collaborative data curation. In this context, despite being targeted to document curation, wikis can also support data curation.

6 Case Study: The New York Times - 100 Years of Expert Data Curation

The New York Times (NYT) is the largest metropolitan and the third largest newspaper in the United States. The Times website, *nytimes.com*, is ranked as the most popular newspaper website in the United States and is an important source of advertisement revenue for the company. The NYT has a rich history for curation of its articles and its 100 year old curated repository has ultimately defined its participation as one of the first players in the emerging Web of Data.

6.1 Data Curation

The history of data curation in The New York Times dates back to 1913 when, fearing competition with the New York Sun, the publisher and owner Adolph S. Ochs decided to provide a set of additions to the newspaper. One of these additions was the New York Times Index, an ambitiously organized catalog of articles titles and summaries (containing the issue, date and column of the original article), published in a period of time, categorized by subject and names. The Index was introduced on a quarterly basis at first, being later produced on an annual basis. With the introduction of the NYT Index, the typically transitory content of the newspaper became an important source of searchable historical data, often used to settle historical debates.

In order to create a high quality catalog, an Index Department was created, marking the start of a systematic data curation and cataloguing effort over the NYT resources (since 1851 the NYT already had a low quality index for internal use). In the following years, the Index Department developed a comprehensive catalog using a controlled vocabulary covering subjects, personal names, organizations, geographic locations and titles of creative works (books, movies, etc), linked to articles and their summaries. As of March 2010 the Index Department is 15 people strong.

The process of consistently and accurately classifying news articles over a large period of time can pose numerous challenges. Over the time span of 100 years the keywords used to express subjects may show some variance due to cultural or legal constraints. The identities of some entities, such as organizations and places, changed over time. Other entities, in particular names derived from non-Latin alphabets may show different lexical expressions. In addition, the NYT controlled vocabulary grew to hundreds of thousands of categories adding considerable complexity to the classification process.

With the increase of importance of the Web to the NYT, there was a need to improve the categorization of online contents. The curation carried out by the Index Department in library-time (days to weeks) was not suitable for real-time demands of online publishing. The print versions of the paper could handle a next-day index, but nytimes.com needed a same-day index. To meet this challenge, the NYT introduced a two stage curation process where the editorial staff performed best-effort semi-automated sheer curation at the point of online publication with the Index Department following up with long-term accurate classification and archiving. This blended approach provides the best of both worlds, with the non-expert journalist's curators providing instant accessibility to online users, and the Index Department providing long-term high-quality expert curation in a "trust but verify" approach.

The editorial staff of the New York Times consists of several hundreds journalists who work as first level curators in the content classification process. Two *taxonomy managers* review the work of the first level curators, providing constant feedback into the classification process.

The basic workflow (see Figure 1) of the first level curation starts with an article getting out of the newsroom. Using a Web application, a member of the editorial staff submits the new article through a rule based information extraction system (in this case, SAS Teragram[11]). Teragram uses a set of linguistic extraction rules which are created by the taxonomy managers based on a subset of the controlled vocabulary used by the Index Department. Teragram suggests tags based on the Index vocabulary that can potentially describe the content of the article. The member of the editorial staff then selects the terms that better describe the contents and inserts new tags if necessary. The classification is reviewed by the taxonomy managers and the content is published online. In a later stage the article receives a second level curation by the Index Department, which appends additional tags and a summary of the article to the stored resource.

6.2 Publishing Curated Linked Data

In 2009 the NYT announced the publication of a subset of nearly 10,000 tags of its indexing vocabulary as Linked Open Data (LOD), becoming one of the early companies to open their data as Linked Data. The NYT LOD initiative[12] intends to expand its vocabulary coverage to a larger set of the index.

As of March 2010, the NYT dataset consists of people, organizations and locations. The published data is complemented by the NYT Restful API, where appli-

---

[11] SAS teragram http://www.teragram.com Last Accessed on 8th June 2010

[12] The NYT Linked Open Data http://data.nytimes.com, Accessed on 9th March 2010

cation developers can use a set of different search services to consume data about articles, movies, best sellers, Congress votes, real estate, among other uses.

The NYT LOD initiative inherits the quality that is the consequence of almost 100 years of investment in careful data curation. The publication of its curated Linked Data unleashes a set of potential benefits to the NYT including: improvement of the online traffic by third party data usage, lowering of the cost of development of new applications for different verticals inside the website (e.g. movies, travel, sports, books), creation of better online contents by links and the potential for Search Engine Optimization.

7 Case Study: Thomson Reuters - Data Curation, a Core Business Competency

Thomson Reuters is an information provider company created by the acquisition of Reuters by Thomson Corporation in 2008. In 2009 the company had over 50,000 employees and a commercial presence in more than 100 countries. Thomson Reuters business is focused on the provision of specialist curated critical information and information-based services which can enable strategic decision making in different domains, including Healthcare, Science, Financial, Legal and Media. Thomson Reuters is among the early corporate adopters of Semantic Web technologies, progressively incorporating these on its data and services.

Thomson Reuters utilize Semantic Web Technologies to provide better contextualized, meaningful, interoperable and machine readable contents to its customers. Since the main customers of Thomson Reuters are information consumers, Semantic Web Technologies are seen as a way to bring information with integrated context to end users. The acquisition of ClearForest (by Reuters in 2007), a company focused on information extraction through Natural Language Processing, shows solid evi-

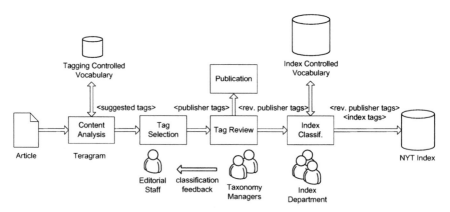

Fig. 1 The NYT article classification curation workflow

dence that improving the organization and semantics of the information can provide a competitive edge for the company

7.1 Data Curation

The objective of data curation at Thomson Reuters is to select the most relevant information for its customers, classifying, enriching and distributing it in a way that can be readily consumed. The curation process at Thomson Reuters employs thousands of curators working over approximately 1000 data sources. In the curation process, automatic tools provide a first level triage and classification which is further refined by the intervention of human curators. A curator inside Thomson Reuters is a specialist in a specific domain, who collects, aggregates, classifies, normalizes and analyzes the raw information coming from different data sources.

Since the nature of the information analyzed at Thomson Reuters is typically high volume and near real-time, data curation is a big challenge inside the company and the use of automated tools plays an important role in this process. One of these tools, OneCalais, is a platform which uses Natural Language Processing (NLP) over unstructured text to automatically derive tags for the analyzed content, enriching it with machine readable structured data. The tags enrich the original text with the general category of the analyzed contents, while also providing a description of specific entities (places, people, events, facts) which are present in the text. OneCalais was a product developed at ClearForest.

Since 2008 OpenCalais, a free public version of the extraction service provided by OneCalais, was made available to the public. By March of 2010 OpenCalais had over 20.000 users executing an average of over 4 million transactions per day. The corporate users of OpenCalais includes CNET, CBS Interactive, The Huffington Post, The Powerhouse Museum of Science and Design, which use the system as a platform to reduce the workload involved in the classification of digital collections.

Both OneCalais and OpenCalais use the Linked Data principles[13] to describe entities. Every entity inside the systems has a de-referenceable URI. From the perspective of Thomson Reuters business, Linked Data can provide a high impact data distribution strategy. However, deploying Linked Data to corporate customers brings additional challenges. Business users will not rely on an unmanaged linked data ecosystem. Thomson Reuters address part of this problem creating its own 'branded' Linked Data containing information about companies, geography, etc.

---

[13] T. Berners-Lee, "Linked Data Design Issues.", http://www.w3.org/DesignIssues/LinkedData.html Last Accessed on 8th June 2010

8 Case Study: ChemSpider - Open Data Curation in the Global Chemistry Community

ChemSpider[14] is a search engine that provides free service access to the structure centric chemical community. Available since 2007 ChemSpider has collated over 300 data sources from chemical vendors, government databases, private laboratories and individuals, providing access to 25 million records. Used by chemists for identifier conversion and properties predictions, its datasets are also heavily leveraged by chemical vendors and pharmaceutical companies as pre-competitive resources for experimental and clinical trial investigation. Pharmaceutical companies are starting to realize the benefits of the open data model and contribute in kind, Glaxo Smith Kline[15] is an example of an enterprise intent on making its proprietary malaria dataset of 13,500 compounds available for community consumption.

Using the Open Community model, ChemSpider distributes its curation activity across its community using crowd-sourcing[16] to accommodate massive growth rates and quality issues. Integrating online services (e.g. PubMed[17], Google Scholar, Google Books and Microsoft's academic search) allowed ChemSpider move towards an environment that provides all additional required resources such as patent structured search. In addition, The Concept Web Alliance, a partner of the ChemSpider Initiative, is looking to linked data as a strategy to organize scientific data on the Web.

Driving its community vision was the provision of an environment where the community could participate in data curation, and validation that would help the chemical structure community to solve problems. Anthony Williams, ChemSpiders' VP of Strategic Development, attributes successful community participation levels to engagement and feedback through the use of social networking (e.g. blogs, forums, twitter, friend feed). The interactions, Anthony noted, led to better understanding of the community needs and an accommodation shift on ChemSpider's part which helped guide the project path. In curation terms, gaining access to knowledge skills and understanding that otherwise would not have been possible, proved to be critical.

---

[14] http://www.chemspider.com/ Last Accessed on 8th June 2010

[15] European Bioinformatics Institute Press Release, "GSK and Online Communities Create Unique Alliance to Stimulate Open Source Drug Discovery for Malaria", http://collaborativedrug.com/blog/news/2010/05/20/gsk-opens-up-2/ Last Accessed on 8th June 2010

[16] Jeff Howe, "The Rise of Crowdsourcing", Wired Magazine, Issue 14.06, June 2006

[17] http://www.ncbi.nlm.nih.gov/pubmed/ Last Accessed on 8th June 2010

8.1 Community Objectives

The majority of ChemSpider's data curation challenges are concerned with the identification of chemical identifiers, adherence to nomenclature structure standards, associated layered information such as experimental data, and establishing dataset record links to publications. With 25 million unique compounds across 300 sources, even simple data imperfections such as spelling errors can quickly make the curation effort unfeasible. Drawing upon experiences with Wikipedia's chemical data curation, ChemSpider engaged its community to assist with curation resources and quality.

8.2 Curation Approach & Types

ChemSpider uses a flat meritocracy model for their curation activities. Normal curators are responsible for deposition which is checked and verified by master curators. Normal curators in turn, can be invited to become masters after some qualifying monitoring period. The curation process is iterative, with normal curators receiving correction comments on rejected structures to apply before any new deposition.

ChemSpider blends human and computer based curation approaches to extract maximum knowledge from its community participants. *Robotic Curation* uses algorithms for error correction and data cleansing at deposition time. The algorithms automatically factor in a higher rank for previous manual edits with master curators occupying the most powerful rank position.

Leveraging novel approaches to curation *Blink* or *Game Based* curation used the gaming paradigm to extract curation effort. A spectral game[18] powered by chemical data from ChemSpider is used as a teaching tool on NMR spectrum interpretation. Game activity is actively monitored to identify problematic issues and paths which are fed back into the curation process to re-check existing spectrum analysis efforts and improve the data set quality. Spectrum analysis also represents *Focused curation* which specifically looks at a particular type of data. Focused curation relies upon targeted expert curators to help specify specific algorithmic and rule development. All curated data tracks specific provenance, including that of change through its deposition parameters.

Recognition of community curation effort and contribution to the wider community as done by Wikipedia is considered as a necessary next step by ChemSpider.

---

[18] http://www.spectralgame.com/ Last Accessed on 8th June 2010

9 Case Study: Protein Data Bank, Pre-competitive Bioinformatics

The Research Collaboratory for Structural Bioinformatics Protein Data Bank (RCSB PDB)[19] is dedicated to improving understanding of the function of biological systems through the study of the 3-D structure of biological macromolecules. Started in 1971 with 3 core members it originally offered free access to 7 crystal structures which has grown to the current 63,000 structures available freely online. In 2003, the RCSB PDB joined with sister organizations from Europe (PDBe) and Japan (PDBj) to promote outreach, education and standardization through the wwPDB foundation[20]. Today, the PDB has had over 300 million dataset downloads and continues to curate and annotate data with the support of its community. Its tool and resource offering has grown from a curated data download service, to one that serves complex molecular visualized, search, and analysis capabilities.

9.1 Serving the Community

Community uses of the data are varied; structural biologists and crystallographers starting a project find it useful to check if similar or identical structures are already in place. This can accelerate investigations to the next phase of the experimental process. Protein investigators searching for the 'holy grail' of protein sequence prediction, use the PDB as a knowledge base (assisted by analytics) from which to try and predict structure from sequence. Others use it as a storage and archival mechanism. Pharmaceutical companies frequently download the entire dataset and combine it with proprietary data as an essential tool for their internal drug development.

From PDB's perspective open data sharing is key as it encourages a wider audience in solving the same problem due to basic data and most often pre-competitive data availability. In fact this was the approach taken to combat the Aids virus. Protein - protein interaction and structure comparison represents a field that emerged from having an open structured data set that readily lent itself to structured informatics. PDB invested heavily in community engagement and education to get the point across that progress can be made faster by increasing data availability.

9.2 Curation Approaches & Types

Making available molecular representation, their 3-D coordinates and experimental data requires massive levels of curation to ensure that data inconsistencies are identified and corrected. A central data repository and sister sites accepts data in

---

[19] http://www.pdb.org/ Last Accessed on 8th June 2010

[20] http://www.wwpdb.org/ Last accessed on 8th June 2010

multiple formats such as the legacy PDB format, the mmCif introduced in 1996 and the current PDBML valid since 2005. Operating a global hierarchical governance approach to data curation work flow, wwPDB staff review and annotating each submitted entry before robotic curation checks for plausibility as part of the data deposition, processing and distribution. Distributing the curation workload across their sister sites helps to manage the activity.

A significant amount of curation process is performed with the use of vocabularies. Vocabularies provide identifier and access support for resource mapping and relationships between biological datasets, varying from organ tissue to structure description. The use of standardized vocabularies also helps with nomenclature used to describe protein and small molecule names and their descriptors present in the structure entry. Nomenclature standardization affects experiment descriptors, information sources and names that also change over time and across different theme lines. Tracking the identifiers across multiple databases even with taxonomic support is a challenge. While large portions of metadata is represented as RDF triples core atomic coordinate data is not. PDB are also involved in the development of experimental science-based ontologies through the Open Biology and Biomedical Ontologies (OBO) project[21] to further assist with the integration effort. The internal curation processes also uses a data dictionary to manage and translate the data into semantic enabled visual representations.

Robotic curation automates data checking with curators contributing to rule definition for inconsistencies. The process is iterative and corrections to discovered mistakes such as those against current standards are applied retrospectively to the archives. Versioned weekly schedules and periodic full datasets are released to keep all sources consistent with the current standards and ensure curation quality.

PDB provenance model was developed prior to the advent of any open public model and a separate project is looking at the Open Provenance Model.

9.3 Observations

Persistence in promoting the open data idea was the single biggest contributor to PDB's success. The PDB engaged community stakeholders from the start to determine what they wanted. Both producers and consumers of the data were engaged in dialogue and outcomes articulated as white papers. This early stakeholder buying, along with patience proved crucial for acceptance. The idea of data sharing was not initially popular but the drive to share important data beyond an individual group has since gained acceptance.

What is of particular interest is that while the wwPDB operate a consortium-type governance structure where consensus decision making is required, its member sites employ a *friendly competitive approach* to the provision of services and software offerings available from their site which they feel better serves the community. Pack-

---

[21] http://www.obofoundry.org/ Last accessed on 8th June 2010

aging of unique information only available at a particular site "supports innovative use of data and also further helps discovery of representation inconsistencies" observes Helen Berman, Director of PDB, feels that channeling creativity into the web sites is the best way to extract the richness of data usage. The approach of a no cost friendly competitions where you compete with the people you collaborate with "is an example of a lightly regulated community getting what they deserve".

10 Case Study Learnings

Learnings from case study practitioners fell into the broad categories of being either insights or practicalities. Of the two, insight, relating to social best practice was consistently emphasized as the key success factor for project success, and community participation. Practicalities confined to a technical focus were deemed important for project success only. The social elements of community participation along with technical best practices are next discussed.

10.1 Social Best Practices

The successful communities observed had social best practices in common:

- **Participation:** Stakeholders involvement for both data producers and consumers must occur early in the project. This will help provide insight into the basic questions of what they want to do, for whom, and what it will provide. White papers are an effective means to present these ideas, and solicit opinion from the community. They can be used to establish an informal 'social contract' for the community.
- **Engagement:** Outreach activities are essential for promotion and feedback. Social communication and networking forums are useful but be aware that with typical consumers-to-contributors ratios of less than 5%, the majority of your community may not communicate using these media. The communication by email still remains important.
- **Incentives:** For a community to participate in sheer curation there must be a line of sight from the data curating activity, to tangible exploitation benefits. If the general community lacks awareness of the value proposition, a collaborative contribution environment will be slow to emerge. Recognizing contributing curators through a formal feedback mechanism will help reinforce the contribution culture and directly increase output quality.
- **Community Governance Models:** An effective governance structure is vital to ensure the success of a community. Internal communities and consortium perform well when they leverage traditional corporate and democratic governance models. However, these approaches are not appropriate for open communities

where there is a need to engage the community within the governance process. Successful governance models for open communities follow less orthodox approaches using *meritocratic* and *autocratic* principles.

- A *meritocratic* community is lead by an elected leadership team or 'board'. In the meritocratic mode appointments are made and responsibilities assigned to individuals/organizations based upon demonstrated talent and ability. The community operates with an almost completely 'flat' structure, which means that any participant willing to contribute can engage and gain influence in recognition of their contributions. Examples include Apache Software Foundation and ChemSpider.
- An *autocratic* benevolent dictatorship is a community controlled in a hierarchical fashion with a single person or organization leading the community and has final say in decisions. A hierarchical model requires the leader to be strong in diplomacy and community building skills.

10.2 Technical Best Practices

In terms of infrastructure and process support the following were highlighted across the case studies as key practices:

- **Data Representation:** Data representations that are robust and standardized will encourage community usage, and tools development. Support for legacy data formats should be considered, as is the ability to translate all data forward to deal with emergent technology and standards is important.
- **Balancing Human- and Computer-based Curation:** Arriving at a balance between orchestrating automated and human assisted curation will improve data quality. For large datasets robotic curation should be used for validating data deposition and entry, while the community targets focused curation tasks. Robotic curation should always defer to, and never override, human curation edits.
- **Track Provenance:** A user consuming data generated from third parties needs mechanisms to assess the entities and process involved in the generation and publication of this data. Provenance is a key aspect in the process of mapping the historical trail behind an information artifact and can help determining if the data is high quality, trustworthy and compliant. Different users can lead to different perspectives of provenance. A scientist may need to evaluate the fine grained experiment description behind the data, while for a business analyst the 'brand' of data provider can be sufficient for determining quality. The ability to provide a provenance description attached to the data plays an important role in the data quality process. All curation activities including edits, especially where human curators are involved should be recorded and maintained as part of a larger data provenance effort.
- **Data Consumption Infrastructure:** As open datasets become more prevalent, companies will need to develop appropriate internal infrastructures to consume,

curate, manage and integrate third-party data. External data can be generated by business partners, expert communities or from the open web, the organizations data governance policies will need to cater for this consumption.

11 Conclusion

With increased utilization of data within their operational and strategic processes, enterprises need to ensure data quality and accuracy. Data curation is a process that can ensure the quality of data and its fitness for use. Data curation teams have found it difficult to scale the traditional centralized approach and have tapped into community crowd-sourcing and automated and semi-automated curation algorithms.

The emergence of pre-competitive data collaborations is a significant development: pre-competitive data is information that can be shared without conferring a commercial advantage. Within these collaborations, competing organizations share data and the effort required to curate data. With ever increasing data volumes, and continuing pressure on resource availability, these collaborations will become more prevalent within the enterprise information landscape.

Effective community based data curation is highly dependent on the community it serves. Early involvement of key stakeholders, a continuous community communication channel, clear incentives, and an effective governance model are important social aspects for community development. Persistence in promoting the idea of open data is the biggest contributory factor for a successful community.

Acknowledgements In writing this chapter we were fortunate to be have access to a number of thought leaders in the area willing to share their time, insights and experiences. We would like to thank Evan Sandhaus (Semantic Technologist), Rob Larson (Vice President Product Development and Management), and Gregg Fenton (Director Emerging Platforms) from the New York Times, Krista Thomas (Vice President, Marketing & Communications), Tom Tague (OpenCalais initiative Lead) from Thomson Reuters, Antony Williams (VP of Strategic Development) from ChemSpider, Helen Berman (Director), John Westbrook (Product Development) from the Protein Data Bank and finally Nick Lynch (Architect with AstraZeneca) from the Pistoia Alliance. The work presented in this chapter has been funded by Science Foundation Ireland under Grant No. SFI/08/CE/I1380 (Lion-2).

References

1. Davenport, T.H., Competing On Analytics, in Harvard Business Review. 2006. p. 98-107.
2. Wang, R. and D. Strong, Beyond Accuracy: What Data Quality Means to Data Consumers. Journal of Management Information Systems, 1996. 12(4): p. 5-33.
3. Knight, S.A. and J. Burn, Developing a Framework for Assessing Information Quality on the World Wide Web. Informing Science, 2005. 8: p. 159-172.
4. Ball, A., Preservation and Curation in Institutional Repositories. 2010, Digital Curation Centre.

5. Bourne, P. and J. McEntyre, Biocurators: Contributors to the World of Science. PLoS Comput Biol, 2006. 2(10): p. 142.
6. Uren, V., et al., Semantic Annotation for Knowledge Aanagement: Requirements and a Survey of the State of the Art. Web Semantics: Science, Services and Agents on the World Wide Web, 2006. 4(1): p. 14-28.
7. Appelt, D.E. and D.J. Israel, Introduction to Information Extraction Technology. in International Joint Conference on Artificial Intelligence. 1999.
8. Ekins, S. and A.J. Williams, Reaching out to Collaborators: Crowdsourcing for Pharmaceutical Research. Pharmaceutical Research. 27(3): p. 393-5.
9. Bingham, A. and S. Ekins, Competitive Collaboration in the Pharmaceutical and Biotechnology Industry. Drug Discovery Today, 2009. 14(23-24): p. 1079-81.
10. Barnes, M.R., et al., Lowering Industry Firewalls: Pre-competitive Informatics Initiatives in Drug Discovery. Nature Reviews Drug Discovery, 2009. 8(9): p. 701-708.
11. Giles, J., Internet Encyclopaedias go Head to Head. Nature, 2005. 438(7070): p. 900-901.
12. Emigh, W. and S.C. Herring. Collaborative Authoring on the Web: A Genre Analysis of Online Encyclopedias. in System Sciences, 2005. HICSS 2005. Proceedings of the 38th Annual Hawaii International Conference on System Sciences.
13. Mons, B., et al., Calling on a Million Minds for Community Annotation in WikiProteins. Genome Biology, 2008. 9(5): R89.
14. Stvilia, B., et al., Information Quality Work Organization in Wikipedia. Journal of the American Society for Information Science and Technology, 2008. 59(6): p. 983-1001.
15. Kollock, P. and M. Smith, The Economies of Online Cooperation: Gifts and Public Goods in Cyberspace, in Communities in Cyberspace. 1999, Routledge. p. 220-239.
16. Bryant, S., A. Forte, and A. Bruckman. Becoming Wikipedian: Transformation of Participation in a Collaborative Online Encyclopedia. in GROUP '05: Proceedings of the 2005 international ACM SIGGROUP Conference on Supporting Group Work. 2005. Sanibel Island, Florida, USA: ACM.
17. Viegas, F., et al. Talk Before You Type: Coordination in Wikipedia. in System Sciences, 2007. HICSS 2007. Proceedings of the 40th Annual Hawaii International Conference on System Sciences.
18. Bizer, C., et al., DBpedia - A Crystallization Point for the Web of Data. Web Semantics: Science, Services and Agents on the World Wide Web, 2009. 7(3): p. 154-165.
19. Hepp, M., K. Siorpaes, and D. Bachlechner, Harvesting Wiki Consensus: Using Wikipedia Entries as Vocabulary for Knowledge Management. IEEE Internet Computing, 2007. 11(5): p. 54-65.

Few doubt the impact of the great quantities of new information now flooding enterprises. Technologists, however, cannot provide any part of a solution without two critical criteria; budget and buy-in. This part provides material to make business cases and an account of the politics necessary to shepherd a mission-critical Linked Data project through a Fortune 500 company. Never easy, the navigation of large enterprise politics is nevertheless critical to the success of any large project.

Preparing for a Linked Data Enterprise

Bernadette Hyland

Abstract

The cost of building a business application in the early 1990's that was both resilient and could handle additional data sources, let alone third party content, was many times the cost of building a simple application. The use of Web tools and techniques has changed that. The use of Web architecture within enterprises started in the mid-1990's and continues today. The introduction of Web architecture within the enterprise has had many benefits which include shortened development cycles, improved product innovation and increased product and service quality. The Semantic Web, a concept introduced in 2000, introduced the concept of machine-understandable content. The benefit of having computers (or computer programs) understand content is to retrieve and present more relevant information to people. Linked Data, a concept introduced in 2006, is the next evolution and uses the Semantic Web to *link related but previously unconnected content* in new and meaningful ways. Later chapters in this book discuss both early and current efforts to showcase enterprise data and drive new value and insights.

In a world that contains vast amounts of digital data, Linked Data is emerging as the *scalable and generalized* approach to link previously unconnected information. This chapter highlights the characteristics of an organization that is prepared to embrace this decentralized approach for wrapping and exposing content for data discovery. Linked data brings us closer to the benefits touted by proprietary data management and analysis vendors, but in an open, non-proprietary and ground-up manner. The successes enjoyed by the early adopters suggest that Linked Data techniques are likely to have a major impact on enterprise architectures in the near future.

Bernadette Hyland

3 Round Stones Inc., Fredericksburg, VA 22408, USA, e-mail: bernadette.hyland@3roundstones.com

D. Wood (ed.), *Linking Enterprise Data*, DOI 10.1007/978-1-4419-7665-9_3,
© Springer Science+Business Media, LLC 2010

1 Introduction

Expectations by customers, partners, suppliers and the public have increased for highly available online services and accurate information. The expanding reach of Google, Facebook and other personal online services has resulted in greater expectations within enterprises, especially by the younger generations of workers. Web approaches are expected. The Web, of course, is still evolving and the pace of change is increasing.

The next big thing for the Web regards the handling of machine-understandable data. The Web is becoming a huge distributed database, in parallel to its scope as the worlds file system. Human and machine-understandable content is moving us closer to the Semantic Web as described by Tim Berners-Lee in his 2006 publication, "Linked Data Design Issues"[1]. Linked Data, those aspects of the Semantic Web most suited to the immediate task, is the means by which this evolution of the Web is occurring. Linked Data techniques, like the earlier aspects of Web technology, are beginning to impact enterprise IT systems[2]. Commercial and government organizations, several of whom are discussed in this book, are making significant contributions, and commitments, to the Linked Data cloud.

The benefits of Linked Data have been described as a means to ensure the public trust and establish a system of transparency, public participation, and collaboration[3]. The benefits include decentralizing and exposing legacy silos of data thereby enabling new applications and better resource discovery. Improved discovery and re-use is particularly relevant in the news and media industries, which we discuss in later chapters of this book. Additionally, Linked Data is seen as critical means to satisfy emerging government mandates for transparency and accountability.

The amount of high quality, trusted data for decision making throughout the enterprise has increased. In recent years, Oracle, IBM, Microsoft and SAP have collectively spent in excess of US$15 billion on acquisitions of software companies that focus on data management and analytics, an industry estimated to be worth $100 billion and growing at the rate of 10% annually[4]. Budgets to solve large enterprise data problems are constantly being allocated. Linked Data techniques are some of most effective tools in the toolbox to address enterprise information integration issues.

2 The Cost of Linked Data

Linked Data projects demonstrate real business value in a small fraction of the time earlier Web-based applications required. For decades data has been created in legacy databases, silos, and industry and enterprise-specific controlled vocabularies. Enterprises have data and it is generally well described. The process of linking data is generally one of reformatting, organizing and exposing existing data. Data is exposed by making it available via a Web server, connected to either the public network or a private one.

Based on our consulting experience within Fortune 2000 organizations, application of Linked Data tools and techniques allows developmental teams to show results in short timeframes. Developers and business users can quickly determine the usefulness of a linked data approach, define deliverables and acceptance criteria. Repeated 6-8 week sprints work well to move from demonstrating value to eventual production applications. Much of this book is dedicated to the successes of Linked Data in practice, however, it is important to recognize that the benefits of Linked Data do not come without some cost. Costs to participate on the Linked Data cloud may be expressed in terms of:

1. Cost of Services and support
2. Cost of Education and training
3. Infrastructure Expense

2.1 The Cost of Services and Support

Organizations often have a specialist in information analysis, access and data curation. This individual is trained in procedures and best practices for making data available as a Web service. Their role is to increase consistency, make re-purposing of content straightforward and empower data owners within the enterprise to published quality data sets. This key resource should be factored into a business case as an expense.

2.2 Education and Training

Education and training for application developers and IT support groups should be accounted for in the business case for a Linked Data project. There is a significant amount of free information available on the Web, along with a helpful Linked Data community that is growing on a daily basis. There is opportunity cost however in culling through Web content and advice on mailing lists and online forums. A number of the enterprise case studies examined for this book included the use of an outside expert for training and mentoring of IT and executive management teams.

Management requires mentoring and advice on establishing a Linked Data strategy within the enterprise. External consultants with a track record in providing advice to corporate and government organizations can help navigate and avoid the pitfalls. Consultants can play a useful role in identifying what are the aspects of an appropriate first Linked Data project, how to accelerate time to delivery and importantly, what infrastructure would be useful for deployment.

2.3 Infrastructure

Leverage Open Source wherever possible. If your organization leverages Open Source, consider supporting an Open Source project on a part time basis. Alternatively, budget for development work undertaken by a commercial company that specializes in creating and publishing Free/Libre/Open Source Software (FLOSS) projects. If you are using Open Source, be sure your personnel and/or contractors contribute back the changes they make. If they do not contribute the changes and the Open Source project is upgraded, then changes made for your project may be lost. This is an expensive and often overlooked mistake organizations made by not understanding how to operate with the Open Source community and FLOSS projects. Leverage Open Source projects where there is an active development community, preferably not a sole contributor. If you are part of a government organization, find out what other agencies and departments are using the Open Source project too and leverage financial resources for Open Source development activities.

An example of a well-proven Open Source technology for linking data is the use of Persistent URLs (PURLs). The use of Persistent URLs can greatly reduce the long term costs of linking data by ensuring longevity of identifiers. Standing up a PURLs Server allows enterprise identifiers to be maintained, monitored and their usage reported. For more information on PURLs, go to the PURLs community site.[1] Commercial organizations offer production Linked Data managed services for services including persistent URLs, data conversion and visualization. Outsourcing managed services is an efficient way to stand up Linked Data services for less than the cost of a full time resource.

If your organization is standing up a service that is intended for 24x7x365 use, factor in the expense of standing up development and production server instances. Today, this can be done both quickly and economically using the cloud service providers. The costs for standing up a production service has been reduced by at least one order of magnitude in the last three years.

3 Is your Organization Ready for Linked Data?

A key attribute of Linked Data is that it can begin at any level in the organization. Another aspect is that it is often built on Free/Libre/Open Source software ("FLOSS") components and there are ways to ease that transition, especially at the management and corporate legal level. Strive for clear separation between what is enabling technology (e.g., wikis, data transformation tools, browser plugins, etc.) versus company-confidential business logic and workflows. Management should become familiar with the different types of FLOSS licenses that are appropriate for use within your organization. Federal government agencies and departments typically

---

[1] http://purlz.org

have a stated policy and care should be given to reviewing the proposed FLOSS within the context of existing policy.

There is no such thing as a typical Linked Data project; initial prototypes may be large or small, targeted toward critical data or purely academic in nature. No perfect ontology nor use case need be minted. Valuable results from publishing Linked Data may be achieved with some modest investment in time and planning. The costs for an given organization will vary depending upon the internal skill level, how many other groups are going to be involved, the organization's receptivity to and experience with Open Source software and, critically, the level of executive support provided.

Much of the underpinnings of the Internet and the World Wide Web have been the result of academic research projects. Increasingly, commercial organizations are providing consulting and managed services, software-as-a-service (SaaS), hosting and support. There are online resources, including discussion groups and mailing lists available from the World Wide Web Consortium (W3C). Free or low-cost community activities such as the Semantic Web Meetup[2] groups are a great way to learn what others are doing and who the experts are in your area. The annual Semantic Technology Conference (STC) draws together forward-thinking technology and business leaders from around the world. Leveraging external experts can also reduce the cost of deployment, and increase the likelihood of successful outcomes. Research for this book has shown that all successful Linked Data projects in enterprises to date have leveraged expert advice in some form. Experts can help navigate past dead ends and steer the project team toward best practices.

The Internet is prompting institutional change in the face of an organizations resistance to change, especially within government agencies[5]. Based on the explosion of Linked Data on the public Web over the last three years[3], some commercial enterprises are embracing the promise of Linked Data and are transforming their data management strategies to more fully be compliant with Linked Data principles. Recently, the governments of the United Kingdom[4], the United States of America[5], Canada, Australia and New Zealand defined mandates to publish government data for use by researchers and the public. The focus of the next several years will be on production of high quality content, better tools for discovering and viewing Linked Data, as well as deploying the highly scalable production applications that will be the foundation of early majority uptake.

Linked Data may be exposed in ways that are searchable by major search engines. People, especially younger people, tend to use content they can find using a search

---

[2] SemWeb Meetups have over 10,000 members and are meeting in over 17 countries. http://semweb.meetup.com/

[3] The W3C SWEO Community Project estimated the number of triples to be approximately 13 trillion as of June 2010. http://esw.w3.org/TaskForces/CommunityProjects/LinkingOpenData/DataSets/Statistics

[4] http://data.gov.uk/ is a key part of the Government's Transparency programme for the UK public sector as a whole.

[5] As of June 2010, nearly 200 high value data sets out of 1,500 have been published and 250 new applications based on data.gov datasets have been been written. http://www.data.gov/metric

engine and ignore information they cannot rapidly locate[6]. Indexing by search engines is thus critical to gaining use and acceptance of your information. There are other concerns as well: People tend to turn to experts when facing health problems; government agencies top the list when information about specific programs is of concern[7]. Exposing useful and relevant information is as important as making it searchable.

Think about books as an analogy. Many books are written with varying levels of credibility. Someone looking for high quality information will have to somehow search through the large number of books to find credible authorities on a given topic. That search may be done with the help of search tools or a reference librarian. Librarians, professional curators, are a relatively untapped resource for helping manage the overwhelming context available through Linked Data, directing enquirers and sharing their recommendations into a broader context that increases the value of the corpus of information. We need to engage data curators now more than ever.

Trusted communities and organizations who publish high quality data reinforce their "brand". Over time, they may become a de facto provider of valuable, trusted information about a specific domain of knowledge. Organizations such as the United Nations, federal government agencies and Fortune 2000 companies are now implementing effective and well-considered Linked Data strategies to serve their members, constituents and customers.

Today's enterprises face a unprecedented explosion of data and a highly competitive business climate. While there is no silver bullet for information management, creating the right balance between machine processing and exception handling, can be readily achieved through incorporating the data management strategies outlined in this book.

Combining enterprise data and vocabularies with the architectural principles of Linked Data leads to that "ah ha!" moment for many seasoned executives. Credibility and executive support is far easier to achieve when they can *see their own data linked with related, but previously unconnected content*. The ability to visualize ad hoc combinations of data is why major data and analytics vendors are spending billions to show leadership in decision support solutions. Those responsible for research, drafting policy, performing risk analysis, and doing compliance reviews can see the potential of using Linked Data techniques when the ubiquitous Web browser is the only tool required. That is especially true when the data in question was once distributed across many spreadsheets, business reports and separate Web pages. The ability to drill down on native applications remains, but the new ability to discover (versus search) underlying content is a profoundly important paradigm shift made possible though Linked Data and the Web.

Geoffrey Moores business classic Crossing the Chasm[8] defined terms to track the adoption of products and ideas. Web technologies have, in Moores language, crossed the chasm to reside firmly in the realm of the late majority. That is, even latecomers have Web sites, email, use outsourced Web-based services and use Web techniques internally. Linked Data is at an earlier stage, perhaps in the transition from early adopter to early majority - in the chasm itself. The successes enjoyed by the early adopters suggest that Linked Data techniques are likely to have a major impact on enterprise architectures in the coming months and years.

4 The Linked Data Initiative

The term "Linked Data" was coined by Tim Berners-Lee in his July 2006 publication on Linked Data Design Issues[2]. The term Linked Data refers to a style of publishing and linking structured data on the Web.

The key concept of Linked Data, as it is on the Web itself, is the Uniform Resource Indicator (URI). URIs have two roles - one is to serve as a global identifier for things and the other is to provide somewhere to look for information. HTTP URIs allow content to be located and retrieved via the Web. The SPARQL query language, analogous to the well-known SQL query language for relational databases, may be used to treat Linked Data on the Web as a huge database.

The basic assumption of Linked Data is that the *usefulness and value of data increases the more readily it can be accessed and recombined with other data*. This assumption may sound familiar to the value of the Internet, or the Web, itself. Metcalfe's law, named after the inventor of ethernet, states that the value of a telecommunications network is proportional to the square of the number of connected users of the system. Linked Data is showing us that the same is true with data. A fundamental property of RDF is that RDF graphs may be readily combined, unlike most non-standard data description schemes. The availability of open standards (e.g., RDF, SPARQL, SKOS and RDFa) and the increased availability of both commercial and Open Source software tools has allowed the Linked Data community to grow at an exponential pace.

The last couple of years have seen an unprecedented growth in information creation, and in storage and retrieval systems. Unfortunately, that has also led to fantastically complex information silos and complex knowledge management landscapes. An information revolution is desperately needed to provide knowledge workers, researchers and policy makers the ability to recombine existing information in new and interesting ways. This is true both on the Web and within enterprises. The Web, due to its fully distributed and robust architecture, has evolved an answer that enterprises need to consider: Linked Data. The purpose of the Linked Data project on the Web was to interrelate data in Web-accessible silos so that one might "follow your nose" or follow the path from one data silo to another via hyperlinks. The techniques of Linked Data can now help enterprises interrelate their own silos of information.

5 A Decentralized Approach to Data Management

The recent work of researchers in the advanced Web community[6] is taking a fresh approach to referencing resources on the Web. The intent is to create a more effective framework for information sharing and reuse. By linking data using standard Web techniques (the hyperlink and descriptions of resources on both sides of the links), information systems may be related at very little cost. Each system must simply wrap and expose its data via a Web server and URI addressing.

The central insight is that its not the documents that are important, but rather the things the documents are about that is important. Dan Brickley, a long-time participant in the development of Web standards, has said, "The Web is about links. The Semantic Web is about the relationships implicit in those links." The context of documents, the topics, characteristics, sources and provenance, and especially the interlinking patterns between documents is the true foundation for discovery and assessment of useful resources on the Web. The Semantic Web initiative at the World Wide Web Consortium has been actively developing these ideas for more than a decade. Linked Data techniques have come out of that work.

Linked Data is a way to make it just as easy for people to establish and share context on the Web as it was for them to originally share documents. It looks as much as possible to reduce the burden of the Web developer by building on things that are already widespread on the Web. It focuses on Web identifiers (URIs), linking, and simple expression of the context of documents in the form of standardized metadata (RDF).

Web principles are also the basis of trends such as "Web 2.0", "social computing" and "cloud computing". Social computing tools are aimed at interpersonal and group communication. Cloud computing forms a basis for commoditizing and outsourcing computing resources. These aspects of the modern Web give Linked Data scaffolding for growth, but its important to recognize that while the underlying components may be the same, the goals of Linked Data are more nuanced.

Linked Data builds on the Web foundation, but is emphatically geared towards cooperative decentralization.

The idea is to empower people and institutions to present information of creative and intellectual value in a way that can be readily connected to other Linked Data resources without the intervention of a central aggregator. These techniques may be used on the public Web (as with the Linked Open Data project) or take place completely within the bounds of an enterprise network. Many institutions have been discovering this opportunity on the public Web, and the Linked Data cloud has been growing almost as prodigiously as the original Web. Some recent examples of organizations joining the Linked Data cloud are National Public Radio, the BBC, Newsweek, New York Times, the World Bank, the UK governments data.gov.uk, along with US Governments efforts with recovery.gov and data.gov.

---

[6] Linked Open Data Community Project, http://esw.w3.org/SweoIG/TaskForces/CommunityProjects/ LinkingOpenData and http://linkeddata.org/

Many governments are making commitments to transparency with the Web as the primary publishing interface. They are publishing data as Linked Data because they recognize it to be a workable and inexpensive approach for publishing data and are doing so in gradual and sustainable ways[7]. These examples are a small fraction of a rapidly growing movement of leveraging the Web, and the power of people, for managing and sharing of data.

Linked Data developments have clear benefits for making it easier to share and discover valuable information, and to evaluate the credibility of this information, but some of these benefits obtain more slowly because there are few clear alignments with large commercial interests. Another retardant is the paucity of curators for the large quantities of information that is rapidly coming together in the Linked Data space. To date, almost all curation of the public Linked Data cloud has been done by volunteers.

Linked Data can serve not only as a rich body of information for policy and decision-makers, but also as a flexible framework that makes it easier for internal and third party data providers to organize and curate that information. The richness of information available through Web 2.0 applications such as wikis, blogs and other systems with implied or actual semantics, and the growing interest of Linked Data are a latent fuel, and there is a very unique opportunity at present for governments, non-profits and commercial organizations to spark a true revolution in how individuals discover and utilize valuable data. Linked Data has the potential to greatly empower individuals with timely, relevant information.

6 Being On the Web vs. In the Web

Enterprises who publish a Web site without exposing machine-understandable data are "on the web", but not "in the web." Web pages with HTML, CSS (Cascading Style Sheets) and Javascript are machine-understandable, however relied upon the programmer or Web designer to define how the data would be presented and used. Whereas, preparing Web pages with metadata embedded (RDFa or micro-formats), an RSS or Atom feed for news or publications, or even rich, downloadable data sets, represents the semantics and allows the computer to process it dynamically in order to discover what the content means and how to use it.

Being "in the Web" implies leveraging Web Standards and best practices for publishing content and metadata on the Web. Enterprises contributing to the Linked Data cloud use URIs to identify things, not only documents but *everything*. Everything means:

- **Physical Resources**, in the real world, for example, a car itself;
- **Concepts**, in the real world, the idea of a car; and
- **Information Resources**, a Web page describing a car, or an image of a car.

---

[7] Jeni Tennison, Why Linked Data for data.gov.uk?, January 26 2010, http://www.jenitennison.com/blog/node/140

Ideally, each URI is de-referenceable, meaning that one can point a Web browser to that address and get either content or a description of the thing it describes. Applications that are *in the Web* are changing how commercial, governments and non-profits, operate and communicate. Third parties are able to recombine data, discover new use patterns utilize and leverage the authoritative information for decision making. Linked Data techniques have the network effect; it can be impossible to tell in advance who might use the data and how. That may seem risky at first, until one realizes that empowering people empowers the enterprise.

7 Leverage Vocabularies

It is considered best practice to reuse existing vocabularies whenever possible. Enterprises generally have well refined vocabularies for their own internal use. Some have vocabularies, taxonomies or ontologies useful to others. When reusing existing vocabularies, it is recommended that one convert them to international standard formats (RDF and the vocabulary descriptions built on it). When defining new vocabularies, one should construct small, discrete "micro-vocabularies" related to the general types of resources reflective of a domain (e.g. people, place, topics, etc.)

Two meta-vocabularies prove valuable in most enterprise linked data initiatives:

- **SKOS**, the Simple Knowledge Organization System, is a lightweight language to help migrate existing taxonomies and other knowledge systems to the Semantic Web. Its primary value will be to reduce the cost of migrating existing vocabularies.
- **voiD**, the Vocabulary of Interlinked Datasets, is used to describe data sets as a whole, rather than information about any particular component. The intent is that it be used to advertise the availability of data.

Describing organizational concepts, terms and relationships is challenging. Organizations with experience in vocabulary and terminology projects recognize the value of consistency in describing this information and similarly, appreciate that diverse views and perspectives on concepts, terms and relationships should be embraced.

The real value comes from carefully curated vocabularies and terminologies and made accessible for others to reuse. RDF has come of age in the era of Linked Data partially because many useful vocabularies for common terms have already been developed. It is relatively easy to leverage standard vocabularies to describe common concepts, terms and relationships within a given knowledge domain. A domain expert has the freedom to describe other terms unique to a specific knowledge domain and then align it afterward. Terms may also be combined (specifically, noted that they are the same as another term). Thus, one has the freedom to publish content in RDF and if a new vocabulary emerges in the future, one can equate the previous vocabulary with the new one.

8 A Simple Approach to Linked Data

The first steps in creating a linked data set is to publish data on the Web, preferably in a non-proprietary format such as comma separate value (CSV). Alternatively, publishing data sets in RDF/XML with an XSL stylesheet allows Web browsers to display a nicely formatted page containing URIs to machine-understandable content. The added benefit of publishing data sets in RDF/XML is that it allows scripts or Linked Data clients access to the raw data. The preferred approach to Linked Data consumption is to use data directly from the source. If the data uses standardized formats, a script or Linked Data client can be used to transform the data into an immediately consumable form so that it can be integrated into a target system. However, here is an outline of the initial steps:

- Find some data with reuse potential.
- Describe your data and give it context.
- Use URLs to identify information resources so that others may point to them.
- Plan for persistence, e.g., PURLs
- Publish data on a Web site. That data may be in XML, RDF, or even comma-separated values.
- Create an online catalog of published data so others can find and reuse it.

Linked data is not simply a dump of of a database or a spreadsheet, rather it should be richly described data which it precisely what makes it *high value data.* Descriptions should include schema information, for example, how this data relates to other things, what unit of measure the units are in, and what the data represents. A best practice is to add human-understandable labels and descriptions to describe the data to a human being. Descriptions of where and when data came from, called provenance is still a widely discussed area and there is no standard yet. Do not allow the lack of a standard prevent you from adding provenance information if the use case requires it. Getting started with Linked Data need not be difficult. One may start on the public Web or within the enterprise. Providing context is very important in creating high quality linked data sets.

- Re-use vocabularies wherever possible.
- Preserve provenance, e.g. seeAlso, etc.
- Relate when possible, e.g., owl:sameAs, etc.

Tim Berners-Lee in a keynote at the Gov 2.0 Expo 2010 described a "5 star" system for data that was summarized by Ed Summers[8]. Tim described this system in which the more stars, the better. A key point he made is, one gets one huge star for cutting through the bureaucracy and getting data published to the Web. Do not stop at one star, strive for five stars. Continue with adding structured data to earn 2 stars, preferably in a non-proprietary format (e.g., comma separated value instead of Microsoft Excel) earns 3 stars. Adding URLs so others can point to published data gets 4 stars, and linking data to other people's data earns the coveted 5 star rating!

---

[8] http://inkdroid.org/journal/2010/06/04/the-5-stars-of-open-linked-data/

Unlike any other technology or syntax previously defined, data exposed as Linked Data allows people and machines to select data that is meaningful and useful.

Other best practices include the use of permanent addresses for data elements. Use patterned or best practice URIs in accordance with W3C guidance[9]. Linked data is about following these rules for data production. It is about using URIs to identify resources, providing information at the end of those URIs that is self-descriptive, and linking those resources to other resources using these URIs.

This approach works well from the ground up which fits well with an enterprises model for third party data provision. The Linked Data approach dovetails nicely with governments and NGO initiatives who are publishing information with similar strategies. It does not require a top down approach, rather Linked Data benefits from people on the ground publishing content, one data set at a time.

Many organizations publish non-company confidential content on both their intranet(s) and external website. The goal is to incorporate trusted third party content to drive new insights and services. Researchers, analysts and other users of the data will be able to graft onto your data and add value.

9 Conclusions

The bar has been raised and there is pressure to deploy a Linked Data strategy to reinforce the organization's brand and reach via the Web. If the organization is seen as the de facto source for a specific type of information, it is critical to make that information available both human and machine-understandable formats on the Linked Data cloud.

The transition to being "in the Web" is occurring. Machine-understandable data should be presented as metadata embedded in Web pages (RDFa or micro-formats), an RSS or Atom feed for news or publications, or even rich, downloadable data sets. Expectations have increased along with access for highly available online services and accurate information. Linked Data are a latent fuel for governments, non-profits and commercial organizations around the world to spark a revolution in data discovery, access and re-use.

9.1 Prepare for a Linked Data Enterprise

1. Publish content in both human and machine understandable formats. Publish machine formats that major search engines are able to parse. If content cannot be found via a Web search, it is increasingly being overlooked, especially by younger people.

---

[9] Cool URIs for the Semantic Web, http://www.w3.org/TR/cooluris/

2. Leverage existing controlled vocabularies, terms and relationships which your enterprise has already spent resources to develop.
3. Ensure the longevity of your linked data identifiers, such as by using Persistent URLs (PURLs)[10] to manage their long term resolution.
4. Use Web Standards and Open Source (FLOSS) Software to achieve more effective information sharing, re-packaging and re-use, with the minimum of specialized Web development skills.
5. Follow best practices and document them for others to use.
6. Empower a specialist in information analysis, access and data curation to assist data owners with procedures and support expose data. The benefit is increased consistency and straightforward repurposing of content.
7. Recognize there is no such thing as a typical project; initial prototypes may be large or small, targeted toward critical data or purely academic in nature.

Creating an application that combines linked enterprise content and public data *is very compelling to management.* Executives should view defining a Linked Data strategy and supporting organizational efforts as *leading edge, not bleeding edge.* While there are costs associated with making content available long term on the Linked Data cloud, the benefits outweigh the costs. Linked Data will unlock new sources of economic value, provide new insights and help hold governments to being more accountable.

Acknowledgements The author wishes to acknowledge the efforts of the early pioneers of both the Semantic Web and more recently the Linked Data Community, especially my colleague Eric Miller at Zepheira who always took the time to share his vision. Many thanks to Tony Shaw and his highly competent team at Wilshire Conferences who brought the technical and business communities together to envision how to make this goodness stick and be truly useful. The conversations we share each year at the Semantic Technology Conference go along way to make "open standards, open software, and open society" a reality. Thanks to Jeni Tennison of the data.gov.uk project for blogging about her experiences and helping others to get started. Special thanks go to David Wood who has applied his multidisciplinary engineering skills to foundational parts of the Internet and taught me so very much along the way during the last 17 years. Linked Data is the culmination of thousands of really bright people who took the time to lay the groundwork for building an open and highly connected world, so that billions of people will hopefully benefit.

References

1. Berners-Lee, Tim. Linked Data Design Issues, July 27 2006, http://www.w3.org/DesignIssues/LinkedData.html
2. Mills, Anthony, Collaborative Engineering and the Internet, Society of Manufacturing, 1998
3. Obama, Barack. Memorandum for the Heads of Executive Departments and Agencies on Transparency and Open Government, December 2009, http://www.whitehouse.gov/the_press_office/Transparency_and_Open_Government/
4. The Economist. Data, data everywhere, a special report on managing information, page 4, Feb 27 2010

---

[10] http://purlz.org

5. Anderson, Janna and Rainie, Lee. The Impact of the Internet on Institutions in the Future, Pew Internet & American Life Project, Pew Research Center, March 31 2010, http://www.pewinternet.org/Reports/2010/Impact-of-the-Internet-on-Institutions-in-the-Future.aspx

6. Taylor, Paul and Keeter, Scott (eds). Millennials - A Portrait of the Generation Next, Pew Research Center, February 2010, page 27, http://pewresearch.org/millennials/

7. Estabrook, Leigh, Witt, Evans and Rainie, Lee. In Search of Solutions: How People use the Internet, Libraries, and Government Agencies to Find Help, Pew Internet & American Life Project, Pew Research Center, December 31 2007, http://pewresearch.org/pubs/677/in-search-of-solutions

8. Moore, Geoffrey. Crossing the Chasm, Harper Business Essentials, 2nd Edition, 1999.

Selling and Building Linked Data: Drive Value and Gain Momentum

Kristen Harris

Abstract

Data inside enterprises is exploding. Routinely key decision makers state, "one of the most valuable assets of our organization is actionable information." Paradoxically, it is often challenging to gather the necessary metrics to build a business case to justify a Linked Data initiative for improved data quality in the face of the well-documented shortcomings of traditional enterprise approaches to data management. Internet standards have matured considerably in the last decade. The number of linked data sets is growing daily and already exceeds well in excess of ten thousand data sets, over 400 of which are published via the US Government at http://www.data.gov as of April 2010. Many of these linked data sets are high quality. Best practices for linking data within the enterprise are increasingly being published in articles, blogs and technical books. One of the pioneering linked enterprise data projects was undertaken by a Fortune 500 company in the early 2000 timeframe. The lessons learned about how to navigate the management and organizational dynamics are relevant today. This chapter outlines the successful strategies for a linked enterprise data initiative, including a consistent metadata management strategy across lines of business, definition and documentation of data ownership and the value of cross-functional teams in the definition, development and deployment of the project.

A team of executives, managers and data creators at Sun Microsystems built a business case to transform static enterprise data contained in a large number of data silos to linked enterprise data published on their public Web site. Core to the effort was a cross-functional team focused on defining the business use cases, the data architecture and benefits of reduced data duplication, data re-use and enhancing the web experience for employees, customers and partners. This chapter highlights the

Kristen Harris

Oracle Corporation, 500 Oracle Parkway, Redwood Shores, CA 94065, USA, e-mail: kristen.harris@oracle.com

D. Wood (ed.), *Linking Enterprise Data*, DOI 10.1007/978-1-4419-7665-9_4,
© Springer Science+Business Media, LLC 2010

organizational tactics and strategies employed to build support for this linked data initiative.

1 The Data Burden

Today's business climate requires a competitive organization to identify opportunities in new sectors, support employees, customers and partners, and meet regulatory and compliance requirements, often using Web technologies. Many will admit it is often easier to locate accurate enterprise information on the companys public web site than to source the same information internally on the enterprise intranet. All too often one hears of colleagues painstakingly creating new copies of datasets in order to have it available for re-use. There are many hurdles to overcome. For example, data is often poorly described, not exposed and therefore difficult or impossible to search. If relevant data is found, it is generally coupled tightly to an application with complex business rules. Most likely it is not granular and there is no programmatic interface which makes re-use cumbersome at best.

Increasingly, Linked Data solutions are deployed within the enterprise to overcome the aforementioned problems. Critical to a successful information integration effort is identifying and exposing the most valuable data. Defining a use case and a corresponding data set is a critical first step for any linked enterprise data initiative.

An enterprise is likely to be far more competitive when they are able to analyze, transform and clearly understand potential business opportunities and new markets. In addition, enterprises oftentimes need a cross-functional view of their knowledge. Data must be able to be recombined and viewed through the lens of various business sectors, e.g., regulatory and compliance, legal, finance, marketing, product development, and client support. It is critical to represent data such that the lines of business, data ownership rules and process for the creation, access, updating and deletion of data are understood.

This chapter describes the key lessons learned on a major information integration effort that wrapped and exposed data via the Web, and incorporated semantic technologies, to produce one of the first dynamically created multi-lingual product catalogs available on the public Web. We focus on how linked data concepts were communicated to the executives and woven together to transform the corporation's customer facing Web. While the development team employed various linked data technologies, they were transforming the data inside of the existing Web content management systems (WCM), eCommerce, configuration and other back-end systems across the company. It was important to communicate to the executive management team that employing new technologies is not a silver bullet. Transforming enterprise data takes time; however, productivity gains will be achieved in the increased utilization and re-use of data upon delivery. In fact, transformation of enterprise data and well described metadata required years to change and mature. Throughout this project there was much achieving, pursuing, laboring, and waiting[1], and through the years the team gained great success in the data initiatives. A linked data strategy should be implemented incrementally, striking balance in the alignment of both tactical and strategic business objectives. There are challenges in focusing on good data architecture *and* practical business need, but that is how linked data in the enterprise becomes a success.

2 Driving Value Principles

A Linked Data project must take into account the limitations of the enterprise which may include lack of specific technical expertise (e.g., Web architecture, linked data technologies, ontology development, data curation, etc.) and a culture of inflexibility, while simultaneously driving towards an ambitious information integration project. The key is connecting the vision to clear business drivers and articulating the goals of the project. Quantifiable business results will serve to propel future projects leveraging linked enterprise data, thereby building the "network effect." One of the key reasons projects fail is because of a misalignment between project teams vision and the daily pressures of supporting and running the core business[2]. In addition, if an IT manager makes technology choices a centerpiece of the solution, ahead of defining the business processes or issues to be addressed, the project may fail. The business drivers are also very often missed in Web development and redesign projects because typically very bright Web-savvy developers correctly identify the usefulness of Web-based enterprise solution; however they fail to articulate a clear delivery roadmap that aligns with the needs of the business within a timely manner. Where well-specified and properly implemented linked data projects excel is in keeping pace with the rapidly changing business landscape. Properly implemented, linked data initiatives are all about *future-proofing an organizations core data assets*.

Sun's web data transformation started with a few loosely defined business drivers and was long on vision by several key executives. In the early 2000's Sun was committed to be a leader in global Internet solutions. The portfolio of enterprise network computing products included workstations, servers, software, microprocessors, and a full range of services and support. The company had a Web focus and one of the goals was to provide innovative solutions to help Internet startup companies get up and running quicker and more efficiently. As innovation goes, the products the company was selling were becoming increasingly complex and more numerous. The companys knowledge of and data about their products was becoming more and more difficult for any management team to comprehend the complexity and interdependencies. Their ability to put data in the hands of their critical partner network for sales, education and procurement was lagging behind their competitors. To keep up with the competition and changing business landscape, the Web based product data catalog, needed major improvements, inclusive of improved user experience.

Being an innovative technology company did not excuse Sun from setting out on their data improvement project with ill-defined business objectives. The management of Web data for their large, constantly-updated corporate product sites presented enormous resourcing and quality challenges. The team set out to address the following challenges:

1. Enable customers around the world, to find products and product information quickly.
2. Gather and expose related information, such as comparison of similar products, and companion services or upgrades of those products.
3. Ensure minimal manual Web navigation with consistency of organization and nomenclature.

Reworking of all the publishing processes across the corporation's hundreds of Web publishers was not an option. A purely process oriented answer would not work without being tied to a more fundamental, data architecture driven approach. Architecting a solution using semantic web technologies to build a framework for Web data relationships was envisioned. In the end, some rework of business processes would be needed. The proposed framework, the swoRDFish Metadata Initiative[3], was the first step in changing how data worked in the organization and how the customers would experience researching products through the Web interface. Related and in response to the business drivers above, the components of the swoRDFish Program were outlined as follows:

- Create an RDF Metadata Repository
- Provide a framework of SOAP-based Web services
- Allow viewing of metadata through a simple Ontology Browse Utility
- Enable relationship management through swoRDFish Ontology Management & Administration (SOMA) Utility

In the early days of the project, the team spent nearly a year modeling and prototyping the Web-friendly RDF metadata store, which was modeled using DAML+OIL (DARPA Agent Markup Language and Ontology Interface Layer[1]). Working in the early 2000s, long before Web Ontology Language (OWL) was refined, DAML+OIL as a superset of RDF was able to utilize Jena, a Java API for processing RDF, and an Oracle database to implement the data store. Yet even with the technology framework set, and prototyping well underway, the boundaries for the role of the RDF store, early adopters, ontology owners, and business cases upon which to start driving relationships were yet to be chartered.

One of the most valuable ways to get a quick check on the proposed approach is to do some prototyping. Key to any prototype is that it must be tied to a use case that managers can readily see, preferably with enterprise data with which they are familiar. It drives the point home to use familiar content but to show novel ways of viewing or recombining the data.

Although the project started strong on the technology side, it wasn't making the progress or showing tangible results with the business units. At this stage, core pieces of infrastructure were not yet mature and discussions around technically complex topics bogged down the goals of rapidly showing business value. Additionally,

---

[1] http://www.daml.org

it lacked the buy-in and backing across lines of business due to an undeveloped vision not yet presentable to diverse audiences. To successfully show the vision tied to business value, internal and external experts are required.

At least one internal champion of a linked enterprise data approach is required for success. That executive understands the complex culture of the enterprise and champions the vision, connecting it to the many audiences of the organization. A singular-storyline approach to selling the initiative creates the risk of lagging support across diverse lines of business. Speaking to more than just the enthusiastic supporters is critical. The executive needs to articulate the vision carefully in spite of diametric business cases and complexities.

Most successful early stage projects also leverage an external expert who can help prioritize planning, design, prototype, deployment phases of the project. Importantly, an external expert adds the needed support that executives need - they can answer "what are my competitors doing?", "how has this worked in other projects similar to this one?" A strategic Web consultant is often helpful in articulating the vision and helping to gain momentum across different parts of the organization. Ideally, the executive, someone from the project team and/or the outside expert should each be able to concisely describe how the linked enterprise data project will better position the organization.

Take care not to describe the project too conceptually, be ready to show a prototype and describe the improved workflow, improved analysis and/or visualization capabilities of the resulting linked data initiative. Most importantly, a well articulated vision drives the business to engage with an emphasis on the following:

1. Speak the language of and appeal to the interest of the stakeholders (customers, shareholders, employees)
2. Explain and convey the project's goals with real-world examples.

Selling the vision of the project was not unlike selling change through an organization. Vision is mentioned in many methodologies for enabling change. Kotter International[2] is a group which leads executives and teams through change. With regard to the vision, Kotter says this:

> A good vision can demand sacrifices in order to create a better future for all of the enterprises stakeholders.

Selling the value of a corporate-wide Linked Data program takes more than architecture diagrams and descriptions of modeling languages. Taking the project to the next step requires sound technology coupled with willingness by business teams to make sacrifices in how they work. A key milestone is having data owners, as well as the internal champion support the project while working to understand and mitigate project risks. This is the best way to create tangible use cases to share.

A compelling business case may quantify the cost to maintain data across the various classification systems, and the risks that result from working in silos of complex spreadsheets to structure metadata and content. Correlate business unit objectives with real figures in resourcing costs and costly inconsistencies within and

---

[2] http://www.kotterinternational.com/KotterPrinciples.aspx

across each business unit. Avoid diving into the details of the architecture or the latest buzz on Web technologies, and focus on all the ways in which the organization is storing and proliferating its core data assets, resulting in poor customer experience, lost opportunities, non-compliance or other costly business issues.

If diligent, a few adjustments to process could save millions of dollars through more effective data creation, curation and re-use strategies. Defining a clear path for a linked data initiative involves incorporating current best practices which are readily available through management consulting firms, blogs and recently published books on linked data and the semantic web.

A key aspect of a successful project is defining a metadata management strategy which includes getting the various data owners to sponsor and drive that metadata through legacy systems. A Linked Data project is not about the perfect taxonomy or centralized metadata repository; rather, it is about articulating, documenting and leveraging Web-oriented development tools for building Web-based applications. Once an organization has made their data accessible as linked enterprise data, business users, enterprise data curators, suppliers and partners will rapidly wrap and expose their content in new and unforeseen ways.

3 Building a Team

In building momentum for a successful project, one of the challenges is figuring out how to best mobilize the team to implement the project roadmap. Engaging stakeholders from across the company, encouraging them to review and sanity check the use cases or later asking them to adopt new ways of thinking may prove difficult. In the beginning of the project, the team was centralized. In some ways it was an advantage. The dedicated team of data experts included business and governance experts, modelers, coders, ontologists, engagement managers and more, all reporting into a centralized structure. This team's charter was to establish and maintain standards for repeatable metadata and data process and procedures, as well as influence the semantic layer of various systems across the company. Yet, the centralized team lacked authority to take the linked data initiative deeper into the organization's culture. In any large corporation or organization, centralized teams are often faced with the inevitable organizational politics and associated issues. Risking alienation from the business complexities and facing resistance as they engaged with distributed teams, the centralized team needed a less authoritarian approach.

A strategy that yielded a positive outcome was to solicit the help of the executive sponsors who were working to gain support for the project across business units. Asking the sponsors for support in seeking and engaging experts across business units, the team virally engaged key players from within the company to sow the seeds of linked data and semantics throughout their systems. Creating a project team aligned with a committed business sponsor and a widening set of business unit champions, the core team reduced the risk of alienating themselves from the real business issues. Evolving the backbone of data systems is not done with a centralized team pushing standards downstream, but by the adoption of linked enterprise goals defined by a well connected core team working their way into the organization and expanding reach as a virtual team. The difference is subtle, but critical. With embedded champions emerging around the company, both the project and the team gain credibility.

Getting the new team to align on the project goals is the next step. Accomplishing short-term goals in rapid sprints helps to solidify a virtual team, while rapidly rationalizing the initiative and reducing risk and project costs. Setting up short term goals takes careful consideration. If incremental goals are not tied to the overall business drivers they distract the team from more important long term goals. Added pressure on the team is another risk of rapid sprint pilot projects. However, when well defined and solidly executed upon, short term goals build valuable momentum for the team.

To begin showing tangible results connected to business drivers, the projects executive sponsor mandated that the team build a dynamic, customer-facing Web site with an initial set of data that was to be more than a simple prototype. It was to be a live example on the corporations production Web site. In order to gain significant experience it was decided that even though a marketing focused product ontology was not yet ready in the swoRDFish Project, a real-world, customer-facing pilot project was going to be built. This pilot (called the Hero Pilot) fueled the future of linked data initiative and drove the Web content management ecosystem in new directions. The pilot pushed forward both the internal metadata and Web platforms. Semantic web goals emerged as followed:

- Create authoring environments that evolve with the anticipation and encouragement of data re-use, separating data from design.
- Rebuild a set of related, consistent tools for Web data entry and metadata association.
- Prepare an XML content repository.
- Provide a dynamic presentation system based on the use of the metadata repository.

As the project continued, there were two or three groups working on and replacing old processes to move the Linked Data initiative forward. Web publishers relinquished control of some of their data to be defined in swoRDFish and manipulated by Web engineers to create the dynamic content, while the linked data project team drove relationships to enhance the Web experience.

The Hero Pilot became a short-term big win. It was visible. It was unambiguous. It was a success. The small set of dynamic product pages were live and getting thousands of hits an hour. The team could relish in success for a moment, even though they knew there was much work in front of them to be done. For now, taking the story of the success of the live pilot along with the vision of the Semantic Web they were able to much more concretely describe the value of linked data in the corporation. The executives were able to move from describing only the most high level details of the vision, to adding specific (live in production) use cases for specific linked data sets and could now match that with the key goals of the initiative. They had a clearer story and specific examples of what each group across the organization could really empower by using linked data. Executives now would not just tell the story, but actually show the rest of the company how to get involved. This was changing how people worked, and it would most certainly be changing how their data could work for them.

Not only was the pilot transformational for the message, it was also transformational for building of the team. The team had expanded across organizational, as well as global boundaries, adding credibility and momentum to the initiative. Now, with the continuing momentum across business units, the linked data project was well on its way to becoming a legitimate, company-wide standard.

4 Committing to Something Bigger

The project was gaining momentum, and a steady flow of products and parts were being fed into it from various source systems (product lifecycle, education/training, and support systems). But a well-defined, marketing focused ontology of products within which many relationships would be curated was still incomplete. If this project was going to lay the groundwork for the entire customer facing Web experience, it needed a flexible marketing-focused ontology behind it. This was going to be critical to the success of the overall initiative.

Be careful to not get bogged down developing vocabularies, taxonomies or ontologies in early stages of a project. It is unlikely that "one size" will fit all. Successful linked data projects are a hybrid of standard and custom vocabularies. Simple knowledge object representation allows the project to show results more rapidly versus getting the end-all-be-all ontology created. However, in expanding a projects reach across large sets of data a custom ontology may be required to support the growing goals. A smart, yet practical ontologist must make some tough design decisions in building any ontology. Working through many details of core enterprise data and vocabularies is required before starting to define the ontology relationships.

Maximizing value and leveraging tags across disparate systems the ontologist only classified a subset of the tens of thousands of products, at the appropriate level of granularity, to be sure the custom ontology provided the most value across business units. The ontologist had to think like a customer; carefully weighing and envisioning what a customer might want to know at any stage in their research / buy / support lifecycle and model to those rules. Some calculated guesses and trade-offs were made in hope that fate would be on their side with certain risky decisions. The marketing ontology was widely adopted as the backbone of product relationships and became the single Web marketing view of the products, their associations, structure and nomenclature. Taking a risk to build a marketing ontology of products resulted in being a very important investment. The ontology connected product content, facets for product finding, companion information links, comparison of similar products, configuration rules, and much more.

Along with standard vocabularies, a custom ontology, albeit a large investment in creation and maintenance, can be an important part of the next big steps in making subsequent projects a wider success. Cutting across the data and business rules locked into systems, a custom ontology can link data that was previously impossible to expose or relate. Tagging even the most complex data eventually provides high value.

Table 1 shows a distinct example where different groups maintain some subset of marketing, manufacturing or configuration information; however, before the corporate Linked Data strategy, this information could not be leveraged on a Web page or outside of the original scope of use for the data.

Table 1 Data Types related across systems

Data Type	Example	Managed By
Marketing	Product name, product image, short description Sun SPARC Enterprise T5120 Server Eventually, everyone will have this kind of processing power and efficiency, but you can get it today, in a 1RU server. [ ] Virtualize, consolidate, and accelerate.	Product Marketing via Web Publishers in Web Content Management System
Option Class (Help) Text	Option class text is used to assist the customer configuring the hardware. Help text is specific both to the Option (in this case Memory) and to the product (Sun SPARC Enterprise T5120). It looks like rules, but is not. Presented to users as tips, such as: The Sun SPARC Enterprise T5120 has 16 DIMM slots supporting up to 64 GB of memory. Memory DIMMs are added in pairs. All DIMMs in the system must be the same size. Only memory configurations of 4, 8 or 16 DIMMs are supported.	Store Operations / Data Analysts in Configuration Tuner database
Configuration Rule	An option choice used to build the hardware, governed by a set of rules. 4 GB Memory Expansion (2 x 2 GB FB DIMMs) Low-Profile, Second Gen 2, 1.8 V	Configuration Experts in Oracle Configurator

Although each of these data types were first created for other purposes and are stored in separate databases, a combined view of this data is presented in an eCommerce interface today. The simple example above shows the benefits of reduced data duplication, data reuse and an enhanced experience for employees, customers and partners.

5 Putting it together

At the time, this was one of the earliest examples of a corporate Linked Data strategy. It included storing metadata in RDF to identify and describe the companys products across systems and departments. A successful Linked Data project should review the available modern development platforms specifically designed with and for semantic technologies, e.g., RDF, URL/URIs, persistent identifiers (PURLs), versus shoe-horning metadata into a relational database and older style development platforms. Many of these more modern development platforms are available as Open Source software (FLOSS).

As customers, employees and partners enjoyed locating product data or directly to the product's documentation, based on the shared resource, and they really started to experience the value of the linked data. What they were locating was a mashup of product data presented from a series of structured Web sites, but was transparent to the customer, employee and partner.

Key to success is maintaining quality content upon which others rely and trust. Content curators learned to appropriately tag content and soon they would automatically attract complementary web content on their product pages with little to no effort. Tying together various interface tabs for product content, facets for product searches, companion information links, atomized comparison of similar products, and so much more were the building blocks that a well designed linked data project delivers. With more business (content) owners and back-end systems following the publishing standards, including using the tags, the data becomes more rich in relationships and relevant to employees, partners and customers.

As additional groups started to see the value of recombining content, the business realized that there was a huge momentum building for more than just the customer-facing product Web site. Architects of systems for documentation, service and support knowledge, configuration, eCommerce, software downloads and more moved toward integration with the linked data initiative.

The project has formed the foundation of linking simple to complex content, from product image libraries and marketing content to the most detailed product specifications and configuration rules. One of the unanticipated business benefits is that employees feel they are speaking a similar language and working toward shared corporate goals in their daily efforts. Even though most of the data is stored and maintained by experts in separate teams in a wide variety of repositories, there is a foundation of linking that data such that it can readily be wrapped and exposed, and critically important, used to make important decisions with a higher degree of confidence in the quality of the information.

6 Conclusions

Challenges of integration and pressures of daily operations keep us busy, however, organizations that determine their high value data, and take the step to expose that important data, are more likely to be successful.

Transforming static, unstructured data into linked enterprise data served Sun's employees, customers and partners well. Linked data continues to accelerate meeting new opportunities, serving partners and customers more efficiently and handling rapidly evolving regulatory and compliance requirements.

The success of one linked data initiative inevitably leads to more. No matter what systems are in place today, there will always be another big initiative to define and build next year. Linked data is a future-proofing strategy that cannot afford to be overlooked or postponed within your organization. Always remember that the best ideas are at risk of failing without strategies for how to position an effective plan to obtain executive backing and employee adoption across a complex landscape.

Improve the chances of funding, designing and deploying a linked data initiative by keeping the following in mind:

1. Lead with Vision.

    a. Start with well understood business problems and transform that into business drivers.
    b. Link the vision to tangible business results that resonate with stakeholders.
    c. Be ambitious yet realistic in setting goals.

2. Gain support from executives leading the charge.

    a. Educate executives and tell the story with conviction and preferably a proof of concept with content (data) familiar to the target audience.
    b. The technical details should be covered last & briefly - dont dwell on technology.
    c. Explain the initiative in a way that is relevant to the target audience.

3. Structure the team to succeed.

    a. Understand the pros and cons of building centralized teams.
    b. Enlist at least one internal champion.
    c. Identify an external expert to help define a project with a high likelihood of success given the unique characteristics of your organization. Sometimes it requires seeing with new eyes.
    d. Do not be afraid to add new perspectives to the team to gain credibility, but remain laser focused on delivery.
    e. Require the team to work through hard problems together, gaining trust and credibility.

4. Drive specific, achievable wins to build momentum.

    a. Define small wins that don't distract from, but drive toward the larger project.
    b. Connect incremental projects to the value drivers.

5. Scaling the project.

    a. Don't be afraid to GO BIG. Architect upfront to later scale the project. As much as the beta release should be scrapped and an entirely new application written, it rarely happens that way in practice.

   b. Do not underestimate the time and expense associated with implementing, testing and documenting a scalable platform.

6. Lastly, no matter what the next challenge, keep innovating.

References

1. Longfellow, Henry Wadsworth. Psalm of Life, http://www.poemhunter.com/poem/a-psalm-of-life/
2. Dorsey, Paul. Top 10 Reasons Why Systems Projects Fail, http://www.dulcian.com/
3. Cone, Susie and MacDougall, Kathy. Case Study: The swoRDFish Metadata Initiative: Better, Faster, Smarter Web Content, W3C Semantic Web Use Cases and Case Studies, http://www.w3.org/2001/sw/sweo/public/UseCases/Sun/

Part III
Techniques for Linking Enterprise Data

Even the most capable technologists and ardent supporters of Linked Data techniques are likely to need additional tools to deal with the complexities of enterprise information. This Part contains four such tools.

The recent integration of social networking tools into enterprises has facilitated information dissemination that created yet another integration problem. The Sem-SLATES approach described in the next chapter presents a solution and a series of techniques to enhance information integration of Enterprise 2.0 tools.

The following chapters provide guidance and examples for the translation of existing data sources to Linked Data, the application of logical reasoning techniques to enterprise-scale problems and the use of persistent identifiers to ensure long-term accessibility of Linked Data resources.

Enhancing Enterprise 2.0 Ecosystems Using Semantic Web and Linked Data Technologies: The SemSLATES Approach

Alexandre Passant, Philippe Laublet, John G. Breslin and Stefan Decker

Abstract During the past few years, various organisations embraced the Enterprise 2.0 paradigms, providing their employees with new means to enhance collaboration and knowledge sharing in the workplace. However, while tools such as blogs, wikis, and principles like free-tagging or content syndication allow user-generated content to be more easily created and shared in the enterprise, in spite of some social issues, these new practices lead to various problems in terms of knowledge management. In this chapter, we provide an approach based on Semantic Web and Linked Data technologies for (1) integrating heterogeneous data from distinct Enterprise 2.0 applications, and (2) bridging the gap between raw text and machine-readable Linked Data. We discuss the theoretical background of our proposal as well as a practical case-study in enterprise, focusing on the various add-ons that have been provided to the original information system, as well as presenting how public Linked Open Data from the Web can be used to enhance existing Enterprise 2.0 ecosystems.

Alexandre Passant
Digital Enterprise Research Institute, National University of Ireland, Galway, IDA Business Park, Lower Dangan, Galway, Ireland, e-mail: alexandre.passant@deri.org

Philippe Laublet
STIH (Sens - Texte - Informatique - Histoire), Université Paris-Sorbonne, 28 rue Serpente, 75006 Paris, France, e-mail: firstname.lastname@paris-sorbonne.fr

John G. Breslin
School of Engineering and Informatics, National University of Ireland, Galway, Galway, Ireland, e-mail: john.breslin@nuigalway.ie

Stefan Decker
Digital Enterprise Research Institute, National University of Ireland, Galway, IDA Business Park, Lower Dangan, Galway, Ireland, e-mail: stefan.decker@deri.org

D. Wood (ed.), *Linking Enterprise Data*, DOI 10.1007/978-1-4419-7665-9_5,
© Springer Science+Business Media, LLC 2010

1 Introduction

Blogs, wikis, as well as free-tagging and content syndication principles are now widely used in the enterprise, in a paradigm shift generally referred to as Enterprise 2.0 [23]. In this vision, Web 2.0 tools and their collaborative behaviours (which are now widely accepted on the Web) become part of the enterprise: *"Enterprise 2.0 is the use of emergent social software platforms within companies, or between companies and their partners or customers"*[1]. Furthermore, since the social aspect predominates, the Enterprise 2.0 vision relates to the *Information Ecology* paradigms proposed by [10], in which people play a central role in information systems.

Inside the enterprise, these tools help to enhance information sharing and collaboration between employees, with a global aim to enable collective intelligence in such structures, following the *"We are smarter than me"* idea [21]. When defining Enterprise 2.0, [23] discusses how such tools can transform intranets into dynamic and evolving structures thanks to user involvement. In addition, he characterises how Enterprise 2.0 should respond to user needs by defining the SLATES acronym:

- *Search* — Efficient information retrieval;
- *Links* — Links between (internal and external) content;
- *Authoring* — Easy publishing services;
- *Tags* — Tag-based annotation;
- *Extensions* — Discovery of new content;
- *Signals* — Identification of relevant information.

However, the services usually deployed to achieve this goal introduce various issues regarding how to efficiently use the information they help to produce. First, their nature and diversity emphasise issues regarding information fragmentation, as content about particular objects (projects, customers, etc.) is split within several tools. Moreover, their plain-text nature makes knowledge capture and reuse particularly difficult, while they generally provide valuable and consensual information, in particular within wikis. Finally, free-tagging leads to ambiguity and heterogeneity issues, also constraining the information retrieval task.

In this chapter, we discuss an approach based on Semantic Web and Linked Data technologies to solve the aforementioned issues. In particular, our approach, named SemSLATES (for "Semantic SLATES"), provides a *Social Semantic Middleware* architecture that can enhance existing information systems with these technologies [27]. It relies on different level of ontologies and metadata generated from existing Enterprise 2.0 applications, thus enabling Linked Data in Enterprise 2.0 environments, by forming a complete graph of RDF(S)/OWL annotations on top of existing information systems. Furthermore, once this additional layer of semantics has been provided, new applications can be deployed, ranging from semantic search interfaces to semantic mashups, combining internal data and information gathered from the Linking Open Data cloud, enhancing enterprise information systems by reusing public and open data from the Web.

---

[1] http://andrewmcafee.org/blog/?p=76

The rest of this chapter is organised as follows. In Section 2, we detail the three main issues of Enterprise 2.0 ecosystems that we briefly mentioned earlier. Then, in Section 3, we present our SemSLATES proposal, detailing (1) its global vision and architecture; (2) the ontologies it requires; (3) how existing applications can generate the related data; and (4) how new services can be deployed using it. We then present a related case-study of the SemSLATES implementation at Électricité de France (EDF) Research and Development[2] in Section 4 and we particularly focus on the ontologies we designed, the plug-ins that have been developed, as well as the additional services that we have engineered. Furthermore, since the motivations of our work came from that particular case, the issues described in Section 2 are back-ended by some figures gained in this context [26]. Finally, we conclude the chapter, also discussing how the approach can be extended with further data, such as mobile information or sensor networks deployed in the enterprise.

2 Issues with Current Enterprise 2.0 Ecosystems

As mentioned in the introduction, Enterprise 2.0 can be defined through the SLATES acronyms, and blogs, wikis, RSS feeds — among others — aim to achieve this goal of collaborative knowledge management. However, while they definitely help to reduce the burden of creating and sharing information in the enterprise (simple interfaces, open access, etc.), they raise various issues regarding how to efficiently use this information. To that extent, we believe that Mathes' views regarding folksonomies (*"a folksonomy represents simultaneously some of the best and worst in the organization of information"* [22]) can be applied to Enterprise 2.0 ecosystems in general: more and more information becomes available, but it becomes more and more difficult to make sense of it.

To defend this opinion, we now detail three main issues of Enterprise 2.0 ecosystems, based on our experience at EDF R&D : (1) information fragmentation and heterogeneity of data formats; (2) knowledge capture and re-use; and (3) tagging and information retrieval. In this chapter, we only focus on the technical issues of Enterprise 2.0 systems. There are however other — more social — issues that must be considered to make such systems successful, especially in organisations where generally *"knowledge = power"*. For instance, in our context, we observed that some users were reluctant to open-up their wikis, while they finally changed their mind when realising that other open wikis received valuable contributions. These relationships between the corporate culture and adoption of Enterprise 2.0 principles have also been observed by an AIIM study indicating that 41% of respondents do not have a clear understanding of Enterprise 2.0, as against only 15% for companies with a knowledge management background [11]. Thus, it is important to keep in mind that more than a set of tools and technical prerequisites, Enterprise 2.0 is a

---

[2] EDF is the major electricity company in France — see http://rd.edf.fr for details.

philosophy that can sometimes takes time to be accepted, as noted by Dion Hinch-cliffe: *"Enterprise 2.0 is more a state of mind than a product you can purchase"*[3].

2.1 Information Fragmentation and Heterogeneity of Data Formats

Information sharing and social networking in organisations is generally object-centric: people publish and browse information about particular objects such as projects, research topics, customers, etc. This relates to the "object-centred social-ity" idea [18] that can also be observed on the Web (*e.g.* people connecting through musical artists in last.fm). While some Enterprise 2.0 information systems are pro-vided using dedicated suites, such as IBM Lotus Connections[4], they generally con-sist of an aggregation of services fragmented over a company network. Indeed, the heterogeneity of people and topics in organisations often leads to different ways to share information and hence to different applications being deployed: some people may only need an RSS reader, other will require a wiki or a blog, etc. Furthermore, these services might be setup at different times, which make them even more hetero-geneous (some software architectures may becomes obsolete and are consequently replaced by new ones, etc.).

As a consequence of the fragmentation of services and applications, data and knowledge about particular objects is often spread between various sources in the company network. For example, the description of a project and its deliverables can be edited on a wiki but the latest project news may have been blogged and commented about on another platform, while RSS feeds may also contain valuable information regarding the project partners. Consequently, knowledge workers must query different sources of information to get the global picture regarding a particu-lar topic. Most importantly, users must know that these sources exist in order to be able to reach them — which is not always the case, especially in large-scale organ-isations. Furthermore, different applications imply different APIs and data formats. Hence, information integration is a costly task for developers.

While this is not a new issue *per se*, Enterprise 2.0 strengthens information frag-mentation since it provides users with new means for publishing content, thus en-abling more and more distributed and heterogeneous data, locked in walled-garden applications that do not interact each other. As an example, in our environment, more than 200 users where involved in the creation of more than 4,700 wiki pages and 21,000 blog posts, over a three years period.

---

[3] http://blogs.zdnet.com/Hinchcliffe/?p=143
[4] http://www-01.ibm.com/software/lotus/products/connections/

2.2 Knowledge Capture and Re-use

Wikis are used in many organisations as a way to collaboratively build open and evolving knowledge bases, in areas ranging from project management to software development. Yet, while they contain much valuable information, software agents cannot easily exploit and reuse it easily. A reader could learn from a wiki that EDF is a company producing nuclear energies in France but an application will not be able to easily answer requests such as *"Is EDF located in France?"* or *"List all companies referenced in this wiki"* without using complex Natural Language Processing algorithms. The main reason is that wikis simply deal with documents and hyperlinks and not with machine-readable of real-world concepts, as understood by readers when they are browsing or editing a page. A wiki engine will indeed store the fact that *"There are some hyperlinks between a page titled "EDF", a page titled "France" and a page titled nuclear "energy""*, but it will not be able to deduce anything about the nature of those different objects and their relationships, since the pages do not carry enough semantics about the knowledge they contain, *i.e.* focus on a *document-centric* view rather than on a *data-centric* one.

Hence, there is a gap between documents and their interpretation. Consequently, users must parse and read all the pages from a wiki to answer such queries, which can be a time-consuming task. Moreover, user interpretations can be biased and different depending on their cultural and technical backgrounds.

2.3 Tagging and Information Retrieval

Tagging is a well-known practice on Web 2.0 websites and consists of the attachment of multiple free-text keywords or "tags" as metadata to created content. Tags are often used as a means of categorising similar content from various users for later retrieval and browsing. In addition, an important feature of tagging is its collaborative aspect, since tags can be shared between people, and are often used to retrieve and browse documents produced by others. The collection of these tagging actions and keywords created by many users is generally known as a folksonomy [39].

The limits of free-tagging approaches are mainly due to tag ambiguity and heterogeneity as well as a lack of organisation between tags [22] [34]. Consequently, while tagging can be a time-saving method for end users when publishing and categorising content — since they do not have to apprehend a pre-defined classification — it becomes costly when trying to retrieve relevant information. For example, since tag-based search engines are plain-text only, someone looking for items tagged *"social_software"* will neither get those tagged *"socialsoftware"* (spelling variant) nor *"logiciel_sociaux"* (linguistic variation), and they will not be able neither to find specific tags such as *"wiki"*. While clustering approaches can be used in some cases [2], an analysis of our organisational folksonomy raised other interesting issues regarding that topic.

First, as in many systems, most of the tags used in our blogging platform were used only a few times. In a total of 12,257 tags — used within 21,614 blog posts — it appeared that more than 68% were used twice or less, while only 10% were used more than ten times. As [15] has reported, tag clustering may not be adapted for this kind of distribution, unless combined with other techniques such as, for instance, taking into account the underlying tagged information. This is also a complex issue if dealing with non plain-text documents, such as PowerPoint files or diagrams that can be exchanged in corporate blogging platforms.

In addition, another lesson learnt from our folksonomy analysis is that users tag differently depending on their level of expertise and that these differences in tagging behaviours also raise several issues when retrieving content. For instance, we identified that experts in solar energies used specific tags such as *"TF"*[5], while non-experts would use generic ones like *"solaire"*[6]. This relates to the different "basic levels" of knowledge that people have regarding given domains [38], as also raised by [12] when analysing tagged content from Delicious. Furthermore, we identified that experts often did not use any broader terms when tagging content. Only 1% of the 194 items tagged with *"TF"* in our system were tagged together with *"solaire"*, while less than 0.5% of the 704 items tagged with *"solaire"* were tagged with *"TF"*.

Hence, clustering algorithms cannot be efficiently used to find related tags since they are too weakly related, as discussed in [2]. Thus, lots of valuable content (*i.e.* created and tagged by experts) cannot be retrieved by non-experts, as they use generic keywords in their queries. This entails a real problem in terms of knowledge sharing inside organisations and limits the possibilities offered by these collaborative platforms: most of valuable information (*i.e.* produced and tagged by domain experts) is lost as it cannot be easily retrieved by non-experts.

3 SemSLATES: A Social and Semantic Middleware Approach for Enterprise 2.0

While we agree that most Enterprise 2.0 tools ease the *Authoring* process (from the SLATES acronym), we have shown in the previous section that they are somehow limited regarding some other features, especially *Search* and *Extensions*. To solve these issues and to offer new value-added services to end-users, our proposal consists of using Semantic Web technologies (*i.e.* RDF(S)/OWL, SPARQL, etc.) and Linked Data principles, to enable (1) interoperability between heterogeneous Web 2.0 applications in the enterprise, (2) knowledge capture — by bridging the gap between *documents* and *data* — , and (3) better information browsing and querying *via* additional applications using this machine-readable and structured data. In particular, our approach focuses on:

---

[5] An acronym for *Thin Film*, a particular kind of solar cell.

[6] French for *solar*.

- using lightweight semantics and simple add-ons producing Linked Data from existing tools, rather than building a new monolithic application that would require to rethink existing information systems;
- re-using existing models and data already available on the Web, hence (1) bridging a gap between the open Web and Enterprise 2.0 information systems and (2) taking advantage of structured data available on the Web (especially from the Linked Open Data Cloud) to enrich Enterprise 2.0 information systems;
- considering users as the core component of the system, by being producers and consumers of semantic annotations, hence strongly emphasising the collaborative side of Semantic Web-enabled knowledge management.

This additional stack of semantics on top of existing Enterprise 2.0 information systems led us to define SemSLATES, *i.e.* "Semantic SLATES", demonstrating how Semantic Web technologies can enhance the SLATES approach (Table 1). By applying the SemSLATES principles to existing Enterprise 2.0 systems, a query such as *"List all the blog posts written last week about a project involving a company based in France"* can be answered, while it cannot be carried out using current Enterprise 2.0 systems.

	SLATES	SemSLATES
Search	Plain-text search	Semantic search based on RDF annotations
Link	Hyperlinks between documents	Relationships between resources
Authoring	Documents	Data and metadata
Tags	Tagging	Semantic indexing based on ontologies
Extension	Hyperlinks navigation	RDF graph-based navigation
Signals	RSS feeds	Semantically-indexed RSS feeds

Table 1 SemSLATES: Extending SLATES using Semantic Web and Linked Data technologies.

3.1 The SemSLATES Architecture

In order to achieve the SemSLATES vision, there is a need to provide an additional layer of semantic annotations on top of existing Enterprise 2.0 systems, thus "linking enterprise data" [37] and enabling a new area of Semantic Enterprise 2.0 information systems, since this layer provides the meaningful integration of data from heterogeneous components. It is also important to keep in mind that our goal is not to engineer a new knowledge management suite for Enterprise 2.0, but rather to provide means to integrate various existing components together in a transparent way for end users. Therefore, we consider SemSLATES as providing a *Social and Semantic Middleware* approach for Enterprise 2.0, enhancing existing ecosystems. To that extent, we defined a middleware process [41] comparable to the *RDF*

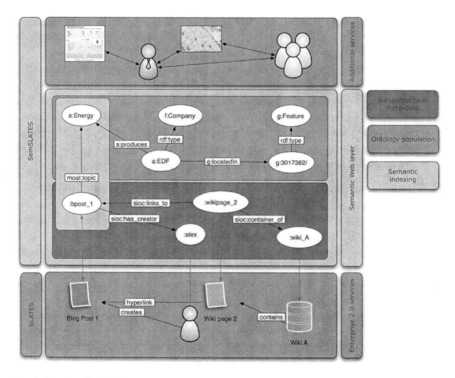

Fig. 1 The SemSLATES approach: Combining different layers of RDF(S)/OWL annotations on top of existing Enterprise 2.0 systems.

bus architecture proposed by Berners-Lee[7]: semantic annotations are produced from existing tools, and these are then interlinked and queried using Semantic Web standards (RDF(S)/OWL and SPARQL).

More precisely, various kinds of semantic annotations are required to enable this SemSLATES layer, as depicted in Fig. 1, and defined as follows:

- **socio-structural metadata** are required to model uniformly (1) structure of existing Enterprise 2.0 applications, (2) metadata about the social interactions happening between users in these applications, and (3) the resulting documents. This layer solves the issue of heterogeneous data formats and APIs between different Enterprise 2.0 applications, by offering a common representation layer for such, wherever they come from. Our vision relies on popular ontologies such as FOAF — Friend Of A Friend[8] [8] — , a lightweight ontology aiming at representing people and their social networks, and SIOC — Semantically-

[7] http://www.w3.org/2005/Talks/1110-iswc-tbl/#(26)

[8] http://foaf-project.org

Interlinked Online Communities[9] [6] — dedicated at representing online communities, their activities and contributions;

- **domain-specific ontologies and semantic annotations** are required to enable representation of the business information stored inside these Enterprise 2.0 systems (*e.g.* information about companies, projects, etc.). Here domain-specific ontologies can be used along with popular existing vocabularies [4]. In order to create the related annotations, semantic wikis are of particular interest, since they combine wiki principles (open editing, versioning, multi-authorship, etc.) and Semantic Web knowledge representation principles for a user-driven, open and evolving population of related knowledge bases, as described in more detail in [9] and [35];

- **semantic indexing** is required so as to allow content to be annotated with URIs identifying meaningful information (such as projects or people) instead of simple and unstructured keywords. This latest layer solves the issues of free-text tagging and enables links between domain ontologies and socio-structural metadata, leading to a complete interlinked graph of structured data on top of existing Enterprise 2.0 systems. It is achieved thanks to models and frameworks as MOAT — Meaning Of A Tag[10] [31] — an ontology and process to bridge the gap between free-tagging and semantic indexing.

In addition, to enable these annotations, enhancements of the original tools must be as lightweight as possible to avoid disturbing users in their existing publishing habits. Considering that transitioning from legacy information systems to Enterprise 2.0 environments can take time (in terms of user acceptance), it is indeed important to build on existing services, rather than providing new applications that can take time to be accepted. Once these enrichments have been enabled, and therefore the annotations being available, new applications can be provided, improving the whole user experience of querying and browsing information in Enterprise 2.0 settings.

To that extent, SemSLATES promotes the use of user interfaces that do not confront end-users with any of the underling modelling features (URIs, Linked Data principles, RDF(S)/OWL, triples, etc.). These interfaces include geolocation mashups and faceted browsing, some of which will be detailed in Section 4. Hence, SemSLATES bridges a gap between Enterprise 2.0 and the Semantic Web in both directions (Fig. 1) by (1) providing a Semantic Web layer for enabling Linked Data on top of Enterprise 2.0 applications, and (2) using user-friendly Web 2.0 interfaces for browsing and querying complex RDF(S)/OWL graphs.

---

[9] http://sioc-project.org

[10] http://moat-project.org

3.2 Ontologies for Enterprise 2.0

As seen in the previous section, various layers of semantic annotations are required to enable the SemSLATES vision, each layer corresponding to a particular kind of ontologies.

With regards to models for representing users, social interactions and the content generated from these interactions, *i.e.* socio-structural metadata, our proposal relies on popular vocabularies used in the Social Semantic Web realm [7]. In particular, we focus on FOAF for representing user information and social networking and SIOC to represent the conversations and interactions happening in their related online communities. By using these models to describe uniformly content from different — and originally heterogeneous — applications, we enable a first common layer of semantics for Enterprise 2.0 ecosystems. Among others, the choice of these models has been motivated by:

- their wide adoption on the Web — and consequently their related community —, which has lead to notable user-feedback and improvements that the enterprise can benefit;
- a large number of tools and APIs available for managing related data, both for generating and consuming it;
- their simplicity, so that they can easily be enhanced and integrated with more specific models if required.

Regarding the ontologies required for modeling business data, they obviously depend on the domain(s) of interest discussed in the information system. It can be quite broad, ranging for simple description of companies to accurate representation of solar cell components. However, the SemSLATES approach focuses on reusing as far as possible existing and public ontologies, notably the ones proposed in the context Linking Open Data initiative[11], as described in [4], for two main reasons:

- first, as for the use of the previous models, enterprises can benefit from a large community feedback instead of building a new model from scratch, hence benefiting from earlier developments regarding these ontologies. In addition, in case they are extended (as we will discuss when presenting our case-study), these extensions can be published on the Web so that the enterprise providing it can benefit from feedback from other communities — and even other enterprises — using it;
- then, it provides means to reuse existing data available publicly on the Web and modeled with these ontologies. For example, using the GeoNames ontology[12] internally permits to reuse the million of entities provided openly in the GeoNames knowledge base[13], with facts such as coordinates, population, etc. We shall see later how this can be used to build low-cost semantic mashup, since data integration can be done in a straightforward way — as the same models

---

[11] http://linkeddata.org

[12] http://sws.geonames.org/

[13] http://geonames.org

are used internally and on the Web, this does not require any ontology or data alignment process.

Furthermore, existing enterprise ontologies can also be reused in this context, as well as taxonomies and thesauri (for instance translated to SKOS — Simple Knowledge and Organization Scheme [24]). That way, background information from the company can be reused in these Enterprise 2.0 settings , bridging the gap between traditional enterprise knowledge management and socially-enhanced information systems.

Finally, and to bridge the gap between these two layers, there is a need for models linking user-generated content to the various objects they are dealing with. Here, our approach relies on MOAT (combined with the Tag Ontology [25])[14], since it offers a vocabulary bridging the gap between free-tagging and semantic indexing. It aims at representing the meaning of tags through identifiers (URIs) of the objects they represent, these objects being modeled with the aforementioned ontologies. Using it, users can associate their tags to structured resource from the previous ontologies (and share these associations), hence solving the ambiguity and heterogeneity issues of tagging, as well as their lack of structure. Then, as we can see in Fig. 1, it enables a complete approach for providing Linked Data in Enterprise 2.0 environments, with a strong emphasis on the user aspect, while not neglecting the business domain.

3.3 Generating Semantic Annotations Through Software Add-ons

In order to generate the semantic annotations corresponding to the previous ontologies, add-ons must be provided to the original applications. As we make a distinction between different levels of ontologies — notably between ontologies for modelling socio-structural metadata and the ones aimed at modelling business data — we also rely on different methods for generating these annotations.

On the one hand, the creation of socio-structural annotations can be fully automated, by using services translating internal data structures or APIs to RDF data based on the previous models. Many exporters and APIs are already available to produce FOAF and SIOC data, and can be consequently used in those contexts[15]. Hence, this first layer of semantics can be provided without any additional user input, in a completely transparent way. We will see in the upcoming section how we enabled it in our context, generating RDF data from existing blogs, wikis and RSS feeds.

On the other hand, the process of creating annotations related to domain ontologies can be seen as a usual ontology population process. However, instead of using tools such as Protégé, our approach benefits from existing Web 2.0 applications and their associated social behaviours to create and maintain ontology instances. In particular, semantic wikis [40] are an appropriate technology as they

---

[14] Note that CommonTag can also be used here, see http://commontag.org/

[15] See for instance http://sioc-project.org/applications.

can be used to create and maintain ontology instances by using the wiki philosophy principles: openness, collaborative access, and versioning. Then, they enable collaborative management of structured knowledge bases, whereas traditional wikis enable the management of document-based repository.

Finally, regarding semantic tagging, one can benefit from existing MOAT applications. MOAT tools provide user-generated semantic indexing capabilities, by letting users associate their tags to the resources they represent (identified by their URIs). Thus, users can link tags and tagged content to the various resources created from the aforementioned semantic wikis. Moreover, MOAT features a collaborative architecture that enable these links between tags and resources to be shared and exchanged in the enterprise. In addition, frameworks such as FLOR (FoLksonomy Ontology enRichment [1]) may be used in combination with MOAT to automatically provide these mappings between tags and URIs, and hence make the process easier for end-users.

Combined together, these applications, extending the initial tools, enable a complete collaborative food-chain of semantic annotation in Enterprise 2.0 environments, where each step can be achieved by different users and communities:

- structured representation of objects (projects, technologies, etc.) is generated *via* semantic wikis;
- content discussing these objects is generated using other applications, such as weblogs;
- semantic tagging provides the glue between these two levels.

3.4 Deploying Additional Services

Finally, the next step of the SemSLATES vision consists in enabling new services that consume the data generated through the previous applications.

Indeed, the whole RDF(S)/OWL annotations produced using these tools form a single Linked Data graph, either *via* direct links between instances or through the use of shared ontologies.

However, that graph — in addition to being relatively complex because of the different representation layers that it involves — is highly distributed since it consists in different sub-graphs spread in the enterprise (since each tool generate a set of RDF documents corresponding to its annotations).

Our proposal relies on using a central RDF-store to aggregate and store this data, a store on top of which new applications can be provided.

This choice was mainly motivated by performance reasons (since response time of distributed querying are not acceptable in enterprise settings), and makes our architecture an hybrid approach between traditional middleware systems (which query original data sources *via* adaptors and re-compose the query results) and data warehouses.

However, using a central storage system also implies to maintain it up-to-date compared to the original services and the data they generate.

Based on the dynamic structure of the tools producing the annotations (as a consequence of their social interactions), we must ensure that there is no temporal gap between the time when data is published and when it can be used, *i.e.* when it is stored in the system.

To enable such synchronisation, SemSLATES uses a notification approach similar to the ping systems often used in the blogosphere (such as `http://blo.gs`), and that we also applied on the Web for RDF data with Ping The Semantic Web [5]. Each time some structured data is created, updated or removed in any of the original tool, a notification is sent from the tool to the RDF store, which immediately adds, updates or removes the related graph.

In addition, we rely on SPARUL (SPARQL/Update [36]), and its related HTTP bindings to provide an additional abstraction layer for data storage[16].

Consequently, interactions between services and the RDF store are achieved (i) on the one hand with SPARQL for querying data and (ii) on the other hand with SPARUL for updating and removing it, both *via* HTTP through the store endpoint. As a consequence, any RDF store supporting SPARQL and SPARUL *via* HTTP can be used in such architectures, offering a dual-abstraction layer where data storage services are completely independent from the other components.

4 Case-study: Enabling SemSLATES at EDF R&D

4.1 Background

Most of the information monitoring and sharing process at Électricité de France R&D used to be done by collecting information from Web sites using tools like WebSite-Watcher[17], capturing knowledge using Lotus Notes databases[18] and delivering information using traditional email processes. Mid-2005, the Athena project started with two main objectives. On the one hand, it aimed at optimising the aggregation and diffusion of information in the company, through innovative solutions. On the other hand, it focused on establishing new collaborative processes in the enterprise, particularly regarding information sharing and collaborative knowledge management between engineers and researchers. In that context, a first Enterprise 2.0 platform was deployed, providing (in chronological order):

- aggregated RSS feeds — enabling (i) information integration from external sources into the enterprise and (ii) open sharing of this information at the workplace;

---

[16] While SPARQL/Update is currently under standardisation process within the W3C, the initial SemSLATES approach was based on the former W3C SPARUL Member Submission — `http://www.w3.org/Submission/2008/SUBM-SPARQL-Update-20080715/`

[17] `http://aignes.com`

[18] `http://www.ibm.com/software/fr/lotus`

- blogs — letting users (i) react to any news from these RSS feeds and write new content, as well as (ii) interact each others through comments;
- wikis — enabling knowledge capture, especially to provide open, user-driven and consensual information, while blog mainly focus on items with a strong temporal emphasis (*e.g.* breaking news).

As mentioned in Section 2, we identified and analysed various issues regarding knowledge management in this particular context. We thus deployed the aforementioned SemSLATES methodology in that ecosystem, and we will now describe how its different steps have been achieved.

4.2 Extending Popular Ontologies

Our first requirement was to agree on a set of ontologies used in this particular Sem-SLATES implementation. While modelling socio-structural metadata is achieved using FOAF and SIOC, particular vocabularies were needed to address the business domain. In our context, our modelling needs mainly involved the representation of organisations, including information such as their location, partners and members, as well as the industrial domains they are involved in.

As we mentioned in the previous section, we relied on popular vocabularies such as FOAF, SKOS or GeoNames to build this representation layer. First, in order to model organisations, we extended FOAF through a lightweight FOAF extension, named FOAFplus, adding classes such as `foafplus:ResearchInstitute` or `foafplus:Company` and properties like `foafplus:acronym` to the FOAF Ontology. One of the reason we extended FOAF rather than using another existing model dedicated to persons and agents was to focus on a lightweight model that we could easily apprehend, extend and reuse, while at the same time conforming to particular ontology engineering best practices [28]. With regards to industrial domains, we relied on SKOS to represent and to organise them hierarchically. SKOS can indeed be used to represent that `d:SolarEnergy` is broader than `d:SolarCells` but narrower than `d:SustainableEnergy`. This hierarchy was also used in a role ontology [28] dedicated to modelling in which industrial domains, and regarding which kind of business (*e.g.* research, sales, etc.) were involved the previous organisations.

Overall, our aim was to focus on modular and lightweight ontologies [13] rather than implementing a single and huge model to cover all our needs, especially in order to reuse some components in other applications (as the aforementioned role ontology). However, combined together, they formed a complete ontology stack to cover our different needs regarding the modelling of business domains.

4.3 Automated SIOC-based Annotations

In order to automatically produce SIOC data from our existing applications, we designed different SIOC data exporters for our blog and wiki systems (both based on the Drupal SIOC exporter, that we co-developed and made publicly available[19]), as well as a service translating incoming RSS feeds into SIOC data. For each exporter, we relied on specific classes from the SIOC Types module[20], e.g. sioct:BlogPost to model blog posts and sioct:WikiArticle for wiki pages, as well as using sioct:Comment to model comments related to such posts (Listing 1[21]). In addition, we also used FOAF for modelling people's personal profile information (name, etc.). Moreover, while these exporters have been build for our particular purposes, we designed a PHP SIOC API[22] so that new plug-ins and exporters of that kind can be engineered with minimal effort.

Listing 1 Modelling a blog post and its reply using SIOC.

```
<http :// athena . der . edf . fr / blog /104> a sioct : BlogPost ;
   sioc : has_creator <http :// athena . der . edf . fr / user /3> ;
   dct : title ''Recent news about EDF" ;
   dct : created ''2009−08−03T22:50:32Z";
   dct : subject ''EDF" ;
   sioc : content ''Today , EDF announced [...]" ;
   sioc : num_replies ''1" .

<http :// athena . der . edf . fr / blog /104#c1> a sioct : Comment ;
   sioc : reply_of <http :// athena . der . edf . fr / blog /104> .
```

As soon as the exporters were online, every new content was automatically provided as RDF using the aforementioned models. Moreover, every content previously generated also became available as RDF, and been integrated in this Semantic Enterprise 2.0 ecosystem. Furthermore, this translation step was done completely transparently for the end-users. Thus, they kept their existing publishing habits and did not have any further action to take in order to enable this first layer of Linked Data in the enterprise.

4.4 Knowledge Capture Using UfoWiki

More than 80 wikis have been created during the lifetime of the Athena project. Valuable information is contained within, however, as we have seen, its reuse is a complex task due to the plain-text nature of the wikis. In order to generate struc-

---

[19] http://drupal.org/project/sioc

[20] http://rdfs.org/sioc/types

[21] Prefixes omitted.

[22] http://sioc-project.org/phpapi

tured and machine-readable data from these wikis, and to enable semantic annotations regarding business data, we focused on the use of semantic wikis to enable collaborative ontology population. Especially, and in order to provide such feature as an extension of our platform, we engineered a dedicated engine, named UfoWiki — Unifying Forms and Ontologies in a Wiki [29] [30] — based on our original wiki system. It enables the definition of form-based templates for wiki pages, mapped to classes and properties of underlying ontologies — in our case, the ontologies presented in the previous section. Forms are constructed in a back-end interface where administrators define widgets (such as "Geolocation") mapped to particular properties (and classes) of the ontologies[23]. Moreover, these widgets can then be reused between different forms using a simple drag and drop interface. While we engineered our own system, in order to provide it as an extension of the original wiki engine, such form-based wiki interfaces are also used in systems such as the Semantic Forms extension for Semantic MediaWiki — `http://www.mediawiki.org/wiki/Extension:Semantic_Forms` —, the Project Halo — `http://semanticweb.org/wiki/Project_Halo` — or Kaukolu [17].

Using UfoWiki, users simply created and maintained instances by editing wiki pages and filling in forms that appeared in addition to the main textarea of each page. For example, instead of writing *"EDF is an organization located in France"*, users filled in a *Company* page template (mapped to our `foafplus:Company` class, subclass of `foaf:Group`) and a *Geolocation* field (mapped to the `geonames:locatedIn` property) so that the following RDF triples would be immediately created when saving the page (Listing 2). In addition, to enable the reuse of URIs between wiki pages, our system features a live auto-completion system (based on SPARQL queries), ensuring a correct interlinking of resources across wikis.

Listing 2 Modelling business data through UfoWiki.

```
athena:EDF rdf:type foafplus:Company ;
    rdfs:label ''Electricit\'{e} de France'' ;
    foafplus:acronym ''EDF'' ;
    geonames:locatedIn <http://sws.geonames.org/3017382/> .
```

Moreover, UfoWiki features a triggering system that queries the GeoNames web service for each *Geolocation* field in order to retrieve its URI — instead of creating a new identifier for each location. This can be seen in Listing 2, where the URI `<http://sws.geonames.org/3017382/>` identifies the city of Paris, capital of France, on GeoNames. While users are required to type in an exact location, *e.g. "Paris, France"*, we allow the reuse of external data in our system to provide advanced browsing features and semantic mashups, as we will describe later. This however has a drawback, since it implies that enterprises rely on public data that they cannot necessarily control and for which the quality of service is not always

---

[23] Note that for domain/range reasons, we were not able to automatically generate the forms, see details in [27].

ensured[24]. To that extent, alternatives could consider in hosting a replica of the required data internally, as for instance done in [16]. In addition, once again, this process could also focus on integrating existing and internal corporate ontologies or taxonomies (and related data) in order to interlink end-user contributions to legacy data from the enterprise.

In terms of statistics, we studied the evolution of one of these UfoWiki-enabled wikis, with 18 users participating and contributing to more than 300 instances during a six-month period. In addition, six users were interviewed and agreed that the additional complexity of filling in forms (rather than using a plain-text wiki interface) was relatively minor compared to the various advantages and features it provided, which we will describe in the next section.

4.5 Semantic Tagging Add-ons

While most of the generic MOAT clients[25] require users to enter the URIs of their tags' meaning(s) to enable semantic indexing when creating and tagging content, we enhanced this approach to make it as user friendly as possible — and do not confront our users to such technicalities. Firstly, users are never shown any URIs as the meanings of tags are suggested via their human-readable labels as soon as tagged content is saved in the system. Moreover, when a user links a particular tag to a resource, this mapping becomes her or his default choice for that particular relationship, making further annotations simpler. Furthermore, if no relevant meaning has been suggested, users can navigate (using a visual browser) through the taxonomy of classes and instances of our internal knowledge base to choose another meaning for their tag, once again without seeing any URI. This is also an innovative aspect of our approach: users create new ontology instances using semantic wikis, and then use these instances to define the meanings of their tags. In case no corresponding resource exists, users can create a new instance (while this step is generally dedicated to wikis as we have shown before). Furthermore, since these two steps can be achieved by different users, we enable a complete social process for instance management, tag meaning identification — and consequently semantic indexing. Finally, the relations between tags and URIs are shared in the corporate environment, so that one can benefit from mappings defined by others, providing an *architecture of participation* component to the semantic tagging approach.

Listing 3 represents the annotations related to the semantic indexing of a given blog post about EDF using MOAT. As we can see, it enhances the global interlinking between the different components of our architecture, linking together a blog post and ontological resources. Thus, by combining this information with the one generated through wikis (Listing 2) and using SIOC (Listing 1), we can identify that this particular blog post is about a company based in France. Therefore, we provided a

---

[24] In addition, confidentiality issues have to be considered, as some information filters out from the enterprise.

[25] http://moat-project.org/clients

complete Linked Data food-chain in the enterprise, using independent components providing distinct but interlinked annotations, as they reuse common URIs to identify the resources they deal with. In terms of statistics, 1,176 tags and about 17,000 instances of sioc:Post (and related subclasses) have been linked to 715 different URIs of resources, these links being represented via MOAT, showing a user willingness to do this manual interlinking step, in spite of the additional efforts it requires. In addition, note that our goal was to keep the initial tagging feature intact in order to let user express their "desire lines"[26] when tagging content, not forcing them to use a particular term to annotate it.

Listing 3 Example of semantically enhanced tagged data with MOAT.

```
<http :// athena . der . edf . fr / blog /104>   a  tag : RestrictedTagging
    tag : taggedResource  <http :// athena . der . edf . fr / blog /104>  ;
    foaf : maker  <http :// athena . der . edf . fr / user /3>  ;
    tag : associatedTag  <http :// athena . der . edf . fr / tags /EDF> ;
    moat : tagMeaning  <http :// athena . der . edf . fr / data /EDF>  .

<http :// athena . der . edf . fr / tags /EDF> a  moat : Tag  ;
    moat : name  ''EDF''  .
```

4.6 Additional Features of the Platform

As we have exposed when describing the SemSLATES architecture, all these services interact with a central RDF-store on top of which new services are deployed. In our context, we relied on 3store[27] and implemented a SPARQL/Update HTTP endpoint, in order to provide that abstraction layer between it and the other services. We will now describe some of the new applications that we engineered and deployed to enhance the initial information system.

4.6.1 Enhancing the Wiki Features

In order to solve the issues of knowledge capture and re-use that we mentioned in Section 2.2, we designed a processor for semantic macros in UfoWiki, inspired by Semantic MediaWiki inline queries [20]. Semantic macros allow to embed the results of SPARQL queries in wiki pages — without requiring users to face the complexity of such queries (especially when combining the different layers of semantic annotations). Macros are defined by wiki administrators and are mapped to SPARQL query patterns and (X)HTML templates, so that they can be integrated in

---

[26]   http://www.adaptivepath.com/publications/essays/archives/000361.php

[27] http://threestore.org

wiki pages using a simple grammar syntax. For example, [onto|members] will be translated into a SPARQL query that will retrieve all the members of the organisation currently browsed, these members being then displayed in the wiki page.

These macros offer a way to integrate information from different wiki pages and are thus used to augment knowledge discovery. Moreover, they also take advantage of the socio-structural metadata layer and of the semantic indexing capabilities of our proposal. As each wiki page is related to a particular instance, some macros are used to include a list of the latest 10 posts (as defined by sioct:BlogPost) that are linked to this instance (via MOAT), once again reusing available Linked Data from the enterprise to enhance user-experience and information integration. That way, it provides users with a direct integration of news and blog posts in wiki pages, so that they can instantaneously browse not only static information but also identify recent news, a novel feature which was particularly appreciated.

4.6.2 Semantic Search

In addition to this macro system, we also developed and deployed a dedicated semantic search engine which uses the whole data available in the RDF store (ontologies and annotations) to answer users' queries [32]. As for content generation, this engine bridges the gap between syntax and semantics [14], *i.e.* it provide means to search information about relevant resources (in particular instances of classes of our domain ontologies), and not only documents.

When users search for a particular keyword, a SPARQL query identifies the related instances, using regular expressions based on the tags and their meanings (via MOAT) as well as using the rdfs:label (and subproperties) values of the instances. If various instances are identified, the system asks the user to select the relevant one. For example, the system asks the user to choose between "Association des Maires de France" (association), "France" (country) or "Électricité de France" (company) if a user searches for the string "France", so that the search is then restricted to the relevant resource only. Once this resource has been identified, the engine lists all information about it, *i.e.* (1) the corresponding tags, (2) the main wiki page, (3) the related wiki pages (*i.e.* pages about instance(s) linked to the current one) and (4) every content item linked to the current resource, thanks to MOAT and an automated RSS indexing process running in the background. This way, the system solves information fragmentation issues as it provides users with a single entry point to access any content regarding a particular object, identified from several sources and initially distributed in the enterprise, avoiding the need to switch between different systems as in the past.

In order to bridge that semantic gap when searching for information, the use of MOAT showed a clear advantage. We indeed identified that 205 resources were linked to more than one tag; in fact, 39 were linked to more than four different tags. Consequently, it implies that four different tag-based queries would have been necessary to identify all the related content, while a single one is sufficient using this search engine, a feature that was also acknowledged by our users.

4.6.3 Semantic Mashups

Furthermore, in addition to this semantic search engine, we enabled advanced browsing interfaces and semantic mashups. In particular, we provided a faceted browsing interface using Exhibit[28] to navigate through the various organisations created using UfoWiki. The novelty of this approach is in the reuse of RDF data from GeoNames to provide a semantic mashup combining internal and external data sources, thanks to the trigger feature in UfoWiki that we explained previously. We can therefore see in Fig. 2 that information from the enterprise (company names and domains) is combined with GeoNames data (coordinates of their location), enabling such advanced navigation features. While this was relatively straightforward to implement, it was also praised by users, notably as it offers a visual representation of their plain-text content, also giving them incentives to publish more data.

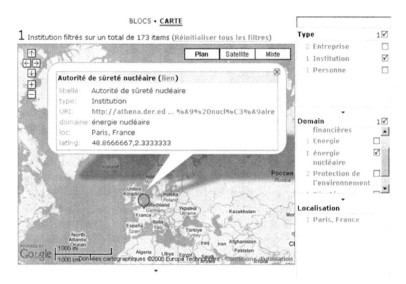

Fig. 2 A semantic mashup and faceted browsing interface for Enterprise 2.0 data, combining internal data and public RDF data from the Web.

We believe that these semantic mashups can be a significant part of the future of Enterprise 2.0 applications and greatly demonstrates the interest of the Linking Open Data initiative for organisations. Similar to how RSS allows companies to benefit from public information (news feeds, blogs, etc.), reusing RDF data brings knowledge about different topics into the enterprise for zero cost (since no data nor ontology alignment is required) — not only for public services as described by [19], but also within intranets as in our case. Furthermore, we can also imagine mashups combining, as said previously, Enterprise 2.0 data with existing legacy data from the enterprise.

---

[28] http://simile.mit.edu/wiki/Exhibit/

5 Conclusion

In this chapter, and based on our work at Électricité de France R&D[29] [26], we presented the SemSLATES approach, extending the original SLATES definition of Enterprise 2.0 by enabling a social semantic middleware architecture on top of existing Enterprise 2.0 ecosystems [27], using Semantic Web and Linked Data technologies. We especially showed how to combine different layers of semantics to provide this additional stack of structured and semantic information on top of social information spaces, without requiring a complete redesign of the information system, but through simple add-ons and plug-ins, and then bringing novel application to end-users, solving most issues of genuine Enterprise 2.0 systems. Then, to quote François-Xavier Testard-Vaillant, formerly senior adviser for corporate collective intelligence at EDF R&D: *"The Semantic Web is one of the tools we have experienced that creates bridges between communities and it does the job provided that it remains almost invisible thanks to a smart and user friendly interface. I do think that the Semantic Web will be a means to encourage our researchers to share more and more knowledge and that it will be easier and easier to use. We do need this"* [26].

In addition, while we focused only on the integration of data from Web-based services, we believe that new data sources could be added to enhance the user experience and information in such Enterprise 2.0 contexts. On the one hand, new internal information could be considered, which could consist in (1) information from the desktop, especially considering Semantic Desktop applications [3], which could integrate calendar of address book information in such services for personalised search, and (2) sensor-based information and data from mobile services, which could also provide some background context when searching for information (*e.g.* geo-locating answers to particular queries). On the other hand, more data from the Linking Open Data cloud could be integrated in these ecosystems, enhancing the initial values of the corporate tools by reusing openly available data to enhance user experience, offering new kind of semantic mashups. Moreover, it could also provide means to integrate different Enterprise 2.0 ecosystems together, providing a global ecosystem of networked knowledge, encompassing data from both the Web and the enterprise [33].

Furthermore, while the work described here was done in the context of a R&D project, many tools and ontologies used, designed and researched during that project are now stable and mature enough to be used in a broader enterprise context and to minimise the associated risks: scalable triple-stores are available on the market, various APIs can be used to deal with RDF(S)/OWL data, ontologies such as SIOC or SKOS got a broader update and hence benefit from large toolkits, query languages are more mature, etc.

Overall, we have thus showed that existing Enterprise 2.0 systems could greatly benefit from Semantic Web and Linked Data technologies, without requiring fundamental changes both in the architectures or in user's habits. We shall however

---

[29] http://edf.fr

remind that, since a main component of the SemSLATES approach is the user itself — as it requires users voluntary sharing their data to enable the semantic annotations and the Linked Data layer — it can be a success only if the Enterprise 2.0 philosophy itself has been acknowledged, understood and appreciated in the enterprise.

Acknowledgements The work presented in this chapter was funded in part by Science Foundation Ireland under Grant No. SFI/09/CE/I1380 (Líon2).

References

1. Sofia Angeletou. Semantic Enrichment of Folksonomy Tagspaces. In International Semantic Web Conference, volume 5318 of Lecture Notes in Computer Science, pages 889894. Springer, 2008.
2. Grigory Begelman, Philipp Keller, and Frank Smadja. Automated Tag Clustering: Improving search and exploration in the tag space. In Proceedings of the WWW2006 Workshop on Collaborative Tagging, 2006.
3. Ansgar Bernardi, Stefan Decker, Ludger van Elst, Gunnar Grimnes, Tudor Groza, Siegfried Handschuh, Mehdi Jazayeri, Cedric Mesnage, Knud Moeller, Gerald Reif, and Michael Sintek. The Social Semantic Desktop: A New Paradigm Towards Deploying the Semantic Web on the Desktop, chapter 7, pages 290312. IGI Global, 2008.
4. Chris Bizer, Richard Cyganiak, and Tom Heath. How to Publish Linked Data on the Web. Technical report, 2007. http://www4.wiwiss.fu-berlin.de/bizer/pub/ LinkedDataTutorial/.
5. Uldis Bojārs, Alexandre Passant, Frederick Giasson, and John G. Breslin. An architecture to discover and query decentralized RDF data. In 3rd Workshop on Scripting for the Semantic Web (SFSW2007), volume 248 of CEUR Workshop Proceedings. CEUR-WS.org, 2007.
6. John G. Breslin, Andreas Harth, Uldis Bojārs, and Stefan Decker. Towards Semantically-Interlinked Online Communities. In Proceedings of the 2nd European Semantic Web Conference (ESWC2005), volume 3532 of Lecture Notes in Computer Science, pages 500514. Springer, 2005.
7. John G. Breslin, Alexandre Passant, and Stefan Decker. The Social Semantic Web. Springer, 2009.
8. Dan Brickley and Libby Miller. FOAF Vocabulary Specification. Namespace Document 2 Sept 2004, FOAF Project, 2004. http://xmlns.com/foaf/0.1/.
9. Michel Buffa, Fabien L. Gandon, Guillaume Ereteo, Peter Sander, and Catherine Faron. SweetWiki: A semantic wiki. Journal of Web Semantics, 6(1):8497, 2008.
10. Thomas, H. Davenport and Laurence Prusak. Information Ecology: Mastering the Information and Knowledge Environment. Oxford University Press, 1997.
11. Carl Frappaolo and Dan Keldsen. Enterprise 2.0: Agile, Emergent Integrated. Technical report, AIIM The Enterprise Content Management Association, 2008.
12. Scott Golder and Bernardo A. Huberman. Usage patterns of collaborative tagging systems. Journal of Information Science, 32(2):198208, 2006.
13. Asunción Gómez-Prez and Oscar Corcho. Ontology languages for the Semantic Web. IEEE Intelligent Systems, 17(1):5460, 2002.
14. Ramanatgan V. Guha, Rob McCool, and Eric Miller. Semantic Search. In Proceedings of the 12th International World Wide Web Conference (WWW2003), pages 700709. ACM Press, 2003.
15. Conor Hayes, Paolo Avesani, and Sriharsha Veeramachaneni. An Analysis of the Use of Tags in a Blog Recommender System. In Twentieth International Joint Conferences on Artificial Intelligence, pages 27722777, 2007.

16. Michiel Hildebrand, Jacco van Ossenbruggen, Alia K. Amin, Lora Aroyo, Jan Wielemaker, and Lynda Hardman. The Design Space Of A Configurable Autocompletion Component. Technical report, CWI Amsterdam, 2007.
17. Malte Kiesel. Kaukolu: Hub of the Semantic Corporate Intranet. In Proceedings of the First Workshop on Semantic Wikis - From Wiki to Semantics (SemWiki-2006), volume 206 of CEUR Workshop Proceedings. CEUR-WS.org, 2006.
18. Karin D. Knorr-Cetina. Sociality with objects: Social relations in postsocial knowledge societies. Theory, Culture and Society, 14(4):130, 1997.
19. Georgi Kobilarov, Tom Scott, Yves Raimond, Silver Oliver, Chris Sizemore, Michael Smethurst, Christian Bizer, and Robert Lee. Media Meets Semantic Web - How the BBC Uses DBpedia and Linked Data to Make Connections. In 6th European Semantic Web Conference (ESWC2009), volume 5554 of Lecture Notes in Computer Science. Springer, 2009.
20. Markus Krötzsch, Denny Vrandecic, and Max Völkel. Semantic MediaWiki. In Proceedings of the 5th International Semantic Web Conference (ISWC 2006), volume 4273 of Lecture Notes in Computer Science, pages 935-942. Springer, 2006.
21. Barry Libert, Jon Spector, and Don Tapscott. We Are Smarter Than Me: How to Unleash the Power of Crowds in Your Business. Wharton School Publishing, 2007.
22. Adam Mathes. Folksonomies: Cooperative Classification and Communication Through Shared Metadata, December 2004.
23. Andrew P. Mcafee. Enterprise 2.0: The Dawn of Emergent Collaboration. MIT Sloan Management Review, 47(3):2128, 2006.
24. Alistair Miles and Sean Bechhofer. SKOS Simple Knowledge Organization System Reference. W3C Working Draft 29 August 2008, World Wide Web Consortium, 2008. http://www.w3.org/TR/2008/WD- skos- reference- 20080829/.
25. Richard Newman, Danny Ayers, and Seth Russell. Tag ontology, 2005. http://www.holygoat.co.uk/owl/redwood/0.1/tags/.
26. Alexandre Passant. Enhancement and Integration of Corporate Social Software Using the Semantic Web. W3C SWEO Case Study, World Wide Web Consortium, 2008. http://www.w3.org/2001/sw/sweo/public/UseCases/EDF/.
27. Alexandre Passant. Technologies du Web Semantique pour lEnterprise 2.0 (Semantic Web Technologies for Enterprise 2.0). PhD thesis, Université Paris-IV Sorbonne, 2009.
28. Alexandre Passant, Antoine Isaac and PhilippeLaublet. Combining Linked Data and Knowledge Engineering Best Practices to Design a Lightweight Role Ontology. Applied Ontology, 2010. To appear.
29. Alexandre Passant and Philippe Laublet. Combining Structure and Semantics for Ontology-Based Corporate Wikis. In 11th International Conference on Business Information Systems, BIS 2008, volume 7 of Lecture Notes in Business Information Processing, pages 58-69. Springer, 2008.
30. Alexandre Passant and Philippe Laublet. Towards an Interlinked Semantic Wiki Farm. In Third Semantic Wiki Workshop The Wiki Way of Semantics, volume 360 of CEUR Workshop Proceedings. CEUR-WS.org, 2008.
31. Alexandre Passant, Philippe Laublet, John G. Breslin, and Stefan Decker. A URI is Worth a Thousand Tags: From Tagging to Linked Data with MOAT. International Journal on Semantic Web and Information Systems (IJSWIS), 5(3):71-94, 2009.
32. Alexandre Passant, Philippe Laublet, John G. Breslin, and Stefan Decker. Semantic Search for Enterprise 2.0. In Proceedings of the WWW2009 Workshop on Semantic Search (Sem-Search2009), 2009.
33. Alexandre Passant, Matthias Samwald, John G. Breslin, and Stefan Decker. Federating Distributed Social Data to Build an Interlinked Online Information Society. IEEE Intelligent Systems, 24(6):44-48, 2009.
34. Alexandre Passant, Jean-DavidSta and Philippe Laublet. Folksonomies, Ontologies and Corporate Blogging. In Proceedings of the 4th Blogtalk Conference (Blogtalk Reloaded). Books on demand, 2006.

35. Sebastian Schaffert. IkeWiki: A Semantic Wiki for Collaborative Knowledge Management. In First International Workshop on Semantic Technologies in Collaborative Applications (STICA 06), 2006.

36. Andy Seaborne, Geetha Manjunath, Chris Bizer, John G. Breslin, Souripriya Das, Ian Davis, Steve Harris, Kingsley Idehen, Olivier Corby, Kjetil Kjernsmo, and Benjamin Nowack. SPARQL Update - A language for updating RDF graphs. W3C Member Submission 15 July 2008, World Wide Web Consortium, 2008. http://www.w3.org/Submission/ 2008/SUBM-SPARQL- Update- 20080715/.

37. Franois-Paul Servant. Linking Enterprise Data. In Proceedings of the WWW2008 Workshop Linked Data on the Web (LDOW2008), volume 369 of CEUR Workshop Proceedings. CEUR- WS.org, 2008.

38. James W. Tanaka and Marjorie Taylor. Object categories and expertise: Is the basic level in the eye of the beholder? Cognitive Psychology, 23(3):457482, 1991.

39. Thomas Vander Wal. Folksonomy Coinage and Definition, 2007. http://www. vander-wal.net/folksonomy.html.

40. Max Völkel and Sebastien Schaffert, editors. First Workshop on Semantic Wikis - From Wiki to Semantics, volume 206 of CEUR Workshop Proceedings. CEUR-WS.org, 2006.

41. Gio Wiederhold. Mediators in the Architecture of Future Information Systems. IEEE Computer, 25(3):3849, 1992.

Linking XBRL Financial Data

Roberto García and Rosa Gil

Abstract One of the main ways of populating the Web of Data is by translating existing data sources. One interesting candidate for this approach is data based on the eXtensible Business Reporting Language (XBRL), a standard for business and financial reporting. Many institutions are making available or requiring data in this format, e.g. the U.S. Securities and Exchange Commission (SEC) through the EDGAR program. However, XBRL data is loosely interconnected and it is difficult to mix and query it. Our contribution is a translation from XBRL filings to Semantic Web technologies, which we have applied to more than 1000 filings obtaining more than 2 million triples. The resulting semantic data is easier to integrate and cross query. Moreover, it can be interconnected with the rest of the Web of Data in order to extract its full potential.

1 Introduction

The main way to populate the Web of Data is by translating existing data sources. The motivation to do so is that usually this data is not offering its full potential because it is isolated, i.e. not connected to other external pieces of data that enrich them. It might even be the case that the data is loosely interconnected internally. Most of the time this is due to the fact that the technological solutions used to publish that data do not make it easy to interconnect it internally and to other external data sources.

Business reporting is a domain where the need for a common data format for reports has already been identified. XBRL (eXtensible Business Reporting Language)

Roberto García
Universitat de Lleida, Jaume II, 69. 25001 Lleida, Spain, e-mail: rgarcia@diei.udl.cat

Rosa Gil
Universitat de Lleida, Jaume II, 69. 25001 Lleida, Spain, e-mail: rgill@diei.udl.cat

D. Wood (ed.), *Linking Enterprise Data*, DOI 10.1007/978-1-4419-7665-9_6,
© Springer Science+Business Media, LLC 2010

is an XML language intended for modeling, exchanging and automatically processing business and financial information. XBRL is being deployed in many different
scenarios, especially thanks to the support of some regulators and government agencies. For instance, there is the EDGAR program promoted by the U.S. Securities and
Ex-change Commission (SEC). It performs automated collection, validation, indexing, acceptance and forwarding of submissions by companies and others who are
required by law to file forms with the SEC.

It has evolved from a voluntary program and now there is a mandate for a three
years phase-in schedule starting 2009 with companies with public float over $5
billion (approximately 500 companies) and ending 2011 with all companies filing
to the SEC doing so using XBRL. Moreover, the Government Information Transparency Act will require federal agencies to collect their data in a uniform, searchable format using XBRL thereby simplifying mandatory financial reporting for companies that receive federal funds.

However, we have observed limited support for cross analysis of financial information in XBRL tools and applications, as it is detailed in Section 1.2. This is
not just among data based on different accounting principles, which are represented
in XBRL using taxonomies. It even happens when comparing filings for different
companies based on the same taxonomies or filings for the same company based on
different versions of the taxonomies.

We argue that this limitation is inherited from the technologies underlying
XBRL, especially XML. XML takes a document oriented approach, where each
document presents a tree structure. This makes it difficult for XML-based tools to
provide functionalities that blur this separation into documents and that overcome
the limitations of a tree structure when mashing-up data from different sources.
Moreover, XBRL does not provide formal semantics that might help to integrate
different taxonomies using logic reasoners.

In any case, the integration of data contained in XBRL into comparable information is a strong requirement for the analysis of business and financial information at
the global level. This might increase the efficiency and effectiveness of the decision
making processes relying on this kind of information. For instance, bankruptcy prediction and other tasks related to the assessment of the solvency of a firm, a business
sector or set of interrelated companies.

Many have already pointed to this issue and propose Semantic Web technologies
as a natural choice for data integration [1] and, in this concrete case, for XBRL data
integration, cf. the related work in Section 1.2 or the W3C Workshop on Improving
Access to Financial Data on the Web[1]. However, this is not enough, the Semantic
Web provides the technologies for data integration but some principles are required
that facilitate Web-wide deployment of highly interlinked XBRL data. Linked Data
[2] provides these principles to publish data in the World Wide Web in a way that
helps making it easily discoverable through the links that connect it to other pieces
of data.

---

[1] Program of the W3C Workshop on Improving Access to Financial Data on the Web,
http://www.w3.org/2009/03/xbrl/program.html

Despite these benefits, currently, financial and business data is being produced using XBRL and it seems that more and more XBRL data is going to be available in the future. XBRL is been promoted by regulators and government agencies like the SEC, as it has been shown before, but also other bodies like the European Union or the Spanish securities commission [3].

Consequently, our opinion is that the best short term approach in order to get financial and business data to the Semantic Web is not to propose and alternative language based on Semantic Web technologies, but to apply methods to map existing XBRL to semantic metadata. This also seems the best option in the short and midterm to populate the Web of Data with business information.

The rest of this chapter is organised as follows. The next subsections introduce the structure of XBRL, then the related work is presented followed by the description of the our contribution in Section 2. It is based on the XML Semantics Reuse Methodology. The first step is to map the XML Schemas that structure XML data to OWL ontologies using the XSD2OWL mapping. Then, the second step is to map XML data to RDF using the XML2RDF mapping.

Once our approach has been presented, the results of the previous mappings are shown in Section 3. They are a set of OWL ontologies for the main XBRL taxonomies used in the EDGAR program. Based on these ontologies, it has been possible to map all the EDGAR instance documents from XML based on these taxonomies to RDF based on the resulting ontologies.

From these ontologies and semantic data, it has been possible to establish some mechanisms, facilitated by Semantic Web technologies, that enrich the dataset with additional links. First, some links to external datasets of the Web of Linked Data. Second, internal links that integrate the different filings by aligning the ontologies they use.

We are currently starting to evaluate this semantic dataset, as it is detailed in Section 4. It is compared to similar undergoing initiatives and it has been made publicly available for querying and browsing through a Web user interface. Finally, in Section 5, the conclusions and future work are presented. The main conclusion is that though RDF data through semantic queries and integration primitives offers a new range of possibilities; it already lacks enough expressive power to substitute XBRL, as it is explained in the conclusion.

We think that the best approach, for the moment, is to combine both approaches and transform XBRL data to semantic form in order to facilitate cross-querying and semantic integration, while keeping the original data in order to benefit from specific XBRL services. Consequently, we concentrate now our future work in completing the mapping from XBRL to Semantic Web, to provide integration facilities at the taxonomy level and to enrich the links of the resulting semantic dataset to other ones in the Web of Linked Data.

1.1 XBRL

XBRL is based on two kinds of documents, instance documents and taxonomies. In-stance documents report business facts and point to a set of taxonomies, which define the meaning of these facts, e.g. under what accounting principles they hold, what other facts they related to or what kind of things do they refer to.

1.1.1 Instances

More concretely, a XBRL instance document contains business Facts. An example of a Fact could be "sales in the last quarter". If the Fact is simple valued, like "the long term debt is 350,000" whose value is just a number, it is called Item. If the Fact has a more complex value, like "for the *preferred stock*, the *preferred stock par value per share* is 0 and the *preferred stock shares authorized* is 2000", it is called a Tuple.

Items are represented in XBRL as a single XML element with the value as its con-tent while Tuples are represented by XML elements containing nested Items or Tuples, i.e. subelements.

However, facts are not isolated entities and it is not enough to provide their values, it is also necessary to contextualize them. Consequently, four more entities are introduced in the XBRL model:

- **Context**: it defines the entity (e.g. company or individual) to which the fact applies, the period of time the fact is relevant and an optional scenario. The period of time can have zero length for instance and its value is based on ISO 8601 for date and time values. Scenarios provide further contextual information about the facts, such as whether the business values reported are actual, projected or budgeted. Contexts are referenced from Facts using the "contextRef" attribute, which specifies that the given Fact is valid for the entity, period and scenario defined in the Context.
- **Unit**: it defines a unit of measure, such as "USD" or "shares". They are referenced from Facts using the "unitRef" attribute, which specifies that the numeric or fractional value of the Fact is based on that unit of measure. Complex units can also be defined, like "USD per share". Currency units are based on ISO 4217.
- **Reference**: The kinds of facts under consideration are defined by taxonomies, which specify their meaning in the context of some accounting principles or purpose, e.g. Facts relevant for banking and savings institutions. These kinds of facts are then used in instance documents in order to specify actual values for them. However, they are linked to their definition in the taxonomies, typically through schema references, in order to be able to retrieve their meaning.
- **Footnote**: it contains some additional support content and it is associated to Fact using XLink[2].

---

[2] XLink, http://www.w3.org/TR/xlink/

Listing 1 shows part of an instance document from the EDGAR program that contains a Context element which defines a company, a time period and the scenario unaudited. Then, there is a Fact that holds in that context. The Fact references the Context and the value unit, while their content is the actual numeric value for that fact.

1.1.2 Taxonomies

The other kind of XBRL document represents taxonomies. A taxonomy defines a hierarchy of concepts, basically kinds of Facts, and captures part of their intended meaning. In XBRL there is a set of base taxonomies that define the core concepts and other ones that extend them in order to particularize these concepts for concrete accounting principles, application domains, etc. Additionally, it is possible to extend existing taxonomies and accommodate them to particular needs.

Taxonomies are based on XML Schemas, which provide the taxonomy building primitives and the extension mechanisms. Moreover, there are also "linkbases", which allow establishing links beyond the tree structure of a taxonomy by virtue of their use of XLink:

- **Schemas** define concepts that are instantiated as Items or Tuples, depending on their complexity, in the instance documents. They are based on XML Schema elements (xsd:element). A concept definition provides the fact name, whether it is a tuple or an item and its value data type (such as monetary, numeric, fractional or textual).
- **Linkbases** define links from concepts in a taxonomy to labels, pieces of content or to other concepts. The XBRL 2.1 specification defines five different kinds of linkbases.
    - **Label Linkbase**: set of links that provides human readable strings for concepts, potentially in multiple languages.
    - **Reference Linkbase**: these links associate concepts with citations of some body of authoritative literature.
    - **Calculation Linkbase**: these are links that associate a set of values of concepts in taxonomies with a mathematical calculation that must be checked for consistency, for instance that a set of concepts with percentage values sum up 100%.
    - **Definition Linkbase**: it provides semantic relations between concepts like is-a, whole-part, etc.
    - **Presentation Linkbase**: This linkbase associates concepts with other concepts so that the resulting relations can guide the creation of a user interface, rendering, or visualisation.

Listing 1 Context and facts examples from an EDGAR filing

```
<context id=''From20080301−To20080530_EnterpriseSolutions_Unaudited">
```

```
<entity>
  <identifier scheme=''http ://www. sec .gov/CIK">
     796343
  </identifier>
</entity>
<period>
  <startDate >2008−03−01</startDate >
  <endDate >2008−05−30</endDate>
</period>
<scenario >
  <adbe : Unaudited />
</scenario >
</context>

<adbe : EnterpriseSolutionsRevenue  decimals=''−6"
contextRef =''From20080301−To20080530_EnterpriseSolutions_Unaudited"
unitRef=''USD">54400000</adbe : EnterpriseSolutionsRevenue>
```

1.2 Related Work

The U.S Securities and Exchange Commission (SEC) offers some online tools that al-low interacting with the data available in XBRL form. There is a tool called Interactive Financial Reports that allows viewing and charting companies financial information. It also provides some functionality that allows comparing different filings and different companies, though it is hard to use and prone to even the slightest differences between the compared filing facts, even when there is just a name change for facts from filings of the same company.

There is also the Financial Explorer[3], which presents company financial data through very informative diagrams. In this case, it is just possible to show data from one company at a time. Finally, there is the Executive Compensation tool, which al-lows comparing just two facts, Public Market Capitalization and Revenue, across all filed companies.

Apart from the SEC tools, there are some other XBRL tools, most of them proprietary and with quite high licensing cost. Among them, the Fujitsu XBRL Tools[4] should be highlighted because they are one of the most popular tool sets and it is available for XBRL Consortium members and academic users. The tools comprise taxonomy and instance editors, viewers and validators.

The most powerful tool in this set, though still in beta and with many usability problems, is the Instance Dashboard. This application can consume multiple instance documents and, by specifying a base taxonomy, users can perform some comparison analysis, though limited to facts in the taxonomy that appears in all the filings.

---

[3] SECs Financial Explorer, http://209.234.225.154/viewer/home/

[4] Fujitsu XBRL Tools, http://www.fujitsu.com/global/services/software/interstage/xbrltools/

As it can be noted from the previous analysis, the main limitation of XBRL tools is their limited support for cross analysis of financial information, not just among data based on different taxonomies, even when comparing filings for different companies based on the same taxonomies.

This limitation is inherited from the technologies underlying XBRL, especially from XML. XML takes a document oriented approach, where each document presents a tree structure. This makes it difficult for XML-based tools to provide functionalities that blur this separation into documents and that overcome the limitations of a tree structure when mashing-up data from different sources.

Consequently, Semantic Web tools are being considered by people like Charles Hoffman, the father of XBRL: *"This field (W3C semantic standards) is rich with possibilities and stands as the next logical step in the natural progression of information technology to seek a higher value proposition"* (emphasis added) [4].

This interest is materializing, and the combination of XBRL and the Semantic Web has been receiving some attention in different blogs[56], mailing lists and web groups[7]. However, it is difficult to find concrete results that put into practice Semantic Web technologies in the XBRL field.

Moreover, most of these results are specific for some parts of XBRL. For instance, there is an ontology about financial information based on XBRL that is specific for investment funds [5] and, though it is generated using a generic XBRL taxonomy to OWL ontology algorithm, there is not and equivalent tool that maps generic XBRL instance data. There is also another tool that maps quarterly and semester accounting information submitted to the Spanish securities commission (CNMV) to Semantic Web technologies [3].

Moreover, both approaches are based on procedural code specially developed in order to extract specific patterns from the XBRL data. Consequently, they are difficult to scale to the whole XBRL specification and sensible to minimal changes in it. We propose an approach that, instead of directly processing XBRL data, takes profit from the fact that it is expressed using XML and specified using XML Schemas. OpenLink XBRL Sponger is the only tool to our knowledge that maps generic XBRL instance data to RDF [6]. However, in this case, there is not and associated mapping from the taxonomies instance data is based on to ontology languages.

2 Approach

There are many attempts to move metadata from the XML domain to the Semantic Web. Some of them just model the XML tree using the RDF primitives [7]. Others concentrate on modeling the knowledge implicit in XML languages definitions, i.e.

---

[5] DuCharme, B. Changing my mind about XBRL again, in: Bob DuCharme's weblog, http://bobdc.blog, 2008.

[6] Raggett, D. XBRL and RDF, in: Dave Raggetts Blog, 2008. http://people.w3.org/ dsr/blog/?p=8

[7] XBRL Ontology Specification Group, http://groups.google.com/group/xbrl-ontology-specification-group

DTDs or the XML Schemas, using web ontology languages [8][9]. Finally, there are attempts to encode XML semantics integrating RDF into XML documents [10][11].

However, none of them facilitate an extensive transfer of XML metadata to the Semantic Web in a general and transparent way. Their main problem is that the XML Schema implicit semantics are not made explicit when XML metadata instantiating this schemas is mapped. This is so because the RDF data produced from XML instance data looses its links to the XML Schemas that structure them and model the relations among different XML entities.

These relations among different XML entities are what carry the XML Schema implicit semantics. They capture part of the meaning intended by the schema developer that, though XML Schema does not provide a way to encode semantics, is recorded in the way XML Schema constructs are used. For instance, by modeling that element "father" is a *substitutionGroup* for element "parent", it is possible to interpret that "parent" is more general than "father" and that "father" can appear where "parent" appears. More details about the implicit semantics of XML Schema constructs as compared to OWL ones are provided in Section 2.1.

Therefore, the previous mappings from XML to RDF do not take profit from the meaning encoded in XML Schemas and produce RDF metadata almost as semantics-blind as the original XML. Or, on the other hand, they capture this semantics but they use additional ad-hoc semantic constructs that produce less transparent metadata.

Therefore, we have chosen the XML Semantics Reuse methodology [12] and the XML Schema to OWL and XML to RDF tools implemented in the ReDeFer project[8]. This methodology combines an XML Schema to web ontology mapping, called XSD2OWL, with a transparent mapping from XML to RDF, XML2RDF. The ontologies generated by XSD2OWL are used during the XML to RDF step in order to generate semantic metadata that takes into account the XML Schema intended meaning.

This approach has already shown its usefulness with other quite big XML Schemas in the Digital Rights Management domain, such as MPEG-21 and ODRL [13], and al-so in the E-Business [14] and multimedia metadata domains [15], where it produced the more complete MPEG-7 ontology to date [16].

2.1 XSD2OWL Mapping

The XML Schema to OWL mapping is responsible for capturing the schema implicit semantics, which is determined by the combination of XML Schema constructs. The mapping is based on translating these constructs to the OWL ones that best capture their intended meaning. These translations are detailed in Table 1 and Table 2 shows an example mapping.

---

[8] ReDeFer project, http://rhizomik.net/redefer

The XSD2OWL mapping is quite transparent and captures a great part XML Schema semantics. The same names used for XML constructs are used for OWL ones, although in the new namespace defined for the ontology. XSD and OWL constructs names are identical; this usually produces uppercase-named OWL properties because the corresponding element name is uppercase, although this is not the usual convention in OWL.

Table 1 XSD2OWL translations for the XML Schema constructs

XML Schema	OWL	Mapping Motivation
element | attribute	rdf:Property owl:DatatypeProperty owl:ObjectProperty	Named relation between nodes or nodes and values
element@substitutionGroup	rdfs:subPropertyOf	Relation can appear in place of a more general one
element@type	rdfs:range	The relation range kind
complexType | group | attributeGroup	owl:Class	Relations and contextual restrictions package
complexType / element	owl:Restriction	Contextualised restriction of a relation
extension@base | restriction@base	rdfs:subClassOf	Package concretises the base package
@maxOccurs @minOccurs	owl:maxCardinality owl:minCardinality	Restrict the number of occurrences of a relation
sequence choice	owl:intersectionOf owl:unionOf	Combination of relations in a context

Therefore, XSD2OWL produces OWL ontologies that make explicit the semantics of the corresponding XML Schemas. Table 2 shows a piece of an XML Schema and the OWL that is generated following this approach.

The only caveats are the implicit order conveyed by *xsd:sequence* and the exclusivity of *xsd:choice*. For the first problem, *owl:intersectionOf* does not retain its operands order, there is no clear solution that retains the great level of transparency that has been achieved. The use of RDF Lists might impose order but introduces ad-hoc constructs not present in the original metadata.

Table 2 XSD2OWL translations for the XML Schema constructs

XML Schema	OWL (Abstract Syntax)
<complexType name="contextOrganisationType"> <complexContent> <extension base="contextEntityType"> <sequence> <element name="Country" type="CountryType"/> </sequence> </extension> </complexContent> </complexType>	Class (contextOrganisationType complete contextEntityType restriction(Country allValuesFrom(CountryType) cardinality(1)))

Moreover, as it has been demonstrated in the Semantic Web community, the element ordering does not contribute much from a semantic and knowledge representation point of view [17] in most cases and when it is a requirement it is more convenient to explicitly represent it using some sort of order attribute or property. For the second problem, *owl:unionOf* is an inclusive union, the solution is to use the disjointness OWL construct, *owl:disjointWith*, between all union operands in order to make it exclusive.

2.2 XML2RDF Mapping

Once all the metadata XML Schemas are available as mapped OWL ontologies, it is time to map the XML metadata that instantiates them. The intention is to produce RDF metadata as transparently as possible. Therefore, a structure-mapping approach has been selected [7] instead of a model-mapping one [18].

XML model-mapping is based on representing the XML information set using semantic tools. This approach is better when XML metadata is semantically exploited for specific purposes. However, when the objective is to obtain semantic metadata from different kinds of input XML data, it is better to follow a more transparent approach.

Transparency is achieved in structure-mapping models because they only try to represent the XML metadata structure, i.e. a tree, using RDF. The RDF model is based on the graph so it is easy to model a tree using it. Moreover, we do not need to worry about the semantics loose produced by structure-mapping. We have formalised the underlying semantics into the corresponding ontologies and we will attach them to RDF metadata using the instantiation relation *rdf:type* later.

The structure-mapping is based on translating XML metadata instances to RDF ones that instantiate the corresponding constructs in OWL. The more basic translation is between relation instances, from *xsd:elements* and *xsd:attributes* to *rdf:Properties*. Concretely, *owl:ObjectProperties* for node to node relations and *owl:DatatypeProperties* for node to value ones.

Values are kept during the translation as simple types and RDF blank nodes are introduced in the RDF model in order to serve as the source and destination for properties. They will remain blank for the moment until they are enriched with semantic information.

The resulting RDF graph model contains all that we can obtain from the XML tree. It is already semantically enriched thanks to the *rdf:type* relation that connects each RDF property to the *owl:ObjectProperty* or *owl:DatatypeProperty* it instantiates. It can be enriched further if the blank nodes are related to the *owl:Class* that defines the package of properties and associated restrictions they contain, i.e. the corresponding *xsd:complexType*. This semantic decoration of the graph is formalised using *rdf:type* relations from blank nodes to the corresponding OWL classes.

At this point we have obtained a semantically enabled representation of the input metadata, a representation that makes the meaning intended by the XML and

XML Schema modelers explicit from a computer point of view. The instantiation relations can now be used to apply OWL semantics to metadata. Therefore, the semantics derived from further enrichments of the ontologies, e.g. integration links between different ontologies or semantic rules, are automatically propagated to instance metadata thanks to inference.

2.3 Algorithm

Listing 2 shows part of the algorithm that implements the XML to RDF mapping. Basically, starting from the root element, it traverses the XML tree and produces triples for all attributes and elements recursively using the "mapResProps" method. All the references to the traversed elements and their attributes are mapped to their equivalent in the OWL ontologies corresponding to the original XML Schemas. This is done by the "map" function.

3 Results

First of all, we have generated an ontological infrastructure for the XBRL core, currently XBRL 2.1. It is composed by the ontologies resulting from mapping the XBRL core XML Schemas using the XSD2OWL mapping: XBRL Instance, XBRL Linkbase, XBRL XL and XBRL XLink.

Apart from the previous generic schemas, the schemas listed at the end of this section have been also mapped in order to be able to map the XBRL data submitted to the SECs EDGAR program. These schemas are part of the EDGAR Standard Taxonomies. The US Financial Reporting - February 28, 2005 taxonomies have been considered as they are used by the input data currently submitted to this program.

Listing 2 XML2RDF Algorithm

```
Model XML2RDF( Document d )
{
  Model rdf ;
  Resource r = rdf . createResource ( doc . url );
  Element e = doc . getDocumentElement ();
  Property p = map ( e . nsURI ())+ e . localName ();
  Class range = map . getPropertyRange ( null , p );
  r . addProperty ( RDF . type , range );
  mapResProps ( r , e , range , rdf );
}

mapResProps ( Resource r , Element e , Class domain , Model rdf )
{
  foreach ( a in e . attributes ())
  {
    Property p = map ( a . nsURI ())+ a . localName ();
```

```
      r.addProperty(p, a.getValue());
  }
  foreach (c in e.childNodes())
  {
    if (c.isTextNode()){
      Property p = map(c.nsURI())+c.localName();
       r.addProperty(p, c.getValue());
    }
    else {
      Resource  rC = rdf.createResource();
      Property p = map(c.nsURI())+c.localName();
      r.addProperty(p, rC);
      Class range = map.getPropertyRange(domain, p);
      rC.addProperty(RDF.type, range);
      mapResProps(rC, c, range, rdf);
    }
  }
}
```

From US GAAP (Generally Accepted Accounting Principles) the schemas, and corresponding ontologies, are: Primary Terms Elements (USFR-PTE), Primary Terms Relationships (USFR-PTR), Financial Services Terms Elements (USFR-FSTE), Financial Services Terms Relationships (USFR-FSTR) and Investment Management Terms Relationships (USFR-IME). For specific industries: Banking and Savings Institutions (US-GAAP-BASI), Commercial and Industrial (US-GAAP-CI), Insurance (US-GAAP-INS) and Investment Management (US-GAAP-IM).

There are also some non-GAAP schemas that have been also mapped to OWL ontologies: Accountants Report (USFR-AR), Management Discussion and Analysis (USFR-MDA), Management Report (USFR-MR) and SEC Certifications (USFR-SECCERT).

Schemas mapped:

- **US GAAP** (Accepted Accounting Principles):
    - Primary Terms Elements (USFR-PTE)
    - Primary Terms Relationships (USFR-PTR)
    - Financial Services Terms Elements (USFR-FSTE)
    - Financial Services Terms Relationships (USFR-FSTR)
    - Investment Management Terms Relationships (USFR-IME)
    - Industry:
        · Banking and Savings Institutions (US-GAAP-BASI)
        · Commercial and Industrial (US-GAAP-CI)
        · Insurance (US-GAAP-INS)
        · Investment Management (US-GAAP-IM)

- **Non-GAAP**:
    - Accountants Report (USFR-AR)
    - Management Discussion and Analysis (USFR-MDA)

      – Management Report (USFR-MR)
      – SEC Certifications (USFR-SECCERT)

Each filing for the companies participating in the EDGAR program contains and XBRL XML file representing the actual financial data and also a specific XML Schema extending the XBRL core. This schema provides specific guides for the corresponding financial data. Both files are mapped using XML2RDF and XSD2OWL respectively.

For instance, for Adobe Systems Inc filing on 2008-07-03, there are the adbe-20080616.xml file containing the instance data and the adbe-20080530.xsd schema for data structures specific for this filing. They are mapped, respectively, to the RDF file for instance data adbe-20080616.rdf and the OWL ontology adbe-20080530.owl for the schema.

All the previous ontologies are available from the BizOntos Business Ontologies web page[9] and the semantic data for all the processed filings can be queried and browsed from the Semantic XBRL site[10]. Currently, 489 filings have been processed from EDGAR. The combination of all these filings once mapped to RDF amounts slightly more than 1 million triples, concretely 1,023,929 triples. A triple is the minimal component of an RDF graph and corresponds to one of its edges connecting two of its nodes.

Table 4 in the Evaluation section shows the RDF metadata resulting from applying the XML2RDF mapping to the XBRL context and fact shown in Listing 1. The RDF metadata references classes and properties from the OWL ontologies resulting from mapping the XML Schemas used in the XML instance. This includes the XBRL schemas and also those specific for the concrete filing being processes.

For a more general view of the resulting semantic dataset, Figure 1 shows a diagram of the resulting RDF model. At this step, it is possible to take profit from semantic web technologies in order to facilitate connecting the resulting data to other datasets, but also to improve the interconnectedness of the dataset. Both processes are detailed in the next subsections.

3.1 Links to External Data

In order to connect the XBRL RDF dataset with other ones in the Web of Linked Data, the entities in the XBRL model have been analyzed in order to detect those also described in other datasets. The more prominent ones are companies, a kind of EntityType present in most EDGAR filings. XBRL data provides an identifier for these entities, the Central Index Key (CIK) number. It is a number given to an individual or company by the U.S. SEC and used to identify the filings of a company, person, or entity in several online databases, including EDGAR.

---

[9] BizOntos, http://rhizomik.net/ontologies/bizontos

[10] SemanticXBRL, http://rhizomik.net/semanticxbrl

However, there are some EDGAR filings that do not use this identifier and use the CompanyName one instead. For most of them it is possible to get the corresponding CIK using EDGARs CIK Lookup service[11]. Unfortunately, as the filings are directly submitted by the participant companies, there are some discrepancies between the names in the filings and those in the lookup service.

Even when a CIK identifier is available in the EDGAR dataset, it might be impossible to directly connect it to company descriptions available in DBPedia because just 23 of them have the "secCik" property that links them to the company CIK. Actually, we have been able to map just 5 companies to DBPedia using the DBPedia secCik property as just some of them are currently using XBRL filings. Consequently, we have explored some alternative ways to connect companies to DBPedia. We have conduced this exploration with the help of the Silk framework [19], a tool for discovering relationships between data items within different Linked Data sources.

Using the Silk - Link Specification Language (Silk-LSL), we have specified which links should be generated between data sources as well as which conditions data items must fulfill in order to be interlinked. These link conditions combine various similarity metrics and can take the graph around a data item into account, which is addressed using an RDF path language.

The simplest case is to define the link specification using the CIK property. In this case, it is just specified to look for pairs of resources, one from the semantic XBRL dataset and the other from DBPedia one, that have the same value for the dbpprop:secCik property. Note that we have used this property during the triplifi-

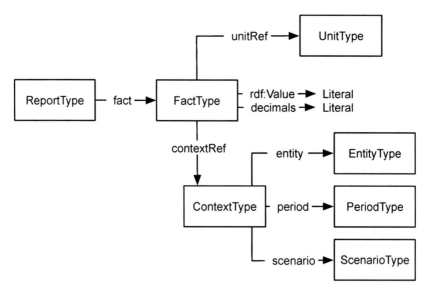

Fig. 1 RDF Model of the semantic XBRL dataset (squares: classes, arrows: properties)

[11] Search EDGAR: CIK Lookup, http://sec.gov/edgar/searchedgar/cik.htm

cation process in order to model the ID in the input XBRL. As mentioned before, from this link specification we are able to get just 5 owl:sameAs links between both datasets.

The next possibility we have explored is to link resources with almost identical company names. We have used a combination of the Jaro and Q-Gram similarity measures implemented by Silk. We have been forced to use a quite high threshold for accepted links because the presence of quite common words in company names, like "Inc.", "Corp.", "Co.", "Ltd.", etc., and their many variants makes it very difficult to get reliable links based on the company name.

After a review of the links generated using the previous approach we have been able to generate 27 new owl:sameAs relations between the datasets. This is also a quite scarce amount given that we currently have 543 companies in our dataset. Our last attempt to date to generate links to DBPedia is to take profit from the fact that for 398 companies in our dataset we have the ticker.

The obvious approach is to use the dbpprop:ticker property to generate links to the corresponding DBPedia resources. However, just 4 of them have this property. Fortunately, we have observer that many DBPedia companies have alternative URI based on their ticker. In this case, the approach to specify the links has been to explore the dbpprop:redirect links pointing to DBPedia public companies and strip the URI in order to get potential tickers. Eg., dbpedia:Microsoft is dbpprop:redirect of dbpedia:MSFT. Using this approach we have been able to generate 64 owl:sameAs links to DBPedia.

This continues to be a quite limited amount so we continue to explore other ways to generate links to dbpedia. Meanwhile, we have also explored other datasets we can link to. A really interesting candidate is the U.S. Securities and Exchange Commission Corporate Ownership RDF Data[12] generated by Joshua Tauberer from SEC and CorpWatch[13] data.

This is a very interesting dataset because it provides information about who is in the board of many of these companies and also the subsidiary relation among companies. We can use this data in order to generate complex queries that aggregate the financial data we are triplifying from SEC taking into account groups of companies that hold different kinds of ownership relations, e.g. are all subsidiaries of the same company or share board members.

In this case it has been easy to generate the links to this dataset because all companies are identified using their CIK. Not all of them are providing XBRL filings so from a total amount of 543 companies in our dataset and 12589 companies in the ownership dataset, we have obtained 398 links. Table 3 shows a summary of the number of links to external datasets and the method employed to generate them.

Finally, the other kind of entities that might be connected to external datasets is units. The easiest kind of entities is currencies because most of the filings use the ISO 4217 code in order to identify them. The rest of the units are specific to the filings, for instance there is the "shares" or "pure" units that do not have equivalents

---

[12] http://www.rdfabout.com/demo/sec/

[13] http://api.corpwatch.org/

Table 3 Summary of the number of links to external datasets

Linking Method	# Links to DBPedia	# Links to Corporate Ownership Data
SECs identifier CIK	5	398
Company name	27	
Company ticker	64	

in other datasets. Consequently, we are just linking currencies to their descriptions in DBPedia.

3.2 Semantic Integration

Apart from the links to other datasets, the EDGAR dataset resulting from the transformation to Semantic Web technologies can be also enriched with internal links. As it has been mentioned earlier, each XBRL EDGAR filing consists of an XML in-stance file accompanied by a XML Schema taxonomy. This taxonomy is specific for the filing, it changes from filing to filing. The taxonomy defines a set of facts specific for the filing. New facts are introduced, other used in previous filings are removed and some of them suffer minimal modifications.

For instance, the 2008-07-03 filing from Adobe Systems Inc. refers to the fact "InvestmentLeaseReceivable" defined in the adbe-20080530.xsd taxonomy while the 2008-09-16 filing refers to "Investment*In*LeaseReceivable" defined in the adbe-20080829.xsd taxonomy. Apart from these slight differences, many facts appearing in the earlier filing do not appear in the later and the reverse. This happens even if both filing are of the same kind; in this case they are both "Form 10-Q – Quarterly report [Sections 13 or 15(d)]" filings.

These differences among filings, even when they are of the same type and from the same company, make it really difficult to integrate them and to perform queries crossing individual filing boundaries. Consequently, we have taken profit from the semantic integration tools provided by Semantic Web technologies. The Web Ontology Language (OWL) provides a set of primitives that allow stating that two classes, two properties or two instances are the same. It is also possible to state that something is a subclass or subproperty of another class or property respectively, that two classes are disjoint, etc.

These semantic integration statements are then used by inference reasoners, which are capable of dealing with their semantics while making their implications totally transparent for the users or applications using them. For instance, it is possible to state that, continuing with the previous example, "InvestmentLeaseReceivable" and "InvestmentInLeaseReceivable" are equivalent. Consequently, when the user queries for any of them, the other will be automatically included in the results.

Unfortunately, the process of detecting equivalent or similar concepts and relations from different ontologies, called ontology alignment, is a very time consuming one. Moreover, in the case of the EDGAR XBRL filings, there are a lot of ontologies to align because, as has been already mentioned, each filing has its own one. Consequently, automatic or semiautomatic alignment tools are required in order to get a scalable solution.

Currently, we have just performed some alignments among the ontologies for the Adobe Systems Inc. filings. This alignment process has not been integrated into the whole XBRL to Semantic Web application yet. For instance, we have applied the alignment implementation provided by the Falcons tool [20] for the two Adobe Inc. ontologies commented in this section getting a equivalence matching quality of 0.988 for the "InvestmentLeaseReceivable" and "InvestmentInLeaseReceivable" properties.

The maximum quality value is "1.0", which is has been obtained for the 26 properties with identical names in both ontologies. Overall, more than 70 have been obtained with a minimum matching quality of "0.741". The amount of concepts and properties with the same or very similar labels seems to indicate that it is possible to achieve a great degree of semantic integration among the ontologies for the filings coming from the same companies. We are currently evaluating the quality of the alignments generated by different tools and for filings from different companies.

In any case, we can currently take profit from the fact that most facts in the filings are not from these filing specific taxonomies. Most of them come from the standard XBRL taxonomies. Consequently, we have focused on integrating and cross querying filings from the point of view of the facts from these standard taxonomies, as it is shown in the Evaluation section, where the results of the previous process of moving XBRL data to the semantic space have been put into practice.

4 Evaluation

The XSD2OWL and XML2RDF mappings have been validated in different ways. First, we have used OWL validators in order to check the logical consistency of the resulting ontologies. Once all the ontologies were validated, which also includes checking that all the dependencies among them are met, we proceeded to put them into practice, together with the semantic metadata generated by the XML2RDF mapping.

In parallel with our efforts, the ontologies we have generated for XBRL using the XSD2OWL mapping are being used by OpenLink Software[14], who has also tested them independently. These ontologies have been chosen by OpenLink as the ontological framework for their software component responsible for translating XBRL data to semantic data based on RDF, which they call the XBRL Sponger.

This parallel effort provides us an independent evaluation of the generated ontologies, which they have found as appropriate in order to structure the RDF data they generate from the XBRL filings. Moreover, they also generate RDF data from XBRL so we have also evaluated our XML2RDF mapping in comparison to their

---

[14] OpenLink Software, http://www.openlinksw.com

mapping. As it is shown below, they have implemented their own mapping for this step thought their and our instance level mappings are based on the same ontologies.

First of all, there is a significant difference in the number of triples generated by the OpenLink XBRL Sponger and XML2RDF. For instance, for the same EDGAR XBRL filing[15], the XBRL Sponger produces 900 triples while XML2RDF produces 4739 triples. One possible reason for this difference is that we have followed quite different approaches relative to how the original XML tree structure is captured in the RDF graph. However, there is also a significant difference in the amount of instance data captured in the output RDF. While XBRL to RDF captures all the data in the original XBRL instance, the XBRL Sponger captures just a small part of it in comparison.

For instance, Table 4 shows in the first row a portion of XBRL XML instance data from the previous filing. This XBRL corresponds to a context and to a fact that references de previous context. The second row contains the RDF generated from the previous XBRL XML by the OpenLink Sponger. As it can be shown, the result is a "sioc:Container" object for the context object that contains just some of the properties of the original container plus the fact and its value. Some of the information for the context and most of it for the fact is not captured. Moreover, the whole structure is flattened.

On the other hand, the third row in Table 4 shows the mapping for the same XBRL XML as generated by our XML2RDF mapping. As it can be seen, the result is much move verbose, even more than the original XBRL. However, it does capture all the original information and keeps the original structure. Even more, the original XBRL does not explicitly refer to the XML Schema *complexTypes* defined in the schemas and used in the instance data. This information is available in the XML2RDF semantic data and can be used, together with the hierarchical relations among complex types, when resolving semantic queries against this data.

Apart from instance data, it is also possible to compare the OWL ontologies generated following the proposed approach to those available from the two other initiatives introduced in the related work section. It has not been possible to compare the instance data generated by these initiatives because it not publicly available nor documented in the corresponding publications or associated documents.

In relation with [5], which focuses on investment funds taxonomies and their corresponding ontologies, they also perform an automatic mapping from XBRL taxonomies to OWL ontologies. However, the mapping is not as complete as the proposed one, especially in relation with cardinalities. The cardinalities in the input XBRL taxonomies do not seem to be taken into account and thus the output ontologies define all properties as FunctionalProperties or cardinalities equal to one.

Finally, comparing with the results reported in [3], they focus on just one taxonomy, the IPP-XBRL taxonomy that was promoted by the Spanish Securities Commission (CNMV) then, and just instance data based on this taxonomy can be generated.

---

[15] Adobe Systems Inc. EDGAR filing 2008-07-03, XBRL file: http://www.sec.gov/Archives/edgar/data/796343/000079634308000005/adbe-20080616.xml

Table 4 XBRL XML instance data example (first row), OpenLink XBRL Sponger mapping (second row) and XML2RDF XBRL mapping (third row) for the previous example

```
<context id="AsOf20061201_Consolidated_Unaudited">
<entity>
<identifier scheme="http://www.sec.gov/CIK">796343</identifier>
<segment><adbe:Consolidated /></segment>
</entity>
<period>
<instant>2006-12-01</instant>
</period>
<scenario><adbe:Unaudited /></scenario>
</context>
<usfr-pte:CashCashEquivalents decimals="-3"
contextRef="AsOf20061201_Consolidated_Unaudited"
unitRef="USD">772500000</usfr-pte:CashCashEquivalents>
```
```
<sioc:Container rdf:about=AsOf20061201_Consolidated_Unaudited>
<olsw:identifier>796343</olsw:identifier>
<olsw:scheme rdf:resource=http://www.sec.gov/CIK/>
<olsw:instant>2006-12-01</olsw:instant>
<olsw:CashCashEquivalents>772500000</olsw:CashCashEquivalents>
<olsw:has_space rdf:resource=&adbe796343;adbe-20080616.xml/>
</sioc:Container>
```
```
<xbrli:context>
<xbrli:contextType rdf:about="AsOf20061201_Consolidated_Unaudited">
<xbrli:entity>
<xbrli:contextEntityType rdf:about="&semxbrl;CIK/796343">
<xbrli:segment>
<xbrli:segmentType>
<adbe20080530:Consolidated rdf:parseType="Resource"/>
</xbrli:segmentType>
</xbrli:segment>
</xbrli:contextEntityType>
</xbrli:entity>
<xbrli:period>
<xbrli:contextPeriodType>
<xbrli:instant>2006-12-01</xbrli:instant>
</xbrli:contextPeriodType>
</xbrli:period>
<xbrli:scenario>
<xbrli:contextScenarioType>
<adbe20080530:Unaudited rdf:parseType="Resource"/>
</xbrli:contextScenarioType>
</xbrli:scenario>
</xbrli:contextType>
<xbrli:context>
<xbrli:item>
<usfr-pte:CashCashEquivalents>
<rdf:type rdf:resource="&xbrli;monetaryItemType"/>
<xbrli:unitRef rdf:resource="http://dbpedia.org/resource/USD"/>
<xbrli:decimals>-3</xbrli:decimals>
<xbrli:contextRef rdf:resource="#AsOf20061201_Consolidated_Unaudited"/>
<rdf:value>772500000</rdf:value>
</usfr-pte:CashCashEquivalents>
</xbrli:item>
```

4.1 Use Case

As a result of how the original XML tree is semantically enriched when it is mapped to RDF and how different XML trees are interconnected when mapped to RDF graphs, it is possible to query and traverse the mix of many XBRL filings in novel and more productive ways.

All this functionality has been put into practice for the semantic dataset resulting from mapping the EDGAR XBRL filings to RDF. The more than 2 million triples re-sulting from the mapping have been published online using the Rhizomer tool [21]. Data can be queried, traversed and edited online[16] through a web user interface for human users. Moreover, through HTTP and content negotiation, Rhizomer also makes data available for machine consumption and makes it possible to integrate it into the Web of Linked Data. The overall architecture of this solution is shown in Figure 2.

For human users, this tool makes it possible to interact with Semantic Web data by posing semantic queries through dynamic forms or by browsing the RDF graph interactively. The entry page provides some sample queries that return an HTML render-ing of the selected parts of the graph, which can be then used as the starting point for the browsing steps.

This sample queries illustrate how semantic queries take profit from the hierarchical relations in the original XML Schemas, i.e. hierarchies of elements and complex types that are translated to property and class hierarchies respectively. Moreover, there is also a query that exploits the fact that some of the Adobe Systems Inc. ontologies have been integrated and returns data from different filings for equivalent facts with different names.

Finally, there are additional views dynamically plugged in depending on the kind of resource being browsed. Many of them are the same available from Exhibit [22] (timeline, map, facets,). In addition to visualization plugins, it is also possible to integrate other kinds of services that manipulate data.

The whole system is built on top of a OpenLink Virtuoso[17] repository that provides scalability to more than tens of millions of triples and provides RDF Schema inferencing and support for OWL equivalence constructs.

5 Conclusions and Future Work

As it has been shown, it is possible to map the XML data for XBRL filings in order to generate RDF semantic data that keeps all the original information and structure. This mapping also includes the involved XML Schemas that structure the XML data. These schemas are mapped to Web ontologies, which make all the seman-

---

[16] SemanticXBRL, http://rhizomik.net/semanticxbrl/

[17] OpenLink Virtuoso open-source edition, http://virtuoso.openlinksw.com/wiki/main/

tics implicit in the original XML Schemas explicit and available when semantically querying RDF data.

Moreover, it is also possible to take profit from Web ontology primitives in order to semantically integrate different filings following different XML Schemas, i.e. XBRL taxonomies. Once mapped to ontology concepts and relations, the XBRL context, facts and other resources defined for different filings can be related as more specific, more general or equivalent.

This approach has been put into practice in the context of the SECs EDGAR program that promotes XBRL filings for USA companies. It has been possible to apply the previous XML to RDF and XML Schema to Web ontology mappings to all the EDGAR filings and more than 2 million triples have been obtained.

Our approach has been independently validated by the OpenLink Software, a company that is currently using the resulting XBRL ontologies in its XBRL to RDF mapping product. However, OpenLink does not follow the same XML to RDF mapping approach. Their approach has been compared to ours showing that our proposal retains much more of the original XBRL information and structure.

We have also have made all this semantic information generated from the EDGAR program available online, so it can be queried and browsed using a Web

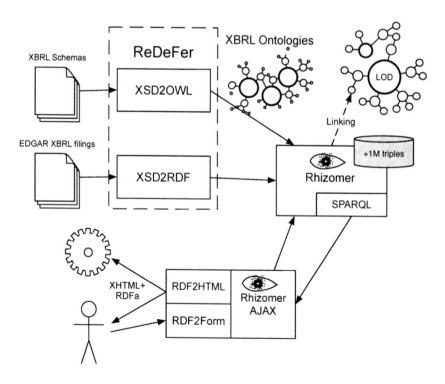

Fig. 2 Architecture of the proposed solution for semantic XBRL generation, linking and publishing

user interface. The proposed semantic queries illustrate the benefits of the semantic integration available once XBRL data is translated to semantic data.

However, it is important to note that we do not see our proposal as an alternative to XBRL. Semantic Web technologies have some limitations that currently do not make them a clear alternative to XBRL. For instance, OWL does not provide the primitives to easily model features available in XBRL like the calculation facilities provided by calculation linkbases. Moreover, the characteristics of the logic formalisms underlying OWL might not be the more intuitive choice in some XBRL use scenarios. For instance, a great part of OWL relies on the Open World Assumption and it is based on restrictions instead of on constraints [5].

On the contrary, we see XBRL and the Semantic Web as clearly complementary. XBRL can be used for business and financial data representation and validation, while its translation to Semantic Web technologies can be the way to make all this data publicly available enabling cross analysis of this data thanks to semantic integration and a graph base model.

This vision must be more deeply tested and validated. In order to do that, we are currently working on integrating ontology alignment tools into the mapping process. This way it is going to be possible to extensively put semantic integration into practice and test the benefits of cross-filings semantic queries and browsing.

Another future plan is to exploit XBRL semantic data beyond querying and brows-ing. In this respect, our idea is to take profit from the Rhizomer human-Semantic Web interaction platform in order to implement additional ways to interact with this data. For instance, we are currently evaluating an interactive mechanism for plotting numeric values available through the Parallax interface to Freebase [23]. This would allow performing semantic queries for specific facts across different filings and then plotting their values.

Acknowledgements The work described in this chapter has been partially supported by Spanish Ministry of Science and Innovation through the Open Platform for Multichannel Content Distribution Management (OMediaDis) research project (TIN2008-06228).

References

1. Lytras, M., Garca, R. Semantic Web Applications: A framework for industry and business exploitation - What is needed for the adoption of the Semantic Web from the market and industry, International Journal of Knowledge and Learning 4(1) (2008) 93-108.
2. Bizer, C., Heath, T., Idehen, K., Berners-Lee, T. Linked data on the web (LDOW2008), in: Proceeding of the 17th international conference on World Wide Web, ACM, 2008, pp. 1265-1266.
3. Núñez, S., de Andrs, J., Gayo, J. E., and Ordoez, P. A Semantic Based Collaborative System for the Interoperability of XBRL Accounting Information, in: Emerging Technologies and Information Systems for the Knowledge Society. Lecture Notes in Computer Science Vol. 5288, Springer, Berlin, 2008, pp. 593-599.
4. Hoffman, C. Financial Reporting Using XBRL: IFRS and US GAAP Edition. Lulu.com, 2006.

5. Lara, R., Cantador, I., and Castells, P. Semantic Web Technologies for The Financial Domain, in: J. Cardoso and M. Lytras (Eds.), The Semantic Web: Real-World Applications from Industry. Springer, Berlin, 2008, pp. 41-74.
6. Erling, O., Mikhailov, I. RDF Support in the Virtuoso DBMS, in: Pellegrini, T., Auer, S., Tochtermann, K., and Schaffert, S. (eds.) Networked Knowledge - Networked Media, Springer, 2009, pp. 7-24.
7. Klein, M.C.A. Interpreting XML Documents via an RDF Schema Ontology, in: Proceedings of the 13th Int. Workshop on Database and Expert Systems Applications, DEXA02, IEEE Computer Society, 2002, pp. 889-894.
8. Amann, B., Beeri, C., Fundulaki, I., Scholl, M. Ontology-Based Integration of XML Web Resources, in: Proceedings of the 1st International Semantic Web Conference, ISWC02. Lecture Notes in Computer Science, Vol. 2342, Springer, Berlin, 2002, pp. 117-131.
9. Cruz, I., Xiao, H., Hsu, F. An Ontology-based Framework for XML Semantic Integration, in: Proceedings of the 8th Int. Database Engineering and Applications Symposium, IEEE Computer Society, 2004, pp. 217- 226.
10. Lakshmanan, L., Sadri, F. Interoperability on XML Data. In Proceedings of the 2nd International Semantic Web Conference, ISWC03, Lecture Notes in Computer Science Vol. 2870, Springer, Berlin, 2003, pp. 146-163.
11. Patel-Schneider, P.F., Simeon, J. The Yin/Yang web: XML syntax and RDF semantics, in: Proceedings of the 11th World Wide Web Conference, WWW02. ACM Press, 2002, pp. 443-453.
12. García, R. XML Semantics Reuse, Chapter 7 in: A Semantic Web Approach to Digital Rights Management, PhD Thesis, Universitat Pompeu Fabra, Barcelona, Spain, 2006. http://rhizomik.net/ roberto/thesis
13. García, R., Gil, R., Delgado, J. A Web Ontologies Framework for Digital Rights Management, Journal of Artificial Intelligence and Law 15, 2 (2007) 137-154.
14. García, R., Gil, R. Facilitating Business Interoperability from the Semantic Web, in: Proceedings of the 10th International Conference on Business Information Systems, BIS'07, Lecture Notes in Computer Science Vol. 4439, Springer, Berlin, 2007, pp. 220-232.
15. García, R., Perdrix, F., Gil, R., Oliva, M. The Semantic Web as a Newspaper Media Convergence Facilitator, Journal of Web Semantics 6, 2 (2008) 151-161.
16. García, R., Tsinaraki, C., Celma, O., Christodoulakis, S. Multimedia Content Description using Semantic Web Languages, in: Semantic Multimedia and Ontologies: Theory and Applications, Y. Kompatsiaris and P. Hobson Eds. Springer, Berlin, 2008, pp. 17-54.
17. Berners-Lee, T. Why RDF model is different from the XML model. W3C Design Issues, 1998. http://www.w3.org/DesignIssues/RDF-XML.html
18. Tous, R., García, R., Rodrguez, E., and Delgado, J. Arquitecture of a Semantic XPath Processor, in: Proceedings of 6th Int. Conference on E-Commerce and Web Technologies, K. Bauknecht, B. Pröll and H. Werthner Eds., EC-Web05, Lecture Notes in Computer Science Vol. 3590, Springer, Berlin, 2005, pp. 1-10.
19. Volz, J., Bizer, C., Gaedke, M., Kobilarov, G. 2009. Silk A Link Discovery Framework for the Web of Data. 2nd Workshop about Linked Data on the Web (LDOW2009), Madrid, Spain.
20. Hu, W., Qu, Y. Falcon-AO: A practical ontology matching system. Journal of Web Semantics, 6, 3 (2008) 237-239.
21. García, R., Gimeno, J.M., Perdrix, F., Gil, R., Oliva, M. 2008. A Platform for Object-Action Semantic Web Interaction, in: Proceedings of the 16th Int. Conf. on Knowledge Engineering and Knowledge Management Patterns, A. Gangemi, J. Euzenat Eds., EKAW08. Lecture Notes in Computer Science Vol. 5268, Springer, Berlin, pp. 404-418.
22. Huynh, D. User Interfaces Supporting Casual Data-Centric Interactions on the Web. Doctoral Thesis at MIT EECS / CSAIL, 2007. Available from http://davidhuynh.net/media/thesis/thesis.php
23. Huynh, D., Karger, D. Parallax and Companion: Set-based Browsing for the Data Web. Submitted to the World Wide Web Conference, 2009. Available from http://davidhuynh.net/media/papers/2009/www2009-parallax.pdf

Scalable Reasoning Techniques for Semantic Enterprise Data

Reza B'Far

Abstract

Semantic Reasoners are the set of applications that can provide inferences over semantic data sets. As the types of data ontologies, the amount of instance data based on those ontologies, and the type of required inferences grow, the problem of reasoning becomes increasingly difficult. Linking of the Data within the enterprise as with the case of external data explodes the scaling problem. In this chapter, we look at various reasoning techniques and how to assure that they can scale properly so that Linking Data results in additional knowledge.

1 Introduction

During my undergraduate studies, every day, I walked in a building with the etching of a quote by T.S. Eliot:

Where is the Life we have lost in living?
Where is the wisdom we have lost in knowledge?
Where is the knowledge we have lost in information?

With each passing of the many years since, it has meant something more, something different, and something new. As I have become fond of artificial intelligence, it has taken more and more meaning. In a single quote, T.S. Eliot answers significant portion of what we know today to be clear differences between human and machines. The last two lines apply in particular to the topic of this text.

Why do we want to have abundant amounts of information linked? How do we make sure that we don't simply get lost in the volume of the information within the

Reza B'Far

Oracle Corporation, 500 Oracle Parkway, Redwood Shores, CA 94065, USA, e-mail: `reza.bfar@oracle.com`

D. Wood (ed.), *Linking Enterprise Data*, DOI 10.1007/978-1-4419-7665-9_7,

systems as we gather and link them? An attempt to answer those questions leads us into reasoning. The most rudimentary step in gaining knowledge from information is some ability to draw inferences from that information given a set of axioms and some way of navigating the information. This chapter focuses on reasoning through data stored in triple stores and/or quad store . Some boundary conditions are put into place on the problem considered to limit the scope of the discussion to applications of reasoning within the enterprise so as to make the discussion manageable within the space of this chapter.

In a nutshell, the goal of this chapter is to help us find knowledge in the vast oceans of information that result from linking enterprise data. In order to do this, our interest is either in building tools or using tools that are built by others. The approach in this chapter is to layout the various aspects of reasoning over large data; it occasionally takes a somewhat academic approach to looking at algorithms at a high-level (for example, there will be references to Big O notation). We'll start the chapter by discussing high-level concepts in reasoning so that the reader has a good overview of the most pertinent feature-sets to extract knowledge from semantic stores. These sections are centered around proven work in both academic and commercial arena's. We spend the middle section of the chapter looking at how to scale these concepts to real environments with linked enterprise data. We end with best practices in applying these concepts.

As this is a practitioner's guide, these segments are intended to enable the reader to either evaluate infrastructure technologies as tools, to decide what high-level design architecture to use in building tools and products, or to decide on specific algorithmic approaches to solving problems. It is crucial that the enterprise practitioner understands what feature-sets are encapsulated within the toolsets that are chosen and how, at the high-level, these toolsets function.

2 Survey of Reasoning Techniques

The concept of reasoning may be considered an umbrella for things such as traditional rule-engines (using simple set of if-then rules to make assertions) to STRIPS[18]-like planners and finally to full-blown infrastructures built on modern artificial intelligence techniques. The first goal of this chapter will be to provide an overview of the approaches to reasoning in short bits. After the introduction, we will delve into some areas which have either proven themselves of great success in reasoning over semantic date within the enterprise or are at the bleeding edge of being applied with great prospects of application within the enterprise.

Let's first consider the conceptual points. It's widely accepted that the best abstract model for thinking about reasoners is that they can look at a knowledge graph, and given a set of instructions can make some inferences. Typically, the knowledge graph needs to be thought of as one single cohesive network of connected nodes where the nodes are connected through "smart" or "rich" edges. Relating this to the Semantic Web concepts, the nodes are subjects or objects and the edges are predicates. So, a triple store is a graph and a quad store can be considered a graph with a series of named subgraphs. This straight-forward mapping is, in fact, one of the main reasons Semantic Web technologies such as RDF and OWL are extremely useful for linking data the fact that they can be represented in form of a graph of nodes, without large amount of difficulty or appealing to mapping techniques such as Object-to-Relational mappings.

In this chapter, we will only consider reasoning done over DAG's[2] (Directional Acyclic Graphs). These graphs are specially important to enterprise data because the great majority information generated in business constructs are causal in nature and this causality gives birth to the directional nature of the graph. If there are cycles in the instance data (important to note that this is instance data we're talking about the actual triples not the ontology on which its based), they are most probably errors and need to be removed. For example, if an instance of an invoice is created by an instance of a vendor, the vendor could not have been created by that same instance of invoice. In other words, the two statements Invoice_111 -> CreatedBy -> Vendor_222 and Vendor_222 -> CreatedBy -> Invoice_111 are mutually exclusive. The key here is to assure that the predicates are all orthogonal and, if they are not, to break the predicates down additively to a point where they are. Here, CreatedBy is a predicate. We don't want to have predicates that state something like OwnedBy where "ownership" may mean one entity (a vendor, for example) can modify, update, or delete another entity. The degree of atomicity of the predicates in the ontology here is the key in being able to have some automated manner with which to remove cycles.

Furthermore, reasoning over non-directional graphs and/or graphs that have cycles is a significantly more complex problem that presents challenges beyond the scope of this chapter.

We now have to take a quick detour and discuss so-called Open World versus Closed World assumptions. Consider for a moment that we have a database of patient information that can be represented in terms of semantic statements. An example of such a statement may be:

Zara is a Flu patient

Now, let's assume we also make the statement

Zara is a 4 year old female

In the case of Closed World assumption, the reasoning system basically says that its universe of facts is limited to what is exactly known and there is nothing beyond that. Therefore, for the Closed World case, any 4 year old female is a Flu patient (there is a bit of generalization here, but we'll clear that up later). In the Open World assumption, the reasoner simply says that it doesn't know anything about the the category of patients that are Flu patients. Clearly, Open World assumption is a much more "intelligent" model. But, Open World assumption results mostly in unsolvable or np-complete (nondeterministically polynomial time)[19] problems. So, for enterprise data, we will take some steps to make the Closed World assumption more intelligent to a point where we can draw conclusions such as "there is a high probability of being a Flu patient if the patient's immune system is compromised, she has a runny nose, and she has a fever". The reason for our detour is that it is not possible to create a mental model of the Open World in terms of a DAG. Conversely, we can do so in a Closed World.

DAG's are essential to the conversation of Semantic Web reasoning in the enterprise. Since Semantic Web stores are some realization of a triple store (and higher encapsulations of triples such as quads), then they provide the right conceptual orientation for reasoning through a sea of triple instances and their meta-models. Let's take, for example, 1-N sources of triples for patient data residing in various triple stores or quad stores can be made available with the goal of drawing new inferences. As a side point, mining data for new information is a typical reason for linking data and this is a typical need regardless of the implementation techniques. Next, we need to reason through this data to find the information we're looking for. We can do this in two different ways:

1. Link the data first, build a larger DAG, and then reason through the large DAG. We'll refer to this method as *Combine Then Reason* (CR)
2. Reason through the individual stores by building one DAG for each triple store or quad store. Then, take the resulting inferences from each store, along with all the relevant connections between the stores, and reason through those to get more inferences. We'll refer to this method as *Reason, Combine, then Reason* (RCR)

Both methods have their advantages and disadvantages. In both cases, however, performance becomes a serious issue as the size of the individual triple store or quad stores grow. Later in this chapter, we will look at attacking the performance problem via distribution, parallelization, and improving algorithmic efficiency. This is not to say there are not other approaches, merely that these are the approaches we will consider.

2.1 Traditional Rule Engines

The casual reader can think of the term Rule Engine as any piece of software that can interpret a set of rules and create a set of assertions (conclusions) based on those rules when it's given a set of data. Traditionally, in the business application realm, these rules are limited to "If-Then" type rules. When the "If" part of the expression is satisfied, the "Then" part of the expression is fired off to build an assertion. Inference engines are a more formal term used in computer science and are considered to provide the super-set of functionality of the aforementioned rule engines implement. Inference engines are programs that can draw a set of inferences about a knowledge based when asked certain questions. The difference is subtle, but very significant. Inference engines, for example, encompass the ability to do probabilistic reasoning. For example, you can ask an inference engine "What time will the train arrive?" and it can look at the last 100 arrival times for a train, average them, eliminate the anomalies, remove potentially incorrect answers, then come up with an answer. A traditional rule engine can answer "Will the train arrive between 1 and 2 PM?". We continue to use the word "traditional" because the definition of rule engine seems to be expanding as it is becoming synonymous with inference engines.

An example of a traditional rule engine is the Drools[1] rule engine authored in Java. Drools provides a scripting language with which to specify the definition of the rules. Data is then provided to it and it makes a set of assertions based on the rules. Example of a rule may be:

Company (name == ''Oracle'' || name == ''Peoplesoft'')

Drools then iterates through all of the available data and keeps the data where the expression qualifies and returns them.

Traditional rule engines not only limit all of their assertions to closed world, but also are very limited in the type of reasoning. Much like other traditional rule engines, Drools has an implementation of the RETE[20] algorithm. In fact, a hallmark of today's traditional rule engines is typically having an implementation of RETE which will be discussed in the next section. The other problem with using these rule engines with triples is that implementor can run into problems writing rules that sometimes have to deal with choices made in the taxonomy of the instance data (whether something is a property of a class or a predicate, for example). With all of their limitations, traditional rule engines are pervasive as they provide useful abstractions for specifying simple if/then style rules by business users. There are ample use-cases where the only need for reasoning within the enterprise data is to perform if/then style reasoning.

Traditional rule engines also often deploy some sort of chaining (forward or backward rule chaining) in processing the rules which we will also describe in the next sections.

2.2 Forward Chaining and the RETE algorithm

The RETE algorithm was invented in 1974 by Charles L. Forgy and published in the paper "A network match routine for production systems". It is at the heart of many different rule engines. It is optimized for computing cycles by building a network of nodes where matching the pattern of nodes is the goal. RETE has been implemented by Open Source Software projects Jena, Drools, Pellet[9], and many other traditional rule engines.

The RETE algorithm falls within a broader class of algorithms called *Forward Chaining* algorithms. Forward Chaining is a very straight forward idea: take a series of atomic logic segments, move through them sequentially, and build a knowledge base by adding the inference of these atomic segments together. Let's go back to our previous example where we have a rule that states

Child (p) ^ Fever (p) ^ RunnyNose (p) ? Flu (p)

The rule states that if a patient is a child, he/she has a fever, and also has a runny nose, then we conclude that the patient has the flu. Now, let's assume we have an instance of patient data Anna who is a child, has fever, and has a runny nose.

The reasoner would first evaluate that Zara is a child and that the first segment is true so it would continue. Then that she has a fever, causing it to continue, and finally that she has a runny nose. The segment above is atomic because if any of the segments are false, then the entire segment becomes false so there is no reason to continue evaluating the individual conditions. The RETE algorithm looks for patterns of literals within the atomic segments and if those literals already exist, then they are shared within different atomic segment evaluations. For example, if we have another rule that says

Child(p) ˆ Fever(p) ˆ Coughing(p) ? Bronchitis(p)

The two atomic segments share the literals Child(p) and Fever(p). With RETE, the reasoner first recognizes that Child(p) F̂ever(p) is a pattern that is shared across multiple rules, then the result of these literals are cached for use as the reasoner goes through the various rules and instance data to evaluate against the rules.

The central problem with RETE is in memory requirements. By caching interim results, it avoids repeated evaluation of same facts. However, the results have to be stored somewhere permanently. From a performance perspective, the need for storage in memory grows as a function of the matched patterns.

Forward chaining and the RETE algorithm are important to Semantic Web reasoning because they are frequently used to draw assertions within a triple store. In fact, in the example we presented, it's easy to see that we have a triple store of patient data that says

Anna has Fever
Anna is Patient
Anna is Coughing
Anna is a Child
Joey is a Child
Joey is a Boy
Joey has broken arm
. . .

Another form of drawing inferences from enterprise data is using a Backward Chaining reasoner.

2.3 Backward Chaining

In forward chaining, we started with the literals in the atomic expressions and evaluated our way to get the assertions (or goals) that we need. Backward chaining is the opposite as the name indicates: we start from the end (or goals) and see if the facts (in our case our triple in our triple store or quad store) support those. The advantage of backward chaining is that, in similar ways to Depth First Search algorithms, its memory needs grow only linearly as a function of the depth of the triple graph.

In general backward chaining is useful when the memory needs of forward chaining methods are too large. But, the disadvantages include, similar to Depth-First search, that there is no cache of previous work done so redundant work may be done over and over. Various techniques have been added to plain backward chaining to overcome these problems that we won't cover in this chapter.

Most advanced reasoners implement both forward and backward chaining and deploy them in a manner that is optimal for the usage of the application sector for which they are designed. Forward and Backward chaining provide us with techniques to draw inferences from triple stores based on "First Order Logic" rules. The reader can think of these as deterministic statements that relate two objects together similar to a triple (this is not the formal definition, but for the purposes of this chapter, it will suffice). There are other reasoning methods where the inferences are not 100% conclusive. These include probabilistic reasoners such as those that deploy Bayesian networks .

3 Bayesian Networks

In a very generic sense, a Bayesian network is a DAG where the nodes and edges are associated with conditional probability tables. They are DAG's that encapsulate a probabilistic model of causality between the nodes on the graph. Figure 1 shows the classic example where a Bayesian network is used to represent causality of a disease.

In a Bayesian network, every node has a conditional probability of occurring based on the existence of its parent. For example, in Figure 1, if a patient is coughing, then there is a 0.05 probability that he/she has an asthmatic condition. The direction of the DAG in a Bayesian Network indicates the direction of causality. For example, if a parent of the Fever node is Flu, then it means that the Flu caused the fever (as opposed to the Fever causing the Flu). Therefore, the construction of the Bayesian Network is not just about graphing out a series of probabilities. We also have to know something about which object caused which object. The significance to ontological representations, and in particular to Semantic Web presentations, is that the predicate that connects the Subject and Object must not violate causality and has at least one conditional probability that describes the probability of occurrence of the subject or object on the other.

Fukushige[3] was one of the first to explore modeling Bayesian Networks (which referred do as Probabilistic Knowledge Graphs) using RDF. Some of the most important scenarios where the usage of Bayesian Networks provides high reasoning value when looking at enterprise data:

1. A taxonomy is known and the Bayesian Network serves to provide either a probabilistic model for prediction or an analysis model for verification of the taxonomy causality. Let's take our patient model. In this case, we can use a Bayesian

Network to determine the causal relationships, probabilistically speaking, between different facts. In other words, it can help us build the direction of the arrows in our graphs since predicates don't inherently have direction with which
we can build a DAG.

2. The second scenario is where there is no ontology (taxonomy) of the meta-data,
but enough data so that reliable conditional probabilities can be obtained. In
this case, we can first draw a set of conditional probabilities, then build the
ontology based on the probabilistic model represented by the data. Pan et. al.[4]
were one of the first to explore this approach. Huttenhower et. al. [7] show
a very successful application of this approach to leveraging this approach for
modeling biological processes.

3. Removal of cycles in the instance data. Since there are often errors in the instance data (can be semantic errors, physical errors, etc.), and since we're considering DAG's to be the ideal model for reasoning through enterprise data,
one of the steps in processing the data is to remove any cycles. For example,
we don't want to have a ontological model where there is a causality relationship from patient class to fever class and then another causal relationship from
the fever class back to the patient class. In this case, being given a significant
data set, if there is a 99% probability that all people with fever are patients and
only a 15% probability that all patients have fever, then we simply remove the
predicate that says all patients have fever from our ontological model when reasoning (note that the cycles are not necessarily mutually exclusive, therefore
probabilities associated with cyclical predicates may not add up to be 1). Unfortunately, the application of Bayesian Networks for probabilistic reasoning

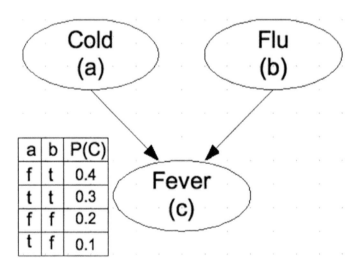

Fig. 1 Conditional Probabilities Associated with Nodes in a Bayesian Network

through Semantic Web data is still fairly limited. Sometimes the sources of data used to populate the triple store and quad stores don't have the necessary data available, sometimes the triple stores don't provide the infrastructure necessary to store conditional probability tables for the predicates, and other times, the reasoners don't have sophisticated probabilistic capabilities. In the next section, we'll look at some attempts at extending OWL to encapsulate the conditional probabilities necessary to store the overlay of a Bayesian Network on the top of vanilla ontological data stored in OWL and/or other relevant standards.

3.1 Representing Probabilities within the Ontological Model

Ding and Peng[6] were one of the first to explore the idea of extending the meta-model standard of the triplestore (in their case OWL) to accommodate for storage of additional information that makes up the Bayesian Network. In particular, Ding and Peng as below

```
<prob:PriorProbObj rdf:ID= P(Animal) >
  <prob:hasVariable>
    <rdf:value>&ont;Animal</rdf:value>
  </prob:hasVariable>
```

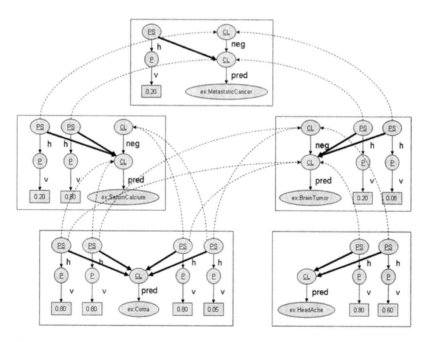

Fig. 2 Sample Probabilistic Model of Cancer Patients in RDF[3]

```
<prob:hasProbValue>0.5</prob:hasProbValue>
</prob:PriorProbObj>
```

This approach allows the conditional probability tables associated with each node to be encoded directly encoded to the semantic store that persists the data.

An important note here is that if the Bayesian Network approach is used (given some data set) in some way in the initial construction of an ontology, we should have some additional data to verify the ontology. This is the same approach as one would take to a neural network: we need data to verify the construction of the neural network after the training step. If only one data set is available, then it's suggested that this data set be broken into multiple random parts, the first part is used to build the ontology using a Bayesian Network, then the resulting ontology is tested by the data that was not used in the first run.

Approaches such as Ding and Peng's have not been standardized, but they present undebatable benefits in providing a semantic data set that has, embedded within it, a Bayesian Network.

Generally speaking, Bayesian Networks and their capabilities are underutilized within the enterprise. This is mostly caused by the fact that there is a gap in functionality offered by reasoners suitable for enterprise applications as they race to catchup with the bleeding edge of technology. Bayesian Networks are highly useful for inferencing within the financial arena, health-care arena, and other domains where probabilistic reasoning can lead to better decision making.

4 Unsupervised Reasoning

Unsupervised reasoning is a recent term used to encapsulate several other areas which include application of pattern-based algorithms for reasoning, reasoning that follows unsupervised learning, application of fuzzy neural networks, and some others. Within this chapter, we will consider a subset of these types of reasoning:

1. **Pattern-based reasoning**: We define pattern-based reasoning as any reasoning types that is based on an indirect criteria in form of a set of pattern-matching instructions instead of looking for triples or quads that match some deterministic criteria. For example, we can tell the reasoner Find diseases that seem to have causal correlation. The reasoner can then use various correlative algorithms to find candidates. Using pattern-based algorithms to build reasoners can be quite useful, particularly when the amount of data that we're dealing with is very large and/or when there is a mismatch between the conceptual model for which the end user wants to get inferences and the ontological model in which the data is stored. We will leave the first case to a later section in this chapter where we discuss performance techniques. The second case is a common problem: for example, we have an enterprise system within which exist potentially millions of financial transactions and the end user may need to discover fraud in them. But, the end user may not know how fraud is being committed (fraudsters are

always coming up with new schemes, some schemes are extremely complex, etc.). In such a case, pattern based algorithms can look for seemingly random correlations and at least point to us potential areas of problems.

2. **Clustering** is a division of data into groups of similar objects; representing data by fewer clusters necessarily loses certain fine details, but achieves simplification[8]. While clustering itself is not a reasoning technique, it's invaluable in enabling or enhancing other reasoning techniques. For example, given a perspective density-based clustering can be used in building a taxonomy or for running a given algorithm within each cluster, then aggregating the inferences. A real-life application could be something like looking at a repository of legal documents and asking a frequency based reasoner where exposed risk may exist. In this use-case, clustering can be used to find those documents which have an affinity to each other or to a 1-N sections of an ontology which represents the semantic definition of risk.

Note that we're intentionally staying away from the concepts surrounding "learning". Machine learning is a concept that extends beyond the scope of this chapter though it can be utilized in reasoning and inferencing through triple stores and quad stores.

5 Semantic Reasoning

So far, we have looked at variety of techniques used in reasoning and what the general ideas around reasoning are. Our focus has been in understanding the high-level ideas of how reasoners are built and how they apply to Semantic Web applications. Semantic reasoning through semantic data can use any one of these techniques, other techniques, or a collection of them in practice. The end user, at the end of the day, doesn't care what technology we use. Our contention has been that the approach of using reasoners and Semantic Web technologies provide more value to the end user. To that end, we're now going to look at a commercially driven view of reasoning in the Semantic Web world. There are four typical perspectives of reasoning:

1. **End Users** : Organizations or users that need to use an existing software application, with minimal implementation effort, to reason through existing data.
2. **Systems Integrators** : Organizations or users that offer service-based infrastructures using more than one software application, not integrated out-of-the-box, to provide the facade of a single product or reasoning infrastructure to the end users. Implementation times can be significant as, in some cases, the integrator may essentially be creating a custom reasoning infrastructure for the end user based on existing technology.
3. **Tool Developers** : Organizations or users that build software components and/or whole reasoners which are not meant for consumption by the end users, rather by either System Integrators and Application Developers.

4. **Application Developers** : Organizations or users that want to build a specific application, providing a specific set of reasoning features to the end users. Application Developers may or may not use tools built by Tool Developers.

In the previous sections of this chapter, we have mainly looked at topics of interest to Application Developers and Tool Developers. There are a large set of semantic reasoning tools such as Jena [21], Sesame [22], Mulgara [23], FaCT, KAON2, Oracle 11gR (which reasons based on Oracle's database), Oracle's GRCC, OWLIM, and many others. It can become a challenge for end users and system integrators to evaluate what the right tool or application is for their requirements. Likewise, it can be difficult for an application developer to decide whether to use tools built by tool developers or to build from scratch. Keep in mind that the end users of Semantic Web applications don't want to understand what goes on under the hood. A physician who wants to know the probability of a particular patient having a disease given a set of symptoms regards the implementation of the tool-set as completely irrelevant. As such, successful Semantic Web applications are all end user applications. Successful Semantic Web applications in the future are sure to be focused on solving specific problems for end users versus providing some generic functionality for the smaller application development and/or system integrator markets.

Having said that, we can evaluate the existing applications via dimensional analysis:

1. **Source Code Availability**: Jena, Sesame and Mulgara are examples of Open Source tools that make their source code available for tool developers and application developers to inspect.
2. **Licensing Model**: Directly or indirectly, licensing translates to cost for the end user. If you're an application developer, you must be well aware of the licensing model of the toolset you use (whether open source or not since many open source tools are not - many open source tools come with hidden costs such as cost for support and documentation).
3. **Usage Model**: Understand the ethnography profile of the user(s) using the application, how often they use it, how they use it, etc. An application such as Oracle 11gR1 database offering Semantic Web storage and reasoning features is designed as a development tool. Another application such as Oracle GRCC, from the same vendor, is designed as a point solution for business users looking for financial fraud. The requirements for these applications are completely different. The way the products are used are different. Certainly the user-base ethnography vary.
4. **Performance Requirements**: Most applications and tools have limitations on what type of data they can reason over, what type of inferences they can produce, and how they perform depending on the inferences expected over the provided data. When looking at performance statistics, dig deep. Most commercially produced performance metrics about reasoners are fairly meaningless since they don't provide crucial relevant information such as handling of graph complexity (the topology of the meta-model and instance data), relationship to triplestore or quadstore performance and other variables.

Semantic reasoning features are a superset of the traditional rule engines that are able to do if-then-else style logic or first-order logic execution. Semantic users can include features we haven't discussed such as Natural Language Processing (NLP) and those that we've discussed such as pattern recognition, probabilistic reasoning, and others. As an end user, the most important decision you will make in your tool or application selection is to assure that it will provide you with the right-sized (not too many and not too few) set of features to accomplish what you need. In general, users should stay away from using tools directly as they are too technical and require technical expertise to operate hence raising the total cost of ownership. It is application developers' job to make the applications they provide end users and system integrators so that the applications sacrifice configurability in exchange for better usability when the balance is required. Only the will semantic reasoning applications will begin to gain mass-market traction.

5.1 Performance and Reasoning

Today, reasoning performance is perhaps the single biggest challenge relating to reasoning and Semantic Web topics. The fact is that we know of many techniques to organize information, but we know much less about how to get the performance we need to build complete and correct reasoners. By complete, we mean a reasoner that produces all of the possible inferences that exist in the data set based on the rules that we've been given. By correct, we mean that all of the inferences are correct. If we relax either or both of those requirements, performance tuning is easier. When it comes to practicality of enterprise reasoning, relaxing of the completeness requirement is much more feasible than correctness. Incorrect inferences are typically unacceptable by businesses, regardless of domain while having some inferences are better than none and various ranking algorithms can help in finding the more important inferences first.

Based on that, we're going to assume that relaxation of correctness is not feasible and that completeness is the only constraint we can relax to ease the problem of performance. Li et. al.[9] recognize the important characteristics of performance and we present them here, with some slight modifications and simplification, to be:

1. **Triple Throughput**: how fast can the reasoner go through the triples?
2. **Query Throughput**: how many queries (reasoning modules are probably a better term since some reasoning may not be query-related) can run at any one time?
3. **Maximum Input Size**: what is the size of the triple store and quad store that the reasoner can process?
4. **Applied Logic Types**: what are the types of reasoning that the reasoner can perform?

If you're an application or tool developer building a a reasoner, these are the metrics you should build into your integration and unit tests up-front in the development cycle. If you're an end user or system integrator, these are the metrics you should ask the tool and application vendors for. Not only is the goal that we are able to parallelize reasoning as much as possible, but also we want to make sure every atomic reasoning module runs as efficiently as possible. We'll start by looking at MapReduce applied to semantic reasoning and then look at algorithmic efficiency at the reasoning module level (we have already touched on this lightly by mentioning RETE).

5.2 Applying Best-First Search (A* Search) to Semantic Reasoning

The idea behind A* (pronounced A Star) search is simple and elegant, presenting one of the main breakthroughs in the field of artificial intelligence. A* search builds on Dijkstra's algorithm. Its essence relies on two principles: first that we can categorize the data that we're trying to search through and second that for that category we can come up with some admissible (admissibility is a fairly complex concept that we need not address in this chapter) heuristic function that describes a cost associated with every edge in the graph. In short, A* search uses what we know about the structure of the data to make it faster.

Be it medical information, a social network, or business applications within an enterprise, any triple store or quad store holds a set of triples based on ontology models it holds. The ontology is the meta-model and the triples are the instance data for the ontology. The ontology, then, is the basis for our heuristic function. The applicability of A* search to the semantic reasoning problem is then in enabling an algorithm that has a cost model associated with the triples that can take advantage of the information within the triples and appropriately weigh them versus treating all triples equally. Now, let's try to apply A* search with some of our previous concepts.

Let's assume that we're looking for financial fraud within a large set of triples residing in multiple triple stores and quad stores. In such a case, we may want to first find the fraud that is of the highest risk or highest cost. So, the heuristic model would provide us with the appropriate bias.

5.3 High-level View of Distributed Reasoning

Works such as DRAGO[12] look at processing of large heterogeneous ontologies that can be semantically decomposed to smaller ontologies, each of which can be processed individually and the whole of which can be recomposed using bridge rules[12][14]. Yet, other approaches such as KNAML treat ontologies as knowledge domains that happen to be of the ontology domain; using an ontology of ontologies to define the concept and relation types available in an ontology[13][14].

There are parallels in the various approaches taken to date to other problems solved in distributed computing. Namely, techniques such as divide and conquer

(D&C)[24], data replication, graph partitioning, and other tools and algorithms are used to distribute the computation of reasoning over large data sets so that the inferences are obtained within the time-requirement expected.

In this chapter, we will focus only on Map-Reduce[15] as a specific technique. The main reason for this approach being there are increasing number of infrastructure works such as Apache's Hadoop[16] which provide the pieces needed to build distributed applications and focus on the core functionality of the application (in our case semantic reasoning) versus the mechanics of distribution. Of course, with this tooling approach comes restrictions that bind the semantic reasoning model to certain restrictions. But this will give the reader a good idea of what all is entailed in creating a distributed reasoning infrastructure.

5.4 Map-Reduce and Similar Techniques

Many architectural approaches to semantic reasoning use various divide-and-concur attacks so that the problem of reasoning over a very large DAG is broken up to either reasoning over smaller DAG's, modularizing reasoning operations into multiple orthogonal operations that can run simultaneously, or a combination of both. A good example of these approaches is the now popular MapReduce algorithm which was invented by Google engineers. MapReduce was not invented to operate on semantic data, but it can be applied to the problem of reasoning over semantic data without much creativity being required.

There are two simple steps to MapReduce. The Map step is about breaking up the dataset so that many nodes (these can be processes running on the same CPU, different CPU's on the same hardware, or many different CPU's in different places) can operate on the dataset simultaneously. The Reduce step takes the result of the operations that the nodes produce and combines them to get the final intended results.

You may recall that in the first section of this chapter, we looked at CR and RCR techniques for reasoning over triple store or quad stores that are somehow linked. As such, MapReduce can be applied so that:

1. Using the CR method, one large DAG is produced so that is the starting point for the reasoner. The reasoner than has to partition the graph in someway. Various partitioning techniques such as bipartite graph partitioning and heuristic partitioning techniques (where some knowledge of the data composing the DAG provides for some hints in how to do the partitioning). The selected partitioning method here would comprise the majority of what goes into the Map portion of MapReduce. The nodes then do the job of reasoning over each partition and produce some results. The Reduce is then comprised of a collection of algorithms that takes the results of the nodes and gets the final set of inferences needed. Though graph partitioning is a so-called np-complete problem, there have been many algorithms defined for partitioning graphs whose content and

structure is somewhat known before partitioning takes place. Particularly, enterprise data is typically very well know in its structures and content, and even
when combining many disparate sources of such data, the combined DAG can
be well-characterized with reasonable certainty.

2. The CRC method introduced earlier essentially provides us with a pre-
   partitioned data set. CRC is clearly more effective if the number of triples
   crossing boundaries between two different triple stores (relationships between
   subjects and objects that exist in different stores) is insignificant. In such cases,
   CRC takes advantage of the natural partitioning of the data. For example, in
   a setting where we have a medical database of diseases for patience in one
   triple store and patient payment information in another datastore, there are
   some triples that extend across boundaries (such as the treatment cost where
   the treatment is a subject in the first triple store and the cost is an object in the
   second triple store), but the purpose of the triple stores (and their underlying
   ontologies) are fundamentally different.

MapReduce is sometimes referred to as Map-Combine-Reduce. This is because
some combination of the results is some time needed. In our case here, combine
could be useful in creating the set of inferences that cross the boundaries between
partitions, so that the reduce steps merely combines all of the finalized set of inferences. Map-Reduce is important in that it allows reasoning over a single set of
instance data, which could be based on a single ontology, over multiple processes.
While there may be some inefficiencies in how the computing cycles are used, the
end cost is less since the platform (hardware and software) on which the reasoning is
done can be made of more commoditized equipment and not specialized mainframe-
like hardware.

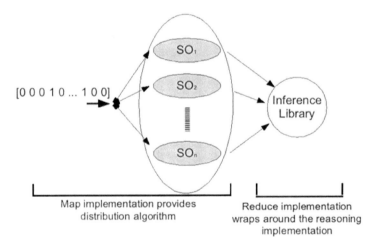

Fig. 3 High-Level role of Map and Reduce functions in providing a distributed reasoning system
for ontologies[14]

5.5 *Performance and Ontology Engineering*

There are various approaches and techniques used to formulate taxonomies of concepts to build ontologies. Missikof[25] and Gruber[26] provide some starting points while there is a large amount of literature for other reference points. As an example, when does one take a "strongly typed" approach to classification versus a "weakly typed" approach: is a white fox its own class or is it an instance of fox class with color attribute whose range includes white?

When designing your taxonomy, keep in mind that it's most likely that your data must be reasoned over at some point. At its simplest form, the instance data for your ontology will be stored in a database under the covers and there is a layer of abstraction that converts requests to retrieve the data to SQL queries at some point. More sophisticated schemes deploy various reasoning and search algorithms some of which we have mentioned in this chapter: for example, a probabilistic reasoner can run over a DAG stored in the file system or memory. When you design your taxonomy, keep in mind that best-case and worst-case performance of the reasoner will be bound by the structure of the instance data. You will want to design your ontology so that the worst case scenario for your reasoner is not a limiting factor for feature implementation or inferencing. The average performance scenario should be acceptable for most of the use-cases. While you want to avoid a common anti-pattern (designing your ontologies to fit some physical layer manifestation such as an RDBMS schema), keep in mind potential performance ramifications during your ontology design. Better yet, when you're selecting your tool set(s) for reasoning, make sure that the tool set can accommodate your approach to ontology design.

6 Semantic Reasoning vs. Business Intelligence

Within the realm of commercial enterprise applications, we have seen the rise and plateau of business intelligence applications during the 1990's and then 2000's. Business intelligence applications allow slicing and dicing of data, typically in some RDMBS store, via dimensional analysis. The goal of these tools is to provide a mechanism to improve decision making, be it to optimize performance or for any other set of reasons. The central issue around business intelligence applications is that they are tools and take significant expertise and time to apply to specific problem sets. As opposed to vertical search tools and applications that attack very specific problems, BI tools provide platforms on which end users can figure out how to solve their problems. And why do we mention them in the context of reasoning?

At the end of the day, semantic reasoners achieve some of the same things as BI tools, but as applications versus tools. Semantic reasoners look at goals (for a naive example, the corporate executive's objective being maximizing profits) instead of providing a tool-set on the top of which to build that (providing a dimensional analysis tool). As the Semantic Web reasoning tools and applications evolve, they will offer richer feature sets that will satisfy more and more of the business intelligence requirements. Likewise, so called "Business Intelligence 2.0" applications are now incorporating semantic concepts. The convergence point will become in the persistence mechanisms (triplestores, quadstores, and/or RDMBS), the scope of reasoning features, and the extended ability to perform advanced algorithms that fall within the realm of modern artificial intelligence techniques[10]. The competition with semantic reasoning is pushing BI applications to become richer and more semantic, moving them out of the realm of tools and into end user applications.

7 Best Practices for Application Developers and System Integrators

To conclude this chapter, we'll provide a succinct list of lessons learned through building various semantic reasoning applications as tool and application developers as well as using them as system integrators and end users. The list introduced here is not conclusive as the extreme youth of the field has not allowed for formal studies of methodologies. Nevertheless, it should be a useful list you can treat as patterns and anti-patterns:

1. **Semantic Reasoning Anti-Pattern: Avoid Duct-Tape Engineering.** There are a large set of tools using varying technologies in any nascent field. Each set of tools, architectures, technologies, and approaches may have fundamental differences. Failure of many Semantic Web projects are caused by trying to paste these various pieces together with some magical duct-tape (be it programming language such as Java, technology stack such as J2EE or .NET, or others) while not considering fundamental software engineering principles. Given the age of Semantic Web, the probability of a failed project is much higher than that of a successful project. So, if you don't understand how the tools you've chosen (as an application developer) work, the technical benefits of the approach of the application you've chosen (as an end user or system integrator), or the algorithmic approaches you're using (as a tool developer), you're probably better off not even starting the project. For example, if you want to build a custom reasoner from a collection of off-the-shelf reasoners such as Jena, Sesame, and others, understand the taxonomy of their API's, what algorithms they use, how building adapters between them will effect performance, and other factors.

2. **Semantic Reasoning Anti-Pattern: Tool overuse.** Understand what it is that you're trying to achieve with the Semantic Web application. Semantic reasoning exists to give you conclusions about your semantic data. Be clear, up front, with not just the use-cases that your application needs to solve, but also how the use-cases tie together both technically and functionally. Keep in mind that with nascent technologies, use-cases will change often and frequently as the end customer searches for the most optimal way of achieving the end goal. If you don't understand the underlying motivation for your use-cases, you'll under end up with mangled control structures that bloat over time (commonly referred to

spaghetti code) as you organically add code. Also, clearly understand that there can be a gap between the functional problem you're trying to solve and the tool set that you choose (or have available) to solve that problem. If there are things that the tool is not able to solve, don't try to force the issue. It's better to write custom code to augment your tool set features than it is to make the tool do something it's not meant to do since you have more control over the behavior of your custom code.

3. **Semantic Reasoning Pattern: Always keep in mind software entropy.** Ivar Jocobson[7] showed that "The second law of thermodynamics, in principle, states that a closed system's disorder cannot be reduced, it can only remain unchanged or increase. A measure of this disorder is entropy. This law also seems plausible for software systems; as a system is modified, its disorder, or entropy, always increases. This is known as software entropy." Without considering software entropy, you will spend a huge amount of time up-front designing what seems to be the perfect system, implement it, and then have to redesign and reimplement by the time your application is in the market. Carefully balance the consideration of software entropy with duct-tape engineering: do your due-diligence, but don't overdo it. This seems common sense, but just think of all of the various frameworks built for web applications, by very capable engineers, that at the end of the day add no value and merely provide layers of unneeded abstraction.

4. **Semantic Web and Reasoning Anti-Pattern: Don't design your ontologies like RDMBS entities.** Many developers and users are much more familiar with concepts in designing RDBMS schema's than they are with ontologies, folksonomies, and others. If you're going to design an ontology that has either 1-to-1 or near 1-to-1 correlation with an entity model in an RDBMS, there is probably no good reason to do what you're doing other than satisfying your technical curiosity. RDBMS schemas should be, if designed correctly, optimized for usage scenarios such as transactional schema's, analytic schema's, and others. Ontologies, reasoning, and concepts discussed in this book are intended to provide a semantic layer of abstraction where data is dealt with by its meaning rather than its physical structure. If you're defining your ontology based on entity design in an RDBMS, then you're defining the meaning of things based on how they are stored - a rather absurd proposition.

5. **Semantic Web and Reasoning Pattern: For best results, apply fundamentals of computer science and software engineering.** Try to avoid anecdotal information and ask for metrics and references. For example, when looking at performance, don't rely on statements such as this is the fastest OWL reasoner in the market. Instead of relying on the vendor to make such statements, ask for concrete information such as $O(n)$ analysis paper on the product. Though Big O notation is somewhat of an academic concept, it's an absolute and well-defined means of discussing performance. It provides an objective metric for measurement of performance versus discussing hardware (such as how many MIPS a given processor is able to handle, how many cores it has, how many machines

are chained together, etc.), software (abilities of the operating system, etc.), the data set used in testing, etc.

6. **Semantic Reasoning Pattern: Poor Atomicity and Orthogonality within the predicates.** The concepts of Atomicity and Orthogonality are very important concepts in general in software engineering. Atomicity, within object oriented systems, refers to things that can not be broken down any further to smaller things. Orthogonality refers to the things that don't have overlap (similar to orthogonal vectors in mathematics where the inner product of 2 orthogonal vectors is zero). To create reasoning systems that are distributable and scalable, it's highly desirable that the predicates in the ontologies are atomic and orthogonal. This is also important in other aspects of dealing with instance data such as automated removal of cycles.

8 Summary

Reasoning over semantic data is an evolving subset of the field of artificial intelligence. This chapter provided a survey of semantic reasoning as applied, within the commercial consideration of enterprise applications, to semantic data. Performance is a concern we addressed specifically as it is often neglected until it becomes a problem. This chapter provided a brief survey of most relevant artificial intelligence concepts to distributed reasoning and presented some emerging best practices for application developers and systems integrators. To delve further into the background of some of the concepts, there are host of sources such as Norvig and Russell's[10] text book. The growth of enterprise linked data will provide increasing opportunities in creating added value via better reasoning, and hence providing better knowledge.

References

1. http://www.jboss.org/drools
2. Thulasiraman, K.; Swamy, M. N. S. (1992) 5.7 Acyclic Directed Graphs, Graphs: Theory and Algorithms, John Wiley and Son, p. 118, ISBN 9780471513568
3. Fukushige, Yoshio. Representing Probabilistic Knowledge in the Semantic Web, 2004. Matsushita Electric Industrial Co., Ltd., http://www.w3.org/2004/09/13-Yoshio/PositionPaper.html
4. Rong Pan, Zhongli Ding, Yang Yu, and Yun Peng. A Bayesian Network Approach to Ontology Mapping, Proceedings of the Fourth International Semantic Web Conference. November 06, 2005
5. Reza BFar, Tsai-Ming Tseng, Ryan Golden, Yasin Cengiz, Nigel Jacobs. SDR: An Architectural Approach to Distribution of Complex Ontology Processing, SWWS 2009: 10-18
6. Zhongli Ding and Yun Peng. A Probabilistic Extension to Ontology Language OWL, Department of Computer Science and Electrical Engineering, University of Maryland Baltimore County, Proceedings of the 37th Hawaii International Conference on System Sciences 2004
7. Curtis Huttenhower and Olga G. Troyanskaya. Bayesian data Integration: A Functional Perspective, Department of Computer Science, Lewis-Sigler Institute for Integrative Ge-

nomics,Princeton University, Proceedings of 2006 LSS Computational Systems Bioinformatics Conference

8. Pavel Berkhin, Survey of Clustering Data Mining Techniques, http://www.cs.unc.edu/Courses/comp790-090-s10/Papers/clustering_survey.pdf

9. Evren Sirin, Bijan Parsia, Bernardo Cuenca Grau, Aditya Kalyanpur, and Yardan katz. Pellet: A practical OWL-DL reasoner. Web Semant., 2007

10. Peter Norvig and Stuart Russell. Artificial Intelligence, A Modern Approach, Second Edition. Prentice Hall, ISBN-0-13-790395-2, 2003

11. Peiqiang Li, Yi Zeng, Spyros Kotoulas, Jacopo Urbani, and Ning. The Quest for Parallel Reasoning on the Semantic Web, Proceedings of the 5th International Conference on Active Media Technology, 2009. 430-441. ISBN:978-3-642-04874-6

12. M. Fiedler. A property of eigenvectors of non-negative symmetric matrices and its application to graph theory. Czechoslovak Math. J., 25:619633, 1975.

13. Karen Devine, Sandia National Laboratories, Erik Boman, Sandia National Laboratories, Umit atalyürek, Ohio State University, Lee Ann Riesen, Sandia National Laboratories Partitioning and Dynamic Load Balancing for Petascale Applications, 2007

14. Reza B. Far, Tsai-Ming Tseng, Ryan Golden, Yasin Cengiz, Nigel Jacobs: SDR: An Architectural Approach to Distribution of Complex Ontology Processing. SWWS 2009: 10-18

15. Jeffery Dean and Sanjay Ghemawat, MapReduce: Simplified Data Processing on Large Clusters, Sixth Symposium on Operating System Design and Implementation, 2004. Page 1

16. http://hadoop.apache.org/

17. Ivar Jacobson, Magnus Christerson, Patrik Jonsson and Gunnar Övergaard, Object-Oriented Software Engineering: A Use Case Driven Approach. ACM Press. Addison-Wesley, 1992, ISBN 0201544350, pp. 69-70

18. R. Fikes and N. Nilsson (1971). STRIPS: a new approach to the application of theorem proving to problem solving. Artificial Intelligence, 2:189-208.

19. Garey, M.R.; Johnson, D.S. (1979). Computers and Intractability: A Guide to the Theory of NP-Completeness. New York: W.H. Freeman. ISBN0-7167-1045-5. This book is a classic, developing the theory, then cataloguing many NP-Complete problems.

20. Forgy, C.L. (1974) A Network Match Routine for Production Systems, Working Paper.

21. http://jena.sourceforge.net/

22. http://www.openrdf.org/

23. http://mulgara.org/

24. Radu Rugina and Martin Rinard, Recursion unrolling for divide and conquer programs, in Languages and Compilers for Parallel Computing, chapter 3, pp. 3448. Lecture Notes in Computer Science vol. 2017 (Berlin: Springer, 2001).

25. A. De Nicola, M. Missikoff, R. Navigli (2009). A Software Engineering Approach to Ontology Building. Information Systems, 34(2), Elsevier, 2009, pp. 258-275

26. Gruber, T. R. 1993. A translation approach to portable ontology specifications. In: Knowledge Acquisition. 5: 199199.

Reliable and Persistent Identification of Linked Data Elements

David Wood

Abstract

Linked Data techniques rely upon common terminology in a manner similar to a relational database's reliance on a schema. Linked Data terminology anchors metadata descriptions and facilitates navigation of information. Common vocabularies ease the human, social tasks of understanding datasets sufficiently to construct queries and help to relate otherwise disparate datasets. Vocabulary terms must, when using the Resource Description Framework, be grounded in URIs. A current best practice on the World Wide Web is to serve vocabulary terms as Uniform Resource Locators (URLs) and present both human-readable and machine-readable representations to the public.

Linked Data terminology published to the World Wide Web may be used by others without reference or notification to the publishing party. That presents a problem: Vocabulary publishers take on an implicit responsibility to maintain and publish their terms via the URLs originally assigned, regardless of the inconvenience such a responsibility may cause. Over the course of years, people change jobs, publishing organizations change Internet domain names, computers change IP addresses, systems administrators publish old material in new ways. Clearly, a mechanism is required to manage Web-based vocabularies over a long term.

This chapter places Linked Data vocabularies in context with the wider concepts of metadata in general and specifically metadata on the Web. Persistent identifier mechanisms are reviewed, with a particular emphasis on Persistent URLs, or PURLs. PURLs and PURL services are discussed in the context of Linked Data. Finally, historic weaknesses of PURLs are resolved by the introduction of a federation of PURL services to address needs specific to Linked Data.

David Wood

3 Round Stones Inc., Fredericksburg, VA 22408, USA, e-mail: david@3roundstones.com

D. Wood (ed.), *Linking Enterprise Data*, DOI 10.1007/978-1-4419-7665-9_8,

1 Introduction

The serving of Linked Data terminology on the World Wide Web is considered a best practice. Linked Data terms must, when using the Resource Description Framework, be grounded in URIs. Vocabulary terms are served as information resources and addressed via Uniform Resource Locators (URLs). Both human-readable and machine-readable representations are typically served.

Linked Data terms thus become a critical form of metadata, interlinking and relating other information resources served on the Web or within enterprise systems based on Web architecture.

Metadata itself is not a new concept. In fact, there is some archeological evidence that the use of metadata preceded the use of full written language [52]. Ancient Assyrians inscribed notations on clay cylinders to denote the material inside before 3,000 B.C.E. The applications of metadata developed alongside writing and later alongside other advances in the presentation and organization of writing, such as bibliographies, encyclopedias, novels and epic poems and eventually the World Wide Web.

Work on identifiers and other metadata began with early libraries and continued there until the advent of computing. Libraries were somewhat sidelined as computing and communications technology was developed by others during the twentieth century. The current standards for metadata and identifiers by computer scientists has only just begun to seep back into libraries and other holders of large-scale collections of information. Large enterprises now rival libraries as holders of information.

Today, metadata on the Web is applied in very particular ways to facilitate the operations of the Web. Persistent identifiers are used by organizations interested in retaining addresses to information resources over the long term. Most recently, persistent identifiers have been used to uniquely identify objects in the real world and concepts, in addition to information resources. For example, persistent identifiers have been created by the United Nations Food and Agriculture Organization (FAO) to provide URIs for major food crops. The National Center for Biomedical Ontology provides persistent identifiers to unify and address the terminology used in many existing biomedical databases.

The remainder of this chapter traces the means by which our view of persistent identifiers have developed and how they may be made to serve the needs of today's Linked Data enterprise.

2 Metadata Before the World Wide Web

The philosopher Aristotle (384 - 322 BCE) and his student Alexander (later to become "the Great", 356 - 323 BCE) assembled some of the first large personal libraries in the fourth century BCE. The Greek historian Strabo said of Aristotle that "He was the first to have put together a collection of books and to have taught the kings of Egypt how to arrange a library." That may not be literally the case. The "kings of Egypt" referred to are generally considered to be the Ptolemaic rulers following the collapse of Alexander's empire in the last years of the fourth century BCE and the "library" is most likely to be the great Library of Alexandria, in a city created by Alexander to avoid the treacherous Nile Delta. Historians disagree whether it was Aristotle or his student Demetrius of Phalerum who was responsible for Strabo's first century CE assertion [16]. Regardless who taught the kings of Egypt, it seems that Aristotle did produce the first hierarchical categorization system for library organization. Variations on that theme (with relatively minor non-hierarchical adjustments) dominate library categorizations through to the present time.

Aristotle's hierarchy caused problems for Callimachus of Cyrenae (ca. 305 BC-ca. 240 BC), who worked at the Library of Alexandria and began several early bibliographic projects. Callimachus' efforts earned him remembrance as the "father of bibliography". Callimachus, though, wrote poetry and also prose. How did he categorize himself using Aristotle's classification scheme? Were his entries duplicated or cross-referenced or collapsed or simply left out? [16] There is no way to know his solution to this problem since his bibliographies have not survived. It is clear, though, that the problem was introduced by use of hierarchies. We refer to this problem as Callimachus' Quandary. It would not be solved in the general case for twenty-four centuries. For a solution, we needed to wait for a scalable, non-hierarchical information system like the World Wide Web.

The Belgian Paul Otlet presaged some of the key concepts of the Web in 1934 [55]. Otlet articulated a vision for a "universal book" and is credited with coining the now- familiar terms "link" and "web" (or "network" from the French *reseau*) to describe the navigation of his "book". He was able to get substantial funding from the Belgian government for the realization of his work (the Mundaneum), which operated between 1910 and 1934 in the form of a massive collection of index cards and responded to queries by postal mail. A museum version of the Mundaneum was opened in 1996 with the surviving elements of the original. Otlet's web was a web of metadata; his index cards provided multi-subject faceted classification across and between resources. Although implemented in physical form, the faceted classification system pioneered by Otlet is the intellectual precursor to modern systems using metadata-based information organization, including the World Wide Web.

Vannevar Bush followed Otlet, although there is no indication that the two knew of each other's work. Bush's well-known treatise As We May Think set the tone for the application of then-modern technologies to both library science and non-library holdings [14]. He noted the problems with finding and organizing knowledge resources and the lack of recent progress in the field:

> The difficulty seems to be, not so much that we publish unduly in view of the extent and variety of present day interests, but rather that publication has been extended far beyond our present ability to make real use of the record. The summation of human experience is being expanded at a prodigious rate, and the means we use for threading through the consequent maze to the momentarily important item is the same as was used in the days of square-rigged ships.

Bush's suggestions were not just of recording knowledge resources, but of organizing them better for search and retrieval. He suggested that the individual human memory be augmented with an external device that he famously called a "memex". The concept of the memex is considered by many to be the intellectual precursor to today's hypertext systems (e.g. [43] and [2]) However, the memex was specifically intended to be a device used by an individual; in this Bush revealed his own heritage of Greek individualism. The librarians had larger problems connecting knowledge resources, but it took decades for digital computers to become mature enough for librarians to contemplate them as meaningful alternatives to card-based indexing systems.

Bush did not explain precisely how the memex was to be implemented, nor did he mention the term "metadata". He did, however, intimate that a form of metadata would be collected, stored and used for later retrieval: "Wholly new forms of encyclopedias will appear, ready-made with a mesh of associative trails running through them, ready to be dropped into the memex and there amplified." [14] There may be a good reason to use an associative model to describe information: Human memories have been claimed to be associative in nature [18], and recent functional magnetic resonance imaging studies lends credence to that view [41]. Viewed from the modern perspective, it is difficult not to suggest that Bush's "associative trails" are a collection of metadata.

By 1965 the librarian Jesse Shera was ready to formulate some "axiomatic principles for the classification of bibliographic materials". As a librarian, he thought that "*every attempt*" (emphasis in original) to analyze bibliographic materials must be made upon the basis of classification. This was a traditional and non-controversial thought in his field and dated back directly to Aristotle. In other ways, though, he was years ahead of his time. He noted the problems caused by hierarchical thinking and suggested a solution:

> The Aristotelian concept of the hierarchy must be rejected as a basic principle of classification if classification is to adapt itself to constantly changing needs, uses, and points of view. This is so because a hierarchy, of whatever structural design, implies a specific philosophical orientation, and the crystallization of a hierarchical structure into a *particular* orientation precludes, or does violence to, all others. [50] (emphasis in original)

Shera had established the need for a general classification scheme that was non-hierarchical (like Otlet's) and, in the terminology of logic, "Open World". He made a call, twenty-four centuries in the making, for a general solution to Callimachus' Quandary. The call could not be heeded until the digital computer made adequate inroads into both libraries and the general public. The "See Also" references in encyclopedias and categorization systems may implement a poor man's hypertext, but a general solution required a more flexible medium than paper.

Shera also noted that bibliographic classification be "completely independent of physical objects (books), for no arrangement of such objects can reveal the complex of relationships that may exist among the many separate thought-units that make up the subject content of these books." His solution was for librarians to give up not only hierarchical thinking but also any idea that their job was the protection of books. He wanted to redirect their dedication to "the ideas the books contain." Shera, alone of library theorists, presaged the changes that would come over the discipline of library science with the advent of digital computers.

The idea that ideas matter more than form was compelling, but the means to reorganize library holdings around such a concept could not be implemented without inexpensive digital computers. Knowledge resources, regardless of their physicality, would have to be stored and maintained in a manner consistent with their content. Their form matters less. The preservationist Paul Conway put it this way, in 1996 (nearly a half century after Shera's call to arms):

> The digital world transforms traditional preservation concepts from protecting the physical integrity of the object to specifying the creation and maintenance of the object whose intellectual integrity is its primary characteristic. [26]

The canonical source for the above quote is no longer available on the World Wide Web, highlighting the new classes of difficulty in digital reference and preservation.

Librarians adopting computers initially carried over the types of metadata used during the last two millennia (attached metadata like indexes and external metadata like catalogues). Physical card catalogues became virtual card catalogues. Librarians, once the keepers of metadata formats and standards, became somewhat sidelined as computing technology developed. Libraries became users of the new technologies, but not developers of it. The Online Computer Library Center (OCLC), for example, was founded in 1967 to use computer networking to facilitate sharing of resources between U.S. libraries. Today, the inter-library search product World-Cat is used by more than 57,000 libraries in 112 countries. OCLC is a non-profit corporation supported by its member libraries. The World Wide Web, widely seen at that time as a threat to the very existence of libraries, spurred OCLC researchers to facilitate the adoption of metadata for the "finding, sharing and management of information". The Dublin Core Metadata Initiative was founded partially by OCLC to do that in 1995. The Dublin Core element set, consisting of tags to describe both physical and virtual knowledge resources, was later adopted by the International Organization for Standardization (ISO) as ISO standard 15836. Dublin Core metadata is now used as the basis for both Open Source and proprietary card cataloguing systems (e.g. the Vital and Valet products from VTLS, Inc and the Fedora digital content repository). Dublin Core metadata is verbose enough for human readers, unlike MARC, and has become widely used for other purposes by Semantic Web applications, including Linked Data.

Hypertext systems use metadata (hyperlinks) to associate different information resources. Hypertext systems predated the World Wide Web by many years. Ted Nelson coined the term hypertext in 1965 (in [42]) and envisioned a complex hypertext system called Xanadu [44]. Xanadu was a complicated system that attempted to transcend properties of physical books, such as the notion of pages, and was to include automated management of bi-directional hyperlinks. Xanadu's concepts have not been fully implemented, although periodic software releases are accessible via, ironically, the World Wide Web.

Nelson's celebrated invention of the hyperlink should be seen in context, as Otlet's links implemented in software. Nelson's Xanadu should also be viewed in context, as iteration on Bush's Memex that allowed multiple users to share a centralized data store.

Important, early implementations of the hypertext concept included Doug Englebart's oN Line System (NLS) in the late 1960s [9], Randy Trigg's Notecards [31], Akscyn's KMS [1] and Apple Computer's HyperCard system started in 1985 and released in 1987 [55]. Lesser-known, but important in the development of the World Wide Web was Enquire, Tim-Berners-Lee's first attempt at building a hypertext system in 1980 [9]. Englebart, at least, was directly inspired by Bush [45].

Early hypertext systems were centralized applications that stored information in a single repository. Hyperlinks, as in Nelson's vision, were bi-directional and maintained; both linking and target entities were updated when one of them changed. Berners-Lee's later iteration of the ideas from Otlet, Bush, Nelson and Englebart led to his changing a single presumption that would lead to the World Wide Web; distribution of hypertext information across multiple locations, which in turn necessitated the Uniform Resource Locator (URL) to address those locations [6].

Berners-Lee's breakthrough simplification, hypertext through distribution, solved a long- standing limit to scalability of hypertext systems. That simplification was also responsible for a so- called "link maintenance problem"; hyperlinks became unidirectional in practice. Although some Web servers attempt to track references from hyperlinks ("back-links") within the confines of their own data sets (notably wikis), the link maintenance problem led hypertext pioneer Ted Nelson to sneer, "The reaction of the hypertext research community to the World Web is like finding out that you have a fully grown child. And it's a delinquent." [25]

Hyperlinks, either as a standalone URL or embedded within a hypertext document, act as external metadata. External metadata in the form of hyperlinks are relatively difficult to find, collect and identify on the World Wide Web due to the link maintenance problem and one reason Web search engines have gained widespread popularity in recent years. The Linking Open Data project proposes an alternative form of finding information that is also reliant upon metadata; that of explicitly hyperlinking resources to one another. Other forms of metadata exist on the Web, including rich descriptions of resources, but the humble hyperlink may be the most powerful of all. Metadata, initially considered by librarians as a way to find information, thus became a critical component in the way information was structured, described, prepared for reuse and presented to human readers.

3 Metadata on the World Wide Web

The World Wide Web is an information retrieval system built upon a foundation of metadata. Metadata was a first class component in the earliest proposal for the Web, although it was not then called "metadata" [4]. Berners-Lee intended that metadata take on a wider role as the Web matured [7]. He introduced the concept of machine-understandable metadata, which he defined as "information which software agents can use in order to make life easier for us, ensure we obey our principles, the law, check that we can trust what we are doing, and make everything work more smoothly and rapidly. Metadata has well defined semantics and structure." The concept of machine-understandable metadata led to a "road map" for its implementation [8] and eventually to standardization efforts at the W3C.

Otlet noted the social value of metadata in his *reseau*, although mostly the World Wide Web's implicit relationships remain untracked and unexploited, as noted by historian Alex Wright:

> In the Web's current incarnation, individual "authors" (including both individuals and institutions) exert direct control over fixed documents. It takes a meta-application like Google or Yahoo! to discover the broader relationships between documents (usually through some combination of syntax, semantics and reputation). But those relationships, however sophisticated the algorithm, remain largely unexposed to the end user, never becoming an explicit part of the document's history. In Otlet's vision those pathways constituted vital information, making up a third dimension of social context that made his system so potentially revolutionary. [55]

Exploitation of relationships between resources on the Web remains incomplete for an excellent reason: The very design decision that allowed the Web to scale (distribution of resource servers) removed the ability to monitor links bidirectionally (the link maintenance problem). Some services exist to track and retain inter-resource metadata, such as Technorati, a service for tracking the relationships between information resources (especially Web logs ("blogs") and social content tagged with microformats). Technorati requires a publisher to register with them so that inter- resource monitoring may be accomplished. The majority of Web resources are not so registered and thus may not be monitored; Google claimed to have indexed roughly 6 billion documents in 2004[1] whereas Technorati monitors roughly 110 million blogs (each consisting of multiple documents)[2].

Use of metadata on the Web has not been a linear process. Research and implementations have used metadata in varying ways. Key to the differing approaches is who controls the metadata and which metadata is required. Some metadata is required (such as necessary HTTP headers and the use of URLs) and is necessary to ensure consistent interactions between Web clients and servers. Required metadata is also known as authoritative metadata [23]. Other metadata is optional (such as the HTTP "Accept" header or various ways to describe a document's author, provenance or meaning). In the early Web, authors were also publishers, a situation that is not as generally true today, and metadata was seen as the province of authors.

Early attempts to describe resources on the Web using rich metadata included the author-centric HTML META tag. The META tag was quickly abused for the purposes of gaming search engine result ordering. The World Wide Web Consortium attempted to develop an improved metadata standard for the Web known as the Platform for Internet Content Selection (PICS). PICS was standardized by the W3C in 1996 and included a new feature for metadata management; the ability for end users to subscribe to third party "rating services" [40]. Rating services were to provide

---

[1] Retrieved February 10, 2008 from http://www.news.com/Google,-Yahoo-duel-for-documents/2100- 1038_3-5160480.html

[2] February 10, 2008 from http://technorati.com/about/

metadata about content that users could trust (a "brand"). PICS attempted to add third-party (external) metadata to the Web. PICS failed to gain widespread acceptance, in spite of being implemented by many pornographic content providers and search engines. The primary reason was that URL-based censorship schemes were rendered less effective by changing URLs for given resources (E.J. Miller, personal communication, January 26, 2008). Browser makers ignored arguments by the PICS community that PICS' third-party rating services could provide trust without censorship [48]. Lack of client support doomed widespread use of the PICS standard. The W3C is trying again to create community consensus around a PICS-like standard for Web content control with the Protocol for Web Description Resources (POWDER) Working Group [3]. POWDER's future standardization and use remains uncertain as of this writing.

Ramanathan Guha, while working on the Cyc knowledge base [37], developed an iteration of the knowledge base formulation most commonly used in symbolic artificial intelligence systems [28]. Guha introduced the notion of context into AI knowledge bases and formalized a description for context information. He later used those ideas to develop metadata descriptions of Web site changes, first the Meta Content Framework (MCF) [29] and later RDF Site Summaries (RSS) [30].

Lessons learned from the implementations of Guha's work on contexts, PICS and Dublin Core metadata [54] led to a standard for the description of metadata on the World Wide Web, the Resource Description Framework (RDF). RDF [38] is a standardized mechanism for deploying metadata on the World Wide Web.

Lessons from the deployment of the HTML META tag led supporters of RDF to conclude that some issues of trust are best solved socially (E.J. Miller, personal communication, January 26, 2008). In RDF, as in PICS or RSS, the author or publisher of information may choose to lie and the consumer of the information may choose whether to believe. Trust relationships, a social consideration, are necessary to determine how to use the information contained in metadata. Trust relationships must exist for metadata to be useful (e.g., trust of a curation source such as an employer or service provider, trust that a user wouldn't lie about their own contact information in a Friend of a Friend (FOAF)[3] document, or trusting the aggregate judgment of a many people in a social network) [27]. The RDF standard attempts to facilitate trust relationships by allowing metadata to be attached, separated and/or external, so that authors, publishers and users may each have some ability to describe Web-based resources. Authors, publishers and users may all add RDF metadata to Web resources. Metadata may be cached at Web clients and servers.

RDF and the general structure of the Web provide a number of critical enhancements to the art of metadata. Callimachus' Quandary is (at last) addressed with the appearance of international standards based upon a graph data structure. The removal of Aristotle's hierarchical thinking from the library and computer science communities may well be decades in coming, but coming it is. Hierarchies may be seen as they should be; as degenerate conditions of the more general graph structure.

---

[3] Retrieved May 27, 2010 from http://www.foaf-project.org/

Although there is little disagreement about the use of metadata in protocols or machine-readable formats such as HTML layout tags (as opposed to descriptive tags or attributes), there is substantial disagreement on the use of user-defined metadata to describe the meaning of resources or suggest potential uses. Bulterman has suggested large-scale comparisons of binary data (such as a mathematical hash function on a resource's bytestream, or geometric modeling of image content) for the purposes of replacing the use of textual metadata on the Web [13]. It is interesting to note that Bulterman would like to do away with all metadata used for describing virtual image resources "other than perhaps required citation information and a URI"; even as a harsh critic he did not deny the need for some descriptive metadata.

Doctorow presented seven criticisms of the use of metadata to describe virtual resources on the Web[4]. Doctorow's criticisms are summarized in Table 1 alongside the positions suggested by the RDF community in relation to them.

Each of Doctorow's criticisms is valid for the case of metadata added by an author (attached/separated metadata). The history of the HTML META tag illustrates every one of the failures suggested by Doctorow. However, metadata is known to avoid each criticism in some social environments both on and off the Web. The use of external metadata in PICS (via rating services) was intended to broaden the social discourse to address those criticisms. RDF, by addressing resources by URL (unidirectional hyperlinks), also encourages external metadata. External metadata may include vocabulary descriptions (schemas), content descriptions, and metrics. External metadata may also come from a source more trusted than the source of the content to which it refers.

Table 1 Metadata Criticisms and Responses

Doctorow's Criticisms	Web Approaches
"People lie"	Allow users to choose a social trust model
"People are lazy"	Automate where possible and encourage authoring where needed
"People are stupid"	Automate where possible, check where possible
"Mission: Impossible know thyself"	Allow multiple sources of metadata
"Schemas aren't neutral"	Allow multiple schemas
"Metrics influence results"	Allow multiple metrics
"There's more than one way to describe some-thing"	Allow multiple descriptions

One of Doctorow's most stinging criticisms was that users must know themselves in order to create metadata worth having. This criticism makes an assumption about the relationship between metadata and the content to which it refers; the assumption is that a resource's author also creates the metadata.

There are at least two mechanisms that can produce high-quality metadata without reliance upon the motivations of an individual user. Professional ontologists

---
[4] Retrieved May 27, 2010 from http://www.well.com/ doctorow/metacrap.htm

within corporations, such as at Yahoo!, Google and many corporate information technology departments, routinely provide trusted, quality metadata in the same way that librarians have done for millennia. A more recent approach is the so-called "hive mind" of social networks. Many individual categorizations are combined and weighted, with the most popular tags being given precedence. Web-based systems that use the latter include the Web bookmarking community del.icio.us and the book review system at Amazon.com. Doctorow claimed that knowing ourselves was impossible, but it appears that we need not all know ourselves, after all.

The reasons that individuals donate their time and attention contributing to online social networks was studied by Smith and Kollock [51], [36]. They determined that individuals contributed for both economic reasons (anticipated reciprocity and increased recognition) and psychological reasons (a sense of efficacy and a sense of community). These reasons, also present in traditional social networks, work to build trust in the aggregate [27].

Both Doctorow and Shera complained about the lack of neutrality in schemas and noted that different people naturally describe resources differently. The Web addresses these concerns for data directly by (a) making schemas optional, (b) allowing multiple (possibly overlapping) schemas and (c) allowing the arbitrary application of schemas.

Doctorow's criticisms, although accurate, are shown to be bounded. People do lie, but the Open World assumption coupled with the ability to combine RDF graphs has provided technical infrastructure for distributed trust. RDF metadata may be applied to resources by others, not just the author of the resource. Social networks, within or outside of an organization, may be used to assign trust levels to a resource or to override metadata provided by an author.

Implicit metadata on the Web includes the interpretation of URL components to suggest content that will be returned. Such a practice is dangerous, at best. For example, the URL http://example.ca/toronto/images/cntower.jpg might suggest that the resource to be returned is an image of the Canada National Tower in Toronto. Unfortunately, that might not be the case. The idealized architectural style of the World Wide Web is known as Representational State Transfer (REST) [22]. A key concept in REST is the late binding of addresses (URLs) to resources. Late binding, at the time the resource must be served, allows a Web server to return any type of content for a URL. Our example URL may return an HTML page of today's news or an audio recording of Beethoven's Ninth Symphony. Apparently worse, a URL may return many different types of content at different times. It may be considered impolite, but such actions are not excluded by Web architecture. The dissociation of a URL from the content that it returns is known as the Principle of URI Opacity [33]. The application of URI opacity has been a topic of much discussion for the last decade and is widely violated. It does suggest, however, that one may not rely on implicit metadata on the Web.

4 Persistent URLs

The problems of trust related to author- and publisher-centric metadata highlighted by Doctorow may be partially addressed in at least two ways: by allowing resource users and/or third parties to manage the process of URL resolution or the provision of metadata independently of Web resource author and publishers. An implementation of third party URL resolution management is the Persistent Uniform Resource Locator (PURL) scheme [49]. This chapter describes how the public PURL service has been extended to allow third party control over both URL resolution and resource metadata provision.

A URL is simply an address of a resource on the World Wide Web. A Persistent URL is an address on the World Wide Web that causes a redirection to another Web resource. If a Web resource changes location (and hence URL), a PURL pointing to it can be updated. A user of a PURL always uses the same Web address, even though the resource in question may have moved. PURLs may be used by publishers to manage their own information space or by Web users to manage theirs; a PURL service is independent of the publisher of information. PURL services thus allow the management of hyperlink integrity. Hyperlink integrity is a design trade-off of the World Wide Web, but may be partially restored by allowing resource users or third parties to influence where and how a URL resolves.

A simple PURL works by responding to an HTTP GET request with a response of type 302 ("Found"). The response contains an HTTP "Location" header, the value of which is a URL that the client should subsequently retrieve via a new HTTP GET request.

A public PURL service has been operated by the Online Computer Library Center at http://purl.org since 1995. The source code was released under an Open Source Software license and now forms the basis for several other PURL services, both public and private.

PURLs implement one form of persistent identifier for virtual resources. Other persistent identifier schemes include Digital Object Identifiers (DOIs) [47], Life Sciences Identifiers (LSIDs) [46] and INFO URIs [53]. All persistent identification schemes provide unique identifiers for (possibly changing) virtual resources, but not all schemes provide curation opportunities. Curation of virtual resources has been defined as, "the active involvement of information professionals in the management, including the preservation, of digital data for future use." [56]

For a persistent identification scheme to provide a curation opportunity for a virtual resource, it must allow real-time resolution of that resource and also allow real-time administration of the identifier. PURLs provide both criteria, as do DOIs. DOIs resolve to one of many possible repositories that provide administration capabilities, but have been criticized for their commercial nature (E.J. Miller, personal communication, January 26, 2008). LSIDs may be mapped to a URL scheme and an administration service [17], in which case they would be functionally similar to PURLs. INFO URIs provide neither real-time resolution, nor real-time administration.

PURLs have been criticized for their need to resolve a URL, thus tying a PURL to a network location. Network locations have several vulnerabilities, such as Domain Name System registrations and host dependencies. A failure to resolve a PURL could lead to an ambiguous state: It would not be clear whether the PURL failed to resolve because a network failure prevented it or because it did not exist [39].

PURLs are themselves valid URLs, so their components must map to the URL specification. The scheme part tells a computer program, such as a Web browser, which protocol to use when resolving the address. The scheme used for PURLs is generally HTTP. The host part tells which PURL server to connect to. The next part, the PURL domain, is analogous to a resource path in a URL. The domain is a hierarchical information space that separates PURLs and allows for PURLs to have different maintainers. One or more designated maintainers may administer each PURL domain. Finally, the PURL name is the name of the PURL itself. The domain and name together constitute the PURL's "id".

PURLs require a Domain to hold them. Domains have to be created before PURLs may be placed in them. Some PURL servers automatically create domains when a PURL is created and others require domains to be created separately. A domain maintainer is responsible for administering a PURL domain record. Domain "writers" are allowed to add or remove PURLs from a domain.

The original PURL service thus provided a general mechanism for third party URL curation using established elements of the HTTP standard. It was, however, simplistic in its scope. A more general solution to common issues of metadata trust may be found by extending the scope of PURL services.

5 Extending Persistent URLs for Web Resource Curation

The most obvious extension to PURL services is the creation of a greater number of PURL types. PURLs are categorized into different types depending on how they respond to a request. Simple PURLs that redirect to another URL (the "target" URL) via an HTTP 302 (Found) response are known as type 302. The new PURL service includes nine different types of PURLs that return six different HTTP response codes. Figure 5-3 illustrates the behavior of the new Typed PURL service and Table 5-1 summarizes the different types of PURLs and their response codes.

The most common types of PURLs are named to coincide with the HTTP response code that they return. Not all HTTP response codes have equivalent PURL types. Some HTTP response codes (e.g. 401, Unauthorized) have clear meanings in the context of an HTTP conversation but do not apply to the process of HTTP redirection. Three additional types of PURLs ("chain", "partial" and "clone") are given mnemonic names related to their functions.

Some have argued that a PURL server should return an HTTP 301 (Moved Permanently) response instead of a 302 (Found) response. OCLC chose to use the HTTP 302 response code in 1995 in an attempt to encourage the further use of the PURL; a 301 response would suggest that a client should use the target URL in

Table 2 PURL Types

Type	PURL Meaning	HTTP Meaning
301	Moved permanently to a target URL	Moved permanently
302	Simple redirection to a target URL	Found
Chain	Redirect to another PURL within the same server	Found
Partial	Redirect to a target URL with trailing path information appended	Found
303	See other URL	See Other
307	Temporary redirect to a target URL	Temporary Redirect
404	Temporarily gone	Not Found
410	Permanently gone	Gone
Clone	Copy the attributes of an existing PURL	N/A

future requests. The controversy between 301 and 302 response codes continues as of this writing. The new PURL service allows sites or individual PURL maintainers to choose between 301 and 302 response codes. Major Web browsers currently handle HTTP 301 and 302 responses identically; an implicit redirection to the target URL results regardless.

A PURL of type "chain" allows a PURL to redirect to another PURL in a manner identical to a 301 or 302 redirection, with the difference that a PURL server will handle the redirection internally for greater efficiency. This efficiency is useful when many redirections are possible; since some Web browsers will stop following redirections once a set limit is encountered (in an attempt to avoid loops).

The introduction of type 303 PURLs has particular significance for Semantic Web techniques. The World Wide Web Consortium's (W3C) Technical Architecture Group (TAG) attempted to settle a long-standing debate about the things that could be named by HTTP URLs. The debate is formally known as the range of the HTTP dereference function (and called "http-range-14" for reasons of TAG issue numbering). After three years of debate from March 2002 to June 2005, the TAG ruled as follows[5]:

> The TAG provides advice to the community that they may mint "http" URIs for any resource provided that they follow this simple rule for the sake of removing ambiguity:
>
> - If an "http" resource responds to a GET request with a 2xx response, then the resource identified by that URI is an information resource;
> - If an "http" resource responds to a GET request with a 303 (See Other) response, then the resource identified by that URI could be any resource;
> - If an "http" resource responds to a GET request with a 4xx (error) response, then the nature of the resource is unknown.

The principal design goal for the support of typed PURLs was to allow PURLs to be definable within the scope of the TAG guidance.

The TAG made a very subtle point. The idea was to cleanly separate those resources that are referred to by an HTTP URL and those that cannot be referred to directly, but might have an HTTP URL assigned to them anyway. The latter include

---

[5] Retrieved May 27, 2010 from http://www.w3.org/2001/tag/issues.html#httpRange-14

physical and conceptual resources in the real world. Importantly, many of the objects assigned URIs in Semantic Web descriptions are given HTTP URLs but cannot be directly referred to on the Web. The TAG's guidance, having nearly the weight of a standard until such time as a standard may override it, insists that physical and conceptual resources addressed by HTTP URL return HTTP 303 responses. They may not return a 301 (Moved permanently), 302 (Found) or 200 (OK) response since they are not information resources.

Programmatic resolution of an HTTP URL may refer to an object in the real world (that is, a physical or conceptual resource) or a virtual resource (such as an HTML page or an image or a movie). In that case, the HTTP response code would be 303 (See Other) instead of 200 (OK). A 303 is an indication that the thing referred to may not be an information resource, it may be either an information resource or a "real" object. The body of the 303 (and the Location header) can provide information about the resource without encouraging one to think that what was returned really was a representation of the resource (as one would with a 200 response).

The W3C characterization of an information resource is that the entire content of the referred object may be "conveyed in a message". But what about resources that cannot be conveyed in a message? My dog is a resource, as is my car, or myself. These things cannot be conveyed in a message, they can only be referred to. That is where HTTP 303 response codes come in.

RFC 2616 [21] defines HTTP version 1.1 and its response codes. Section 10 defines a 303 thusly:

> The response to the request can be found under a different URI and SHOULD be retrieved using a GET method on that resource. This method exists primarily to allow the output of a POST-activated script to redirect the user agent to a selected resource. The new URI is not a substitute reference for the originally requested resource. The 303 response MUST NOT be cached, but the response to the second (redirected) request might be cacheable.
>
> The different URI SHOULD be given by the Location field in the response. Unless the request method was HEAD, the entity of the response SHOULD contain a short hypertext note with a hyperlink to the new URI(s).

RFC 2616 clearly predated the TAG guidance on http-range-14. The TAG (mildly) extended the use of an HTTP 303 without changing the manner in which it is generally currently applied. Further, the TAG guidance does not preclude the complete lack of a Location header in a 303 response referring to a physical or conceptual resource. RFC 2616 allows a Location header to be missing (by the use of "SHOULD" and not "MAY", terms used in accordance with RFC 2119 [12]). Typed PURLs referring to physical or conceptual resources may thus be distinguished from typed PURLs referring to virtual (information, knowledge) resources by the presence or absence of a resolvable URL in a Location header.

A PURL of type 307 informs a user that the resource temporarily resides at a different URL from the norm. PURLs of types 404 and 410 note that the requested resource could not be found and suggests some information for why that was so. Support for the HTTP 307 (Temporary Redirect), 404 (Not Found) and 410 (Gone) response codes are provided for completeness.

There are some differing interpretations of the HTTP specification and hence some decisions were made in the implementation of PURLs. For example, an HTTP server may respond with a 404 response code if a resource is not found, if it is temporarily not present or if it simply does not want to provide it to a requester. The new PURL service treats a 404 as representing a temporarily gone status and uses a 410 for those resources that are permanently not resolvable. Similarly, Eric Miller and David Wood have noted the need for a way to ground non-information resources into the World Wide Web and supported that concept with PURLs by suggesting that any resource addressed by a 303 PURL and returning a "See also URL" be explicitly considered not to be an information resource if the response does not include a resolvable URL in the Location header. This decision allows physical resources (such as your car) or conceptual resources (such as the idea of a car) to be given a PURL and referred to in a sharable manner (as when using Semantic Web techniques). Where a particular interpretation of the HTTP status code definitions differs from the way an HTTP response code is used by a PURL server, the intent of the PURL should be interpreted via the Meaning column in Table 5-1.

It should be noted that two other HTTP response codes indicate that a resource may be found elsewhere without providing a URL to such a location. They are 304 (Not Modified) and 305 (Use Proxy). Those response codes were not implemented as PURL types because their meanings within the context of URL curation is unclear. Overloading the meaning of the presence or absence of the Location header in a type 303 PURL addressed the range of HTTP responses without otherwise applying meaning to the 304 and 305 response codes.

The new PURL service includes administrative functionality, such as the ability to create and manage user accounts, assign users to groups for convenience and create and manage PURL domains. A new PURL may be created with the same values as an existing PURL (via the PURL type "clone"). PURLs may also be created or modified in batches by the submission of an XML document complying with a published XML schema. The new PURL service[6] has been released under an Apache License version 2.0 (an Open Source license) and is available for download at the PURL community site http://purlz.org.

To allow Web clients to programmatically determine when they have resolved a PURL, the new PURL service adds a non-standard header to HTTP responses called X-Purl. A PURL header reports the base URL for the PURL server and the version number of the PURL server release. A PURL header for a PURL version 2.0 service running on localhost at port 8080 looks like "X-Purl: 2.0; http://localhost:8080".

The addition of a typing system to PURLs provides greater descriptive and managerial capability to URL curators. The specific addition of type 303 PURLs provides a way to cleanly and programmatically separate addresses for virtual resources from addresses for physical and conceptual resources, thus overcoming the objections made by Chimezie Ogbuji in regard to the overuse of the HTTP URI scheme for the addressing of non-resolvable resources[7].

---

[6] Retrieved Mary 27, 2010 from http://purlz.org/

[7] Retrieved March 1, 2008 from http://copia.ogbuji.net/blog/2007-05-26/linked-data-is-overseling-http

6 Redirection of URL Fragments

The original PURL service included a concept known as partial redirection. If a request does not match a PURL exactly, the requested URL is checked to determine if some contiguous front portion matches a registered PURL. If so, a redirection occurs with the remainder of the requested URL appended to the target URL. For example, consider a PURL with a URL of http//purl.org/some/path/ with a target URL of http://example.com/another/path/.

An attempt to perform an HTTP GET operation on the URL http//purl.org/some/path/and/some/more/data would result in a partial redirection to http://example.com/another/path/and/some/more/data. The concept of partial redirection allows hierarchies of Web-based resources to be addressed via PURLs without each resource requiring its own PURL. One PURL is sufficient to serve as a top-level node for a hierarchy on a single target server. The new PURL service uses the type "partial" to denote a PURL that performs partial redirection.

Partial redirections at the level of a URL path do not violate common interpretations of the HTTP 1.1 specification. However, the handling of URL fragments across redirections has not been standardized and a consensus has not yet emerged. Fragment identifiers indicate a pointer to more specific information within a resource and are designated as following a # separator in URIs [10].

Partial redirection in the presence of a fragment identifier is problematic because two conflicting interpretations are possible [11]. If a fragment is attached to a PURL of type "partial", should a PURL service assume that the fragment has meaning on the target URL or should it discard it in the presumption that a resource with a changed location may have also changed content, thus invalidating fragments defined earlier? Bos suggested that fragments should be retained and passed through to target URLs during HTTP redirections resulting in 300 (Multiple Choice), 301 (Moved Permanently), 302 (Found) or 303 (See Other) responses unless a designated target URL already includes a fragment identifier. If a fragment identifier is already present in a target URL, any fragment in the original URL should be abandoned. Unfortunately, Bos' suggestion failed to navigate the IETF standards track and expired without further work. Dubost et al. resurrected Bos' suggestions in a W3C Note (not a standard, but guidance in the absence of a standard) [20]. Makers of Web clients such as browsers have "generally" failed to follow Bos' guidance.

The new typed PURL service implements partial redirections inclusive of fragment identifiers by writing fragments onto target URLs in an attempt to comply with [20] and avoid problematic and inconsistent behavior by browser vendors.

7 Using Persistent URLs and Retrieved Metadata

The typed PURL service may be used in a manner similar to, or slightly more flexible than, the original PURL service. That is, the service allows simple redirection of URLs to content provided elsewhere and the ability to manage (curate) the URL resolution process. Other opportunities for management of Web-based services exist, however, by making use of the combination of curation services and published metadata.

Primary goals of URL curation are the ability for a user to choose a curator of choice and for a curator to choose a metadata provider of choice. These goals were first articulated for PICS. When PURLs are used to implement a curation service that meets these goals, they are called "Rich" PURLs to denote the widening of metadata choices. Rich PURLs were first called by that moniker by Uche Ogbuji and first fielded as part of a production metadata service for a Web magazine, Semantic Report (http://purl.semanticreport.com) in 2007. Rich PURLs are an application of typed PURL services that particularly redirect to structured metadata on the Web. No code changes were made to the typed PURL code to implement Rich PURLs.

In a typical Rich PURL application data flow a user has a URL to a Web resource that resolves to a PURL service. The PURL service resolves the URL and returns the HTTP response code appropriate for the URL (typically 301 (Moved Permanently), 302 (Found), 303 (See Other) or 307 (Temporary Redirect). The user's Web client is redirected to a target URL that resolves to a metadata description of a Web service, typically published in RDF. The Web client is responsible for understanding how to parse and take action on the RDF metadata. If the client is so capable, it will have a rich description of the content held at the final resource, the Web service.

The term "Web service" is used here to include any Web-based service providing answers to queries and is intended to include, but not be limited to, Web Services (typically capitalized) based on the Web Service Description Language (WSDL) and the Simple Object Access Protocol (SOAP).

Rich PURLs of the form described above have the obvious disadvantage that most Web clients do not natively support the parsing or even meaningful display of RDF metadata as of this writing. Even some Semantic Web applications require non-generic formatting or use of particular vocabulary descriptions to operate fully. Rich PURLs are therefore limited to building the data set available for semantic processing on the Web and do not by themselves implement a user-directed experience.

It is possible to extend Web clients to handle Rich PURLs via their existing extension mechanisms, such as JavaScript. A Rich PURL client could, for example, display metadata about an information resource and link to or retrieve the resource itself as well. Since the metadata may include additional resolvable URLs, a display of the metadata may include hyperlinks based on those URLs. This is the approach taken by Semantic Web applications such as Exhibit, a JavaScript in-browser presentation application for semantically structured information [32].

Naturally, native Semantic Web applications already implement support for resolving URLs, following HTTP redirections, parsing and taking action on RDF metadata and following hyperlinks to referred content. Examples include the Haystack [35] and Longwell Semantic Web browsers [15]. Rich PURLs may be used directly by tools implementing those features.

8 Federations of PURL Servers

Addressing the most frequent criticism of PURLs (that PURLs need to resolve a URL, thus tying a PURL to a network location) seems downright silly when discussed in the context of Linked Data. All of Linked Data requires and is in fact built upon the live resolution of identifiers. However, much can be done to enhance the robustness of that resolution, especially for commonly used vocabularies and terms.

The oldest PURL server, purl.org, is also one of the largest. Many Linked Data vocabularies are hosted there, including the Dublin Core element set and FOAF. Twice so far in 2010 the number of responses for those terms, especially Dublin Core terms, overwhelmed the server's ability to respond. As Linked Data traffic increases, the viability of hosting critical vocabularies on a single site must be brought into question. One approach to addressing robustness of response is the concept of a PURL server federation.

The National Center for Biomedical Ontology and Zepheira announced work on a PURL Federation in March 2010 (http://purlz.org/pipermail/purl-interest/2010-March/000124.html). A dynamic DNS resolution is used to allow PURLs to be resolved by proxies to one member at a time of a federation of PURL servers. PURL servers in a federation are to be monitored (in near real time) for availability. The stated goals of the PURL Federation were:

1. PURLs are both URIs and URLs and must be treated as such. Each PURL must be addressable solely by its URL and yet be resolvable by any proxy. We recognize that some PURL service operators have spent significant amounts of time and money getting users to "buy into" their namespaces.
2. Any member of the federation must be able to leave at any time, and new members must be able to join at any time, without impacting the ability of the federation to resolve the total set of PURLs from members past and present.
3. PURL service operators will remain in control of their DNS registrations and operation.
4. PURL service operators will remain in control of their user accounts and internal policies relating to the creation and modification of PURLs. The federation serves solely to resolve existing PURLs.
5. If any third party service is used to operate any component of a PURL federation, members of the federation must be free to switch out that provider without disruption to the operations of the federation.

Naturally, the architecture for a PURL Federation made some presumptions. The presumptions were:

1. Some PURL service operators (e.g. grant-funded research organizations) may wish to join a PURL federation to enable ongoing resolution of their persistent identifiers in the case of a funding loss.
2. Some PURL service operators (e.g. those providing government or non-profit library services) may wish to join a PURL federation to amortize the costs associated with operating a fully redundant Web service in multiple geographically-

separated locations with hot backup and failure capabilities or to gain those capabilities in the absence of sufficient institutional support.

3. It is important to minimize the cost (in terms of equipment, operations, systems administration complexity and relationship management time) of developing and operating a PURL federation for all participants.

4. Speed of response (i.e. network efficiency) is not a design criterion, but may be treated as an available optimization in certain deployment scenarios.

A PURL Federation is anticipated that will consist of multiple independently-operated PURL servers, each of which have their own DNS hostnames, name their PURLs using their own authority (different from the hostname) and mirror other PURLs in the federation. The authorities will be "outsourced" to a dynamic DNS service that will resolve to proxies for all authorities of the PURLs in the federation.

Caching proxies are inserted between the client and federation members, but may be coincident with a PURL server host. The dynamic DNS service responds to any request with an IP address of a proxy. The proxy attempts to contact the primary PURL member via its alternative DNS name to fulfill the request and caches the response for future requests. In the case where the primary PURL member is not responsive, the proxy attempts to contact another host in the federation until it succeeds. Thus, most traffic for a given PURL authority continues to flow to the primary PURL member for that authority and not other members of the federation.

It is envisioned that proxy servers may be virtual machines located in a cloud computing environment or co-located with PURL servers. The proxy implementation need not require on-disk storage of any PURLs or related material. Proxies are expected to acquire their configuration upon startup from the dynamic DNS service for a federation (the location of which need be their only configuration option).

So, let's say a client wants to resolve the PURL http://purl.zepheira.com/team/dave/. The dynamic DNS resolver resolves the authority purl.zepheira.com to the IP address of a caching proxy (either by random selection, geographic closeness or other criteria). The client makes an HTTP GET request for the PURL path to the IP address of the caching proxy using a HOST header of purl.zepheira.com (or an HTTP GET on the fully-qualified PURL). The proxy looks at the HOST header or fully-qualified PURL to determine the entire PURL URI and searches its cache to determine whether it can respond immediately. If it cannot, it attempts to contact the primary PURL member for the PURL in question with the intent of proxying its response. If the canonical PURL server cannot be reached, other PURL servers in the federation are tried until a response is found. If a PURL member that is mirroring the PURL is used to satisfy the request, an HTTP "Warning" header will be included in the response.

In this way, each PURL proxy would be able to respond to requests for any PURL held by members of the federation. Because each PURL is only ever resolved using its full and complete URI, a PURL can only be identified by its full and complete URI, regardless of the authority responding for it at any given time.

The act of "being in the federation" would be as simple as (a) operating a PURL server and (b) participating in the dynamic DNS operation. Participating in the dynamic DNS operation is as simple as adding a DNS CNAME entry to the organization's DNS servers for the name of their PURL authorities, pointing to a dynamic DNS service. Such a dynamic DNS service is intended to be operated by the federation as a consortium or by a vendor or partner agreed to by the members.

Individual PURL members may be directly contacted by clients making requests directly to the server's IP address or non-authority host name and including the appropriate authority in the HOST header. This use case, while allowed, should not be encouraged outside of directly testing the responsiveness of a given host because it by-passes the automated failover service provided by the federation.

All changes (writes) to PURLs would be made on their primary PURL members. Recognizing that DNS resolution as described above would resolve to a proxy, administrative actions (HTTP PUT, POST or DELETE operations) could be redirected from a receiving proxy to the primary PURL member as required.

Writes (additions and changes) will be made to the primary PURL member and promulgated to its mirrors. PURLs are never deleted (but may be "tombstoned"), so changes resulting in the tombstoning of a PURL entail the addition of metadata to a PURLs existing record. In other words, the number of PURL records are designed to only increase in time and never decrease. Such an environment facilitates data mirroring because, although state still needs to propagate through a federation, complex issues of data integrity are kept to a minimum.

Non-administrative actions (HTTP GET) requests would be handled directly by a receiving proxy or PURL server. We also envision the assignment of DNS A records to all hosts in a federation. In other words, it knows itself by the service name (its hostname).

A simpler architecture without the use of caching proxies was considered and rejected. Dynamic DNS resolution directly to a non-canonical PURL server allows for a poorly- behaved host to make all PURLs served by a federation to appear to be inaccessible for a period of time for some clients. This can occur when a server is unstable or overly busy and cannot respond to requests for PURL resolution. Periodic monitoring of server availability by the dynamic DNS service is envisioned to reduce the likelihood of this scenario by removing a bad server from the list of hosts used for DNS resolution. However, if such an unstable host fails for short periods of time and thus appears available as of the next time a monitoring request is made, and DNS caching is used by clients or their network providers such that the unstable host continues to receive requests, the entire federation can appear to be unresponsive to any clients attempting to resolve PURLs via that host. The use of caching proxies to receive dynamic DNS resolution and to direct most traffic to the authoritative PURL server reduces such risks considerably and ensures that a poorly-behanved host effects the resolution of its own PURLs more than others.

Even if service monitoring catches a poorly-behaved or failing host, DNS caching can continue to make the entire federation appear unresponsive to some clients until the DNS caches expire. The dynamic DNS service is thus motivated to set low or null times-to-live on DNS responses. However, the use of proxies eliminates this risk.

Advantages of the PURL Federation architecture are:

- Meets all stated goals and complies with all stated presumptions.

- Request loads are spread fairly throughout the federation. A dominant PURL service with many requests will generally handle their own requests. Significant loads on other servers in the federation will only be encountered in the case of a systems failure.
- Allows for a one-time, low-administration method for joining or leaving a federation; operate a PURL server and make a single DNS CNAME entry for that server.
- Protects against poorly-behaved or unstable hosts that could make the entire federation appear inaccessible for a period of time for some clients.
- Caching proxies may enable better network efficiency for repeat requests for PURLs in their cache.

Disadvantages:

- Greater cost than a more simplistic architecture (without the caching proxies).
- The use of proxies may cause difficulty with certificate validation for any PURL servers using the HTTPS protocol, depending on the detailed implementation. This is not considered an important scenario for public federations, but should be kept in mind for private PURL services.

The PURL server RESTful API will need to be augmented to support operations for data mirroring including both full and partial updates, and the resolution of PURLs based on the HOST header of a request. Some amount of configuration information will need to be provided at a PURL server to ensure that its operators can control whether or not to participate in a federation.

Members of a federation undergo some cost when other members join because the new member's data must be mirrored, stored and maintained. Therefore, some social and technical mechanisms should be put in place to prohibit unwanted members and denial-of-service attacks. Ideally, this mechanism should be a simple administrative approval and not require a software change or server restart.

Data mirroring between servers in the Federation will be accomplished via a "pull" strategy. Each PURL server will publish two sources of data: The first of these sources will, upon invocation by an HTTP GET request message, return representations of each PURL domain (or collection).

The second data source published by each server will provide the list of PURL domains (or collections) that the server is contains and is configured to poll, as well as the last datetime and entity tag a successful poll response was received from each server. This will permit debugging of the state of the federation as a whole.

The existing format used to represent PURLs is a custom XML vocabulary that was not designed for use outside of the scope of a single PURL server. Also, the existing format includes maintainer information which is neither necessary nor desired for passing to PURL mirror hosts. Therefore, a new data format is required. We suggest using Turtle, a compact, non-XML based serialization of RDF. Regardless of a PURL server's data persistence implementation, an RDF serialization can be parsed and transformed appropriately. A suitable RDF vocabulary for representing a complete PURL wil be developed.

Some PURL providers (e.g. OCLC and the US Government Printing Office) require the ability to mirror a PURL at an alternate address; for example,

- http://purl.example.com/purl/abcdef
- http://example.com/purl/abcdef

The RDF vocabulary will use skos:exactMatch to relate the canonical and alias URIs to meet this objective.

A PURL server will need to be provided the following information (via an administrative user interface) in order to join a federation:

- the canonical URIs for each PURL server it will mirror;
- its own authority and any aliases.

It is envisioned that each PURL server will advertise URIs for its PURL data sources, batch upload endpoint and management interface at its canonical URI (http://*authority:port/*) for the purposes of bootstrapping initial configurations into operations and enabling Linked Data client operations.

9 Conclusions and Further Work

Metadata identifying information resources has been shown to a be concern since the earliest days of writing itself. Resolvable persistent identifiers such as PURLs have been shown to be fundamental to addressing the lack of back links on the Web. PURLs have been used to address persistent identifier needs in the library and Linked Data communities for the past fifteen years. PURLs have thus been placed on a solid footing in both theory and practice.

The continued development of the PURL concept has resulted in a very different conception of the value of the approach. PURLs were initially conceived as a convenient method of redirection for the purpose of URL longevity. Although URL longevity is still a primary use case, a modern PURL server acts as a specialized Web server for the curation and management of arbitrary URL resolution processes. PURL services allow the Web's back link problem to be addressed for any content important enough to warrant its use. The introduction of the 303 PURL substantially modernizes the PURL concept and provides an important foundation for describing conceptual and real-world resources on the Web.

Community development of the both a PURL server and the PURL concept continues. The most recent development has been the implementation of the PURL Federation described in this chapter. The project is Open Source Software under an Apache 2.0 license and is available on the PURL community site at http://purlz.org.

Further work regarding the application of PURLs to Linked Data identifiers is anticipated to be along the lines of developing best practices for the publication of human- and machine-readable representations of both terms and instance data. The greater usage of PURLs of Type 303 is explicitly anticipated as the amount of machine-readable data on the Web grows.

Acknowledgements The author wishes to acknowledge Nigam Shah of NCBO, Alan Ruttenberg and Jonathan Rees of Science Commons and James Leigh and Mark Baker of Zepheira for their contributions to the definition of the the the PURL Federation architecture and James Leigh for its implementation. The PURLz Open Source Software project has received support from the On-line Computer Library Center (OCLC), the National Center for Biomedical Ontology (NCBO), Zepheira LLC and 3 Round Stones Inc.

References

1. Akscyn, R., McCracken, D. and Yoder, E. (November 1987). KMS: A Distributed Hyperme-dia System for Managing Knowledge in Organizations. Proc. HYPERTEXT '87, pp. 1-20.
2. Alesso, H. P. and Smith, C.F. (2006). Thinking on the Web: Berners-Lee, Godel, and Turing, Wiley, Hoboken, New Jersey.
3. Archer, P. (ed.) (2007, October 31). POWDER: Use Cases and Requirements, W3C Working Group Note. Retrieved March 13, 2008 from http://www.w3.org/TR/2007/NOTE-powder-use-cases-20071031/.
4. Berners-Lee, T. (1989). Information Management: A Proposal, Retrieved February 17, 2008 from http://www.w3.org/History/1989/proposal.html.
5. Berners-Lee, T. and Connolly, D. (1995, November). Hypertext Markup Language - 2.0, In-ternet Engineering Task Force, Network Working Group, RFC 1866. Retrieved February 8, 2008 from http://www.ietf.org/rfc/rfc1866.txt.
6. Berners-Lee, T., Fielding, R. and Frystyk, H. (1996, May). Hypertext Transfer Protocol – HTTP/1.0, Internet Engineering Task Force, Network Working Group, RFC 1945. Retrieved February 8, 2008 from http://www.w3.org/Protocols/rfc1945/rfc1945.
7. Berners-Lee, T. (1997, January 6). Metadata Architecture. Retrieved February 20, 2008 from http://www.w3.org/DesignIssues/Metadata.html.
8. Berners-Lee, T. (1998, September). Semantic Web Road Map. Retrieved February 20, 2008 from http://www.w3.org/DesignIssues/Semantic.html.
9. Berners-Lee, T. (2000). Weaving the Web. The Original Design and Ultimate Destiny of the World Wide Web. Harper Business, New York, pp. 4.
10. Berners-Lee, T., Fielding, R. and Masinter, L. (2005, January). Uniform Resource Identifier (URI): Generic Syntax, Internet Engineering Task Force, Network Work-ing Group, RFC 3986 (STD 66), Section 1.2.3. Retrieved March 1, 2008 from http://tools.ietf.org/html/rfc3986#section- 1.2.3.
11. Bos, B. (1999, June 30). Handling of Fragment Identifiers in Redirected URLs, In-ternet Engineering Task Force, Expired Internet Draft. Retrieved March 1, 2008 from http://www.w3.org/Protocols/HTTP/Fragment/draft-bos-http-redirect-00.html.
12. Bradner, S. (1997, March). Key Words for Use in RFCs to Indicate Requirement Levels, Internet Engineering Task Force Best Current Practice (BCP) 14, RFC 2119. Retrieved March 1, 2008 from http://www.ietf.org/rfc/rfc2119.txt.
13. Bulterman, D.C.A. (2004). Ïs It Time for a Moratorium on Metadata?,ÏEEE MultiMedia, 11(4), pp. 10-17.
14. Bush, V. (1945, July). As We May Think, The Atlantic Monthly, pp.101-108.
15. Butler, M., Huynh, D., Hyde, B., Lee, R., Mazzocchi, S. (2006) Longwell Project Page. Re-trieved March 3, 2008 from http://simile.mit.edu/wiki/Longwell.
16. Casson, L. (2001). Libraries in the Ancient World, Yale University Press, New Haven & London.
17. Clark, T., Martin, S. and Liefeld, T. (2004, March). Globally Distributed Object Identification for Biological Knowledgebases, Brief Bioinform, 5 (1), pp. 59-70.
18. Collins, A.M. and Loftus, E.F. (1975, November). A Spreading-Activation Theory of Seman-tic Processing. Psychological Review, 82, pp. 407-428.

19. Communications Decency Act of 1996 (1996) Section 5 of Telecommunications Act of 1996, 104th Congress of the United States of America, Retrieved February 17, 2008 from http://www.fcc.gov/Reports/tcom1996.txt.

20. Dubost, K., Haas, H. and Jacobs, I. (2001, February 6). Common User Agent Problems, W3C Note, Section 4. Retrieved March 1, 2008 from http://www.w3.org/TR/2001/NOTE-cuap-20010206#uri.

21. Fielding, R.T., Gettys, J., Mogul, J., Frystyk, H., Masinter, L., Leach, P. and Berners-Lee, T. (1999). Hypertext Transfer Protocol HTTP/1.1, Internet Engineering Task Force, Network Working Group, RFC 2068. Retrieved February 19, 2008 from http://www.w3.org/Protocols/rfc2616/rfc2616.html.

22. Fielding, R.T. (2000). Architectural Styles and the Design of Network-based Software Architectures. Doctoral dissertation, University of California, Irvine.

23. Fielding, R.T. and Jacobs, I. (2006, April 12). Authoritative Metadata, W3C TAG Finding. Retrieved March 6, 2008 from http://www.w3.org/2001/tag/doc/mime-respect-20060412.

24. Furrie, B. and The Follett Software Company (2003). Understanding MARC Bibliographic: Machine Readable Cataloging, Seventh Edition, Cataloging Distribution Service, Library of Congress. Retrieved June 12, 2007 from http://www.loc.gov/marc/umb/.

25. Gill, T. (1998). Metadata and the World Wide Web in Introduction to Baca, M. (ed). Metadata; Pathways to Digital Information, Getty Information Institute, pp. 11.

26. Gilliland-Swetland, A.J. (1998). Defining Metadata, in Baca, M., ed., Introduction to Metadata, Pathways to Digital Information, Getty Information Institute.

27. Golbeck, J. (2005). Computing and Applying Trust in Web-based Social Networks, Ph.D. dissertation, Department of Computer Science, University of Maryland College Park, pp. 30- 34. Retrieved February 17, 2008 from http://trust.mindswap.org/papers/GolbeckDissertation.pdf.

28. Guha, R.V (1995, February 10). Contexts: A Formalization and Some Applications, Ph.D. thesis, Department of Computer Science, Stanford Univesity.

29. Guha, R.V. and Bray, T. (1997, June). Meta Content Framework Using XML, W3C Technical Note, Retrieved February 17, 2008 from http://www.w3.org/TR/NOTE-MCF-XML/.

30. Guha, R.V. (1999, March 15). RSS 0.90 Specification, Netscape Communications Corporation, Retrieved February 17, 2008 from http://www.rssboard.org/rss-0-9-0.

31. Halasz, F.G., Moran, T.P. and Trigg, R.H. (May 1987). Notecards in a nutshell, ACM SIGCHI Bull., 17, SI, pp. 45-52.

32. Huynh, D.F. (2007, August). User Interfaces Supporting Casual Data-Centric Interactions on the Web, Ph.D. Thesis, Department of Electrical Engineering and Computer Science, MIT.

33. Jacobs, I. and Walsh, N. (eds.) (2004). Architecture of the World Wide Web, Volume One, W3C Recommendation, Retrieved June 7, 2007, from http://www.w3.org/TR/2004/REC-webarch-20041215/.

34. Japan Electronics And Information Technology Industries Association (JEITA) (2002, April). JEITA CP-3451: Exchangeable Image File Format for Digital Still Cameras: Exif, Version 2.2. Retrieved February 16, 2008 from http://www.digicamsoft.com/exif22/exif22/html/exif22_1.htm.

35. Karger, D., Bakshi, K., Huynh, D., Quan, D. and Sinha, V. (2005). Haystack: A General Purpose Information Management Tool for End Users of Semistructured Data. Proc. 2nd Biennial CIDR, Asilomar, CA, pp. 13-27.

36. Kollock, P. (1999). The Economies of Online Cooperation: Gifts and Public Goods in Cyberspace.In Communities in Cyberspace, edited by Marc Smith and Peter Kollock. London, Routledge.

37. Lenat, D., Guha, R.V., Pittman, K., Pratt, D. and Shepherd, M. (1990, August). Cyc: Towards Programs with Common Sense, Communications of the ACM, 33/8.

38. Manola, F. and Miller, E. (eds.) (2004). RDF Primer, W3C Recommendation, Retrieved July 29, 2007 from http://www.w3.org/TR/rdf-primer/.

39. Martin, S. (2006, June 30). LSID URN/URI Notes, W3C ESW Wiki. Retrieved February 24, 2008 from http://esw.w3.org/topic/HCLSIG_BioRDF_Subgroup/LSID_URN_URI.

40. Miller, J., Resnick, P. and Singer, D. (1996, October 31). Rating Services and Rating Systems (and Their Machine Readable Descriptions) Version 1.1, W3C Recommendation, Retrieved February 17, 2008 from http://www.w3.org/TR/REC-PICS-services.

41. Mitchell, T.M., Shinkareva, S.V., Carlson, A., Chang,K.-M., Malave, V.L., Mason, R.A. and Just, M.A. (2008, May 30). Predicting Human Brain Activity Associated with the Meanings of Nouns, Science, 320 (5880), pp. 1191-1195.

42. Nelson, T.H. (1965). Complex Information Processing: A File Structure for the Complex, the Changing and the Indeterminate. Proc. 1965 20th National Conference of the ACM, ACM Press, New York, pp. 84-100.

43. Nelson, T.H. (1972). As We Will Think, in Nyce, J.M. and Kahn, P. (1991). From Memex to Hypertext. Academic Press, Boston, pp. 245-260.

44. Nelson, T.H. (1987). Computer Lib; Dream Machines. Redmond: Tempus Books of Microsoft Press.

45. Nyce, J.M. and Kahn, P. (1991). From Memex to hypertext : Vannevar Bush and the Minds Machine, Academic Press, 1991.

46. Object Management Group (OMG) (2004, April). Life Sciences Identifiers, OMG Adopted Specification dtc/04-05-01. Retrieved February 24, 2008 from http://www.omg.org/docs/dtc/04-05-01.pdf.

47. Paskin, N. (ed.) (2006, October 6). The DOI Handbook, Edition 4.4.1, International DOI Foundation, Inc., Oxford, UK. Retrieved February 24, 2008 from http://www.doi.org/handbook_2000/DOIHandbook-v4-4.pdf.

48. Resnick, P. and Miller, J. (1996). PICS: Internet Access Controls Without Censorship, Communications of the ACM, 1996, 39 (10), pp. 87-93.

49. Shafer, K., Weibel, S., Jul, E. and Fausey, J. (1996). Introduction to Persistent Uniform Resource Locators, OCLC Online Computer Library Center, Inc. Retrieved February 23, 2008 from http://purl.oclc.org/docs/inet96.html.

50. Shera, J.H. (1965). Libraries and the Organization of Knowledge, Archon Books, Hamden, Connecticut.

51. Smith, M. (1992). Voices from the WELL: The Logic of the Virtual Commons, Master's thesis, Department of Sociology, University of California at Los Angeles.

52. Stockwell, F. (2001). A History of Information Storage and Retrieval, McFarland & Company, Jefferson, NC.

53. Van de Sompel, H., Hammond, T., Neylon, E., Weibel, S. (2003, September). The ïnfoÜRI Scheme for Information Assets with Identifiers in Public Namespaces, Internet Engineering Task Force, Internet Draft (expired). Retrieved February 23, 2008 from http://info-uri.info/registry/docs/drafts/draft-vandesompel-info-uri-00.txt.

54. Weibel, S., Kunze, J.,Lagoze, C. and Wolf, M. (1998, September). Dublin Core Metadata for Resource Discovery, Internet Engineering Task Force RFC 2413, Retrieved February 17, 2008 from http://www.ietf.org/rfc/rfc2413.txt.

55. Wright, A. (2007). Glut: Mastering Information Through the Ages. Joseph Henry Press, Washington, D.C.

56. Yakel, E. (2007). Digital Curation, OCLC Systems & Services, 23, (4), pp. 335-340. Retrieved May 26, 2008 from http://www.ingentaconnect.com/content/mcb/164/2007/00000023/00000004/art00003.

Linking Enterprise Data has been tried and has, in certain places, proven extremely successful. The lessons learned from the organizations who have gone first may help those who come later. The success stories presented in this Part are diverse and yet each one represents a repeatable real-world scenario.

The United Nations Food and Agriculture Organization collects data from all over the world. They epitomize the distribution problem of the world's largest enterprises. The UK company Garlik was one of the first large-scale startups to employee a fully Linked Data infrastructure, not because they were Semantic Web researchers but because they required certain features and functions that only that approach could provide. The large legal publisher Wolters Kluwer created a nightmare of disparate content formats and required a way to integrate their production pipelines. The Cleveland Clinic needed to integrate many information sources into a single view. Finally, the BBC decided to invest fully in the World Wide Web as their content management system. Each of these stories provides a unique perspective while at the same time defining the commonalities of Linked Enterprise Data.

Linked Data for Fighting Global Hunger: Experiences in setting standards for Agricultural Information Management

Thomas Baker and Johannes Keizer

Abstract FAO, the Food and Agriculture Organization of the UN, has the global goal to defeat hunger and eliminate poverty. One of its core functions is the generation, dissemination and application of information and knowledge. Since 2000, the Agricultural Information Management Standards (AIMS) activity in FAO's Knowledge Exchange and Capacity Building Division has promoted the use of Semantic Web standards to improve information sharing within a global network of research institutes and related partner organizations. The strategy emphasizes the use of simple descriptive metadata, thesauri, and ontologies for integrating access to information from a wide range of sources for both scientific and non-expert audiences. An early adopter of Semantic Web technology, the AIMS strategy is evolving to help information providers in nineteen language areas use modern Linked Data methods to improve the quality of life in developing rural areas, home to seventy percent of the world's poor and hungry people.

1 Agricultural information and Semantic Web

The Food and Agriculture Organization (FAO), headquartered in Rome, is a specialized United Nations agency leading international efforts to defeat hunger. FAO serves as a neutral forum for discussing policy and agreements aimed at ensuring good nutrition through improving agriculture, forestry, and fishery practices, with special attention to developing rural areas, home to seventy percent of the world's poor and hungry people.

Thomas Baker
Washington DC, USA, e-mail: tbaker@tbaker.de

Johannes Keizer
FAO, Viale delle Terme di Caracalla, 00153 Rome, Italy e-mail: Johannes.Keizer@fao.org

D. Wood (ed.), *Linking Enterprise Data*, DOI 10.1007/978-1-4419-7665-9_9,

One of the primary tools in FAO's fight against hunger and poverty is Knowledge, and FAO has defined itself as a Knowledge Organization. FAO collects, analyzes, interprets, and disseminates up-to-date information on nutrition, food, and agriculture in a variety of genres and formats — from statistics and databases to bibliographies and workshop proceedings — for an audience of decision makers, technical specialists, agricultural "extension workers," and end users (farmers) in 190 member countries and territories around the world.

With six technical departments in Rome, each with a distinctive disciplinary culture, and field offices in many countries, FAO shares the knowledge management challenges common to any complex, global organization, with the additional challenge of targeting an audience in areas that are poor in resources and IT expertise and that require the use of many local languages in the service of end users that may be illiterate.

This chapter assesses the experience of the Agricultural Information Management Standards (AIMS) activity in FAO's Knowledge Exchange and Capacity Building Division over the past decade in promoting the use of Semantic Web standards to improve the dissemination and use of information on nutrition and technical innovation in agriculture. It is based on meetings and interviews held in 2009–2010 for an "autoevaluation" undertaken to critically assess the achievements, impact, and strategic direction of this activity at the start of a new programme cycle.

The story begins in the early 2000s, when a series of workshops with experts and international partners encouraged FAO to work with Member Countries to become "a key enabler and catalyst to establish a new model of agricultural information management in the 21st century" based on decentralized information management and using "Web-enabled" standards for interoperable data exchange. The guiding theme was provided by Tim Berners-Lee's seminal keynote at XML2000[1] outlining his vision of a Semantic Web based on "ontologies." Under the banner "Agricultural Ontology Server" (AOS), and supported by the Agricultural Information Management Standards (AIMS) community Website[2], a team in the Knowledge Exchange Facilitation Branch (KCEW) at FAO developed a program with three main components:

- The use of simple descriptive metadata for integrating access to agricultural information in both developed and developing countries and, to a lesser extent, in FAO's own technical departments.
- The development and maintenance of thesauri and ontologies — especially FAO's flagship vocabulary of agricultural terminology, AGROVOC[3] — as descriptors for structuring access to agricultural information and as "building blocks" for application-specific ontologies.
- Networking, capacity development, and outreach aimed at promoting the uptake and use of these standards by FAO information providers and partner organizations.

---

[1] http://www.w3.org/2000/Talks/1206-xml2k-tbl/

[2] http://aims.fao.org/

[3] http://aims.fao.org/website/AGROVOC-Concept-Server/sub

As an early adopter of Semantic Web technology, the AIMS team has been years ahead of the curve in porting its legacy information management standards from the print world into Web formats and is well-positioned to benefit from current technological trends. In some areas, however, the team is paying a price for having been a bit too far ahead of the curve. This chapter summarizes the work done, lessons learned, and outlines some course corrections decided as a result of the autoevaluation:

- The concept of application profile it used has allowed the AIMS team (and others) to merge information from diverse sources into central databases but now needs to be loosened to accommodate input that is either simpler (where resources are scarce) or more complex (where requirements are more comprehensive) — something which more flexible technological approaches now support.
- The metamodel custom-designed in-house for upgrading AGROVOC and other AIMS thesauri into Web-enabled ontologies, while novel and innovative in 2004, has been superseded by an international standard that serves the same function but with the promise of tool support and compatibility with a rapidly growing number of other Web-enabled vocabularies.

Promoting trusted URIs for use in Linked Data

The Semantic Web vision outlined in 2000 achieved its breakthrough when Tim Berners-Lee radically redefined the message in 2006 around the notion of Linked Data[4]. The term Linked Data refers to a style of publishing structured data on the Web in which all elements of an ontology (properties, classes, and value vocabularies), as well as things described by the ontology (publications, events, people), are identified by Uniform Resource Identifiers (URIs), allowing data to be extensively cross-referenced ("linked") with other data sources.

The vision of Linked Data is succeeding where Semantic Web did not because it conveys a simple message that can be understood in very concrete terms. People can see that it has to do with how things relate to each other and about making such links resolvable on the Web for practical purposes such as structured browsing and data integration.

In Linked Data terms, an ontology is a conceptual structure represented as data. Services can be built over that data. Using HTTP URIs and resolving those URIs to useful information that people can look up replicates the function of a dictionary. By promoting use of the URIs of AIMS standards for tagging (annotating) Web content worldwide, AIMS can empower resource providers to bypass centralized aggregators and search engines, which seek to position themselves as gatekeepers, and connect their resources directly to a growing Linked Data cloud. URIs provide language-neutral hooks for labeling shared concepts in any of the languages used

---

[4] http://www.w3.org/DesignIssues/LinkedData.html

in FAO member countries, enabling coherent access to information across language areas.

As the technological approach which AIMS helped pioneer now matures, AIMS will be able to benefit from generic software tools developed in the commercial world and open-source communities. With mainstream search engines and applications adopting the Linked Data approach, AIMS can transition from the role of technological innovator to that of developing capacity to help information providers in member countries benefit from the Web revolution.

The sections which follow review technical achievements, user feedback, and planned course corrections with respect to:

- Metadata based on application profiles that use open, Semantic Web vocabularies to describe documents and other objects of interest, such as events, people, and learning materials.
- Thesauri such as AGROVOC, upgraded for publication and use in a networked environment, and their alignment with specialized vocabularies in domains such as fisheries.
- Collaboration among partner organizations in the creation, maintenance, and deployment of standards for sharing knowledge related to food and agriculture, notably in the context of an umbrella initiative, Coherence in Information for Agricultural Research for Development (CIARD).[5]

All of the standards and projects discussed below are documented or linked on the AIMS Website.[6]

2 Integrating access using Dublin Core metadata

Work on the standards that now fall under the banner of AIMS began under an Agricultural Metadata Standards Initiative (AgStandards) in 2000. Inspired in part by the Dublin Core Metadata Initiative, then five years old, the AgStandards Initiative took the fifteen elements of the Dublin Core Metadata Element Set (DCMES) — basic elements such as Title, Subject, and Date — as a starting point and defined itself as an umbrella under which additional elements could be created. A new namespace for describing document-like resources relevant to agriculture, Agricultural Metadata Element Set (AgMES), was published in 2005 as the first output of the initiative.

The flagship implementation of AgMES is the International Information System for the Agricultural Sciences and Technology (AGRIS), FAO's database of bibliographic references to literature produced by agricultural research centers around the world. From its beginnings in 1969 — the name "AGRIS" dates from 1975 — through the late 1990s, AGRIS was maintained by FAO as a centralized database with its own unique database structure, exchange formats, and software.

---

[5] http://www.ciard.net/

[6] http://aims.fao.org/

With the rise of the World Wide Web and its new paradigm of distributed information management, the AGRIS database was by 2000 looking old-fashioned and unsustainably centralized. Between 2000 and 2003, a series of workshops with experts and international partners encouraged FAO to diversify institutional participation in AGRIS through capacity development, which aimed at empowering local and regional AGRIS centers to improve information management in their own institutions. The workshops endorsed the role of FAO in supporting common standards and protocols for achieving this goal.

The renewed AGRIS effort focused on the use of a simple application profile based on Dublin Core — the AGRIS Application Profile — as the basis for conversions from a wide range of local database formats into a common XML format (Document Type Definition, or DTD). To facilitate the adoption of the AGRIS profile by AIMS partners such as the Global Forestry Information Service and the research centers of the Consultative Group on International Agricultural Research, the AGRIS team defined mappings from legacy data formats and developed simple data input tools ("WebAGRIS" and "MetaMaker").

The AGRIS Application Profile, which was originally designed published with an RDF variant, was intended from the start as a means for gathering data from partners that could be expressed in triples. The problem was that most AGRIS partners were and continue to be unprepared to generate RDF data on their own. The AGRIS DTD served as an aid for generating a repository of data that could straightforwardly be converted into RDF.

By 2005, the AGRIS team had converted the entire repository of three million records from its legacy library-catalog-based "AGRIN3" format into XML records based on the AGRIS profile. Over the years, data has accumulated in AGRIS from over two hundred institutes, and of today's one hundred AGRIS providers, roughly sixty remain "very active." Some AGRIS data is delivered by motorbikes over dirt roads on thumb drives. Institutions have been encouraged to configure their databases to generate conformant XML data for harvesting and transformation by the central AGRIS team. The introduction of the AGRIS AP as a common exchange format dramatically reduced the need for editing and cleaning incoming data, which before 2000 had been done by a team of more than ten people at the AGRIS processing unit in Vienna.

The AIMS team followed up its publication of the AGRIS profile by developing or promoting profiles for other types of information – e.g., for News (using the standard RSS news format) and Events (a simple profile with starting and ending dates, location, type, and organizer). These were used for an alert service, AgriFeeds[7], which was launched in 2007. The team also created a profile for brief descriptions of organizations which, when published on their own Websites in XML, can be referenced in metadata or harvested for automatic compilation into lists.

In 2006, work began on a profile for providing structured access to learning resources in a Capacity and Institution Building Portal[8]. This profile uses results from

---

[7] http://www.agrifeeds.org/

[8] ftp://ftp.fao.org/docrep/fao/010/ai154e/ai154e00.pdf

an ongoing effort by DCMI and the Institute of Electrical and Electronics Engineers (IEEE) to harmonize the simpler approach of Dublin Core metadata with the more comprehensive and complex specification of the IEEE Learning Object Metadata standard on the basis of a Linked-Data-compatible representation.

Feedback from application profile users

The renewal of the legacy AGRIS database as a Web repository is generally seen as a big success, and the AgriFeeds service is widely used. The repository has exposed local research results to a global audience. The AGRIS center in South Korea, for example, has been delighted at the surge in requests for its publications, especially since AGRIS has been picked up by Google.

The AGRIS Application Profile 1.1 of July 2005[9], however, prints out at eighty-one pages, and as various users attest, the profile is widely perceived as "heavy" and "cumbersome" to implement, requiring a higher level of control than users in low-budget situations can afford:

> We do not use the AgMES application profile. Not that we reject it, but we see that such applications are too heavy-duty for people in developing countries. They do not have the staff to do detailed things, and we do not want to push them to adopt anything. At our home office we have even less capacity for adding metadata or mapping.

An AIMS partner confirms that even the task of mapping from existing formats presents a significant barrier:

> Today we have over 170 information provider partners from around world, but only half have created RSS feeds links to us — and only because we could show that it did not take much working time. We have had even less success in getting partners to create AGRIS data from their native records — it is a bigger job for them to understand the records and make the mapping.

A minority of users see the problem less as one of excessive complexity than of excessive simplicity and lack of flexibility. Work on an application profile for describing projects ran up against the limits of simple, flat (and therefore more easily interoperable) descriptions with the need to provide contact information for project coordinators and recipient institutions — information that requires descriptions about additional entities, such as people and organizations, to be embedded in records about publications.

However, a larger number of users would prefer to see AGRIS lower the bar by promoting simpler, lighter alternatives, perhaps even using just a handful of Dublin Core elements:

> In order to justify the working time, our information providers want to see how this will help them get more users, like offering a simple search tool. Maybe FAO could make the profile simpler and more flexible. Start with something very simple, like RSS, before introducing more comprehensive metadata solutions.

---

[9] http://www.fao.org/docrep/008/ae909e/ae909e00.htm

> We would like to submit data to AGRIS. The problem is that the data is very dirty — it is collected from different sources. The funder collects things they no longer fund, and you have to accept everything and get very dirty metadata. We require something a bit lighter than the AGRIS application profile.

AGRIS staff point out in response that "the AGRIS profile is perceived as complicated because people see the fifty or sixty fields but do not realize that only five or six of those fields are mandatory." The AGRIS team does in fact accept data in whatever granularity it is provided. Many descriptions provide just a minimum, with Title, Subject (typically with an AGROVOC value), Date, Availability (location), Language, and often Conference Name. This message, however, has not been widely understood, so future Web guidelines and training sessions will highlight simple examples.

AGRIS staff also note that the role of metadata is shifting in ways which de-emphasize the importance of information about the location of a resource. In the Web world resources are, in practice, often moved around or replicated on multiple servers. Google, on the other hand, excels at finding "known entities" — resources for which an exact title, authors, or other publication information is known if not the location. In the new division of labor between search engines and curated collections, bibliographic databases can help users discover that a resource exists, then Google can help them find and retrieve it. One user suggests that, if nothing else, tagging resources by subject would by itself be a big win:

> Focus less on application profiles than on using AGROVOC well. If people could pull elements from AGROVOC just to tag their things, it would be fantastic.

Other users caution, however, that even minimal requirements can be hard to meet. They report that "with the AGRIS profile, people are sometimes intimidated by the big words, even if it is just their own data fields that are getting mapped." The underlying problem, according to many, is the lack of basic information management skills:

> In our experience with RSS and the AGRIS profile, the main problem is not with the specifications themselves. The biggest problem is that organizations which maintain and create information on the Web do not have knowledge or skills to maintain metadata. They have old-fashioned Web sites — hand-made, not dynamically generated. Behind those Web pages, some developers have learned to maintain Web pages, but the structure as a whole is not well prepared. Only a few providers know how to create RSS or AGRIS XML data, upload to the Website, and link to our service.

The solution, expressed in many ways by the people interviewed, lies in capacity-developing measures for bringing users up to speed with the technology:

> Ninety percent of our users are in developing countries. The key is capacity building. It is one thing to publish a specification, but to get uptake in twenty institutions, you need to hold face-to-face meetings, identify champions, and train the trainers.

Metadata enrichment and conversion to Linked Data

The AIMS team is currently exploring ways to leverage AGRIS in the Web environment by publishing the entire repository in the form of RDF "triples" — the fundamental unit of Linked Data. The process involves "metadata enrichment" — the progressive enhancement of descriptions, where possible, with explicit links (URIs). This turns each AGRIS record into an entry point to a web of authors, institutions, and topics — a "hub" for drawing together a global collection of information and, by extension, the community of its authors.

The new role of URIs in weaving the Web changes the role of metadata itself by de-emphasizing its function for finding information, for which people often turn to Google. Rather, metadata functions increasingly as a bundle of links that embed a given resource in a web of relationships, thereby giving that resource a context.

With help from the information management company Talis and a team from the Okkam Project[10] at the University of Trento, the AGRIS team is testing the "triplification" of AGRIS XML records. Talis is testing the conversion of string values for Creator, Publisher, Language, and Type into URIs from authority files for authors, journals, languages, and resource types. The Okkam Project is testing algorithms for disambiguating between authors, given inconsistently entered names, by using contextual information such as affiliation, co-authorship, or country. Subject, arguably the most important field in AGRIS descriptions because it links resources to FAO's areas of interest, is also one of the "cleanest" in the dataset because it was populated largely using tools which copy subject strings directly from AGROVOC online.

Before the conversion of strings into URIs, data must often first be cleaned by normalizing variant strings to the "termspell" (normalized string) of a target vocabulary. The process of cleaning, normalizing, and enriching cannot be fully automated — people need to control the results at every step — and the procedure is intended to be a one-way migration, not something that is carried out repeatedly and on-the-fly. It greatly helps that the XML data files of AGRIS are already partitioned according to year and month of ingest, country, and institution because the quality of records systematically improved as AGRIS centers acquired better data-entry tools.

Moving forward, the AGRIS team aims at facilitating the use of URIs by increasing tool support. AIMS partners are developing small utilities and plug-ins, for example, to tag content with AGROVOC descriptors ("AgroTagger"), enhance string-based record fields with URIs in DSpace repositories, and identify concepts in texts for annotation with URIs in Drupal content management systems ("Agro-Drupal"). As one AGRIS manager explained, the AGRIS profile can be taken as a foundation and, starting with a minimal record, tools can be used to enrich the data, automatically, with information extracted from the content of the resource or inferred from its context.

---

[10] http://www.okkam.org/

Accepting "whatever you can get"

For many years, the dominant paradigm for the interoperability of digital information has been syntactic conformance with specific data formats encoded as XML DTDs or XML Schemas. AIMS application profiles were based on a set of well-defined data elements semantically compatible with RDF properties and classes. Transforming AGRIS partner data into the AGRIS XML format was a process of mapping local data elements of AGRIS data providers to common target elements. As the concept of Linked Data had not been developed in 2005, and most AGRIS partners lacked and continue to lack the experience for publishing their data directly in an RDF representation syntax, the AGRIS DTD has served as a transitional aid for creating data that is conceptually and semantically (though not syntactically) interoperable with RDF.

The emerging paradigm of Linked Data, in contrast, explicitly avoids requiring that information providers expose identical formats. RDF provides an abstract model for data that can be serialized in one of several interchangeable syntaxes for representing data as generic "statements" (RDF "triples") that can be joined automatically on the basis of shared global identifiers (URIs). The "Open World Assumption" underlying Linked Data avoids assuming that any one source provides complete and exhaustive information about a given resource and anticipates that information sources may only partially overlap. Whereas formats such as DTDs can be "broken" by omitting data, triples constitute a language in which "missing is not broken" [1]. By anticipating the future integration of new sources even if they are not completely aligned, the architecture of Linked Data is more resilient to imperfections and diversity, while the syntax-independent model of triples makes data more "future-proof."

In the new paradigm, interoperability is an unbroken continuum that depends on the "coherence" of merged triples. Coherence is provided best by shared URIs — URIs for identifying the resources described, for naming the properties used to characterize the relationships between resources, for citing the classes used to characterize types of resource, for defining the datatype of string values, and for characterizing values as members of specific controlled vocabularies. Taken together, these URIs serve to "qualify" data by putting its values into the context of known standards. Qualified data can more easily be integrated across multiple sources because URIs provide a firm basis for alignments and mappings.

String values — sequences of alphanumeric characters such as names, dates, and publication abstracts — are inherently less precise as a basis for merging data due to natural variations in spelling or punctuating subject headings and titles, representing names, or formatting dates. To improve their value for Linked Data, it is important that string values be qualified, when possible, with descriptive context. Date strings, for example, can be expressed as RDF datatypes (in Dublin Core terminology, Syntax Encoding Schemes) by providing a URI identifying the ISO or W3C standard that specifies the pattern used for sequences of months, days, and years.

Value vocabularies are most effective for use in Linked Data when their individual terms are identified using URIs, as with AGROVOC. However, a URI identifying a Vocabulary Encoding Scheme, or VES (in Dublin Core terminology) can be used to put a string value into the context of a controlled vocabulary. Using a VES URI together with a string is not as precise as using a URI for a specific term, but for controlled vocabularies that have not yet been "Webified," it is better than providing no context at all.

Shifting the emphasis from shared data formats to the coherence of underlying triples will allow the AGRIS team to relax the requirements for data ingest and more flexibly accommodate data from a growing diversity of providers. Providers using RDFa to embed structured descriptions "invisibly" into normal Web pages, for example, will be able to use tools such as Yahoo SearchMonkey to extract the underlying triples for ingesting into AGRIS. This shift redefines the function of the AGRIS DTD, and other such constructs, from that of ensuring interoperability through uniformity of format to that of providing a validatable template that is cleanly convertible into RDF triples. In the context of Linked Data, templates and application profiles of this type will continue to ensure that data are created with enough "qualification" to support more-precise, higher-quality data integration.

3 AGROVOC and specialized domain ontologies

AGROVOC, a multilingual thesaurus of agricultural topics, was created by FAO and the Commission of the European Communities in the early 1980s. It consists of "terms" (natural-language phrases) in multiple languages cross-referenced with other broader, narrower, and related terms. The thesaurus standardizes term codes and "termspells" (spelling and punctuation) in order to improve the quality of indexing and search.

From 8,660 descriptors (preferred terms) in 1982, AGROVOC grew to 16,607 descriptors by 2000 and has roughly 32,000 descriptors today. Initially available in English, French, and Spanish, AGROVOC is now available in nineteen languages, with additional translations in the works. Periodic releases of AGROVOC can be freely downloaded in its native relational database format or in alternative formats such as Microsoft Access, and the latest version can be accessed by applications via Web services for looking up terms or expanding queries. AGROVOC terms have been mapped to terms in the Chinese Agricultural Thesaurus, the Schlagwortnormdatei Thesaurus of the German National Library, the US National Agricultural Library Thesaurus, the General Multilingual Environmental Thesaurus of the European Environment Information and Observation Network, and the CAB Thesaurus of the UK-based technical agency CAB International.

In 2001, the (future) AIMS team envisioned an Agricultural Ontology Server as "a reference tool that structures and standardises agricultural terminology in multiple languages," providing modules of terms that can serve as "building blocks" for developing more specific domain ontologies. Starting in 2005, the AIMS team focused on "refining" AGROVOC's standard thesaurus relationships ("Broader Term,"

Agrovoc OWL model today

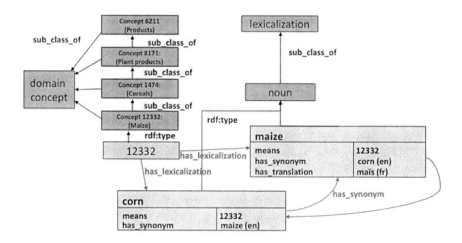

Fig. 1 Metamodel for the AGROVOC Ontology, 2006–2010 (simplified)

"Narrower Term," "Related Term," and "Used For") into semantically more specific relationships such as "hasIngredient" or "growsIn."[11]

This refinement of thesaurus relationships was undertaken with the implicit assumption that a more precisely engineered ontology would support more intelligent queries — for example, to determine whether a specific farming method has been used in a dryland area for a given crop and to find any relevant research reports in whatever language they may be available. Most of the refinements have been defined by experts at the International Crops Research Institute for the Semi-Arid Tropics (ICRISAT) in Patancheru, India.

The AGROVOC project team formulated a conceptual model with "the necessary structure to create precise semantics to facilitate the transition from traditional thesauri to ontologies" — in effect a "metamodel" for thesauri. [10] In the final form of the metamodel (see Fig. 1):

- The natural-language Terms of the AGROVOC Thesaurus are re-conceptualized as Lexicalizations (Labels) for underlying Concepts. Lexicalizations include preferred and alternative labels, synonyms, spelling variants, and translations

---

[11] http://agrovoc.icrisat.ac.in/agrovoc/relationstree.php

in multiple languages. Descriptors are conceptualized as "preferred" Lexicalizations.

- Concepts are modeled as OWL Classes (i.e., as sets of things). [7]
- Each Concept-Class is associated with one Instance of that Class as a means of relating a Concept to its Lexicalizations. (This was done to meet a perceived need for description-logic-based computability, as declaring one Class to be an Instance of another Class sacrifices conformance with "OWL DL," a constrained, description-logic-conformant sub-set of the more expressive but computationally intractable variant "OWL Full.")
- Relationships can also be specified between Concepts (such as "isUsedIn" or "causes") or between Lexicalizations (such as "hasAcronym"). In 2006, this was considered a significant and innovative feature of the metamodel.

Converting the metamodel of AGROVOC into a class-based ontology, however, was only part of the AIMS vision. Equally important was the notion of enabling AGROVOC to evolve dynamically, in response to technical innovation, scientific advances, regional specialization, and linguistic evolution. Just as AGRIS member institutions were empowered to submit bibliographic data directly, decreasing dependence on the central team in Rome, there was a strong push to enable expert users in AGROVOC's twenty-some language areas to maintain the ontology directly online. Aside from relieving the central AGROVOC team of the cumbersome and relentless task of processing change requests — a frustrating bottleneck both for the team and for its users — the idea of moving maintenance to the Web addressed what Martin Hepp refers to as the trade-off between "ontology engineering lag versus conceptual dynamics" [4] — the insight that knowledge itself is continually evolving, that the process of ontology development is necessarily iterative and dynamic, and that for semantic applications, the most important concepts are frequently also the newest.

In 2005, requirements were developed for a Web-based platform — the AGROVOC Concept Server Workbench — to allow experts in many countries to add or translate concepts in their specific areas of interest. The Workbench was conceived as a distributed, Web-based maintenance environment that would enable participants in multiple countries to edit parts of the central AGROVOC ontology simultaneously — adding term translations, adding or refining relationships between terms, or performing batch modifications on the basis of pattern matching. The Workbench was also seen as a platform for plug-in tools that could proactively populate AGROVOC with new concepts extracted by corpus analysis from breaking news stories ("ontology learning"). The move to a distributed architecture was seen as a way to loosen the dependence of AGROVOC on terms entered canonically in English, then "translated" into other languages, towards an environment in which users could create new locally-specific terms in any language.

The system was intended to support levels of authorization ranging from Guest Users through Term Editors, Ontology Editors, Validators, and Publishers, to System Administrators. It was designed to support the extraction and export of sub-sets of concepts for personal use and the upload of entire ontologies for sharing with others. It was conceived of as a generic tool in principle adaptable to other domains, such as health care and medicine. Part of the vision was eventually to provide add-on services such as automatic or semi-automatic translation, ontological reasoning, guided search, and concept disambiguation.

In 2006, having formulated Workbench requirements and finalized the OWL-class-based ontology model, the AIMS team, finding no software capable of fully implementing this vision off-the-shelf, undertook the development of a customized interface to a backend ontology database, Protégé[12]. This software development project has been led since 2006 by Kasetsart University in Thailand with input from implementation testers in Rome and Patancheru. An alpha version of the Work-bench was released in June 2008, and development has accelerated in 2010 with the involvement of a development team at MIMOS Berhad in Malaysia. AGROVOC has in the meantime been maintained in the original thesaurus database, with snap-shots periodically exported to the Workbench for testing. After a final migration, the original thesaurus database will be retired and maintenance of AGROVOC will continue on a production basis in the Workbench.

In the meantime, AGROVOC term codes and "termspells" have been widely used in agricultural portals and repositories worldwide. At FAO itself, AGROVOC terms have been used in AGRIS; in an International Portal on Food Safety, Animal and Plant Health; in an Emergency Prevention System for Transboundary Animal and Plant Pests and Diseases; in Geonetwork, a repository of geospatial information; and in the Electronic Information Management System, a workflow database used at FAO to track publications.

Although AGROVOC has not yet been used in its "ontological" form for production databases, it has been extensively used for research, most notably in the NeOn Project[13], an EU-funded project of 14.7 million Euros involving fourteen partners in seven countries for four years starting in March 2006. The NeOn Project aimed at providing "lifecycle support for networked ontologies" in large-scale, distributed applications.

FAO's role in the NeOn Project — carried out by the AIMS team in coopera-tion with FAO's fisheries department — was to implement a prototype Fish Stock Depletion Alert System in support of the long-term goal of sustainable fisheries. The task of the AIMS team was to integrate a diversity of data sources into a deci-sion support system — sources ranging from land and fishing areas (identified using geographical coordinates), to biological entities (including family and species), fish-eries commodities (using global statistical codes), fishing vessels (types and sizes), fishing gear (using a global classification scheme), and images from a variety of Websites. Related concepts needed to be aligned; water areas needed to be related to neighboring land areas. The objective was to federate the independent ontologies under a common queryable data infrastructure.

In 2003, a previous project in-house at FAO had attempted to build a comprehen-sive monolithic fishery ontology as a central focus for mappings from stand-alone databases, but work had bogged down with modeling issues, and the resulting con-

---

[12] http://protege.stanford.edu/
[13] http://aims.fao.org/website/NeON/sub2

struct was impractical and unwieldly. The NeOn approach, in contrast, was that of a "network of ontologies." It assumed that datasets would continue to evolve within specialized communities of practice, each of which in turn reflected the diverse perspectives of managers, biologists, IT systems administrators, and thesaurus maintainers.

User experience of AGROVOC and AIMS ontologies

The AGROVOC Thesaurus was a loose, sprawling collection of terms added over of the course of many years by innumerable unnamed contributors and encompassing common and scientific names for bacteria, viruses, fungi, plants, and animals, as well as geographic names, acronyms, and chemicals. The terms all have something to do with agriculture or nutrition in a broad sense, but the thesaurus does not reflect any particular context, viewpoint, or application requirements. "Petroleum," for example, is narrower than "mineral resource" and related to "fuels"; the related term "oil spills" is narrower than "pollution," and "pollution" is narrower than "natural phenomena."

One important achievement of the re-engineering process of the past few years has been to "clean" the ontology by consolidating hundreds of top terms, linking hundreds of "orphaned" concepts, and correcting thousands of other inconsistencies.

The process of refining semantic relations, described above, has added more precise relationships, though the process has not been guided by an overarching standpoint — e.g., viewing the entities consistently from the standpoint of business, science, farming, or the environment. The semantic multivalence of the terms is augmented further by the subtle differences of perspective and interpretation introduced by their translation into nineteen languages.

Advanced reasoning, however, presupposes a commitment to an ontologically well-defined point of view. One user finds the effort to refine relationships useful in principle but hard to exploit in practice:

> For our resource-discovery purposes, we cannot really apply the more refined relationships. I do not see how they can work — at least we do not have the technology to use them for resource discovery. You need an inference engine that can use them. Without an inference engine and a purpose, it is not clear what to do with them.

Another believes the effort is useful but explains that their particular application required relationships to be refined *differently*, so they ended up extracting a sub-set of AGROVOC concepts as a starting point and refining it into an ontology in their own particular way.

A recurring theme in user feedback is the case in which developers set out to create expert systems using well-engineered ontologies for text mining or decision support systems and ended up falling back on less sophisticated uses for the ontology such as simple query expansion and structured browsing. One FAO partner recounts the challenge of building a sophisticated ontology application with domain experts in the field:

A group of extension officers in plant protection first tried to make a sophisticated portal on pesticides — a resource that extension officers could consult to help farmers diagnose plant diseases. They tried some complex solution and at some point, they completely gave up. They know the reality, they know their plants and all the relationships — the reality they know is so complex — but they couldn't use it to build an information system. They lacked the knowledge for creating a search assistant with an inference engine. The lesson we learned was that getting the various experts together, identifying the relevant material, and submitting it to the system, was actually more important than the highly codified system that resulted. In the end, we're talking here about references to just 1,000 research reports — and that is quite a lot for a specialized field! Once we identified those 1,000 reports, we did not need overly refined discovery methods.

One FAO technical officer with experience in ontology projects feels the requirements for reasoning functionality were never properly clarified:

The few ontologies in FAO are not exploited fully in terms of reasoning capability, and there are no real specific requirements for reasoning. The real requirements, like language independence and collaborative maintenance, do not require rules and reasoning. Maybe we should investigate whether we really want to have a basis for full-fledged ontologies. Maybe researchers were pushing for more functionality than really required.

Other users confirm that their needs are quite simple — better navigation, search refinement, or ranking hits:

We have used ontologies in vertical portals to index or classify things. We use OWL formats, but more like thesauri. With mappings, we can continue using legacy thesauri. We find we get better navigation; they help in ranking hits and refining searches.

One colleague in a FAO technical department would like to use AGROVOC to tag reports and publications:

Increasingly we have stuff to tag: meeting reports, publications, duty travels, case studies. Much mundane, day-to-day stuff. If we had it "in AGROVOC," we could do interesting things. "Where are meetings duty travel reports, institutions, and Web pages we have done about, say, fungus?"

Fishery experts in the NeOn Project express enthusiasm about the potential of ontologies to guide decision-making but recognize that the methods may take a few years to mature. For the AIMS team, the project confirms that the maintenance of alignments within a "network of ontologies" is time-consuming and error-prone, especially between ontologies based on different underlying models (e.g., class-versus instance-based) and between ontologies that are themselves independently evolving. Recognized bottlenecks are the lack of tools for automating such tasks and the lack of reliable corpi with which to test automatic alignment methods.

AGROVOC as a "quarry" of terms

The goal articulated for the Agricultural Ontology Server in 2001 was that of providing "building blocks" for application-specific ontologies. Feedback from users strongly confirms that this is indeed how AGROVOC is being used, only not for the sophisticated applications originally envisioned. In practice, AGROVOC serves as a quarry of conceptual blocks to extract as a starting point for customized vocabularies:

> We need specific vocabularies in many areas. Making derivative products from AGROVOC — terms relevant for a particular area — is what people want to have: go one level down, slice up the pie with very specific terms in a particular area.

Sets of AGROVOC terms often provide a starting point for creating specialized portals about topics like "crop pests" or "bananas." The Organic Edunet[14] used AGROVOC as a starting point for their own set of categories, mapping to AGROVOC wherever possible and inventing the rest. It is simply more efficient to re-use an existing vocabulary than to try to invent one from scratch:

> We need something between Yahoo and Dewey and more specific. It would take alot of discussion to come up with our own. We use taxonomies both for indexing and for creating the structure of Web pages. For each entry in the browsing structure, we want to have a query to the database using subject headings.

In its entirety, however, AGROVOC is simply too big:

> Using all of AGROVOC is cumbersome — putting whole thing into peoples' hands is too much. We want to make a sub-vocabulary. We are moving towards full-text indexing and need vocabularies for very specific portals.

Given the wide range of audiences for which AGROVOC is used, however, the semantic multivalence of its terms is actually desirable. The Agropedia Project in India needs to customize browsing structures for users ranging from scientists to agricultural extension works and semi-literate farmers. Another user reports:

> We have customers who produce portals for regional development — specific birds, sheep, things in meadows, how to manage meadows in specific ways. We need taxonomies to create a browsing structure for our portals, and not just from a scholarly perspective.

Many users see an inherent tension between centralizing quality control over AGROVOC maintenance with experts in the AIMS team as opposed to decentralizing control over the expansion of AGROVOC to user groups and language communities with their own local requirements:

> I see a need for lots of country-specific AGROVOCs — for India, Brazil, etc. Everyone has very specific terminology. It is not doable to capture all of these variants in the central AGROVOC ontology. We need distributed vocabularies.

Decentralizing maintenance control, however, implies capacity development — instruction about ontological principles and training in the use of specific tools and procedures:

> AGROVOC is understaffed for the task of maintaining AGROVOC, allowing new concepts without duplicating or creating a mess. One always has to check and think before entering a term — it is not a mechanical job for a clerk but involves brainware. KCEW could explain tagging as a capacity-building effort. This could be useful but would conflict with the maintenance task. There is possibly a built-in friction between the two roles.

---

[14] http://www.organic-edunet.eu/

Users see this as a crucial role for the AIMS team:

> FAO provides AGROVOC to download and use, but just as important have been the people who provide support. This is extremely helpful! They bring new ideas. As a UN organization, FAO should have this role — to help solve problems.

Users also feel that decentralizing maintenance would free the vocabulary to grow more quickly:

> AGROVOC is very strong, especially in geographic areas — we like it — but it evolves too slowly to keep pace with emerging research terms. Maybe we need vocabularies in a wiki or blog thing, like Wikipedia, where people can quickly post these things and start to adopt terms quickly — where terms can be proposed and used immediately.

That more sophisticated ontology applications imagined in the early 2000s have not materialized in the AIMS user community has been, to some extent, both a barrier to understanding and a source of tension between visionaries and practitioners. Ontologies have been seen as bleeding-edge research — a noble undertaking but impractically complicated for the average implementer. The simpler and straightforward goals of today's Linked Data movement, however, are seen by many users as a crucial way forward. In this regard, the developments in the AIMS community have simply followed the trajectory of the wider Web world. It would seem that the goal of honing the precision of well-engineered ontologies stands at cross purposes with the goal of accommodating a broad diversity of language communities and user perspectives.

Correcting the model for *less* precision

Since the 2006 finalization of a metamodel for expressing a term-based thesaurus (i.e., AGROVOC) as an ontology of Concepts linked to Lexicalizations, the World Wide Web Consortium has finalized a W3C Recommendation for precisely this purpose: Simple Knowledge Organization System (SKOS) [8]. Indeed, a computer scientist from the AIMS team participated in the W3C Semantic Web Deployment Working Group which developed SKOS, and AGROVOC provided a key use case for the requirement that Labels (Lexicalizations) be defined as first-class resources [6]. It is indeed fortunate that AIMS team has not yet finalized the conversion of AGROVOC from thesaurus to ontology or promoted the URIs of its concepts, modeled as OWL classes, for use in Linked Data, because the shift to a SKOS metamodel can still be undertaken without breaking existing applications.

Figure 2 shows how AGROVOC can currently be expressed in SKOS: AGROVOC Lexicalizations (Terms) are modeled as instances of the class SKOS Label, AGROVOC Concepts as instances of the class SKOS Concept, and the AGROVOC Concept Scheme itself as an instance of the class SKOS Concept Scheme (see Fig. 2). This shift solves several problems with the 2006 AGROVOC metamodel, most crucially because SKOS provides a vocabulary for expressing the legacy thesaurus relationships between concepts not as ontologically strong sub-class relationships, but as ontologically weaker "broader" and "narrower" relationships. This is

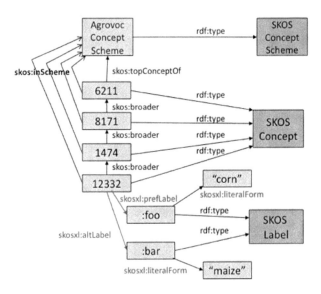

Fig. 2 AGROVOC modeled as a SKOS Concept Scheme (proposed)

more appropriate for AGROVOC because the mechanical translation of thesaurus terms into OWL classes violates the design principle of *minimal ontological commitment*. As explained by Thomas Gruber [3]:

> An ontology should require the minimal ontological commitment sufficient to support the intended knowledge sharing activities. An ontology should make as few claims as possible about the world being modeled, allowing the parties committed to the ontology freedom to specialize and instantiate the ontology as needed. Since ontological commitment is based on consistent use of vocabulary, ontological commitment can be minimized by specifying the weakest theory (allowing the most models) and defining only those terms that are essential to the communication of knowledge consistent with that theory.

SKOS concepts make a minimal ontological commitment to the nature of concepts and of relationships between concepts. Constructs consisting of SKOS concepts do not support reasoning as extensively as do sets of tightly defined and constrained OWL classes, but they more faithfully reflect the flexible way that people actually think. SKOS concepts, by default lightly specified, prevent modelers from introducing false precision into their models, and they prevent inferencers from drawing unwarranted conclusions.

We have seen above that in practice, concepts are often extracted from AGRO-VOC, like building blocks from a quarry, for uses that more often than not are quite basic. Erring on the side of under-specifying concepts avoids imposing inappropriate ontological commitments and reduces the risk of their being reused incorrectly. Users of SKOS concepts in applications downstream do not inherit the transitivity and entailments of OWL sub-classing.

Declaring AGROVOC concepts as SKOS Concepts, on the other hand, does not *preclude* the use of OWL properties for defining relationships between concepts with more precision than the basic set of SKOS properties, e.g., as transitive, inverse, or symmetric. When appropriate, SKOS concepts may also be upgraded to OWL classes, with additional constraints, for use in local ontologies. (It is worth noting that the likewise lightly specified Dublin Core Metadata Terms are often upgraded locally from RDF into OWL properties, then more tightly constrained to support reasoning. As there are endlessly different ways to do this, the minimal commitment of the Dublin Core specifications in this regard is considered a basis of their success.) Defining AGROVOC in SKOS does not, in other words, preclude the development of applications that use reasoning.

Putting the Workbench onto a SKOS basis means that its developers will be able to benefit from software libraries and interfaces being developed for what is already the most widely deployed standard for Linked Data vocabularies. This will, in turn, make the Workbench more attractive for the open-source development community. Users will be able to process the RDF representation of AGROVOC, or an extract thereof, not just with the Workbench but with any SKOS-enabled software. Use of the Workbench will not depend on support for a metamodel unique to AGROVOC.

The conversion into SKOS will also resolve another issue that has emerged as a problem for AGROVOC — the presence of "concepts" that should arguably be conceptualized as "instances." Examples include living species, chemicals, languages, and geographic place names, such as AGROVOC Concept 3253 ("Ghana"). In SKOS, every Concept is by definition an instance of the class SKOS Concept — in other words, every concept is by definition an instance, and the only question is whether there is a meaningful difference between "concept-like" instances and other, "non-concept-like" instances. Although it has been suggested that SKOS Concepts be reserved for "concepts" instead of "real-world" things — or for "universals" rather than "particulars" — such distinctions are not understood widely enough to provide a basis for consistent distinctions. By design, therefore, nothing in the SKOS data model prevents AGROVOC Concept 3253 ("Ghana") from being considered a SKOS Concept.

Forcing a distinction between classes and instances may, in fact, force ontological overcommitment. In order to map AGROVOC to an ontology for Aquatic Sciences and Fisheries Abstracts (AFSA), for example, the NeOn Project had to make AFSA comparable to AGROVOC by mechanically converting it into an ontology of OWL classes. On the other hand, while it seemed logical to the NeOn team that a species of fish be considered a class, and that actual fish be considered instances of that class, they found that when mapping to statistical time series, they needed needed to map species as instances. Indeed, the project team concluded "that the domain of interpretation of fisheries can contain entities as well as types of entities, and distinguishing them in a logically sound way would require a huge amount of fishery experts time, and only after they are organized in a team sided by ontology designers and are taught design tools adequately." [2] Thanks to their ontologically light specification, in other words, SKOS vocabularies can more safely and easily be mapped.

This ontologically more flexible approach to concept schemes also addresses a difficulty that has emerged in AIMS capacity-developing activities. AIMS team members holding seminars at FAO partner institutions report that words like "ontology" and "concept server" are perceived as "confusing," even "scary," and that the finer points of ontologies, such as the distinction between classes and instances, are lost on many audiences. The distinctions are, of course, hard to teach in part because they are hard to nail down or justify in reality. SKOS should be easier to teach, and with the rapid uptake of SKOS, AIMS trainers should benefit from the growing availability of tutorial materials.

The effort to refine AGROVOC concept relationships has underlined a need to standardize some frequently used properties such as "hasAcronym." The popularity of lightly defined concepts suggests, however, that the push to refine AGROVOC as a whole be given lower priority, moving forward, than the gradual extension of the concept set into new languages and subject areas. Mark van Assem reports that the reluctance of vocabulary maintainers to complexify their vocabularies ontologically may be based on healthy "investment versus gain considerations," as it is not always clear how refinements improve performance and user support. He suggests that vocabulary developers follow the adage "no innovations without clear applications."[15]

The AIMS namespace for AGROVOC currently defines 198 refined relationships, two-thirds of which constitute a "long tail" of properties used less than twenty times, or even just once or twice, as with "isAfflictedBy" or "hasBreedingMethod." The AIMS team will publish these properties as Linked Data, enabling their re-use in other projects, but the AIMS team will not have the resources to pursue their standardization in the global arena. Ideally, this task should be undertaken in the context of a standards organization, perhaps with the goal of starting with a manageable core of, say, fifteen popular and well-understood properties — a "Dublin Core" of thesaurus refinements. In the meantime, specifying all of the existing refinements as sub-properties of the original thesaurus relationships (Broader, Narrower, and Related) would allow an application to "dumb down" the refined relationships for simple purposes such as query expansion.

Guus Schreiber points out that vocabularies cannot simply be "merged" because they reflect a diversity of perspectives. Rather, the best one can realistically hope for is to make the vocabularies usable jointly by defining a limited set of mappings in a process of "vocabulary alignment." Published as Linked Data as a part of AGROVOC (or as a separate module), mapping assertions effectively increase the reach of AGROVOC concepts, allowing queries to be expanded to resources indexed with terms from related agricultural vocabularies such as the CAB Thesaurus (see above) or more general vocabularies such as Wordnet or the Library of Congress Subject

---

[15] Personal communication.

Headings. Facilitating the creation of such alignments has been identified as a new priority for the Workbench project.

4 Networking, capacity development, and outreach

A significant part of the AIMS initiative falls under the heading "capacity development" — building partnership among international colleagues through distributed teamwork, workshops, and training seminars in member countries or at headquarters. Capacity-developing efforts typically focus on the formation of information managers, local champions, and educators at regional universities and research centers ("training the trainers"), often with an effort to involve agricultural extension workers or reach out to farmers directly. Capacity development may involve on-site training sessions by FAO staff or research sojourns by visitors in Rome.

The AIMS team has helped build or provided training for regional initiatives such as the following:

- Red Peruana de Intercambio de Información Agraria, a network of public and private institutions for supporting agricultural science and innovation in Peru with an emphasis on technical exchange and information management standards.
- The Kenya Agricultural Information Network, a three-year project funded by the UK Department for International Development, which among other things provided training in the use of metadata to participate in AGRIS.
- The Thai National AGRIS Center, established in 1980 as part of the Kasetsart University Central Library, which was an early adopter of the AGRIS application profile as the basis for merging content from twenty national research institutes and making it freely available on the Web.
- The National Agricultural Research Information Management System (NARIMS) in Egypt, a bilingual Arabic-English Web portal for information about research in Egypt related to agriculture, which was developed in cooperation with FAO staff and using FAO tools and standards, notably an Arabic version of the AGRIS application profile. Starting in 2010, NARIMS data will be harvested by Near East Agricultural Knowledge and Information Network, a platform for agricultural research organizations in the wider Near East region and, from there, ingested into the central AGRIS database.
- The Global Forest Information Service[16], a portal for information sources related to forestry, from maps and datasets to grey literature and journal articles.

The story of several related projects in India exemplifies the role that the AIMS team can play in developing capacity on several levels. Starting in 2002, the Indian Institute of Technology in Kanpur experimented with using the Web to help semiliterate farmers bypass intermediaries to sell their commodities online. The initial

---

[16] http://www.gfis.net

idea of promoting digital commerce failed for lack of uptake, but the project did confirm a need to transfer knowledge about crops (such as dal and sugar), farming methods (sericulture and pest control), and agrarian legislation from India's 11,000 or so PhD-level agronomists to its 100 million farmers to address issues such as crop rationalization, declining soil fertility, the after-effects of chemical use, and pest pathologies.

The initiative enlisted the collaboration of village-level agricultural extension workers in bridging this gap and aimed at disseminating information in broadly consumable forms such as radio broadcasts, comic books, and SMS alerts, written or spoken in the rural vernacular. One strategy for making research outputs accessible to a broader range of participants was to tag available materials with familiar concepts, so parts of the AGROVOC Thesaurus were translated into Hindi and Telugu.

A larger National Agriculture Innovation Project, "Agropedia,"[17] was launched in January 2009 to empower farmers and extension workers with crop- and region-specific information and "accelerate technology-led, pro-poor growth and diffusion of new technologies for improving agricultural yield and rural livelihood." A brainstorming workshop with seventy participants of diverse background generated knowledge models reflecting scientific, clinical, and practical perspectives on the management of key crops such as rice, pigeon peas, and sorghum.

Taking AGROVOC concepts as a starting point, the participants used simple open-source software to define entities and relationships. Experienced ontologists from FAO helped apply standard naming conventions and map the emerging relationships to existing properties in AGROVOC. The workshop served both as a capacity- and a community-building experience. The resulting knowledge models link local terminology to standardized, language-independent concepts usable for tagging research outputs and learning materials, whether by manual metadata creation or automated keyword extraction, and to access those materials from a variety of perspectives.

Fishing in a Sea of Agrovoc?

In 2004, an autoevaluation with focus groups at FAO identified the need for "a prolonged effort to monitor the departmental sites, put a coherent layer of metadata over the different information systems (building on already existing metadata), and do some quality assurance in order to bring some order to the FAO site and better index it." The evaluator reported that previous efforts to put order to the proliferating departmental sites "was never a pretty process; a lot of tension was involved between divergent departments. Everybody is so busy with service/divisional work that coordination is viewed as a burden."

There have been a few cases of successful cooperation between the AIMS team and technical departments within FAO, notably with Fisheries (in the NeOn Project)

---

[17] http://agropedia.iitk.ac.in

and Forestry, involving primarily the use of AGROVOC for indexing, Agrifeeds for disseminating information about events, and the use metadata for describing departmental outputs. Overall, however, the observations made in 2004 appear still to apply five years later.

One technical colleague at FAO, however, offers a compelling metaphor for what might possibly be achieved in such a diverse institution:

> There is absolutely a need for more communication between departments at FAO. Everything we do can be seen from multiple angles: Capacity Building, Research, Women and Development, Democracy. If we were swimming in a Sea of AGROVOC, and we were to cast our hook for Climate Change, what things might we pull up?

The same colleague argues that such an approach is essential for preserving and transmitting institutional knowledge in a faster and more mobile age:

> There is quicker turnover now. With quicker staff turnover, institutional memory becomes a bigger problem. I used to be the youngest person in my department, but in the past three or four years, there have been more retirements. Who can tell me what meetings were held?

How might such a vision be achieved in practice? One well-developed model is offered by the VIVO service, managed since 2003 by the Cornell University Library as a structured view of information about people and academic resources at Cornell University.[18] The sample of VIVO suggests the following lessons:

- Start small, with a few common content types — people, departments, courses, publications — and extend the supported types organically, based on growing relationships to people, activities, and organizations.
- Work with departments and administrators to promote a more uniform approach to self-reporting and demonstrating Return On Investment in the form of improved data consistency and higher public visibility.
- Invest data from departments and databases with as little manual intervention as possible, adapting automated ingest procedures to specific local data structures and using simple inferencing to enrich data records with information not explicitly encoded in the source databases (e.g., "member of life science field") and, where possible, enriching or replacing text values with URIs.
- Convert data into an open and consistent format, using explicit semantic relationships, and publish the data according to accepted Linked Data principles, avoiding a requirement that any one tool be globally accepted and anticipating instead the future availability of innovative alternatives.
- Present users with a clean, Google-like search box in recognition of the fact that people typically submit queries of just one or two words.
- Take the user from a single-word query to a page that assembles links clustered by type — people, events, publications, institutions, and topics — efficiently exposing the searcher to response sets of high quality and providing a structured browsing experience based on semantic relationships.

---

[18] http://vivo.cornell.edu

The global "coherence" of information about food

The AIMS initiative sees itself as part of a broader movement for improving the management of, and access to, agricultural information. FAO is part of an initiative that has coalesced under the banner of Coherence in Information for Agricultural Research for Development (CIARD), the result of expert consultations held in 2005 and 2007.

CIARD presents a broader context in which AIMS can be effective. Where AIMS focuses on information standards, especially the AGROVOC thesaurus and AgMES-based application profiles, with AGRIS as a key implementer, CIARD represents a broader community, institutional base, and scope of action, with Task Forces on Advocacy, Capacity Building, and Content Management. The CIARD Content Management Task Force advocates the use of common standards for enabling the integration of information across institutions. The CIARD Pathways to Research Uptake offer concrete advice on broader issues, such as licensing and open access, techniques for retrospective digitization, policies for sustainable repositories, digital preservation, the exchange of information about news and events, and effective Website management (Web 2.0, search engine optimization, social media, and the use of Web analytics).[19]

The notion of "coherence" fits beautifully with the message of Linked Data. We live in a diverse and rapidly evolving world in which it is unrealistic to expect that interoperability can be tightly coordinated on the basis of mandatory data formats and specific technical solutions, whether by "lock-step" agreement among big institutions or by the de-facto dominance of specific software platforms. RDF provides an open-ended data model that explicitly avoids requiring that providers information in identical formats — a goal which can only remain, in the best of circumstances, elusive.

Rather, the watchwords of this more loosely-coupled vision of interoperability are "alignment," "harmonization," and "partial understanding." The best we can hope for is "coherence" in the underlying data itself — to ensure that the data can be expressed as, or translated into, RDF triples that can be coherently merged on the basis of shared descriptive properties, shared value vocabularies, and shared resource identifiers. The language-neutral nature of URIs turns vocabularies such as AGROVOC into platforms for extending concept schemes into new language areas.

History shows that all technology is transitional. Most of the applications and data formats we use today will become obsolete in the coming decade. RDF triples represent knowledge in the form of a simple sentence grammar, using noun-like classes and verb-like properties to make statements about things in the world — statements that are expressible in, and freely convertible among, multiple concrete syntaxes.

As of 2010, there are no other compatable models for representing knowledge with the uptake and traction of RDF. For the foreseeable future, RDF offers our best hope for "future-proofing" our cultural and scientific memory. As our applications

---

[19] http://www.ciard.net/index.php?id=607

and formats inevitably lapse into obsolescence, we can only hope to retain the ability to interpret what remains. We must ensure that information about so existentially vital topics as food and nutrition be expressed in a form that we can flexibly re-use today and pass to the next generation tomorrow.

References

1. Brickley, Dan. 2003. Missing isn't broken: data validation and freedom on the Semantic Web. FOAF Project Blog, http://blog.foaf-project.org/2003/07/missing-isnt-broken-data-validation-and-freedom-on-the-semantic-web/.
2. Caracciolo, Caterina. 2009. D7.2.3. Initial Network of Fisheries Ontologies. NeOn Project. http://www.neon-project.org/web-content/images/Publications/neon_2009_d723.pdf
3. Gruber, Thomas. 1995. Toward Principles for the Design of Ontologies Used for Knowledge Sharing. *International Journal Human-Computer Studies* 43(5–6): 907–928.
4. Hepp, Martin. 2007. Possible Ontologies: How reality constrains the development of relevant ontologies, Martin Hepp. *IEEE Internet Computing* 11(1): 90-96.
5. Independent External Evaluation of FAO. 2007. Rome: FAO. ftp://ftp.fao.org/docrep/fao/meeting/012/k0827e02.pdf.
6. Isaac, Antoine, Jon Phipps, Daniel Rubin. 2009. SKOS Use Cases and Requirements. [W3C Working Group Note, 18 August 2009]. http://www.w3.org/TR/skos-ucr/#UC-Aims.
7. McGuiness, Deborah, Frank van Harmelen, eds. 2004. OWL Web Ontology Language Overview. [W3C Recommendation 10 February 2004]. http://www.w3.org/TR/owl-features/.
8. Miles, Alistair, Sean Bechhofer, eds. 2009. SKOS Simple Knowledge Organization System Reference. [W3C Recommendation, 18 August 2009]. http://www.w3.org/TR/skos-reference/.
9. Sauermann, Leo, Richard Cyganiak. 2008. Cool URIs for the Semantic Web [W3C Interest Group Note 03 December 2008]. http://www.w3.org/TR/cooluris/.
10. Soergel, Dagobert, Boris Lauser, Anita Liang, Frehiwot Fisseha, Johannes Keizer, and Stephen Katz. 2004. Reengineering thesauri for new applications: the AGROVOC example. *Journal of Digital Information* 4(4). http://journals.tdl.org/jodi/article/view/112/111.

Enterprise Linked Data as Core Business Infrastructure

Steve Harris and Tom Ilube and Mischa Tuffield

Abstract This chapter describes Garlik's motivation, interest, and experiences of using Linked Data technologies in its online services. It describes the methodologies and approaches that were taken in order to deploy online services to hundreds of thousands of users, and describes the trade-offs inherent in our choice of these technologies for our production systems. In order to help illustrate and aid the arguments for the adoption of Semantic Web technologies this chapter will focus on two of our customer facing products, DataPatrol, a consumer-centric personal information protection product, and QDOS a Linked Data service that is used to measure peoples' online activity.

1 Introduction

This chapter presents how and why the online identity and privacy startup Garlik[1] built is own Semantic Web infrastructure to power its core business. The chapter will aim to present insight into how Semantic Web technologies are utilised internally, highlighting the advantages gained over other more traditional technology stacks and whilst providing motivating factors to our early adoption. The chapter will also describe our two primary technological developments in terms of storage solutions

Steve Harris
Garlik Ltd, 1-3 Halford Road, London TW10 6AW, United Kingdom, e-mail: steve.harris@garlik.com

Tom Ilube
Garlik Ltd, 1-3 Halford Road, London TW10 6AW, United Kingdom, e-mail: tom.ilube@garlik.com

Mischa Tuffield
Garlik Ltd, 1-3 Halford Road, London TW10 6AW, United Kingdom, e-mail: mischa.tuffield@garlik.com

[1] Garlik Ltd, Online Identity Experts http://www.garlik.com/

D. Wood (ed.), *Linking Enterprise Data*, DOI 10.1007/978-1-4419-7665-9_10,
© Springer Science+Business Media, LLC 2010

for data represented in the Resource Description Framework (RDF)[2] [6], namely the open-source 4store[3] (see section 5.1) and its proprietary successor 5store[4] (see section 5.2).

In order to help illustrate and aid the arguments for the adoption of Semantic Web technologies this chapter will focus on two of our customer facing products, Data-Patrol[5], a consumer-centric personal information protection product, and QDOS[6] a Linked Data [1] service that is used to measure peoples' online activity. These two systems are presented in section 3.

DataPatrol is a system which scans various sources of information, databases, online resources, open web data, and data held in closed communication systems such as IRC traffic. These sources of information are scanned for instances of customer data which is either appearing in places where it should not, such as an IRC channel known to be used for the sale of personal information, or in combinations which expose the user to a risk of financial fraud.

As the nature and methods used in personal information trading change frequently it is necessary for any system attempting to solve this problem to be easily adaptable to changing environments, and new sources of information.

The rest of this chapter will be broken down as follows. Following this introduction Garlik's core motivating factors for the adoption of Semantic Web technologies are listed in section 2. Section 3 details two of Garlik's main services, these are introduced to as real-world applications of Semantic Web technologies. This is followed by an example of Garlik makes use of Semantic Web Technology to deploy schema driven Software Development that allows for new functionality to be deployed whilst avoiding service down time (see section 4). The motivating factors coupled with the characteristics of the two services described are used to illustrate our arguments for the adoption of Semantic Web technologies, and are revisited in the conclusions and future work section of this paper (see section 6).

2 Motivations

Garlik's use and development of Semantic Web technologies have been driven by a number of core motivational factors that are summarised by the following points. These are used to contextualise the decisions made during the development of Garlik's core technologies, and will be revisited throughout the rest of the chapter.

- **Flexibility** Given that Garlik's core business revolves around the capture of personal information, whether it be specific data sources provided by partners or information collected from the World Wide Web, the ability to adapt and

---

[2] Resource Description Framework `http://www.w3.org/RDF/`

[3] 4store scalable RDF storage `http://4store.org/`

[4] 5store scalable RDF storage `http://4store.org/trac/wiki/5store`

[5] DataPatrol `http://www.garlik.com/products.php`

[6] QDOS `http://qdos.com/`

index new information in an agile manner is key. DataPatrol (section 3.1) needs to be able to index new sources of data as and when they become available. The ability to react to the existence of a new source of compromised data in order to effectively protect our customers' personal information from being abused by criminals is presented as one of the key motivating factors to our development and deployment of Semantic Web technologies. The flexibility of RDF to allow for arbitrary knowledge to be encoded in a triple format is presented at the key reason for why Semantic Web technologies are presented as core to DataPatrol's success.

- **Scalability** In order to meet the demands of a high-volume consumer facing service both DataPatrol and QDOS are required to be able to index and query large amounts of RDF data in real time. As a result of this requirement Garlik was motivated to produce its own RDF storage technology to support the flexibility promised by the RDF data format. The ability to index and run SPARQL[7] queries across high volumes of RDF data in real-time have led to the development of Garlik's two clustered RDF database solutions (these are presented in section 3).

- **Data Centric: Ontology/Schema Driven** The core services provided by Garlik, are all data-centric, and as discussed in the first point the ability to be flexible to search and integrate new forms of information has been fundamental to our success. Garlik makes use the expressive power of RDF by implementing schema driven software solutions that allow for functionality to be added and removed by virtue of adding and removing triples from an RDF schema. An example of such an interaction is presented in section 4, this allows for new functionality to be added to a system, often without the need to redeploy any pre-existing systems. This ability to add new services as desired is said to be core to Garlik's desire to able to react quickly to the need to index new information.

- **Use and Promotion of Standards** This point relates to all of the previous ones. The adoption and promotion of Web Standards have always been high on Garlik's agenda, this is evident by the decision to release and support 4store under the GPLv3 open-source license[8]. The promises presented by the energetic Linked Data community, that can be seen in ever growing Linked Data Cloud[9] has driven Garlik's desire to produce scalable RDF storage solutions. 4store was released into the community to help developers consume the vast amounts of RDF being produced by the Linked Data community. Furthermore, our needs regarding the ability to update RDF via the SPARQL language has motivated Garlik to be at the forefront of the design of SPARQL 1.1[10], the next iteration of the query language, at the W3C. The decision to release 4store as an open-source project is seen as an example of how Garlik is promoting and

---

[7] SPARQL Query Language for RDF http://www.w3.org/TR/rdf-sparql-query/

[8] GNU General Public License v3 http://www.gnu.org/licenses/gpl-3.0.html

[9] Linked Data Cloud http://richard.cyganiak.de/2007/10/lod/

[10] SPARQL Working Group http://www.w3.org/2009/sparql/wiki/Main_Page

furthering the state of the art. The ability to easily setup development environments for coding purposes is another good reason for deciding to work with an many standards as possible. As it stands Garlik's developers can choose to prototype systems on any operating system they wish and are not limited to work on UNIX-like environments, though all production system run the CentOS[11] Linux distribution. Given our heavy use of standards, such as HTTP[12], and the SPARQL Protocol[13], developers are free to build software and prototype using any RDF store that implements the SPARQL Protocol. These include but are not limited to: Jena[14], or Sesame[15].

3 Garlik's System Architectures

In this section we present two of Garlik's live services, DataPatrol (section 3.1), and QDOS (section 3.2). DataPatrol is used to help describe some of the software design decisions employed within Garlik. QDOS will be used to illustrate publicly accessible examples of some of the techniques used within DataPatrol. From a business perspective the information stored within DataPatrol's and QDOS's respective knowledge-bases (KBs) are treated extremely differently, to begin with they are on separate physical networks, one stores private highly-sensitive data, and the other stores facts pertaining to users, obtained from the public Web. One thing both systems share is that they make use of Semantic Web technologies: DataPatrol is presented as a Semantically Driven Web Application, and QDOS a Public Linked Data Service. As described below the ability to flexibly add and remove data, whilst maintaining the ability to query the data stores in a live environment has been central to all of our design decisions.

DataPatrol's requirement to be able to add new data sets easily, coping with constantly changing data, whilst maintaining provenance information used to gather business-critical Management Information (MI) was one of the reasons why the Resource Description Framework (RDF)[16] was selected as the data format of choice. The flexibility that RDF provides when used to represent data, namely that of being able to express arbitrary graphs through the adoption and reuse of unique identifiers, the encoding of knowledge in the form of triples, allows Garlik the ability to add new data sources in an ad-hoc basis, without the need to constantly make changes to one's database schema. This is due to the fact that RDF can be used as a schemaless data representation format.

---

[11] Community ENTerprise Operating System http://centos.org/

[12] Hypertext Transfer Protocol http://www.w3.org/Protocols/

[13] SPARQL Protocol for RDF http://www.w3.org/TR/rdf-sparql-protocol/

[14] Jena - A Semantic Web Framework for Java http://jena.sourceforge.net/

[15] Sesame - An open-source framework for storing and querying RDF data http://www.openrdf.org/

[16] RDF http://www.w3.org/RDF/

Another core driver to the development of services with in Garlik is the exploitation and adoption of open web standards, as proposed by the World Wide Web (W3C) consortium[17]. Use concept of developing software as services has matured over the past few years, that coupled with the power of RDF as a knowledge representation language helped Garlik decide that it would adopt and actively participated in the development RDF of open-sourced tools and open standard to help the realisation of the Semantic Web. RDF is not the only piece of the Semantic Web puzzle that Garlik employs, SPARQL [7], SPARQL-Protocol, HTTP, RESTful APIs [3], and ontologies are but a few of them.

From the many adopted serialisations of RDF, i.e. RDF/XML, n-triples, Turtle, Garlik tends to make use of the "turtle"[18] serialisation. Turtle is a human-friendly serialisation and makes debugging our software much easier. At this point it is important to note that both 4store and 5store do not perform any automatic inferencing whatsoever. Unlike their predecessor 3store[19] [4] which implemented RDFS reasoning upon the RDF data it stored, a decision was made to simply store RDF triples as imported. This decision is based on the desire to be as efficient, and as scalable as possible. Furthermore deleting triples from an RDF graph that supports reasoning is a computationally expensive task, and did not fit in with our motivation of being to index, add, and remove data in an agile manner. This does not mean that Garlik does not apply reasoning methodologies to the RDF it stores, an example of how reasoning is performed via SPARQL is presented in section 3.2.1.

Finally, both QDOS and DataPatrol are presented as Linked Data Applications, insofar as they make use of HTTP resolvable URIs[20], and run off of SPARQL stores – as apposed to being mere transforms on top of relational data. All of the publicly available user pages on QDOS allow for content negotiation to be performed in order to get back RDF describing a given person. Such requests make SPARQL CONSTRUCT[21] queries to the 4store instance and the result is returned to the issuer. The key difference between the two systems is that QDOS is an Linked Open Data resource, which publishes data to the Web whereas, DataPatrol's Linked Data resources are used for internal Customer Service, provenance, and debugging purposes and it not exposed to the Web.

3.1 DataPatrol

DataPatrol is focused on delivering real-time information to its customers protecting them from identity theft by harvesting and searching through both publicly available and privately acquired data about individuals. There have been a number of funda-

---

[17] The W3C http://w3c.org/

[18] Turtle - Terse RDF Triple Language http://www.dajobe.org/2004/01/turtle/

[19] 3store RDF storage http://threestore.sourceforge.net/

[20] Uniform Resource Identifiers http://www.ietf.org/rfc/rfc2396.txt

[21] SPARQL's CONSTRUCT verb http://www.w3.org/TR/rdf-sparql-query/\# construct

mental business driven requirements that have dictated the design and development of our systems and our Semantic Web platforms, DataPatrol influenced all of them. Key to our consumer focused DataPatrol service is the requirement of a highly available software platform, where both flexibility to index new data upon discovery and service uptime were both central. DataPatrol runs on low-cost networked servers and has to support around the clock, 24x7, operation for hundreds of thousands of customers. It should be noted that DataPatrol is currently live and operational in the United Kingdom, Germany, and the United States of America – and is constantly expanding into new geographical regions.

DataPatrol is a Web based consumer focused service powered by Garlik's 5store (see section 5.2), and is built using the Java programming language. Figure 1 presents an overview of DataPatrol's software architecture, which in short is made up of a number of web services interacting via HTTP and that use RDF as a data exchange language. Firstly, it is important to stress that end users never come across RDF, or any mentions of Semantic Web Technology in their day-to-day interactions with DataPatrol. The end users need not know about the underlying technology, and from their point of view DataPatrol's user interface is like any other Web Application.

DataPatrol in short indexes information about people, whether it comes from UK registries or whether it is compromised personal information collected by Garlik, and then acts as a notification system for its users. Users' are alerted when DataPatrol deems that there is too much information about them available in the public and digital domain and suggests a course of action which should be taken by the user in order to safe guard there identity.

DataPatrol integrates information from a number of different sources, these are presented in the figure 1 as "RDF Translators". The UK versions of DataPatrol indexes the following non-exhaustive list of data sources: The Companies House Register, The Births, Deaths, and Marriages Register, Euro Direct Marketing Database, The Royal Mail Redirects Database, as well as harvesting personal information acquired by accessing compromised data distributed via botnet networks, as well as data found on the World Wide Web. The aforementioned sources of information are converted into RDF, and stored within a 5store cluster which is subsequently queried via SPARQL over HTTP. In the architectural diagram (figure 1) these services that issue SPARQL queries over the RDF indexed by DataPatrol are illustrated as "Processing Services". These "Processing Services" are nothing more than simple web services, that when called via a HTTP GET request, issue SPARQL queries to 5store and if they come back with a hit a small RDF document is returned. This RDF document identifies the nature of the information found, and includes provenance information regarding the source of the data and the time in which the data was indexed by DataPatrol. This notion of outputting results in RDF, is illustrated by the label "RDF over HTTP" in DataPatrol's architectural diagram.

This use of "RDF over HTTP" (Turtle being the specific serialisation of RDF adopted by Garlik), and the "SPARQL Protocol" allows for flexibility in terms of the rapid development of new "Processing Services" given the identification of new sources of information deemed critical to protecting individuals from identity theft,

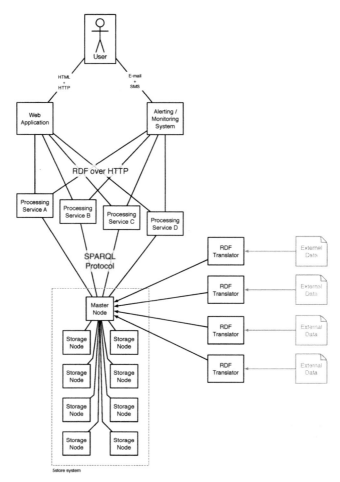

Fig. 1 DataPatrol Architecture

and other online fraud. The two parts of the DataPatrol system that interact with users are the "Web Interface" and the "Alert/Monitoring Systems", these components receive RDF from the various "Processing services" or *searchers* and subsequently inform the user about how their personal information may have been compromised. Garlik has written its own lightweight RDF Parser which parses "turtle" and then makes a decision to alert the customer if the customer is deemed to not have been informed of the alert before; this parser is incorporated into all of the components which may interact with a user. This model of bringing together the various searchers in a service orientated architecture allows for the easy setup and addition of new services. As long as the services can be called via the HTTP protocol, and as long as they return their results in RDF, against the DataPatrol alert schema they can be easily integrated.

The web-service based nature of the DataPatrol makes it easy to debug, allowing for developers to make various HTTP calls to the different services available, in case there is ever an issue. This means that all of the backend services can be invoked individually via HTTP GET requests and they do not require complicated test scripts that make use of Object Models or other database abstraction techniques.

Another advantage of deploying the various backend components as HTTP services makes it easy to add redundancy to the live system. Given that the various processing services are merely web services, if a machine were to crash due a hardware fault or similar the requests will fail over to a duplicate service, and it is but a mere configuration change of adding the location of an additional HTTP service to regain full strength.

There are a numerous other advantages to developing software as HTTP services, such as the fact that RESTful APIs are well established in the developer community and a lot easier for to work with than technologies like SOAP[22]. Mature open-source Web hosting tools, such as Apache[23] and Tomcat[24] incorporate a number of existing features load balancing, caching, proxies which all make managing a busy system with multiple users more straight forward. HTTP services also help get around the issue of connection pooling, as each HTTP based interface ensures that connections to backend services are short lived.

The data which DataPatrol searches over comes from a variety of different sources, some of which Garlik has contractual obligations regarding the manner in which that the data is used. For example, DataPatrol indexes certain pieces of information that has to be discarded after a fixed period of time, this is supported by the inclusion of provenance information relating to the origin and the time in which new data is added to DataPatrol's 5store infrastructure. This provenance information is attached to the Named Graph [2] of every RDF document imported into DataPatrol, and as a result all of the RDF imported is held as quads within 5store. This use of Named Graphs along with the SPARQL query language allows us to track the provenance of all of the data held within it, this is advantageous given that Garlik has strict reporting requirements from our various business partners and data providers. Some of our partners require that data only be accessed within a given duration of time, sometimes DataPatrol needs to count how many times results are found, and sometimes Garlik has to pay per time the data is queried. The ability to be agile when it comes to generating MI is made possible due to RDF's ability to attach triples providing provenance to Named Graphs. Given the numerous third-party data sources integrated within DataPatrol, the fact that 5store indexes all data imported to it, in the form of quads this caters for the simple generation of MI information, whereas certain queries would not be feasible if the data was held in a Relational Database Management System (RDBMS). Traditionally system run off of RDBMSs tend to have to require a separate data warehouse system in which data is imported into, 5store's quad based index relieves DataPatrol of such a subsystem.

---

[22] SOAP Specification http://www.w3.org/TR/soap/

[23] Apache HTTP Server http://httpd.apache.org/

[24] Apache Tomcat Java Servlet Server http://tomcat.apache.org/

3.2 QDOS

We all have a presence in the online world whether we use the internet or not and protecting yourself from identity fraud is just one side of the story. Our digital presence also increasingly opens up new opportunities and influences real world decisions made about us. We now have a means of measuring and therefore managing the way we look online, we call it digital status. QDOS was developed as a exemplar Linked Data application whose aim was to provide a means of measuring and therefore managing ones' digital status. QDOS measures digital status by calculating how active one is in the online world. A given QDOS score is made up of four different components:

- **Popularity** Who you know and the extent of your online network.
- **Impact** How many people listen to what you say online.
- **Activity** What you do online e.g. shop, chat, blog.
- **Individuality** How easy you are to find online according to your name, your age etc.

Recent research has shown that more and more British citizens are making decisions based on digital status[25]. Already 16% have chosen their new home based on how their prospective neighbours appear online. 1 in 5 (20%) have researched a prospective boss online before accepting a job and 32% have searched online to find out more about trades people and professionals, from plumbers to lawyers, before hiring them to do a job.

As illustrated in figure 2 QDOS's architecture is very similar to that of DataPatrol insofar as it is powered by a clustered RDF store, namely 4store. One major differences between QDOS and DataPatrol is that QDOS exposes the contents of its RDF store as publicly available Linked Data[26], via SPARQL endpoints[27], and via a number of RESTful APIs as described in section 3.2.1. QDOS is written in PHP[28] and Perl[29], and makes use of SPARQL, the SPARQL protocol, and HTTP.

As it stands the QDOS 4store instance holds approximately 10 million RDF documents describing people and their social graphs. These RDF documents are of the type `foaf:PersonalProfileDocuments` an RDF class that is defined by the Friend-Of-A-Friend ontology (FOAF)[30]. More information regarding the FOAF based services provided by QDOS can be found in the following section 3.2.1. Work is currently underway to collect more personal profile documents from the Web. A

---

[25] Garlik commissioned PCP market research consultants to conduct research among 2000 UK adults in November 2007

[26] See for example `http://qdos.com/user/5acc361496df109a7c2967760d5d9792/rdfxml`

[27] Once logged in as a QDOS user a SPARQL endpoint can be found at `http://qdos.com/query`

[28] Hypertext Preprocessor `http://php.net/`

[29] Perl Programming Language `http://www.perl.org/`

[30] FOAF ontology `http://xmlns.com/foaf/0.1/`

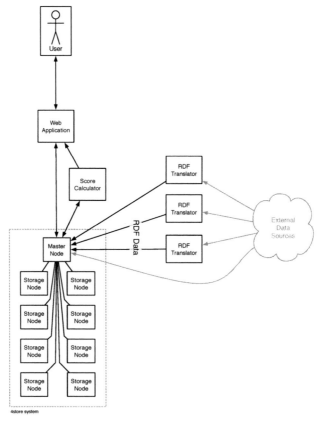

Fig. 2 QDOS Architecture

decision will also be made to port QDOS over from 4store to 5store, and given that both of them implement the SPARQL protocol, and all interacts with the RDF stores are performed via HTTP, this should be a trivial upgrade.

In figure 2 one can see that as in DataPatrol, QDOS is primarily a Web Application, whereby users interact with the system via a web-frontend.QDOS has a module known as the "Score Calculator" which is a background batch process that is constantly refreshing its cache of personal web pages, and publicly available FOAF documents from social networking sites such as, Twitter[31], Flickr[32], Lastfm[33], Facebook[34], and so on. This constant recalculation of individuals' QDOS scores has meant that 4store has had to able to cope with constantly updating RDF, which as it stands averages approximately 10 writes per second. Just like in DataP-

---

[31] Twitter Social Networking Site http://twitter.com/

[32] Flickr Photo-Sharing Site http://www.flickr.com/

[33] Lastfm Online, Social Radio Site http://www.last.fm/

[34] Facebook Social Networking Site http://www.facebook.com/

atrol, all of the interactions between the QDOS system and its RDF store are via the SPARQL protocol, and are performed over HTTP.

The "Score Calculator" iterates through all of the users with QDOS profile pages, and looks at QDOS's RDFS[35] schema[36] in an attempt to classify the various accounts held by a QDOS user in order to extract numbers that are in turn used to calculate the given user's final score. This mechanism used to process each of the individuals within the QDOS system is described in further detail in section 4 and is presented as a public example of how Garlik makes use of schema driven software.

3.2.1 foaf.qdos.com

foaf.qdos[37] is the experimental part of QDOS, and has a number of publicly available services[38]. The services provided under the foaf.qdos domain run on top of the same 10 million individual strong 4store instance that powers QDOS. foaf.qdos presents application developers and Semantic Web enthusiasts with a number of services that can be used to help make the world of FOAF data a more interconnected experience. There are a large number of FOAF emitting sites which can be found on the Social Web[39] but as it stands, FOAF documents in isolation are not said to be of much use. FOAF documents provide information about an individuals, the `foaf:primaryTopic`, and information regarding people which they claim to know. In order for a social graph to be useful, a list of people claiming to know an individual is said to make all the difference, and this is not possible without an index of FOAF documents. foaf.qdos.com is presented as a perfect example to why, Linked Data on its own, will not suffice, the ability to be able to store high volumes of RDF data, in a quad-format, preserving the document URIs from the data was extracted is presented as key to being able to find information from the Linked Data Cloud – FOAF is only useful when one can both find information about who a given `foaf:Person` knows, and information regarding who claims to know the given `foaf:Person`[40].

The nature of the information stored within the QDOS 4store instance provides a perfect example of why Garlik's motivation to not include reasoning to our RDF stores was a sensible one. FOAF documents harvested from the public Web come with a number of errors, and reasoners do not react well to scruffy data. Examples of such scruffiness include, cut and paste errors, whereby people cut and paste RDF fragments from each others FOAF files, which in turn would make the two individuals merged into one. Other examples include the fact that many peoples FOAF files' include the URL `http://www.google.com/` as their `foaf:homepage`

---

[35] RDF Schema (RDFS) `http://www.w3.org/2000/01/rdf-schema\#`

[36] QDOS Schema `http://qdos.com/schema`

[37] foaf.qdos `http://foaf.qdos.com/`

[38] QDOS's service list `http://qdos.com/apps`

[39] List of FOAF Emitting Site `http://esw.w3.org/FoafSites`

[40] Making FOAF useful slides: `http://foaf.qdos.com/slides/london011209/index.html`

properties, which in turn is an Inverse Functional Property (IFP)[41] of the FOAF ontology, and the semantics of the property state that a `foaf:homepage` is a page describing a `foaf:Person`. If a RDF store with reasoning was used, all of the `foaf:Persons` with the same, incorrect, `foaf:homepage` would be merged into one person. This does not go to say that foaf.qdos does not do any reasoning, it just performs all of its reasoning at query time using the SPARQL query language. Querying are executed over QDOS's 4store instance, that in turn merge `foaf:Persons` based if they share IFPs or if they are said to be `owl:sameAs`[42] of another `foaf:Person` – this is referred to as IFP Triangulation and it is this triangulation that powers most of the services listed below.

The services described below are practical examples of an applications which run off of our 10 million individual strong FOAF based 4store. The current size of our QDOS 4store instance is approximately 2GT.

- **FOAF Index**[43] Provides an ability to search through the 10 million FOAF files harvested, searches can be made for any of FOAF's IFPs[44].
- **FOAF builder**[45] Is a user-interface that allows for people to merge their various FOAF profiles into one, and then to save the RDF data back to their servers, or to a Garlik server if the user does not have access to their web-space.
- **FOAF Validator**[46] Allows for FOAF files to be validated against the FOAF ontology.
- **FOAF Reverse Search**[47] Is a RESTful API, which allows one to find out who claims to know a given FOAF Person.
- **FOAF Forward Search**[48] Is a RESTful API, which allows one to find out who a given FOAF Person claims to know.
- **FOAF SameAs Search**[49] Is a RESTful API, which allows one to find out which other FOAF People are the same as given FOAF Person.
- **Social Verification**[50] This is a RESTful API[51] that can help you use FOAF data to act as a whitelist for blog, email, and other online activity.

---

[41] Inverse Functional Properties `http://esw.w3.org/InverseFunctionalProperty`

[42] `owl:sameAs` relationship from the OWL ontology `http://www.w3.org/TR/owl-ref/\#sameAs-def`

[43] FOAF Index `http://foaf.qdos.com/`

[44] FOAF's IFPs `http://mmt.me.uk/blog/2009/09/07/foaf-ifps/`

[45] FOAF Builder `http://foafbuilder.qdos.com/`

[46] FOAF Validator `http://foaf.qdos.com/validator/`

[47] FOAF Reverse Search `http://foaf.qdos.com/reverse`

[48] FOAF Forward Search `http://foaf.qdos.com/forward`

[49] FOAF SameAs `http://foaf.qdos.com/sameas`

[50] FOAF Social Verification `http://foaf.qdos.com/verify-about`

[51] FOAF Social Verification Demo `http://foaf.qdos.com/verify-about`

4 Schema Driven Software Deployment

As mentioned earlier on the chapter, both DataPatrol and QDOS make use of what we will refer to as "Schema Driven Software Deployment". This technique is employed within Garlik's services in order to be able to deploy new functionality without having incurring any service downtime. Given DataPatrol's requirement of being agile, insofar as being able to search through and index new sources of compromised data as and when they are discovered, allowing for the highest level of protection for its users, the ability to add search rules in an ad-hoc fashion is seen as core to its success. DataPatrol's "Processing Service" (see figure 1) that specialises in finding our customers' personal information in DataPatrol's feeds of compromised data, performs its searches based on an RDF schema that defines the list of data types it wishes to identify. This means that given the identification of a new source of compromised personal information, all that is needed is for a new "RDF Translator" to be implemented, which would capture this new source of potentially harmful data by converting it to RDF, and adding it to DataPatrol's 5store instance. This would be followed by a change to the RDF schema that dictates the functionality of the "Processing Service". Once the change has been made to the search schema, and the new search rules have been added to the 5store instance, the "Processing Service" will then start to search for the newly added information.

A public example of this can be found in the QDOS schema, which in turn operates in a similar fashion. The QDOS schema, which can be found at the following URL `http://qdos.com/schema` contains definitions of a number of service properties[52], e.g. `http://qdos.com/schema\#twitter`, each of which have a canonical URI pattern[53], and a parsing module[54] associated to them. Each of the modules are also described in the QDOS schema, whereby the statistical data in which a given service property generates is listed[55]. As each of the QDOS users are processed by the "Score calculator" backend process, all of their online accounts are matched against the QDOS schema, where the backend process identifies which "RDF Translator" module should be used to gather statistics relevant to that user's given online account. The RDF generated by the various "RDF Translators" is publicly accessible and can be fetched by concatenating `-ext/rdfxml` to the end of given QDOS user's URI, e.g. `http://qdos.com/user/5acc361496df109a7c2967760d5d9792-ext/rdfxml`. It is this statistical data that is used to calculate a given QDOS user's digital status.

The process described above allows Garlik to deploy and add new functionality to its services without the need to restart or re-deploy any of its existing software allowing for maximum service uptime. This gives our developers greater freedom to rapidly deploy software updates, allowing Garlik the ability to react, in an agile manner, to new business requirements as and when they come about.

---

[52] QDOS Service Property `http://qdos.com/schema\#serviceProperty`

[53] QDOS Canonical URI Pattern `http://qdos.com/schema\#canonicalUriPattern`

[54] QDOS Parsing Module `http://qdos.com/schema\#module`

[55] This is listed via the `http://qdos.com/schema\#producesDatum` property

5 Technology and the Need to Scale

Garlik's RDF stores provide facilities over the HTTP protocol to allow access to information held within them. We have already discussed the SPARQL protocol which allows queries to be run over HTTP, but in addition 4store and 5store allow data to be added and removed using the HTTP PUT and DELETE verbs[56].

Using existing, widely implemented HTTP features for data management means that updates can be made by lightweight, asynchronous, loosely coupled parser processes which have little knowledge of the rest of system. An example of this can be seen in figure 1.

The dataset required to run DataPatrol for the current userbase comprises around fifteen billion triples (15 GT) of RDF data. This data comes from a variety of sources, with a variety of different conditions on its use, so tracking of the use of this data is key requirement. When data is imported into the DataPatrol RDF store, meta-data relating to its provenance is imported along with it.

The use of this meta-data for enforcing licencing conditions and providing MI reporting has been previously discussed in section 3.1 however there are additional uses. As new data sources, and new releases of the software do not necessarily happen in synchronisation queries can be written target specific data sources, or exclude ones that are not yet ready for production use.

The schema-less nature of our use of RDF allows these new data sources to be imported into the RDF store without changes to any schemas, or affecting the operation of existing processes. RDF namespacing is used to distinguish new types of data, so existing queries, designed before the inclusion of the new data items will not be presented with new results.

5.1 4store

When Garlik was founded, around 2006, it was realised that RDF data representation would be appropriate for the data problems that the company would face. The expected business requirements were for a system capable of storing one billion RDF triples, and answering queries over this dataset in under ten milliseconds.

In order to meet these goals it was felt it was necessary to engineer a new RDF store (4store [5]), based on clustered software in order to allow access to enough main memory to allow the indexes for the RDF data to be held in RAM, in order to meet the processing speed requirements.

For a RDF dataset consisting of one billion triples, a sustained import speed of seventy thousand triples per second (70kT/s) is required in order to allow the dataset to be restored from backup data in four hours. This meant that import speed was a

---

[56] Infomation on 4store's SPARQL server `http://4store.org/trac/wiki/SparqlServer`

major consideration as it must be possible to restore any business-critical system with a minimum of downtime.

Similarly, it must be possible to make the system tolerant of hardware, or operating system faults, and so the software was made resilient against the loss of a node in the cluster.

As it happens the requirement for one billion triples was optimistic, and the final production system running under 4store contained approximately fifteen billion triples.

In order to keep hardware costs to a reasonable level 4store was designed to run on tens of low cost x86-64 servers running the Linux operating system. Using commodity servers it is possible to run at a density of around 500 million triples per cluster storage node, while maintaining the required import and query performance.

Since its initial development 4store has been replaced within Garlik by a new clustered store with even greater scalability and efficiency. The 4store source code has been made available under the GNU General Public Licence version 3. The ANSI C99 source code and documentation can be found in the project's source code repository[57].

5.2 5store

As 4store's capacity was being stretched by holding fifteen billion triples, and the import performance, of around 150 kT/s was felt to be insufficient it was decided to develop a new generation of RDF store for internal use in Garlik. This new store is named 5store, and has been in production use inside Garlik since June 2009.

5store was developed with extreme scalability in mind. It is designed to operate with clusters of many hundreds of machines, and approaches double the triples per machine density of 4store. Its strengths are performance, scalability and stability in the domain of RDF storage and SPARQL queries. It does not attempt to implement additional features beyond this.

As both 4store and 5store adhere closely to the SPARQL standards, upgrading from one to the other was reassuringly straightforward. No software changes were required within the application layer, and all the data generated by the conversion processes could be used without change. This contrasts starkly with our experiences of working with differing RDBMS storage systems, where migrations from one system to another brings a host of incompatibility issues.

5.2.1 Platform

5store was designed from scratch for clusters of up to 1,000 machines and scale of over 1 Trillion (10^{12}) triples should be easily achievable given a large enough

---

[57] 4store source code repository http://github.com/garlik/4store

cluster. Given the new indexing algorithms deployed, there is no effective limit on the number of triples stored, rather it is constrained by the practicalities of cluster size, network speed and so on. 5store is implemented in ANSI C99 and C++. It makes use of custom discovery and clustering technologies and proprietary, novel indexing algorithms. It is primarily intended to run on 64-bit Linux platforms with high RAM density.

5.2.2 Performance

5store maintains similar query performance to 4store, but even greater emphasis is placed on import performance. With increasing sizes of production RDF stores the time taken to reimport data into a system is becoming even more important. 5store comfortably achieves sustained import speeds of a million triples per second on a 16 node cluster, allowing a ten billion triple store to be restored in under three hours.

6 Conclusions

- **Practicality** The capabilities of the SPARQL 1.0 query language are somewhat limited compared to typical SQL[58] implementations. This often means that more processing work is required in the application layer, and can mean that more queries are required to answer the same question, compared to a SQL-based implementation. However, this is offset by the convenience of the high degree of standardisation between stores, and the high degree of flexibility in data representation.
- **HTTP+RDF** All of our services communicate using RDF. The consequences of this are that we achieve a high degree of flexibility with respect to staged deployments incorporating new capabilities.
- **Cost Effectiveness** Despite the high engineering effort involved in developing two cluster-based RDF stores, we feel that overall this effort was well justified. The data volumes that can be held by 5store in particular are similar to those held in Key-Value stores, but yet we have access to a standard, and relatively sophisticated query language that supports very efficient join operations.
- **Reliability and Uptime** There is inevitably some concern when deploying software on top of a newly developed database system, however we have been operating our production system on 4store and 5store for several years now, while retaining high uptime, and without data loss. Engineering of the storage system for robustness, and the use of redundant clusters has helped in this area, and we do not feel that we suffered any more downtime that if we had gone for a more traditional RDBMS.

---

[58] Standard Query Language http://en.wikipedia.org/wiki/SQL

7 Future Work

Future work in this area includes further work in the 5store RDF store, increasing the storage density, scalability and query performance. Increasing the efficiency has a direct impact on the operating costs of the business and is a high priority.

The increasing use of RDF data in public sector data publishing[59] has the potential to be a great benefit to the business, and we will be pursuing opportunities to make use of this data within the company in the near future.

We are also exploring the implementation of the SPARQL 1.1 standard, while retaining the high performance and scalability that is essential to the operation our business.

Acknowledgements This work described in this chapter has been undertaken by Garlik Limited, Garlik was founded by Mike Harris, founding CEO of Egg plc, former Egg CIO Tom Ilube, and former British Computer Society president Professor Nigel Shadbolt. As the first company to develop a web-scale commercial application of Semantic Technology, Garlik enables consumers to find and understand what personal information is in the public domain about them and manage how their identities appear online.

Garlik appointed world-class technology experts to advise the business, including Professor Dame Wendy Hall CBE from the University of Southampton and Sir Tim Berners-Lee.

Garlik is backed by three of the UK's leading blue chip investment firms, Encore/DFJ Esprit, Doughty Hanson, and Noble Venture Finance.

References

1. Bizer, C., Cyganiak, R., Heath, T.: How to publish linked data on the web. Web page (2007). URL http://www4.wiwiss.fu-berlin.de/bizer/pub/LinkedDataTutorial/. Revised 2008. Accessed 07/08/2009
2. Carroll, J.J., Bizer, C., Hayes, P., Stickler, P.: Named graphs, provenance and trust. In: WWW 05: Proceedings of the 14th international conference on World Wide Web, pp. 613622. ACM, New York, NY, USA (2005). URL http://portal.acm.org/citation.cfm?doid=1060745.1060835
3. Fielding, R.T., Taylor, R.N.: Principled design of the modern web architecture. ACM Trans. Internet Technol. 2(2), 115150 (2002). DOI 10.1145/514183.514185. URL http://dx.doi.org/10.1145/514183.514185
4. Harris, S., Gibbins, N.: 3store: Efficient bulk RDF storage. In: PSSS03, pp. 115. Sanibel, Fl (2003)
5. Harris, S., Lamb, N., Shadbolt, N.: 4store: The design and implementation of a clustered RDF store. In: ISWC 2009 SSWS Workshop 09. Washington DC (2009). URL http://4store.org/publications/harris-ssws09.pdf
6. Manola, F., Miller, E.: RDF primer: W3C recommendation (2004). URL http://www.w3.org/TR/rdf-primer/
7. W3C: SPARQL query language for RDF, working draft. Tech. rep., World Wide Web Consortium (2005). URL http://www.w3.org/TR/rdf-sparql-query/

---

[59] UK Public Sector Data http://data.gov.uk/

Standardizing Legal Content with OWL and RDF

Constantine Hondros

Abstract

Wolters Kluwer is one of the largest legal publishers in the world. Its various publishing units use a multitude of different formats to mark up what is effectively similar content. We describe a common content architecture based on OWL, RDF and XHTML that is used to build a standard representation of legal content, allowing publishable assets to be integrated across the enterprise. This architecture is governed by an OWL ontology that models the (occasionally complex) behaviour of legal documents and acts as a domain model of common legal metadata. How do OWL and RDF scale up to real-world publishing? We describe practical issues in producing and validating RDF on an industrial scale; in performance management; in handling fragmented ontologies; and the challenge of using RDF in a performant XSLT pipeline.

1 Introduction

1.1 The problem domain

Wolters Kluwer is one of the biggest Legal, Tax and Regulatory (LTR) publishers in the world. With dozens of business units publishing in at least a dozen languages to mainly vertical markets, it relies on content formats as diverse as XML, SGML, relational data, RTF, and comma-separated-values to drive its editorial and publishing activities. This diverse data landscape obstructs the reusability of content across its

Constantine Hondros

Wolters Kluwer, Zuidpoolsingel 2, 2408 ZE Alphen aan den Rijn, The Netherlands, e-mail: `Constantine.Hondros@wolterskluwer.com`

D. Wood (ed.), *Linking Enterprise Data*, DOI 10.1007/978-1-4419-7665-9_11,

vertical markets and presents a challenge to streamlining the content supply chain technology stack used by business units.

Standardizing the content formats used by the various publishing units could unleash tremendous benefits. Product innovation would be stimulated by allowing novel combinations of content to be assembled, catering for the long tail of publishing. Content supply chains could be built around standardized technology components, realizing cost savings by centralizing development and maintenance. Further, by standardizing around the W3C standards OWL (Web Ontology Language)[1] and RDF (Resource Description Framework)[2], Wolters Kluwer would be positioned to take advantage of paradigm shifts such as Linked Data, which are based on the same standards and which may turn out to be game-changers for the publishing world.

1.2 Application of Semantic Web technologies

Semantic Web technologies are a promising match for this problem, and an ongoing project within Wolters Kluwer has used the standards OWL, RDF and RDFa to define a common standard to represent legal content. Most legal content is textual, designed to be read by humans; however its most complex aspect is the metadata that publishers enrich it with. We take the approach of modeling this metadata in an OWL ontology which serves, in a data integration sense, as a reference model. Metadata captured in any syntax and deriving from any publishing unit can - as long as it shares the same semantics - be abstracted into the concepts defined in this ontology.

RDF is a useful framework for data integration. By using URIs to identify entities and model relationships between them, it simplifies integrating data from heterogeneous sources that implicitly share those entities. For example, every publishing unit maintains controlled vocabularies of courts and geographic regions that overlap with other publishing units'; however since everyone uses different formats and identifiers, the data cannot be combined. RDF ensures that the data from one publishing unit is compatible with the data from another, and where the same entity is being referred to (for example, the European Court of Justice) the same URI can be used to identify it.

OWL meanwhile offers a set of modeling features that allow ontologies - effectively domain models - to be created. Features such as the ability to define class hierarchies and the ability to define restrictions such as cardinality constraints offer sufficient expression to describe the metadata domains used by legal publishers. Certainly, an RDF predicate vocabulary alone could not provide a satisfactory modeling space.

Our common standard is used internally in Wolters Kluwer as an intermediate content format that can be used to integrate and aggregate content from multiple publishing units. Although we make heavy use of OWL and RDF, resources are not linked as such since they are not dereferenceable over HTTP. We also do not (yet) attempt to push RDF content to customer-facing sites, or to link our RDF data to the LOD cloud. These activities will hopefully come within the scope of future applications for our standard.

2 Toward a Common Legal Content Format

Legal content follows a different life-cycle to other content forms. Much of it is created by governmental or legal institutions which release, or sell, a constant stream of legislative material such as legal Acts, amendments to existing Acts, details of court cases, and articles of Jurisprudence. The role of publishers in this scenario is to add value to this content, primarily by aggregating and enriching it with metadata, and then to repackage it and sell it on. By adding useful facts and classifications to the data, they enable customers to interact with the information in useful, time-saving ways. For example, publishers spend great effort maintaining a history of all the revisions and amendments to legal Acts so that customers can have an intuitive overview of all the previous states of a Law. An online product that leverages this state history offers productivity to a lawyer, and is a compelling purchase.

As electronic publishers, all Wolters Kluwer publishing units perform some sort of content modeling that allows them to enrich source content with a layer of meta-data. The more traditional publishing units use proprietary DTD or XSD grammars to capture the original legal text with inline metadata where it is required. More sophisticated publishing units on the other hand have evolved a different approach. Source content, which consists mostly of block-level text, is captured efficiently by light-weight tagging schemes that effectively mark up document structure. The metadata that semantically annotates this content for example, by classifying it, and explicitly associating it with related content - is held separately in rich, complex databases. This latter approach - the logical separation of content from its metadata is considered a best-practice within Wolters Kluwer. It offers a flexibility that is not present with monolithic XML grammars, and is reflected in the ability to innovate new products with a shorter time-to-market.

This observation inspired the use of RDF to model a common content standard. The separation of textual content from its annotating metadata sounds remarkably similar to the vision of using RDF on the Semantic Web, where web resources, both text and binary, can be freely annotated by a cobweb of RDF metadata drawn from any number of RDF vocabularies. The strongly-typed data model and URI-based addressing of RDF provide a standards-based approach to separate metadata from its content.

However, the metadata models used by different business units - that is, the set of properties and annotations they use to enrich and classify their own legal content have evolved separately to serve different markets, and may be fundamentally in-compatible. Is there way to unite them? This is where OWL comes into play. One of OWLs use cases is to bridge between heterogeneous information models by providing an explicit, unambiguous view of a domain. The motivation behind using OWL was to create a single domain ontology to capture the common, overlapping parts of the metadata models being employed by different business units. In data integration terms, it could act as a reference model: by mapping the metadata of any business unit to the reference model, it should be possible to create an abstraction of that metadata using a common, standardized vocabulary of OWL classes and RDF predicates.

So our approach towards a common legal content format is based on the observed best practice of a strong separation between content and metadata. While XHTML provides a mature vocabulary of elements to mark up primary legal content, RDF provides the framework to annotate that content with metadata. Finally OWL provides the modeling sophistication to unify different metadata models with a common RDF representation.

3 OWL Ontology

The backbone of our common standard is a multi-module OWL ontology. This has number of purposes. It contains a rich set of common metadata properties which can be used to provide an RDF representation of a legal documents metadata. Further, it models what you might call the structural behaviour of legal documents: it contains predicates and classes which bind XHTML structural elements to a complex document model, where for example the status of particular fragments (pending, in force, repealed) needs to be tracked in time. Thirdly, it models knowledge structures such as controlled vocabularies through specialization of SKOS[3] properties.

3.1 Creating the ontology

The ontology itself was created in the OWL-Full dialect, using the Protégé ontology editor. We deliberately took a modular approach where each module is assigned a different namespace. This aids the overall maintainability of the ontology. For example, we create small extensions when new publishing unit content models are mapped to the ontology; the generous use of namespaces keeps these properties visibly separate and makes it easier for a working group to take ownership of a module.

3.1.1 Metadata properties

Although a number of OWL ontologies already exist for modeling legal content, we determined that there was no possibility of reusing existing work. None sufficiently captured the domain of common metadata used by Wolters Kluwer publishing units. The only way to model our domain properly was to do our own homework. This involved setting up a cross-border working group of local content experts who pooled knowledge on their respective content models. This expert group was able to distill about 180 semantically unique, but common, legal metadata properties which were captured in the ontology.

Modeling these properties was more complex than creating a vocabulary of RDF datatype and object predicates. For example, domain properties such as "Bibliographic Information" can themselves consist of a number of properties such as multiple Journal citations, page numbers, and various date values. For complex properties like these, we needed to create an ontology class to act as an aggregator for the composite properties.

In other situations we needed to define custom XSD datatypes to handle lexical variants used by different publishing units. For instance, although every publishing unit has metadata properties based on a date-time value, the precision of those values differs; rather than forcing everyone to use the highest precision, we created a custom catch-all datatype that can validate all variants.

Another area which required complex modeling was relationships. Legal metadata is rich with semantically precise relationships. The modifying relation, for example, captures the complex situation that a new Legal Act modifies parts of other Acts, for example by repealing (reversing) them or by causing an amendment to them. This sort of relationship needs to be modeled by an OWL class which identifies the resource performing the modifying (the modifying Act), the resources affected (other Acts, or articles of Acts), and the nature of the modification (for example, repealment). We use intermediate classes called Arcs to link the relationship individual to its various resources, rather than simple predicates. This allows the Arc itself to be annotated with metadata if necessary.

Heavy-weight OWL modeling like this requires some adeptness with the features of OWL and RDFS rather than just RDF. For example, subclass and subproperty hierarchies are extremely useful when trying to create semantic variants of a type. Also the cardinality constraints built into OWL are vital for semantic capture: a modifying relation, for example, must only have one modifying Act.

3.1.2 Document model

The document model is a set of OWL classes and properties which model the structure, and the behaviour through time, of legal documents. While simple legal documents fit easily into the block-level structure of XHTML, more complex legal documents require dedicated modeling. For example, an Act might consist of a large number of articles, each of which can be modified, move into a particular legal state, or be removed at any time and independently of its peers. Our ontology contains a specific module containing classes and predicates that XHTML structures can use to bind themselves to this model. This allows an XHTML fragment such as a div to behave as a more complex document entity, for example as a law article with a particular life-span in the history of its containing Act.

3.1.3 Knowledge structures

All Wolters Kluwer publishing units use knowledge structures to augment their information architecture. These structures are typically used to provide fine-grained classifications of documents and to aid indexing and information retrieval. For example, a publishing unit might maintain a taxonomy of business fields, and explicitly associate legal cases with a point in this hierarchy to provide classifications such as (paraphrased) "Related to regional disputes in exploration & mining rights in the Petrochemical industry".

Knowledge structures like these can be used to drive all sorts of advanced features such as accurate relevancy ranking and faceted search at the content delivery side. When it came to modeling them, rather than reinventing the wheel, our ontology reuses the dedicated W3C standard SKOS. However, we model both controlled vocabularies and individuals (instances) carefully to ensure strong typing of the individuals in these vocabularies. Range constraints on metadata properties which make use of controlled vocabularies mean that only an individual of the correct type can be set as the value.

3.2 Domain Ontology Mapping

A goal of the ontology is to act as a reference model, normalizing metadata models from different publishing units. In other words, we perform a domain ontology mapping: we explicitly map metadata properties from publishing units onto the domain established by the ontology. This, in our experience, is a task that it is impossible to automate, and must be performed by teamwork between local content experts and ontology experts.

We are helped by the flexibility of OWL as a language and the ability to easily create subclasses and subproperties based on entities in the core ontology. Our strategy is this: if the mapping process discovers metadata values that are unique to a business unit and do not yet exist in the reference model, then those new values are either brought into the core ontology, or added to a thin extension layer for use by that publishing unit alone. This extension layer is created as an OWL module that imports and builds on the core ontology modules.

The end result of this mapping process is two-fold. Firstly, we can have some confidence that the full metadata domain of a particular publishing unit is captured in the ontology; and secondly, we have a set of mappings that can act as a specification for publishing units to actually transform their source metadata, whatever its native form - SGML, XML, database dump, CSV file - into RDF. This RDF can be programmatically validated for integrity against the ontology.

4 Content Architecture

The design goal of separating content from metadata, coupled with an ontology that can integrate heterogeneous metadata models has enabled a common content architecture for representing legal content. This is completely based on World Wide Web Consortium (W3C) standards. It uses XHTML to define textual document instances; it uses inline RDFa to identify significant locations in those documents and bind them to ontology classes; and it uses RDF to associate metadata with those document instances and to inter-relate them. All the RDF statements necessary to bind the XHTML to RDF and to annotate it with metadata are governed by our multi-module, extensible OWL ontology.

4.1 Modularized XHTML + RDFa for Textual Content

To represent textual content, we use the XHTML standard. This mature W3C standard is well-suited to the task, with its rich set of block-level and paragraph-level elements. However, since we use it primarily as a vehicle for textual content, we do not require all of its features. So starting from the modularized version of XHTML 1.1[4] we developed our own custom vocabulary which excludes a number of standard modules that are not useful for representing textual content. For example, the script element, the object element, and behavioural inline attributes such as on-MouseClick are all excluded.

We also extended our vocabulary with a module that defines the attributes in the RDFa[5] specification. This is done so that we can use RDFa to bind XHTML elements to the classes and properties of our document model, allowing significant document fragments to be recognised as entities compliant with this model.

For example, a simple XHTML div element might contain content relating to a unique article of Legislation. We use the RDFa about attribute to assign it a globally unique URI; we use the typeof attribute to assign it a particular fragment class from our document model. Now the div is something more than an XHTML element: it is an RDF resource which can be used to anchor whatever metadata the document model specifies should exist for its class. For example, articles of Law can be versioned across time, so each article instance must contain metadata stating the date range for which it is in force.

The document model caters for the fact that legal articles change frequently, although only one may be in force at any one time. Therefore, an entirely different XHTML div element reusing the same resource identifier might be used to carry a different version of this article, which is permitted by the ontology as long as its metadata specifies a different time period for which it is in force.

It is worth emphasising that we do not expect RDFa crawlers to make sense of, or even to see this wire-frame RDF structure we embed in XHTML instances. It is done purely in the context of a closed content supply chain, and it is utilised by our RDF-aware processing software at production time. For example, our software can easily calculate the set of article versions that are in force on a particular date and assemble these into a view (the so-called point-in-time view of a Law) which can be delivered by a web application. In the future, of course, it would be nice to think that intelligent RDF-aware agents could perform this dynamic assembly themselves.

Note too that we do not use RDFa to embed general document metadata. Instead we ask for it to be delivered side-by-side in an RDF/XML file (see next section). This is purely for pragmatic reasons: most legal metadata does not have an equivalent text node in the document it relates to, so there is little to actually mark up with RDFa. So, for a clean separation of concerns, we use RDFa only for marking up document structure.

4.2 RDF for Metadata, Relations and Classifications

With textual content marked up as XHTML and overlaid by a wire-frame structure of resource identifiers with RDFa, we can use RDF to enrich that content with metadata. The set of classes and predicates defined in our reference ontology is used to build for each XHTML document instance an RDF representation of the metadata properties that enrich it.

Such properties range from simple, datatype RDF predicates such as a shortTitle (an abbreviated title that a browser can use when screen real-estate is limited, like in a navigation tree), or language, to more complex properties that need to be modeled with a class. Such a property is applicablePeriod, which needs to have a start-date and an end-date specified to represent a time period for which an entity is legally applicable.

For the purposes of clustering information, we have a number of complex classes that serve to aggregate related data. For example, the class *ltr:ReferenceInformation* is a container for bibliographic information that can contain literally dozens of datatype and object properties.

Where the value of a metadata property is an entity from a known controlled vocabulary such as a specific court or geographic region, those entities are modeled as SKOS concepts. For example, this is how we might set the court that was responsible for a particular judgement:

```
[]  ltr : court  <http :// wolterskluwer . com/ courts / iCourt.1576>
```

The court itself is a SKOS concept which may be defined elsewhere in a controlled vocabulary of values:

```
<http :// wolterskluwer . com/ court / iCourt.1576>
    a  ltr : Court  ;
    a  skos : Concept  ;
    skos : prefLabel  Hoge  Raad @ nl  ;
    skos : prefLabel  High  Court  of  the  Netherlands @ en  .
```

Our complex classes can freely use a mixture of datatype and object properties. In the example below, we use a class called *ltr:Contributor*, which is a richer version of the Dublin Core notion of "contributor". This class has properties for the name of the contributor and their biography, as well as the specific role of that contributor.

```
[]   ltr:contributor   [
rdf:type  ltr:Contributor  ;
ltr:contributorName  John  Adams^^xsd:string  ;
ltr:contributor.Role
  <http://wolterskluwer.com/ltr/roles/iRole.005>  ;
ltr:biography [
  cw:textLiteral  Gained LLB from Oxford in 1983 ;
  cw:textLiteral  Frequently acts as expert witness ;
  ] .
] .
```

The specific role of the contributor is also taken from a controlled vocabulary of values:

```
<http://wolterskluwer.com/ltr/roles/iRole.005>  a  ltr:Role  ;
  a skos:Concept ;
  skos:prefLabel  Expert witness@en .
```

Further forms of metadata are relationships between resources. Publishing units have evolved a rich set of structures to classify the sorts of relationships that typically exist between legal documents. For example, a piece of expert commentary from a legal professional has a particular semantic relationship with the fragment of law that it annotates. Relations like these can be captured using dedicated ontology classes as in the following example:

```
[]  a  ltr:CommentRelation;
  ltr:commentArc [
    a  ltr:CommentArc  ;
    cc:target <http://wolterskluwer.com/Comment001> .
  ] .
ltr:commentedArc [
    a  ltr:CommentedArc  ;
    cc:target <http://wolterskluwer.com/Law/IIC2013> .
  ] .
```

The relation explicitly relates a fragment of legal commentary with the legal Act it comments upon. In real usage, both the relation and the arcs might hold further metadata; for example, the arcs might contain labels giving a human-readable indication of the relation.

5 Working with RDF in a Content Supply Chain

Our current usage of OWL and RDF leverages their ability to enable *data integration*: We use them to define a common content format that any business unit can use to losslessly encode its content, as long as the effort of mapping its metadata domain to our ontology has been made. None of our RDF is actually published to the LOD cloud, or even deployed so that it is dereferenceable by its URI (although I qualify this statement with a '*yet*'), so any RDF we produce lives out its days within the confines of a content supply chain.

Using RDF in a closed-world production environment brings challenges all of its own. We do not have to worry about data provenance (after all, most content management systems track content during its life-cycle), or trust, or entity disambiguation (we do not mesh our data with LOD data). However, both data integrity and performance are critical factors and concerns that we have had to address directly to win the trust of business units.

5.1 The Open World Enigma

A major issue is that OWL makes the so-called open world assumption: it assumes that you always have an incomplete view of data, so limits the conclusions you can draw from the absence of data in your dataset. Absent data is just considered not to have been discovered yet. As a concrete example, if an ontology defines a class called Document with a functional property identifier, no OWL tool will complain if a Document is found without an identifier. The identifier just has not been discovered yet.

This assumption is ideal for agents consuming RDF from distributed knowledge-systems such as the LOD cloud. It lends a certain tolerance to incomplete data that aids incremental knowledge discovery and the ability to merge data from different sources. However, content supply chains are generally closed worlds from end to end, environments where the certitude of data is critical, and the absence of information signifies error. What use is a legal document without an identifier, or a court decision without a court? Such things can never exist in our tightly controlled editorial systems, and should never make their way to delivery platforms. Therefore, in order to guarantee the integrity of data converted into our common format, we were forced to add a layer of custom data sanity checks which are executed in addition to RDF consistency checks.

5.2 Ensuring RDF Data Integrity

To ensure adequate data integrity, we created a Java-based tool that publishing units make use of during content transformations. It imposes a number of constraints on XHTML/RDFa and RDF/XML content packages that, if unchecked, would give rise to fatal production errors in later stages of the content supply chain. For example, it imposes a partial closed-world on the content being validated: we simply cannot permit certain critical data to be missing. For performance, these rules are written in Java when RDF data is being addressed, or in Schematron where XHTML is concerned.

The backbone, of course, of any RDF-aware application is the consistency check, which in our toolset is provided by Pellet. This checks, for a given knowledge base, the logical consistency of RDF instance data () against the theorems contained in the knowledge base (), providing for example datatype checking on literal values, or checks on disjointness. In a data production environment it is tempting to think of this as something similar to an XML-parse against a schema, but it is actually just a prerequisite for inference to take place using the open-world assumption, so does not behave at all in the way that content engineers might expect.

For example, the RDF data model deliberately allows a graph to contain absolutely any predicate or type, as long as it is correctly and uniquely namespaced. But even when such ABox data is consistency-checked in context of a particular TBox, unknown properties are accepted without comment by the reasoner. In other words, your RDF data can contain random garbage triples created by a typing error and no natural trick of reasoning will alert you. While this freedom of expression is entirely in the open world spirit, we felt it prudent to be more rigourous with our core ontology namespaces. We implemented a validation that would flag an error if a predicate or type unknown to those namespaces was encountered in an RDF graph: such things could only exist through transformation error.

Controlled vocabularies provided another scenario where we needed to bolster basic consistency checks. Many metadata properties in our core ontology have their range specified using the owl:AllValuesFrom constraint, where the ontology contains a specific set of individuals typed by the range class. Although this sort of OWL constraint looks and reads like a data constraint ("this property may use only the following set of individuals as a value"), the behaviour of a reasoner is quite different: a Pellet consistency check raises no complaint if a random resource is provided as a value; the inference is that the random resource is also an instance of the range class. This is counter-productive in a closed world scenario, so we impose our own check to ensure that all cited instances of controlled vocabularies are indeed members of those controlled vocabularies.

Another area that requires additional sanity checks is document structure: as described earlier, we embed RDFa statements in XHTML documents to elevate critical document constructs to the RDF level, for example, a base identifier for the document, the document type, the root fragment, and so on. If some of these statements are missing from the graph that is distilled from the document, then it is a serious data problem; however, it is not easy to check for the "completeness" of an RDF graph. Therefore we enforce a Schematron ruleset on the XHTML/RDFa instance to ensure that the graph extracted from it will be complete.

In general, we work hard to impose the sort of data integrity taken for granted in the publishing world. This is not helped by the fact that OWL restrictions such as *owl:AllClassesFrom* and *owl:CardinalityConstraint* look like, but do not behave like, integrity constraints. We believe that our supply chain would be more robust and simpler to set up if constraints could be more easily specified than by coding them. This has been noted by the semantic community[6][7] and there are already some promising developments from semantic technology vendors, such as TopQuadrants SPIN[1] and Clark & Parsias Pellet Integrity Constraint Validator[2]. This is good news, as currently we fear that the lack of obvious constraint checking mechanisms may hamper the adoption of OWL and RDF in scenarios where high data integrity is required.

5.3 Managing Fragmented Ontologies

Running the sorts of checks described above requires a certain nimbleness with run-time ontology handling. Our core ontology is modularized into several dozen OWL files related by imports, and we also maintain a number of extensions containing classes and predicates specific to particular publishing units. Further, each publishing unit provides us with a number of controlled vocabularies, some of which are very large and for performance reasons should only be loaded when needed; the Polish vocabulary of regional districts, for example, contains almost thirteen thousand *skos:Concept* entries.

We have found that a convenient way to manage this tangle of modules and instance data is to create an ontology of ontologies. Using a simple OWL vocabulary, we define instances of *CompoundOntology*, where each instance defines a set of TBox (ontology) modules, ABox (instance) data such as controlled vocabularies, and other crucial files such as custom XSD datatypes. Each such compound ontology defines a working set of common and custom artifacts that is needed to process a single publishing units content.

This method of managing fragmented ontologies gives us the flexibility to only load into memory what is useful given the processing context. For example, a consistency check on document metadata does not bother to load controlled vocabulary instances as the check cannot ensure that cited instances of vocabularies are actually defined. (Instead, we target this with a custom validation).

5.4 Managing Performance

Performance and memory management are still issues in RDF processing. The APIs and tools that our solution depends on, providing services such as data access, persistence, consistency checking and query, are not as performant as equivalent tools from the XML or relational database domains. While it is only a matter of time before mainstream RDF tools offer close or similar performance, it is surprising what performance gains can be made given a talented development team and the incentive to innovate.

---

[1] Retrieved 25 May, 2010 from http://www.topquadrant.com/products/SPIN.html
[2] Retrieved 25 May, 2010 from http://clarkparsia.com/pellet/icv/

One strategy was to create, and cache, our own Java representations of compound ontologies rather than relying on API models such as Jena or Sesame. A cached ontology is a light-weight representation of an ontology serialised as a Java object. Its class and property hierarchies are already calculated, and for many run-time operations it can be used instead of the ontology itself, preventing the expensive operation of loading and classifying ontologies each time they are required. For example, our requirements for reasoning services are limited to materialising certain triples if they are not provided by the publishing unit. We find it very performant to do our own inferencing using the calculated class and property hierarchies available in the cache rather than perform heavy-weight inferencing using Pellet.

We also try hard to streamline consistency checking with Pellet. Since our ontologies are modularized and related via a configuration ontology, we are able to dynamically assemble a for consistency checking. So when an RDF graph only contains predicates and types from certain parts of the ontology, it can be merged with a small, custom TBox containing only the necessary modules for consistency checks. (This fails to produce significant performance benefits, however, and we assume that such optimisations have already been built into Pellet).

Performance profiles of consistency checks also revealed a clear correlation between performance and graph size that can really make itself felt in a supply-chain situation. Processing thousands of small RDF graphs means more time is spent initializing the reasoner than actually checking the data; large graphs on the other hand (hundreds of thousands, or millions of triples) can rapidly cause even high-end machines to run out of memory. Our optimisation is to dynamically merge and chunk RDF graphs into efficient chunks before passing them for consistency checks. This avoids the overhead of initializing the reasoner too frequently, and by capping the model size at 250,000 triples, we avoid exceptionally large RDF serializations causing our validation tool to choke on memory.

5.5 Using RDF with XSLT

At production time, we transform packages containing XHTML/RDFa and RDF/XML into an XML vocabulary recognised by a online delivery platform. This is a typical publishing transformation which closes the loop between a content management or production system and a customer-facing delivery system. We implemented an XSLT transformation pipeline to perform this; however the act of converting RDF to XML (a process called "lowering") with XSLT forced some improvisation.

Firstly, there is no standard way to process RDF with XSLT, although a number of initiatives do exist, including RDF Twig[3] for XSLT-based access to an RDF graph, XSLT+SPARQL[4] which enables SPARQL queries to be executed from

---

[3] Retrieved 25 May, 2010 from http://rdftwig.sourceforge.net/
[4] Retrieved 25 May, 2010 http://berrueta.net/research/xsltsparql

within XSLT, and the XSPARQL language[5] (currently a W3C member submission). Further, the standard XML serialisation of RDF (RDF/XML) is problematic for XSLT processing because it does not provide the sort of consistent, hierarchical structure that the XPath data model requires: RDF/XML permits different serializations of the same graph.

We experimented with a number of ways of selecting and passing RDF to XSLT. The most obvious approach was to use SPARQL within the transformation pipeline to select the RDF to be serialised in the output document. This yields a result-set in the W3C standard SRX format[8].

This approach suffers in a couple of ways. SPARQL is not a particularly efficient way to perform selection or pruning on an RDF graph. Even after optimising the way result-sets were handled (by keeping them in-memory), XSLT-based processing of the SRX result-set was unacceptably slow. This turned out to be due to the structure of the SRX format itself, which is essentially a flat and little-nested list of <result> elements, each containing a variable binding and a value. Typically the XSLT developer needs to query this structure multiple times from different templates, each time accessing a single value; for large result-sets, this equates to spectacularly inefficient XPath execution because of the flat nature of the document tree.

To squeeze better performance out of our XSLT pipeline, we now approach the problem another way. We have defined a number of Java extension functions that can be accessed from XSLT to return the value(s) of a named RDF property. These are essentially a façade to a Jena model containing the full superset of document metadata. If the return value is not just a single RDF literal value but a graph itself, then the graph is put into a canonical RDF/XML form to optimise it for post-processing: for example, any blank nodes are expanded inline to simplify data accessibility with XPath. The RDF/XML fragment is passed back to the calling XSLT template as a DOM object where it can be directly interrogated.

This sort of solution is not for the faint-hearted and was forced upon us given the importance of performance in our pipeline. We feel that there is currently a gap for a standard, performant technology to bridge between RDF and XSLT; whether this ends up being based on SPARQL or some other standard remains to be seen. However, it is also true that while XSLT is a vital tool in the publishing arsenal, it may be of limited value to developers working with RDF in real linked data scenarios, where the graphical demands of mashing up RDF may require more powerful GUI solutions such as Adobe Flex or Microsoft Silverlight.

6 Enabling Large-Scale Triple Production

Our RDF production scenario involves suppliers (publishing units) taking responsibility for transforming their own content to a hybrid of XHTML/RDFa and RD-

---

F/XML. It is rare (although not unknown) to find expertise in either RDF or OWL in such publishing units, and the content engineering skills that we were able to leverage were based on solid experience of DTD or XSD processing with tools such as XSLT and Omnimark, as well as the ubiquitous relational database and SQL.

The flexibility of RDF requires quite a mind-shift for developers. While RD-F/XML is the most obvious delivery format for them to provide, they are surprised to find that it has no XSD schema to validate against; it is also a surprise that equivalent RDF graphs can be serialized in different ways because of the ability to create typed nodes. This just represents ambiguity for a XML content engineer. Which serialization should be used?

Similarly, database programmers are suspicious of a data model that has far less API support than, for example, the area of object-relational mapping (although this shortcoming is currently being addressed by commercial vendors).

It became clear that without waiting for suppliers to embrace RDF - at which point we could presumably just hand them an ontology as a specification - we would have to provide assistance to jump-start the delivery of production-sized RDF batches.

6.1 Experimental XSD generation

One approach we tried was to generate XML schema from our ontology. The idea was for developers to use these to guide the process of creating high quality RD-F/XML document instances from proprietary SGML or XML formats. Essentially, the schema were pre-populated with elements representing typed RDF nodes relating to classes and predicates in the ontology. We tried where possible to model ontology constraints such as cardinalities and functional properties in the schema. We expected the schema to leverage the abundant XSLT skills in publishing units without requiring significant RDF awareness, and also to result in better data integrity, for example by reflecting ontology constraints and validating RDF literal values against their specified datatype.

The approach was well-intentioned but failed for a number of reasons. There is a real problem in trying to wrap a context-free grammar such as XSD around an ontology. The very freedoms that make ontologies attractive for domain modeling make them absurdly hard to constrain using the modeling assertions that are available in XSD.

For example, we were forced to limit the set of elements which could be children of the root element *rdf:RDF* simply to make the schema readable. But this was an artificial constraint: the only way to support the RDF principle that anyone can say anything about anything[6] in XML schema would be to make every type in the ontology available as a child element of the document element *rdf:RDF*. In an ontology containing hundreds of classes, this is simply unworkable.

---

[6]   Retrieved   6   June,   2010   from   http://www.w3.org/TR/2002/WD-rdf-concepts-20020829/#xtocid48014

Consider too the many ontology properties with a domain of *owl:Thing*. These all had to be made available as optional elements underneath every typed node. These repeating blocks of elements for example, the various SKOS label properties - turned up everywhere with little apparent purpose. They made the generated schema resemble a jungle of options and watered down the intended value, which was to provide an unequivocal and informative guide to encoding document metadata in RDF/XML.

In short, while our skilled developers could rapidly prototype XSLT templates using worked examples, they struggled to make sense of the generated schema. Our advice to anyone attempting this route is: dont bother!

6.2 RDFBeans

Another RDF production scenario we faced involved creating RDF from relational databases. This represented a somewhat intractable problem: large-scale RDF generation from databases is an area that is still the focus of research, rather than being addressed by mature, commercial implementations. As noted by the W3C RDB2RDF Incubator Group, a number of different strategies are currently being explored[7].

Our requirement was primarily the fast, large-scale production of serialised RDF/XML using the classes and predicates defined by our ontology. According to the categorization framework developed by the RDB2RDF group, this paradigm is referred to as Domain Ontology Mapping. It is basically data transformation: relational data is extracted from a database as RDF resources, typed by classes and related by predicates defined by a particular domain ontology. We had no need for ad hoc querying of databases for RDF data, or for querying multiple heterogeneous databases simultaneously; these would have involved more complex solutions. We just needed fast dumps of triples.

The closest available tools that suited our needs were [8] and Virtuoso RDF Views. The former was only in version 0.4 at the time of selection, and appeared to perform poorly in the Berlin [9] so was discounted. The latter, although a supported commercial tool, did not offer enough flexibility to perform our domain ontology mapping, and would have required publishing units to host the Virtuoso platform alongside their production systems. (Note that we did not perform an exhaustive assessment of the available options at the time).

Given that and knowledge were plentiful on the publishing unit side, we decided on a solution that leveraged these skills. This involved generating a set of RDF-aware JavaBeans from ontology classes. In the generated API, each bean class represents a class from the ontology, and exposes getter and setter methods for each object or datatype property that the ontology permits on that class. Beans are RDF-

[7] See http://esw.w3.org/Rdb2RdfXG/StateOfTheArt, last accessed 6 June 2010

[8] Retrieved 6 June, 2010 from http://www4.wiwiss.fu-berlin.de/bizer/d2rq/

[9] Retrieved 6 June, http://www4.wiwiss.fu-berlin.de/bizer/BerlinSPARQLBenchmark/

aware in that they expose methods for serializing themselves into a convenient format such as RDF/XML or N3.

Ontology subclass relationships can be easily represented by an object class hierarchy. For example, the fact that an ontology class is a subclass of another can be used to derive a Java extends relationship between two classes:

```
class MasterDocument extends AbstractDocument
```

Datatype properties can be easily represented with get/set methods. For example, a property of type *xs:string* with the domain of a certain class would be represented by a setter method on the bean representing the domain class:

```
public void setLocalId(String localId)
```

Object properties are represented by a setter method that accepts as a parameter the bean class representing the propertys range. For example, a property *ltr:contributor* with the range class *ltr:Contributor* would be represented as:

```
public void addContributor(
    com.wolterskluwer.rdfbeans.ltr.Contributor contributor
)
```

Note that most generated methods are overloaded to allow resources defined elsewhere (such as the LOD cloud) to be set:

```
public void addContributor(URI contributor)
```

The use of this API fits in well with the common skill set of developers in publishing houses. A developer must write custom code to execute one or more SQL queries against a database. This returns a Java result-set object containing the relational data that is intended to be provided as RDF. The developer then writes code to instantiate (create) an RDFBean of the appropriate class. For example, this might be a bean representing a Document, or a bean representing a complex ontology class such as a Court. The developer assigns a URI to the bean, and iterates over the fields of the result-set, setting properties on the bean. The developer can continue to query databases and populate the bean, or serialise it as inherently correct RDF/XML.

To preserve data integrity during the transformation from relational data to RDF, we found it useful to engineer a limited closed world assumption into the RDFBean framework. For example, if a property is declared as *owl:FunctionalProperty*, we make sure that only one instance of that property can be set on the bean. Although the semantics of functional properties are not entirely captured by a setter property of singular cardinality, it makes sense to respect this ontology constraint as much as possible. For example, if a Ruling is made by a Court, represented be the functional property *ltr:court*, with range, *ltr:Court*, we need to prevent the possibility of two different resources being set for property *ltr:court*, as a reasoner will infer that these are the same court!

Similarly, when a propertys range is defined by a set of individuals, and those individuals are themselves generated from a fixed set of entities in a database, it is entirely appropriate to prevent the setting of values outside of that range. For example, developers cannot set the object of the property *ltr:Court* to an arbitrary URI resource: the object has to be one of the resources mapped from court entities stored in their database.

We found that developers rapidly grasped how to use the generated bean API. It contains a number of programmer-friendly features such as method-chaining (the ability to easily set multiple properties on a bean in the same line) and generous amounts of API documentation created from the ontology itself. It also requires practically no knowledge of RDF, which can be seen as a good or a bad thing depending on your point of view. The only interaction with RDF that developers have is when they called a *serialise()* method on the bean which requires them to specify a serialisation method (RDF/XML, N3, Turtle etc.) and an output stream.

There are still a number of improvements we can make. For example, a consequence of the Java Bean approach is that the domain ontology mapping is executed by developers, in code. This is a one-off procedure that has proved to be straightforward; however, a future development might allow the mapping specification to be abstracted into a configuration file. This would limit the coding work and open up the domain ontology mapping to domain experts who are not programmers.

Further, we aim to improve the entity recognition services available in the framework, for example by making use of the growing number of web-based entity recognition services. Currently, all resource URIs are minted within our own namespace, even when they are semantically identical to resources already available in the LOD cloud (for example, courts, judges, languages, geographic areas). If our RDF content is ever to be truly published as linked data, our own resource URIs will at some point have to be reconciled with other peoples identifiers.

7 Conclusions

In the two years that this project has been running the landscape of the Semantic Web has changed significantly. The Linked Data phenomenon is currently the focus of interest from governments, businesses and individuals. For example, the US and UK governments, as well as various European bodies are actively pursuing the linking of vast datasets to the LOD cloud. So, what started as an exercise to use features of Semantic Web technologies to bridge between diverse internal content formats is now looking remarkably prescient, as it offers the ability to catapult Wolters Kluwer publishing units into a new world of data aggregation and integration.

The real value of this project is likely to be when, or if, the LOD cloud contains a critical mass of data that simply cannot be ignored by publishers. Then, as businesses operating in a competitive market, the race will be on with competitors to aggregate, integrate, slice and dice this information in innovative ways that offer real value to our customers. It could be a tremendously exciting, game-changing situation in which the possibilities will be limited only by the availability of datasets and the ingenuity of developers to mould the clouds raw data into useful knowledge. What could we see? In the short term, it should be entirely possible to compile useful statistics on-the-fly showing, for example, the success of appeals against particular judges. In the longer term, intelligent agents could perform time-saving content discovery tasks, compiling must-read dossiers of cases for legal teams.

We have proved that we can utilise the core Semantic Web technologies in a way that adds value to our business. Our standardization effort is beyond a prototype; is it being used in production to drive real content to real customers. We have shown that an OWL ontology can be used to normalise metadata models; we have shown that RDF can be a flexible, performant data format which can be integrated in a production-strength transformation chain.

What were our key lessons? The issue of data integrity and the enigma of the Open World assumption must be better addressed, or better communicated to potential adopters. Without this, semantic technologies may be seen to have too high a risk factor for some industries. It is hard not to notice that solutions for imposing more expressive constraints on RDF data are evolving in several different corners of the semantic world, and we strongly hope that these efforts become mainstream. Also, while OWL is a powerful modeling language, it requires a different mindset that can be hard for people schooled in database and object-oriented technologies to understand. Communication, training, and the high visibility of case studies and success stories will be needed to bridge this gap.

Looking to the future, there is a sense in which we have barely scratched the surface of the issues that will have to be resolved before enterprises can actively make use of - and contribute to - the LOD cloud. Best practices are still emerging from research projects such as ours. For example, does the design of our home-grown ontology help or hinder the integration of content using other vocabularies? What sort of identifier pattern should we use to identify our entities and how can we best ensure that our entities are recognised as the same entities that other suppliers are using? How far back in the content supply chain will LOD supporting technologies have to stretch?

These questions are, of course, in the process of being answered by the growing number of projects using Semantic Web technologies. But one thing is clear: the web is entering a phase of becoming an open data space, and publishers, as data providers, ignore this at their peril. We would like to think that the publishing community should be at the forefront of this change, for while it has much to gain from the world of Linked Data, it has much to contribute too.

Acknowledgements The author wishes to acknowledge the efforts of Barend Jan de Jong, Jack Hoffman and Christian Dirschl of Wolters Kluwer NV and Johan de Smedt, Girts Niedra and Natan Cox of TenForce BVBA for their work on the project described in this chapter.

References

1. Hitzler P, Krötzsch M, Parsia B, Patel-Schneider B, Rudolph F (2009) OWL 2 Web Ontology Language Primer. W3C Recommendation. http://www.w3.org/TR/owl2-primer/. Accessed May 2010

2. Manola F, Miller E (2004) RDF Primer. W3C Recommendation. http://www.w3.org/TR/rdf-primer/. Accessed May 2010
3. Isaac A, Summers E (2009) SKOS Simple Knowledge Organization System Primer. W3C Recommendation. http://www.w3.org/TR/skos-primer/. Accessed May 2010
4. Altheim M, McCarron S (2001) XHTML‡ 1.1 - Module-based XHTML. W3C Recommendation. http://www.w3.org/TR/xhtml11/. Accessed May 2010
5. Adida B, Birbeck M, McCarron S, Pemberton S (2008) RDFa in XHTML: Syntax and Processing. W3C Recommendation . http://www.w3.org/TR/rdfa-syntax/. Accessed May 2010
6. Motik B, Horrocks I, Sattler U (2009) Bridging the Gap Between OWL and Relational Data-bases. Web Semantics: Science, Services and Agents on the World Wide Web. doi: 10.1016/j.websem.2009.02.001
7. Sirin E, Smith M, Wallace E (2008) Opening, Closing Worlds - On Integrity Constraints. http://www.webont.org/owled/2008/papers/owled2008eu_submission_30.pdf. Online document. Accessed May 2010
8. Beckett D, Broekstra J (2008) SPARQL Query Results XML Format. W3C Recommendation. http://www.w3.org/TR/rdf-sparql-XMLres/. Accessed May 2010

A Role for Semantic Web Technologies in Patient Record Data Collection

Chimezie Ogbuji

Abstract

Business Process Management Systems (BPMS) are a component of the stack of Web standards that comprise Service Oriented Architecture (SOA). Such systems are representative of the architectural framework of modern information systems built in an enterprise intranet and are in contrast to systems built for deployment on the larger World Wide Web. The REST architectural style is an emerging style for building loosely coupled systems based purely on the native HTTP protocol. It is a coordinated set of architectural constraints with a goal to minimize latency, maximize the independence and scalability of distributed components, and facilitate the use of intermediary processors. Within the development community for distributed, Web-based systems, there has been a debate regarding the merits of both approaches. In some cases, there are legitimate concerns about the differences in both architectural styles. In other cases, the contention seems to be based on concerns that are marginal at best.

In this chapter, we will attempt to contribute to this debate by focusing on a specific, deployed use case that emphasizes the role of the Semantic Web, a simple Web application architecture that leverages the use of declarative XML processing, and the needs of a workflow system. The use case involves orchestrating a work process associated with the data entry of structured patient record content into a research registry at the Cleveland Clinic's Clinical Investigation department in the Heart and Vascular Institute.

Chimezie Ogbuji
Cleveland Clinic, 9500 Euclid Ave. Cleveland OH 44195, USA, e-mail: ogbujic@ccf.org

D. Wood (ed.), *Linking Enterprise Data*, DOI 10.1007/978-1-4419-7665-9_12,

1 Introduction

There has recently been an increased interest in several architectural paradigms for building distributed, Web-based systems. They all rely on the architecture of the World Wide Web in one form or another. This is no coincidence as the great success of the World Wide Web as a large-scale, distributed hypermedia system has motivated recent advances in approaches to building distributed systems that leverage the protocols that comprise the World Wide Web.

The term *Web Mashups* is often used to refer to a new breed of Web applications that are developed using content and services available online. They aim to combine sources to create useful new applications or services, typically serve a specific, short-lived need, and are comprised of contemporary, easy-to-use Web technologies. A significant component of mashup architecture that eases the challenge of integrating Web-based content into a coherent, value-adding application is the use of the architectural style of the World Wide Web: the Representational State Transfer (REST) architectural style. We will discuss the details of this style, but at its core is the Hypertext Transport Protocol (HTTP).

It is an application-level protocol for distributed, collaborative, hypermedia information systems. It is both generic and stateless. Both of these characteristics will be discussed later. It supports the transfer of typed data representations such that applications can *negotiate* representations appropriate for their use, allowing systems to be built independently of the data being transferred [6].

In many ways, the Web mashup paradigm has much in common with that of *Linked Data*. However, Linked Data facilitates machine-readability through its use of the Resource Description Framework (RDF) to make typed statements that link arbitrary things in the world [2]. We will discuss this distinction later in this chapter.

An alternative architectural approach to building distributed systems has also emerged as a set of Web standards and is typically used for building *enterprise applications*. It is often referred to as Service Oriented Architecture (SOA). Applications built on this framework are often deployed within a commercial organization. This architectural approach is based on an XML communication protocol that is layered on top of HTTP and is called the Simple Object Access Protocol (SOAP). SOAP relies on HTTP only for routing messages on the network and provides a framework for fully customized, remote method invocation. Systems built using this framework rely on an XML dialect that defines the signature of methods associated with a particular service: the Web Service Description Language (WSDL).

Applications built using this paradigm differ from those built to directly use the HTTP protocol as the connection medium. They are different approaches to addressing similar problems in two different contexts (one within an enterprise and another within the larger internet). As a result of the nuances of distributed processing and the subtleties of both approaches, experts in one system rarely understand and appreciate experts in the other. Unfortunately, much of the discussion and literature around contrast to both approaches plays out in an ideological fashion and even where attempts have been made to provide a disciplined set of metrics to contrast both styles. The comparisons have mostly been made in the abstract rather than in the context of deployed solutions.

In this chapter, we will attempt to contribute to this discussion by scrutinizing a deployed, Web-based application that orchestrates the process of structured data collection of content from an Electronic Medical Record (EMR) system into a patient registry for the purpose of clinical research. The application is built on a content repository that incorporates the use of *Semantic Web technologies* in a manner that sheds some light on the contrast of the architectural styles mentioned above.

2 Architectural Styles

2.1 REST Architectural Style

In order to better appreciate the overlap between Web mashups, enterprise applications built using SOA, and Semantic Web applications, we will need to understand the Representational State Transfer (REST) style.

REST is a coordinated set of architectural constraints that capture the properties induced by the architecture of the Web. The collective goal of the various constraints is to minimize network communication latency, maximize the independence and scalability of distributed components, and facilitate the use of intermediary processors [7]. Intuitively, it provides an abstraction of the architectural elements in a distributed hypermedia system such as the World Wide Web: resources, their identifiers and representations, a uniform interface, and the various information processing agents involved. Hypermedia, a term coined by Ted Nelson, describes human-authored media that branch or perform on request from a user.

Two key component of the REST style and the architecture of the World Wide Web are Universal Resource Identifiers (URIs) and Universal Resource Locators (URLs). URIs are global identifiers for the items of interest (resources) in the information space that comprises the World Wide Web. They can be locators, names, or both. URLs are the subset of URIs that provide a means of locating the resource via an access mechanism.

Communication between the information processing agents in the REST style is stateless in the sense that each request includes all the information necessary to understand the request. This rules out the need for and use of data stored in the server to interpret interactions within the protocol. The interface over which invocations are made between the client and server is generic and uniform rather than specific to the needs of an application.

Uniformity is achieved by constraining the semantics of the interface in the following ways:

- Every invocation involves a resource at the server that is identified by way of a URI.

- The identified resources can be manipulated through representations enclosed in a submitted message that capture the current or intended state of that resource.
- Messages are self-descriptive in the sense that they are stateless and associated with a well-defined Internet Media Type (IMT)
- Hypermedia is the engine of application state.

This final constraint is one of the more controversial constraints of the REST paradigm. Much of this controversy stems from the subtlety of this distinction from other distributed frameworks (SOA in particular). It goes hand-in-hand with the constraint of stateless communication. It dictates that (at any point in time) the state of a particular application is determined by the representation a client has on hand and that the paths or transitions from that state to another are determined by the URLs embedded in these representations. In the case where the media is HTML, the state of the Web application is the particular Web page loaded in the browser and the state transitions are the links that the end user clicks to invoke a request back to the server for another representation.

REST allows the functionality of a client to be extended by permitting interactions to include custom programming logic that can be executed by the client. The motivation for this is to simplify clients by reducing the number of required features. This also facilitates an extensible architecture by allowing features to be downloaded after deployment.

2.2 Service Oriented Architecture

Service Oriented Architecture (SOA) is a compositional architectural paradigm comprised of a *Web Service* as its most basic element [13]. Web services are defined by abstract contracts that describe how the services are meant to be invoked. Such definitions are performed at design time. The overall goal of such an approach is to make the coupling between caller and Web service clear and unambiguous [22], separating the function performed by a service from the implementation of the Web service itself.

Typically, SOA platforms promote development centered on Integrated Development Environment (IDE) tools that allow developers to define and orchestrate the invocation of services in a detailed and precise manner through the abstract definition of their interfaces. The Web Service Description Language (WSDL) provides a means to formally define a Web service. WSDL is an extension of the XML Schema specification.

SOAP provides a standard for XML-based Web service messaging with an envelope that can be used to communicate additional information such as security tokens, time stamps, etc. It also standardizes the semantics of handling faults that result from undeliverable messages. This provides certain reliability guarantees that can potentially be of use for optimizing resource usage.

SOAP messages are commonly layered on top of HTTP [23]. SOAP was originally intended as the *Simple Object Access Protocol* and its designers intended it to be used with traditional distributed object technologies such as remote method invocation. When SOAP became popular for Web services the acronym became less relevant because Web service interfaces are agnostic as to whether or not object-oriented implementations are used.

2.2.1 Workflow Systems

Contemporary use of Service Oriented Architecture for enterprise application development typically involves the orchestration of business processes. This extends the ostensible goal of SOA to separate function from implementation by further abstracting the underlying flow of activity of a particular application.

In order to better understand workflow systems in general, we start with a few definitions. A *business process* is a set of one or more related activities that facilitate the realization of an objective or goal. It is typically considered within the context of an organization and involves participation from various *actors* each of whom play a particular *role* in the business process [5]. Actors in a business process can be human or machine alike.

A *workflow* is the automation of a business process in which information artifacts and tasks that drive their management and life cycle are passed on from one actor to another. Workflows are typically subject to a set of procedural rules that dictate the constraints of the underlying business process.

Workflow management systems (WFMS) are information systems that define and manage the execution of workflows through the use of a workflow engine that interprets a workflow definition (typically specified in a particular workflow language) and interacts with the actors involved in the underlying business process.

The primary motivation of workflow management is to separate process logic from application logic in order to make software more flexible and to integrate heterogeneous applications.

2.2.2 Process Representation

In the SOA paradigm, business processes and their respective workflows are formally specified and orchestrated along with the various services they interact with. As with the other ways in which the components of a SOA enterprise architecture are specified, an XML-based dialect has been developed for this purpose. The Business Process Execution Language for Web services (BPEL) has emerged as a standard for specifying and executing processes [20]. It is composable, XML-based, and supported by many vendors and positioned as the *"process language of the Internet."*

A BPEL process itself is a kind of flow-chart, where each element (Table 1) in the process is an activity. An activity is either *primitive* or *structured*. The set of primitive activities include:

To enable the presentation of complex structures the structured activities defined in Table 2 are given:

BPEL Element	Description
invoke	Invoke an operation on a Web service
receive	Wait for a message from an external source
reply	Reply to an external source
wait	Pause for a specified time
assign	Copy data from one place to another
throw	Indicate errors in the execution
terminate	Terminate the entire service instance
empty	Do nothing

Table 1 BPEL elements

BPEL Element	Description
sequence	Define an execution order
switch	Conditional routing
while	A Loop instruction
pick	Race conditions based on timing or external triggers
flow	Parallel routing
scope	Groups activities to be treated by the same fault-handler

Table 2 Complex workflow activities

Structured activities can be nested and combined in arbitrary ways. Within activities executed in parallel, the execution order can further be controlled by the usage of links (sometimes also called control links, or guarded links).

3 Semantic Web Technologies

In both the SOA and REST paradigms, the semantics of the data involved is often encapsulated in the programming logic used to implement the applications and is not specified in any formal way. A declarative approach to programming involves stating *what* is to be computed, but not necessarily *how* it is to be computed [12]. The distributed hypermedia system facilitated by the architecture of the World Wide Web is primarily meant for interaction with humans that read content and traverse hypermedia links. The semantics of HTTP interactions are clearly specified such that an automaton can participate without human involvement. However, there is no common means by which the meaning of the data involved in the interactions can be determined. Enterprise applications built using SOA specify in great detail the orchestration and messaging semantics, however there is no common way for an automaton to interpret the data involved independently.

The Semantic Web [1] is a vision of how the existing infrastructure of the World Wide Web can be extended in such a way that machines can interpret the meaning of data involved in protocol interactions. There is often a distinction drawn from this particular vision and the standards and technologies that have been developed within the World Wide Web Consortium (W3C) to achieve it: Semantic Web Technologies.

Semantic Web technologies can be seen as an extension of the REST style and architecture.

The goal of a universal approach to machine-oriented interpretation of data in the Semantic Web is facilitated through the use of a data representation standard called the Resource Description Framework (RDF). RDF captures meaning as a set of *triples* similar to the subject, verb, and object components of an elementary sentence in a natural language. Typically, the terms in these sentences are resources identified by URIs. Sets of RDF triples comprise an *RDF graph*. In this way, the entities in the World Wide Web can be both manipulated and traversed via human interaction and interpreted and reasoned about by autonomous software agents. The SPARQL specification provides a notion of a collection of *named RDF graphs* (where each graph is associated with a URI) called an *RDF dataset* and a language for querying across an RDF dataset.

The role of RDF in the Linked Data paradigm is what distinguishes it from Web mashups. Whereas Web mashups and other frameworks that rely on the semantics of the underlying protocol add value primarily through connectivity of content and services, Linked Data relies on RDF to provide a general framework for interpreting such connections as logical statements and adds value through this additional dimension of machine understanding.

Another component of Semantic Web technology stack is the ability to interpret a stronger meaning from URIs and typed literals in a specific vocabulary within an RDF graph [8]. There are two frameworks for specifying these stronger vocabulary interpretations: the RDF Schema language (RDFS) and the Web Ontology Language (OWL).

4 SemanticDB Concurrent Data Collection Workflow

SemanticDB[TM] is a *patient registry* implemented on a content repository in the Cleveland Clinic's Heart and Vascular Institute[1]. It is used to manage a cohort of patients who all have a *qualifying procedure* in common for the purpose of clinical research. The Agency for Healthcare Research and Quality (AHRQ) defines a patient registry as

> an organized system that uses observational study methods to collect uniform data (clinical and other) to evaluate specified outcomes for a population defined by a particular disease, condition, or exposure, and that serves one or more predetermined scientific, clinical, or policy purposes.

---

[1] http://www.w3.org/2001/sw/sweo/public/UseCases/ClevelandClinic/

4.1 Requirements

The specific use case that this chapter will discuss represents a subset of the functionality that SemanticDB provides as part of the larger goal of facilitating outcomes research. In particular, once a qualifying procedure has been identified for addition into the population, the content of the Electronic Medical Record (EMR) for that patient needs to be transcribed as structured data (from a possibly unstructured source) into the patient registry. This happens while the patient is still in the hospital and is independent of any other clinical study involving the patient, a more specific set of qualification criteria, or additional data elements. So, the process is referred to as *concurrent data collection* and requires an ongoing electronic interaction with the information systems in the healthcare institution associated with the operating room.

The process of transcribing the content comprising the details of the qualifying procedure from the EMR can be thought of as a business process involving participation from data entry personnel and will be referred to as a *concurrent data collection task*. There are differences in the roles of the people entering data into the registry that depend on the particular section of the EMR they are assigned to transcribe. There is a distinction drawn between those responsible for collecting content that only requires a minimal amount of clinical expertise or interpretation and those responsible for collecting content that requires an understanding of clinical terminology and experience in patient care management. Nurses often play the latter role. Those in the former role will be referred to as *precoders* and those in the latter role will be referred to as *abstractors*. We will refer to data entry personnel collectively as *coders*.

An important characteristic of ideal patient registries is for them to be complete such that one can construct a *longitudinal* (or *birth to death*) record of a patient's care and outcomes[16]. As a result, in addition to transcribing the details of the qualifying operation, coders may also need to perform data entry on the other parts of the medical record for patients who are being added to the patient registry population for the first time.

The overall workflow of concurrent data collection is comprised of an initial part that does not involve any human interaction and a second part that is primarily driven by coders through interaction with a Web-based application in a browser. The second part of the workflow leads the coders through the entire process of concurrent data collection, keeping track of the state of each concurrent data collection case.

The first part of the workflow, however, involves a software module that queries the operating room information system on a nightly basis for those operating room procedures that meet the qualifying criteria relevant to the patient registry. For each such procedure, as much structured information as is available and relevant to the population of the registry is retrieved from the EMR and sent over to the registry to comprise the front of the queue of concurrent data collection tasks that drive the daily workflow. The information retrieved from the EMR includes (but is not limited to):

- Demographic data for the patient involved (name, contact information, etc.).
- The primary staff physician that performed the procedure.
- The name of the qualifying procedure and a common code (the CPT code) associated with the procedure.
- Information regarding the procedure.

4.2 XML and RDF Content Management

What distinguishes SemanticDB from most other patient registries is its use of a content repository (the 4Suite repository) that includes the symbiotic combination of XML and RDF processing as part of its core set of services [15]. From a content perspective, the 4Suite repository can be conceived as a virtual file system of resources each of which is associated with an HTTP IMT. Some media types are considered first class objects in the repository, XML and RDF being the primary ones. Under the category of first class XML resources there are: users, groups, network services, XSLT documents, document definitions, and aliases.

A document definition can be associated with an XML document and is comprised of a set of rules for processing the XML documents they are associated with. These include the type and location of an artifact to use for validation, an indication of whether or not to maintain a full text index of associated documents, and mappings for updating the repository's RDF database with information from the XML file.

Any update to an XML document associated with a document definition with such a mapping will cause the repository to replace the persisted, corresponding RDF graph with the result of applying the mapping to the new XML document in order to obtain an RDF serialization. In this way, not only can the RDF representation of the XML be readily available for clients that prefer RDF, but structured data collection of RDF content can be implemented using technologies such as XForms, which are well positioned to have a significant impact on clinical data collection [14]. This effectively provides a content management paradigm that addresses the purported paradox of having syntactic interoperability without sacrificing semantic interoperability [4].

Another component of the Semantic Web technology stack is the Gleaning Resource Descriptions from Dialects of Language (GRDDL). The GRDDL specification introduces markup for declaring that an XML document includes data compatible with RDF and for linking to algorithms (XSLT typically), for extracting RDF from the document [3]. Document definitions can themselves be XSLT documents and thus can be considered GRDDL transformations of XML content in a 4Suite repository used to manage faithfully rendered RDF as a semantic index of the XML content.

4.3 RESTful XSLT Services

Another distinguishing feature of the content repository that underlies SemanticDB is the HTTP service framework that directly integrates XSLT processing. XSLT is an XML vocabulary for transforming XML documents into resulting XML documents as well as into arbitrary text-based content. The repository's HTTP implementation allows clients to invoke an XSLT transform through an inbound HTTP message that identifies the XSLT stylesheet to be used, includes parameters either in the query component of the URL or embedded in the message body, and specifies the input for the transformation as a parameter of the HTTP invocation as well. The inbound HTTP parameters are passed in as parameters to the XSLT stylesheet. The input document can either be sent as the message payload or a reference to an XML document residing in the repository can be passed in as a parameter in the message. Intuitively, Web content is served from (XSLT) services where XSLT acts as the native language for implementing the functions of the service.

Such a framework appeals to the REST style in several ways. First, the XSLT service is directly addressed by the client by way of a Universal Resource Locator (URL). Second, in the case where the input document is provided by the inbound message, the representations completely determine the service invocation, and the IMT of the result can be specified within the XSLT stylesheet. Finally, the notion of hypermedia as the engine of application state is manifest through the use of XSLT stylesheets that return typed content. The result of the XSLT invocation will contain embedded URLs that the client can follow to trigger subsequent XSLT serices. This is the mechanism by which rich internet application can be built.

XSLT defines an *extension mechanism* that allows namespaces to be designated as *extension namespaces*. While invoking an XSLT stylesheet and upon reaching an element or function in an extension namespace, the element or function is treated as an externally defined instruction. The 4Suite repository provides several extensions that allow the stylesheet to interact with content in the repository.

4.4 Declarative AJAX Framework

The implementation of the concurrent data collection workflow application uses a Web-based framework called Exhibit. Exhibit is a lightweight framework for publishing structured data on standard Web servers that requires no installation, database administration, or programming[10]. It allows authors with relatively limited skills to publish richly interactive pages that exploit the structure of their data for better browsing and visualization. It includes a faceted browsing interface and illustrates how rich user interfaces can be made possible with minimal programmatic intervention through the separation of structured data within a Web page from its presentational elements.

There are two major components in the development of an Exhibit interface: the data source and the presentation template. The presentation is just a regular

HTML document that refers to the data source via a URL. *Lenses* and *views* can be added in the document through the use of *templates* that are fragments of HTML. The fragments include attributes whose values are expressions that refer to various presentation widgets as well as references into the structured data source. In many ways, the lightweight, HTML-based template language of exhibit is similar to the XSLT syntax. Exhibit includes implementations of various kinds of views that are relevant for different kinds of structured data: map, timeline, table, thumbnail, and tile views.

Exhibit includes its own JavaScript Object Notation (JSON) format that data sources must comply with in order to describe the data that feeds the presentation template in a manner that the Exhibit framework can work with. JSON is a lightweight, data-interchange format that was designed to be easy for humans to read and write. It is also easy for machines to parse and generate. JSON is based on a subset of the Javascript programming language.

Exhibit fits well as a component of a larger ecology of mashup data [10]. It also fits well into the paradigm of separating data from presentation associated with both XForms and XSLT. In the same way that an Exhibit template can be generated and served from a *screen-generating service* in the repository with embedded references to a *data transformation service* that transform XML content in the repository into the appropriate JSON format, an XForm can be served from a similar screen-generating service that also directly refers back to an XML document to manage on the client side. This results in a powerful, lightweight, declarative framework for the management and faceted browsing of structured content and RDF graphs (through the use of document definitions).

4.5 Implementation

The framework described in the previous section is the basis for the current implementation of the *case management workflow* application in SemanticDB. It starts with a list of concurrent data collection cases for the patient registry, uses the faceted browsing framework of exhibit to guide abstractors and precoders through the various stages of the workflow, manage the metadata associated with each case, and launch the actual data collection application for the patient record associated with the case.

This is a separate component from another subsystem in SemanticDB that leverages the XSLT-based HTTP service framework and XForms to provide a rich internet application for structured data collection. As such, each patient record is an XML document with a path in the repository that is uniquely specified by the medical record number (MRN) of the patient. The entry point into this separate application is a URL that includes (in the query component) the MRN of the patient whose record will be managed.

The details of this separate component is beyond the scope of this chapter, but it suffices to mention that the concurrent data collection workflow allows the coder to proceed into the data collection workflow for a particular patient through a URL included in the Web pages that present the cases allocated to the abstractor or pre-coder. In this way the case management workflow is connected to the data collection workflow as a function of the progression of the user interaction with the Web page rather than as a result of an a-priori, detailed specification of both workflows as would be the case in a typical SOA approach to workflow management. The merits of this distinction will be discussed later.

In the case of the case management workflow, each concurrent data collection case is represented as an XML document in the repository associated with a *case document definition* that maps the XML content into an RDF graph of statements about the case, and stores the RDF graph in an RDF dataset (a *case management dataset*) where the name of each such RDF graph corresponds to the URL of the XML document in the repository. The name of file corresponds to the primary key of the table in the source operating room database.

We will use the *work* prefix to refer to the namespace associated with the RDF vocabulary used in the case management dataset. There is a *work:Case* class that represent concurrent data collection cases and 4 specializations of this class that represent the various, non-overlapping states a case can be in:

Class	Description
work:UnassignedPrecoding	Accepted into the workflow queue but not picked up by a precoder
work:OngoingPrecoding	Assigned to a precoder
work:UnassignedCoding	Precoder finished but not assigned to abstractor
work:OngoingCoding	Assigned to a precoder

Table 3 Workflow cases as RDFS/OWL classes

Each work:Case instance has statements made about it in their respective graphs using the following predicates:

- work:mrn - A literal property whose value is the MRN of the patient involved.
- foaf:name[2] - The name of the patient.
- dc:date[3] - The date when the qualifying procedure occurred.
- rdfs:label - The human-readable label associated with the case as specified by the source database.
- work:primaryPhysician - A literal property whose value is the name of the primary physician who performed the procedure.
- work:assignedCoder - A resource property that relates the case to the assigned data collection personnel. The object is the URI of a user object in the repository.

---

[2] The **foaf** namespace prefix refers to the Friend of a Friend vocabulary: http://xmlns.com/foaf/spec/

[3] The **dc** namespace prefix refers to the Dublin Core RDF metadata vocabulary: http://dublincore.org/documents/dc-rdf/

- skos:editorialNote[4] - A literal property whose value is an arbitrary note left for the benefit of communication between data collection personnel that share the case.

The details regarding the XML vocabulary of the case documents are not essential to this chapter since (as a GRDDL transform) the mapping from an XML instance to the RDF graph described above produces a *faithful rendition* [3] of the XML content. However, it is important to note that the URI of the case used in the corresponding RDF graph is associated with the corresponding document element in the XML source via a *uri* attribute.

```
<work:Case  uri = ' '..." >
    .. snip ..
</work:Case>
```

The exception to this rule is in the XML structure of *pending cases* that have been identified as candidates for the concurrent data collection workflow but have yet to be selected by a coder. We will discuss this shortly.

In this way, a query can be dispatched against the case management dataset to find cases in a particular state and return the URL(s) of the containing graph. These URLs can then be used by upstream applications to fetch either the XML representation to be managed on the client side via XForms (updating the corresponding RDF graph in the process) or to fetch an Exhibit JSON representation of a case or a list of cases for incorporation into a faceted display .

The starting point of the workflow is single XML document (*inbox.xml*) that contains a list of pending cases identified from the operating room information system as part of the initial phase. The work:Case elements in this document will have an *id* attribute set to the primary key of the case that originates from the source system:

```
<work:PendingCases>
    (<work:Case  id = ' '.. primaryKey ..." >
        .. snip ..
    </work:Case >)*
</work:PendingCases>
```

Most of the infrastructure is in an XSLT service (*workflow-engine.xslt*) that takes an *action* parameter. When action is set to **home**, the service will return an HTML document with a form and table listing all the pending cases with check boxes next to each one. The user can select a set of cases to either accept into the workflow or discard altogether.

Upon submission, the content of the form will be sent back to the workflow engine service via the HTTP POST method, with the *action* parameter set to **accept-cases**. In addition, the identifier of each checked case will be included as a parameter within the submission. When the workflow engine service is invoked with the action set to **accept-cases**, it will iterate over all the work:Case elements in inbox.xml

---

[4] The **skos** prefix is used to refer to the Simple Knowledge Organization System RDF vocabulary: http://www.w3.org/TR/skos-reference/

that correspond to the selected cases and create an XML document under a **/Case-Management/ConcurrentCases/live** directory in the repository. This work:Case element will then be removed from inbox.xml.

The id attribute will be replaced with an uri attribute and each document will be associated with the case document definition. The value of the uri attribute will be a non-resolvable URI of the form:

$$tag : info@semanticdb.ccf.org,2010:ORCases\#DDDDDD$$

where **DDDDDD** is the value of the id attribute. Note that this URI is *non-resolvable* as URIs in the tag scheme can only be used as identifiers, and are not designed to support resolution [11]. For each accepted case, an entry in the corresponding patient record document will be created using this URI as an instance of an *operation event*. Cases can be considered as special kinds of operations undergoing concurrent data collection. In addition, any structured data retrieved from the EMR will also be moved into the patient record (demographic data, details about the procedure, etc.). Instances of work:Case in the case management dataset will also be identified by this URI. We will discuss the architectural ramifications of this and the relation to Linked Data principles later.

The workflow engine can also be invoked with the action parameter set to either **precoding** or **abstraction**. This causes the engine to invoke a template defined in an included *case-workflow-exhibit.xslt* stylesheet, which (as the name suggests) will render the *Exhibit coding presentation page*. When invoked with this action, the workflow engine takes an additional *renderAllCases* parameter that is set to either '1' or '0'.

The Exhibit coding presentation page is comprised of two major sections: a view panel and a list of unassigned cases. The view panel uses the Exhibit tile view to present a faceted list of either just the cases in the precoding or abstraction state assigned to the user currently logged into the repository or *all* the assigned cases in one of those two states, depending on the values of the renderAllCases and action parameters.

The unassigned cases section displays a list of cases that are either in the precoding or abstraction state (depending on the value of the action parameter) in an HTML form with checkboxes so the coder can select one or more cases to assign to themselves. A SPARQL query is dispatched against the case management dataset to construct this list. This particular form will submit the selected cases back to the workflow engine service with an action of **assign-precoder** or **assign-abstractor** accordingly. When invoked this way, the workflow engine will update the XML document (and the corresponding RDF graph in the process), assign the currently logged-in user to the selected cases, and redirect the user back to the Exhibit coding presentation page.

At the top of the Exhibit coding presentation page source is an HTML link element that references an *exhibit data service*. The values of the action and render-AllCases parameters are appended as query components to the URL. This service is responsible for returning a JSON file that conforms to the Exhibit data model and includes the metadata of each case as key-value pair as well as URLs that reference

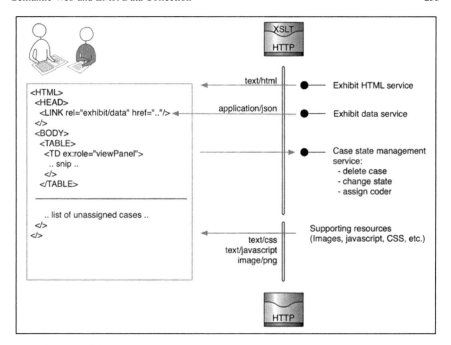

Fig. 1 Exhibit REST topology

invocations of the primary workflow engine service, passing on the following values for the action parameter: delete-case, and change-state. It also includes an entry whose value is the URL that links into the data collection application for the relevant patient record.

The **delete-case** action will cause the workflow engine to remove the corresponding document from the repository (removing the RDF graph in the process). The **change-state** action will cause the engine to transition a case from the ongoing precoding state to the unassigned abstraction state or from the abstraction state to the end of the workflow (indicating the completion of concurrent data collection for this patient record), depending on the current state of the case. This is the primary manifestation of the hypermedia as the engine of state REST constraint. In particular, the returned JSON includes links that allow the user to progress a given case through the workflow by invoking services that render the appropriate, subsequent Web pages.

The exhibit data service retrieves this information from the collection of RDF graphs via one of several SPARQL queries depending on the values of the action and renderAllCases parameters. For example, if it is invoked with a value of 'precoding' for the action parameter and '1' for the renderAllCases parameter, the following SPARQL query will be dispatched against the case management dataset:

```
SELECT  *
{
   GRAPH  ?CASEDOC {
```

```
?CASE  a  ?CASETYPE;
         work:assignedCoder  ?CODER;
         work:mrn  ?MRN;
         rdfs:label  ?PROCEDURE;
         work:primaryPhysician  ?PHYSICIAN;
         dc:date  ?DATE;
         skos:editorialNote  ?NOTE;
         foaf\index{FOAF vocabulary}:name  ?NAME
         OPTIONAL  {  ?CASE  skos:editorialNote  ?NOTE }
         FILTER(
            ?CASETYPE  =  work:UnassignedPreCoding  ||
            ?CASETYPE  =  work:OngoingPrecoding
         )
    }
}
```

If the value of the renderAllCases parameter is '0' then a similar SPARQL query will be dispatched, however, the object of the triple pattern involving work:assignedCoder will be the URI of the user logged into the repository rather than the ?CODER variable. Note that the ?CASEDOC variable will be bound to the (resolvable) URL of the document and the ?CASE variable will be bound to the URI of the operation.

Within the view panel of the Exhibit coding presentation page, an Exhibit lens is specified for each case in the list. The lens renders the metadata returned by the exhibit data service as well as the embedded URLs that facilitate transition through the workflow.

Finally, the exhibit dataset service also returns a URL that references a separate *case management XForm service*. The URL also includes a path to the document as part of the query component. When invoked, this service returns an XHTML container document that includes XForms elements. The XForms view layer includes appropriate control elements that refer to the various parts of the case XML document that correspond to the metadata associated with a case. The XForms model includes a reference to the instance data using the URL of the document. This allows a coder to modify the various aspects of a case such as updating the note, for example. The XForms submission is used to submit the (possibly) modified document back to the repository using the standard HTTP PUT method and the URL of the document:

```
<xf:submission
    id=''update-case"
    ref=''instance('caseDocumentInstance')"
    method=''PUT"
    mediatype=''application/xml"
    .. snip ..
    version=''1.0"
    action=''{$caseDocumentURL}"/>
```

5 General Architectural Observations

Before we go into an assessment of the described architecture, we will summarize some general observations made about the distinctions between the architectural constraints of Service Oriented Architecture and Representational State Transfer. Admittedly, these observations are quite general and not grounded in a use case and are thus hard to quantify. However, they give some reasonable cues to the differences in the two paradigms.

In some respects, the binding of SOAP to HTTP focuses on the transport capabilities of HTTP rather than its function as a framework for building applications. Such an approach is often referred to as *tunneling* and can be considered an abuse of HTTP [18][21]. This is especially the case if the tunneling does not respect the semantics of HTTP. As a consequence, this can break the behavior of HTTP intermediaries that perform a caching or proxy function, since their effectiveness depends on their assumptions about the semantics of the various HTTP methods.

Architectural approaches to distributed systems that rely on an explicit contract to dictate their semantics tend to promote specific and separate interfaces that essentially amount to a fully-specified *conversation* or sequence of method invocations in which the applications must have a-priori knowledge of the implied workflow of the conversation [21] [17] [22]. Languages such as BPEL are positioned as orchestration languages that facilitate this restriction of the sequences of interactions. This is in contrast to the REST approach in which URLs serve as the primary mechanism for steering client participation within a *loosely coupled conversation* [17].

Often, the result of an architectural approach that emphasizes the complete orchestration of the protocol topology and workflow is a platform that tends to promote system development centered on specific programming languages and Integrated Development Environments (IDE), forcing participating applications to use the same underlying platform in order to avoid interoperability problems [22].

On the conceptual level, less architectural decisions need to be made once a SOA approach to building distributed applications has been adopted, but more alternatives are available [17]. From the perspective of technology, the same number of decisions must be made, but fewer alternatives have to be considered when adopting a REST approach to do the same. As a result, the REST approach tends to score better with respect to flexibility and control, but requires a lot of low-level application development. The SOA approach provides better tool support and programming interface convenience, but introduces a dependency on infrastructure vendors.

6 Review of Service-oriented Metrics

In order to contribute to this debate through an assessment of the use case described above, we will need some more specific metrics to do so in a more precise way. Pautasso et al. [17] explored how to apply the concept of coupling to the design of service-oriented systems in greater detail and contributed a better understanding of what people mean when they refer to loose and tight coupling. Their goal was to make explicit the meaning of service-oriented coupling.

The following *facets* from the 12 given in their paper are relevant for the use case we introduce here.

- Identification
- Model
- State
- Conversation

The identification facet is a measure of how the association between representations and their respective resources is managed. A loosely coupled approach to identification is one in which identification is not coupled to a context. From a REST perspective, this is achieved primarily through the use of URIs. Pautasso et al. make the point to admonish the use of opaque identifiers (such as URIs that use the **tag** scheme) as re-creating the problem of requiring a context for proper interpretation of such an identifier.

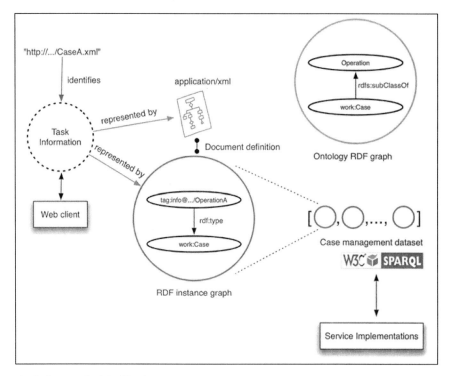

Fig. 2 Contexts for Identification

This critique coincides with the motivation behind the Linked Data requirement that all URIs in RDF are resolvable in order to fetch useful information. However, we have found that this assessment does not necessarily reflect the reality of our use of non-resolvable URIs to identify operation events, for instance (within the case management dataset). RDF, being a full-fledged knowledge representation with a well-specified mechanism for interpretation, provides a sufficient means to interpret the statements made about the resources identified in an RDF graph. This meaning is dictated by the interpretation of the graph rather than any reliance on the representations provided by the underlying protocol as a result of trying to access the resource. This reflects the fact that there are two distinct relationships between names and the things they denote: access and reference. The architecture of the Web (or any similar transport protocol) determines access, but has no influence on reference (or interpretation for that matter) [9].

Consider the diagram above that outlines the roles of a URL used to identify data collection task information and a URI used to identify the operation event that is the target of the transcription performed during the task. It also demonstrates the distinction between task information and an operation event. An RDF ontology graph that defines a case as a specialization of an operation event is also included to illustrate the point.

On the one hand, task information can live on the Web and can be manipulated by a Web client through its XML representation over HTTP. It is therefore appropriate to use an HTTP URL. It is axiomatic that operation events cannot live on the Web. Of course, an HTTP URL can be used as an alias in order to introduce a level of indirection [19]. However, this is more trouble than it is worth since the meaning of the operation instance, the class of cases, and the class of operations can altogether be easily specified in both the case management dataset and a local ontology rather than deriving this from the responses returned when an attempt is made to access each of these via their URIs over HTTP.

The model facet is a measure of whether a particular design assumes there is a common application-level data model shared between services. A loosely coupled approach does not make such an assumption, and exchanged messages are self-contained and designed to be processed as documents in a standardized representation format. In a certain sense, we are able to have the best of both worlds. There is indeed a general assumption that RDF is the common application-level data model. However, at the protocol level, there is no such assumption as XML, JSON, and images are exchanged alike. The only assumption is that the recipient client knows how to handle the representation via the included IMT.

The state facet is a measure of the amount of state a service keeps of an ongoing interaction. As mentioned in the Fielding's description of REST, keeping state can contribute to inefficiencies in a distributed system. A loosely coupled approach coincides with the assumption in REST that all interactions are stateless. In our case, the protocol interactions are indeed stateless in the sense that the hypermedia exchanged determines the state of the application at any time. However, the repository stores the resource representations (as the case management dataset) and the various services in the design have access to the state of each case (and therefore the state of the workflow) through their ability to query the dataset.

Finally, the conversation facet is a measure of how much the architecture requires participating clients to interact with services through a fully-specified sequence of message exchanges. A loosely coupled approach enables clients to discover interaction paths at runtime by means of introspection on the representations returned from invoking the services. In the case of our use case, there is no a-priori specification of the concurrent data entry workflow. The workflow sequence is encapsulated as part of the design of the Web application. This is in contrast to the traditional approach to building workflow applications where an orchestration language such as BPEL is used to fully-specify the interaction paths at design time.

7 Conclusions

The SemanticDB deployment in the Clinical Investigations Heart and Vascular Institute has been successful as the content management infrastructure for a clinical research pipeline. The use of a declarative, Web-based knowledge representation and document management architecture has limited the amount of programming expertise needed to configure and deploy ongoing updates to the system in response to the research demands that change on a weekly basis. In addition, the RESTful service framework of the underlying content repository lowered the cost of integrating mashup frameworks such as Exhibit in order to address the needs of departmental applications.

The role of SOA and REST approaches to architectural design of distributed systems should be carefully considered in the context of the applications being built. It can help ensure that an information system can evolve over time in an iterative fashion that does not require significant and possibly costly changes. In some scenarios, the requirements of a particular use case will appeal to an approach based on the distributed hypermedia paradigm. In other use cases where there is less human interaction, a need for asynchronous activity, and a lack of engineering resources for low-level development, the controlled SOA approach may be more appropriate.

However, in making a determination as to which architecture is appropriate, enterprise architects should also consider how Semantic Web technologies may contribute to the decision process. The Semantic Web provides a framework for machine-interpretation of content that might be relevant for problem domains and use cases where the semantics of the data is a prominent architectural factor.

References

1. Berners-Lee T, Hendler J, Lassila O: The Semantic Web. Scientific American 284(5):34–43, 2001.
2. Bizer C, Heath T, Berners-Lee T:Linked Data–The Story So Far. International Journal on Semantic Web and Information Systems 5(3):1–22, 2009.

3. Connolly C: Gleaning Resource Descriptions from Dialects of Languages (GRDDL). W3C Candidate Recommendation, 2007.
4. Decker S, Melnik S, Van Harmelen F, Fensel D, Klein M, Broekstra J, Erdmann M, Horrocks I. The Semantic Web: The roles of XML and RDF. IEEE Internet computing 4(5):63–73, 2000.
5. Eder J (2009) Workflow Management and Workflow Management System. In Ling L, Tamer O (eds) Encyclopedia of Database Systems.
6. Fielding R, Gettys J, Mogul J, Frystyk H, Masinter L, Leach P, and Berners-Lee T. RFC2616: Hypertext Transfer Protocol–HTTP/1.1. RFC Editor United States, 1999.
7. Fielding R. Representational State Transfer (REST). Chapter 5 in Architectural Styles and the Design of Network–based Software Architectures. Ph. D. Thesis, University of California, Irvine, CA, 2000.
8. Hayes P. RDF Model Theory. Technical report, W3C Recommendation, February 2004.
9. Hayes P, and Halpin H. In Defense of Ambiguity. International Journal on Semantic Web and Information Systems 4(2):1–18, 2008.
10. Huynh D, Karger D, and Miller R. Exhibit: Lightweight Structured Data Publishing. In Proceedings of the 16th international conference on World Wide Web, page 746. ACM, 2007.
11. Kindberg T, Hawke S. The tag URI Scheme. 2005.
12. Lloyd J. Practical Advantages of Declarative Programming. In Joint Conference on Declarative Programming, GULP-PRODE, volume 94, 1994.
13. Mankovski S (2009) Service Oriented Architecture. In Ling L, Tamer O (eds) Encyclopedia of Database Systems.
14. Ogbuji C (2009) Clinical Data Acquisition, Storage and Management. In Ling L, Tamer O (eds) Encyclopedia of Database Systems.
15. Ogbuji U, Ogbuji C. Develop Python/XML with 4Suite, Part 5: The Repository Features. http://www.ibm.com/developerworks/edu/x-dw-x4suite5-i.html, 2002.
16. Olsen L, Aisner D, and McGinnis J. The Learning Healthcare System: Workshop Summary. Natl Academy Pr, 2007.
17. Pautasso C, Wilde E. Why is the Web Loosely Coupled?: A Multi-faceted Metric for Service Design. In Proceedings of the 18th international conference on World Wide Web, pages 911–920. ACM, 2009.
18. Pautasso C, Zimmermann O, Leymann F. Restful Web Services vs. Big Web Services: Making the Right Architectural Decision. In Proceeding of the 17th international conference on World Wide Web, pages 805–814. ACM, 2008.
19. Thompson H. Web Architecture and Naming for Knowledge Resources. Large-Scale Knowledge Resources. Construction and Application, pages 334–343.
20. Wil P, van der A (2009) Business Process Execution Language. In Ling L, Tamer O (eds) Encyclopedia of Database Systems.
21. Vinoski S. Putting the Web into Web Services: Interaction Models, Part 2. IEEE Internet Computing 6(4):90–92, 2002.
22. Vinoski S. Serendipitous Reuse. Distributed Systems Online, 2008.
23. Wohlstadter E (2009) SOAP. In Ling L, Tamer O (eds) Encyclopedia of Database Systems.

Use of Semantic Web technologies on the BBC Web Sites

Yves Raimond, Tom Scott, Silver Oliver, Patrick Sinclair and Michael Smethurst

Abstract The BBC publishes large amounts of content online, as text, audio and video. As the amount of content grows, we need to make it easy for users to locate items of interest and to draw coherent journeys across them. In this chapter, we describe our use of Semantic Web technologies for achieving this goal. We focus in particular on three BBC Web sites: BBC Programmes, BBC Music and BBC Wildlife Finder, and how those Web sites effectively use the wider Web as their Content Management System.

1 Introduction

The BBC is the largest broadcasting corporation in the world. Central to its mission is to enrich peoples lives with programmes that inform, educate and entertain. It is a public service broadcaster, established by a Royal Charter and funded, in part, by

Yves Raimond
British Broadcasting Corporation, Broadcasting House, Portland Place, London, United Kingdom,
e-mail: yves.raimond@bbc.co.uk

Tom Scott
British Broadcasting Corporation, Broadcasting House, Portland Place, London, United Kingdom,
e-mail: tom.scott@bbc.co.uk

Silver Oliver
British Broadcasting Corporation, Broadcasting House, Portland Place, London, United Kingdom,
e-mail: silver.oliver@bbc.co.uk

Patrick Sinclair
British Broadcasting Corporation, Broadcasting House, Portland Place, London, United Kingdom,
e-mail: patrick.sinclair@bbc.co.uk

Michael Smethurst
British Broadcasting Corporation, Broadcasting House, Portland Place, London, United Kingdom,
e-mail: michael.smethurst@bbc.co.uk

D. Wood (ed.), *Linking Enterprise Data*, DOI 10.1007/978-1-4419-7665-9_13,
© Springer Science+Business Media, LLC 2010

the licence fee that is paid by UK households. The BBC uses the income from the licence fee to provide public services including 8 national TV channels plus regional programming, 10 national radio stations, 40 local radio stations and an extensive website, `http://www.bbc.co.uk`.

1.1 Linking microsites for cross-domain navigation

The BBC publishes large amounts of content online, as text, audio and video. Historically the website has focused largely on supporting broadcast brands (e.g. Top Gear) and a series of domain-specific sites (e.g. news, food, gardening, etc.). That is, the focus has been on providing separate, standalone HTML sites designed to be accessed with a desktop Web browser. These sites can be very successful, but tend not to link together, and so are less useful when people have interests that span programme brands or domains. For example, we can tell you who presents Top Gear, but not what else those people have presented. As a user it is very difficult to find everything the BBC has published about any given subject, nor can you easily navigate across BBC domains following a particular semantic thread. For example, until recently you weren't able to navigate from a page about a programme to a page about an artist played in that programme.

This lack of cross linking has also limited the type of user interaction the BBC is able to offer, for example, it is a complex piece of work to recontextualise content designed for one purpose (e.g. a programme web site) for another purpose or to extract the underlying data and visualize it in a new or different way. This has been because of a lack of integration at a data level and a lack of semantically meaningful predicates making it difficult to repurpose and represent data within a different context.

1.2 Making data available to developers

The BBC, since 2005 through its Backstage project[1], has made 'feeds' (mainly RSS) available for third party developers to build non-commercial mash-ups. However, these feeds suffer from the same or similar issues to the microsites namely they lack interlinking. That is, it is possible to get a feed of latest news stories but it is not easy to segment that data into news stories about 'Lions'. Nor is it possible to query the data to extract the specific data required.

---

[1] `http://backstage.bbc.co.uk/`

1.3 Making use of the wider Web

Developing internal Content Management Systems is expensive, both in terms of editorial staff required to add and curate data into them, and in terms of development and integration costs. A tremendous amount of community-curated data is available on the Web, which can be used to make our sites richer, either by providing a navigation backbone (e.g. Musicbrainz[2] for BBC Music) or by enhancing our pages with relevant information (e.g. Wikipedia[3] for BBC Music). Also, by involving our editorial staff in those community-curated datasets, we make sure the community at large benefit from our use of the data.

2 Programme support on the Web

When commissioning hand-crafted programme web sites for specific broadcast brands, only a small subset of programme can be covered. Hence, until recently, only the major BBC brands had a web presence on the BBC web site. Even between programmes that had a corresponding web site commissioned, the disparity in terms of programme support was high. Some programmes would have a very detailed web site, with for example information about cast and crew, about the fictional universe in which the programme takes place, etc. Some other programmes would just have a single web page with upcoming broadcast dates.

As the BBC broadcasts between 1,000 and 1,500 programmes a day, this meant that historically the long tail of programming didn't get any web presence. Hand-crafted web sites are also harder to maintain and they therefore often got forgotten and left unmaintained, or even removed. This meant that when referring to a particular programme from other content on the BBC web site, no persistent link could be used.

As new platforms become ubiquitous (mobile, game consoles, etc.), so the BBC web sites also needed to provide a coherent offering across those platforms. However, without a single, common source of integrated data and an efficient publishing mechanism this increase in platforms could result in a parallel and unsustainable increase in effort.

Hand-crafting programme web sites is inefficient - there is a limited amount of code reuse between sites but it is not only expensive in terms of actual expenditure, but also in terms of opportunity costs. The time spent writing HTML files is lost, and you can't spend it on developing new features or otherwise improving the site for its users.

---

[2] see http://musicbrainz.org
[3] see http://wikipedia.org

2.1 BBC Programmes

BBC Programmes[4] launched in Summer 2007 to address these issues. It provides a persistent web identifier for every programme the BBC broadcasts. Each web identifier has multiple content-negotiated representations, ensuring that a coherent offering is proposed across multiple devices (e.g. desktop and mobile) and that the data used to generate our pages is re-usable in different formats (RDF/XML, JSON and plain XML) to enable building enhanced programme support applications. Other teams within the BBC can incorporate those programme pages into new and existing programme support sites, TV Channel and Radio Station sites, and cross programme genre sites such as food, music and natural history.

2.2 The Programmes Ontology

In November 2007, we launched the Programmes Ontology [11]. The reason for publishing this ontology was three-fold. Firstly, it exposes the data model driving our web site as a formal OWL [5] ontology. As BBC Programmes was built using a Domain Driven Design methodology[5], this ontology can be seen as a 'map' of the different items we publish a web identifier for and of the links between these items. Secondly, it allows us to anchor our data feeds within a domain model. The RDF/XML feeds we provide, as well as the RDFa markup embedded within our HTML pages, refer to terms defined within this ontology. Thirdly, this ontology aims at assisting other organisations or individuals to publish programmes data on the Web. In the following, we give a brief overview of the different terms defined within our Programmes Ontology. A diagram of these terms and their relationships is given in Figure 1.

2.2.1 Main terms

We consider a **Programme** as being the core of our domain model. A programme is an editorial entity, which can either be an **Episode** (e.g. 'Top Gear, first episode of the first series'), a **Series** (e.g. 'Top Gear, first series) or a **Brand** (e.g. 'Top Gear'). All these programmes have multiple **Versions**, where a version is an actual piece of media content, either audio or audio and video. A single episode may have multiple versions. For example, an episode can have an original, unedited, version, a shortened one, a signed one, etc. Versions can have **Broadcasts**, each of them being on a particular **Service** and at a particular time, and they can have **Availabilities** —

---

[4] http://www.bbc.co.uk/programmes

[5] For more details on the methodology used to build BBC Programmes, we refer the reader to http://www.bbc.co.uk/blogs/radiolabs/2009/01/how_we_make_websites.shtml, last accessed April 2010

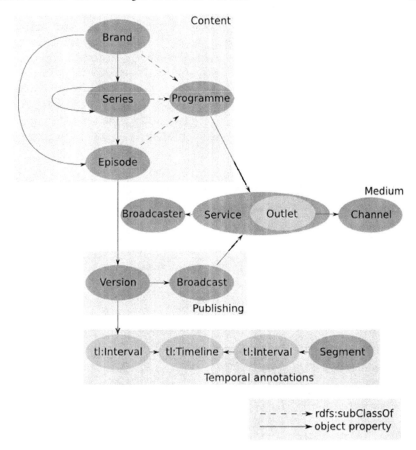

Fig. 1 Main terms within the Programmes Ontology and their relationships

they can be made available through our iPlayer catchup service for a period of time on a particular set of devices.

2.2.2 Tagging programmes

In order to generate simple aggregations of programmes, our domain model has a simple **category** predicate allowing us to relate a programme to a particular item in a SKOS categorisation scheme [8]. The Programmes Ontology defines two different categorisations scheme: genres (e.g. 'drama') and formats (e.g. 'animation'). We also use the **subject** predicate defined within Dublin Core[6] to relate programmes to related subjects (e.g. 'birds'), people (e.g. 'William Shakespeare'), places (e.g. 'Manchester') and organisations (e.g. 'BBC'). Using such

---

[6] see http://dublincore.org/documents/dcmi-terms/, last accessed May 2010

categorisations and subject classifications, we can generate pages such as `http://www.bbc.co.uk/programmes/genres/drama/historical`, aggregating programmes in a particular category (here, in the 'historical' sub-genre of the 'drama' genre). Similarly, we can provide an aggregated view of all BBC Radio 4 programmes associated with the subject 'writer', as depicted in Figure 2. We are currently moving to use DBpedia [1] web identifiers as tags [7], so that we can aggregate richer information about them (e.g. geolocation of places and relationships between artists). By exploiting this ancillary data, we can provide richer ways of navigating our content.

Fig. 2 An aggregation of BBC Radio 4 programmes associated with the subject 'writer'

2.2.3 A flexible segmentation model

When describing a programme, it is critical to be able to describe its actual content. Therefore, a good segmentation model which can accomodate track listings in a music show, points of interest within a programme, or editorially relevant sub-sections of a programme, is critical. The Programmes Ontology defines such a model, making use of the Event and Timeline ontologies[7] created within the scope of the Music Ontology [10]. A version of a programme has a temporal extent, which is defined on a **Timeline**. On the same version timeline, we can anchor **Segments** — classifications of particular temporal sections of a version. Most links to other ontologies are done at the segment level, as we might want to describe e.g. the recipe being described or the track being played. For example, it is at the segment level that we link to the BBC Music web site described in section 3. We can also classify segments using the same mechanism as described above, to associate a segment with a particular place, subject, person or organisation.

2.3 Web identifiers for broadcast radio and television sites

Human-readability is often deemed important when creating web identifiers. In the case of programmes this could mean that identifiers could be created from programmes titles. However, when a programme title changes, the corresponding web identifier would also change, which would make external links to that programme break. Programme titles can also clash — it can happen that two distinct programmes share the same title, e.g. many episodes don't have a distinct title, for example long running weekly shows such as the 'Today programme'[8]. We could imagine creating web identifiers from other literal attributes, such as broadcast dates. However, those identifiers become ambiguous when a programme gets repeated. Those identifiers would also break for off-schedule content — programmes only available through on-demand services such as the BBC iPlayer.

Any web identifier that assumes some structure of the object it is representing is likely to break when that structure changes[9].

In order to keep a level of indirection helping us to deal with such changes, we use opaque unique identifiers such as b00cccvg to construct our web identifiers. Given an opaque identifier, we need to consider several web identifiers for a single programme. We need to identify the actual programme (e.g. a particular episode of 'Doctor Who'), and a page about this programme, as we want to state different things about both of them — the creation date of the page will not the be the same as the creation date of the programme, for example. We adopt the following scheme:

- /programmes/b00cccvg#programme – the actual programme;
- /programmes/b00cccvg – a document about that programme;
- /programmes/b00cccvg.html – an XHTML page about that programme;
- /programmes/b00cccvg.mp – an XHTML Mobile Profile page about that programme;

---

[7] See http://purl.org/NET/c4dm/event.owl and http://purl.org/NET/c4dm/timeline.owl

[8] http://www.bbc.co.uk/programmes/b006qj9z

[9] See the web identifier opacity section in [6]

- `/programmes/b00cccvg.rdf` – an RDF/XML document about that programme

We also need to identify the associated versions, segments, broadcasts and availability windows. We use a similar mechanism for those, by generating unique identifiers and constructing web identifiers from them.

From `/programmes/b00cccvg` to one specific representation (e.g. XHTML or RDF/XML), we use content negotiation [12]. The representation that is most appropriate for the user agent will be sent back, along with a `Content-Location` HTTP header pointing to the canonical web identifier for that particular representation.

The use of content negotiation and the use of the fragment identifiers firstly reduces the number of requests the server needs to process compared to other methods for publishing Linked Data, such as the redirection-based method described in [12]; but more significantly it ensures that there is one web identifier for a resource. We only want users or automated user agents to see and work with the programme web identifier or the generic document web identifier. So that if a user bookmarks a web identifier on a desktop machine they can access that bookmark on a mobile and get an appropriate mobile representation. Similarly, an automated user agent aggregating BBC Programmes data needs information in a more structured format than an HTML document, so it will access an appropriate structured representation, e.g. RDF/XML.

3 BBC Music

The aim of the BBC Music website[10] is to provide a comprehensive guide to music content across the BBC, linking information about an artist to those BBC programmes that have played them. BBC Music follows the same principles as BBC Programmes, and provides a persistent web identifier for primary objects within the music domain, and integrate those with the other BBC domains our audience is interested in, namely programmes, events and users. These primary music objects are: artists, releases and their reviews, and editorial genres.

On the BBC Music Beta, there are three sources of information: Musicbrainz, Wikipedia and the BBC. Musicbrainz is used as the backbone of the site, providing data such as artists' releases, relationships with other artists and links to external websites. Wikipedia is used for artists biographies. The BBC provides additional information, such as audio snippets for tracks, images, album reviews, details about which programme have played which artist and links to related content elsewhere on the BBC site.

---

[10] `http://www.bbc.co.uk/music`

3.1 BBC Music as Linked Data

We are publishing Linked Data for most of the resources on BBC Music using a variety of different ontologies and vocabularies. The Linked Data community has developed several vocabularies around the music domain that we have been able to reuse. For example, we use the music ontology [10] for describing artists and release information, the Reviews Ontology [2] for describing album reviews and SKOS [8] for defining the BBC music genres.

3.2 Web identifiers for BBC Music

As with BBC Programmes, we decided to use opaque identifiers for constructing BBC Music web identifiers to improve their persistence. MusicBrainz uses a globally unique identifier (GUID) scheme for its resources. When it came to BBC Music, instead of coming up with our own identifiers we reused the MusicBrainz artist GUIDs:

- `/music/artists/:musicbrainz_artist_guid#artist` – the actual artist;
- `/music/artists/:musicbrainz_artist_guid` – a document about that artist;
- `/music/artists/:musicbrainz_artist_guid.html` – an XHTML page about that artist;
- `/music/artists/:musicbrainz_artist_guid.rdf` – an RDF/XML document about that artist

For album reviews, we have minted our own URL keys (e.g "b5rj") and use the following scheme:

- `/music/reviews/:url_key#review` – the actual review;
- `/music/reviews/:url_key` – a document about that review;
- `/music/reviews/:url_key.html` – an XHTML page about that review;
- `/music/reviews/:url_key.rdf` – an RDF/XML document about that review

We also have similar scheme for other resources such as reviewers and BBC content promoted through the site[11].

---

[11] respectively at `/music/reviewers` and `/music/promotions`

3.3 The Web as a content management system

The use of Musicbrainz and Wikipedia to provide the underlying data for the site has allowed us to cover a much wider range of artists that would otherwise be possible. It is beyond our resources to maintain a biography for every artist heard on the BBC. It also ensures the data is kept up to date and doesn't go stale. For instance, when an artist dies their profile is updated within a few hours by the community and this change is reflected on our site.

BBC Music takes the approach that the Web itself is its content management system. BBC editors directly contribute to Musicbrainz and Wikipedia, and BBC Music will show an aggregated view of this information, put in a BBC context.

3.4 Using the BBC Programmes and the BBC Music Linked Data

The BBC Programmes Linked Data described in section 2.1 links to the BBC Music data. A programme that features an artist will be linked to that artist within BBC Music, using the segmentation model described above. Moreover, BBC Music artists are linked to corresponding resources within DBpedia. A number of prototype applications demonstrating the use of such links have been built, both within the BBC and outside.

3.4.1 Programmes and locations

When aggregating DBpedia information about BBC artists, we can access related geographical location (current location, place of birth, place of death, etc.). Using this information we can display programmes on maps, according to the locations of the artists played in those programmes. We can also build geographical programme look-up services[12] which, given a place, give a list of programmes featuring an artist related to that place.

3.4.2 Artist recommendations

As mentioned in [9], Linked Data can be used to generate music recommendations. From BBC Music artists, a number of music-related datasets can be reached. By following links leading from one artist to another, we can derive connections between artists (e.g. 'this artist has had his first music video directed by the same person as that other artist') that can be used to drive recommendations. The path leading

---

[12] an example of such a service, using Ordnance Survey, BBC and DBpedia data, is available at http://www.johngoodwin.me.uk/boundaries/meshup.html, last accessed July 2009

from one artist to another can then be used to explain why a particular recommendation has been generated. This is a fundamental shift from most current music
recommender systems which, given an artist, return an ordered list of related artist
without any clue for the user as to how these recommendations were generated. Although recent work has been done in trying to make music recommendation more
transparent, such as the Aura [4] recommendation engine from Sun Microsystems
Labs, the generated explanations are limited by the use of simple textual tags, which
discards explanations derived from potential relationships between such tags.

Two prototypes have been built by the BBC to ilustrate such music recommendations generated from Linked Data. LODations[13] provides a collaborative way to
specify editorially relevant connections between artists. New musical connections,
such as 'if two bands were formed in June 1976 in Manchester, then they are musi-
cally related' can be specified, and music recommendations along with their explanations are derived from these connections. An example of LODations recommendations is depicted in Figure 3. The 'MusicBore'[14] derives connections between
artists in a similar way and use them to generate an original radio programme. An
automated DJ, built using an off-the-shelf text-to-speech software, uses these connections to explain how the next artist in the tracklist relates to the previous one (e.g.
'they were both born in Detroit in the mid-1960s').

Fig. 3 Artist page for Busta Rhymes, along with recommendations generated from Linked Data

---

[13] see http://lodations.heroku.com/, last accessed April 2010

[14] see http://www.bbc.co.uk/blogs/radiolabs/2009/07/the_music_bore.
shtml, last accessed April 2010

4 BBC Wildlife Finder

BBC Wildlife Finder[15], provides a web identifier for every species (and other bio-logical ranks), habitat and adaptation the BBC has an interest in. The information presented is aggregated from data within the BBC and across the Web, including: Wikipedia, the WWF's Wildfinder, the IUCN's Red List of Threatened Species, the Zoological Society of Londons EDGE of Existence programme and Animal Diversity Web. BBC Wildlife Finder repurposes this external data and puts it in a BBC context adding to it with programme clips extracted from the BBC's Natural History Unit archive and links to programme episodes and BBC news articles.

An underlying principle behind the design of Wildlife Finder is the notion that people care more about real world concepts than abstract web pages, by providing web identifiers and associate documents about things that people care about, think about and talk about, it is more likely that the site will be intuitive and more likely to be discovered via search. As a result the Wildlife Finder provides web identifiers for real world natural history objects — animals, plants their habitats and adaptations. Each of these resources are then linked to adjacent concepts within the ontology, for example, a web idenfier for Lions links to web identifiers for the "tropical grassland" (because lions live there) and for "pack hunting" because that's one of the lion's behaviours; this is in addition to BBC programmes and news stories about lions.

Wildlife programmes (clips and episodes) are transcluded and linked to from the Wildlife Finder web site. The programmes are identified by 'tagging' the clip or episode with the appropriate DBpedia web identifier. Programmes are identified as "coming soon", "catch up" or "archived" by checking the BBC Programmes RDF described in section 2.1 to extract the relevant broadcast or catch-up details. RDF was found to be a convenient approach when it came to integrating two separate but related domains within the BBC.

4.1 The Wildlife Ontology

As noted above, BBC Wildlife Finder was designed following similar principles to BBC Music and BBC Programmes - that is modeling the site around real world concepts, in this case that means the animals, plants, habitats and adaptations the BBC films. We recently published the Wildlife Ontology [3], describing how those different concepts we are interested in relate to each other. Our objective in publishing the ontology is similar as what we described in section 2.2 for the Programmes Ontology. It should be noted that although the Wildlife Ontology was designed with the BBC Wildlife Finder application in mind it should be applicable to a wide range of biological data publishing use cases and to that end care has been taken to try and ensure interoperability with more specialised ontologies used in scientific domains such as taxonomy, ecology, environmental science, and bioinformatics.

---

[15] http://www.bbc.co.uk/wildlifefinder/

4.1.1 Main terms

Biologists group organisms based on their current understanding of a species evolution. This has resulted in a hierarchical grouping or taxonomy of species. However, in addition to the absolute hierarchy the relative hierarchy when compared to other species can also be of interest and as a result each of these groups, or ranks, have historically been given their own names. Ranks are useful because they help you know how far down in the tree of life you are (e.g. a Class is further 'down' than Phylum). Certain ranks also allow you to usefully lump groups of organisms together. For example, the rank of "Class" (Class Aves, Class Mammalia, Class Insecta etc.) is convenient and useful to biologists.

Of all the biological ranks that of "species" is the most significant to us. Although there are a number of different definition for species the most common is that of a group of organisms capable of interbreeding and producing fertile offspring of both genders. The classification for all other ranks (e.g. Genus and Class) are not as strictly codified, and hence different authorities often produce different classifications.

In addition to the Linnean taxonomy the wildlife ontology also describes a species's habitat, grouped into terrestrial, aquatic (freshwater) and marine habitats; their adaptations to their environment, their conservation status (as defined by the IUCN[16]) and the habitats and species found within an ecozone[17].

The core to the Wildlife Ontology, however, is the species. Species, in addition, to being for us the most significant biological rank also tend to be the point of interest with regard to other areas of research, for example, both conservation and distribution studies tends to focus on the species. It is therefore the species which links to other classes (habitat, adaptations, conservation status etc.) within the Wildlife Finder application. However, it is worth noting that this level of linking is not enforced within the ontology and it is acceptable to link habitats to other taxonomic ranks.

4.1.2 Species as Classes vs Species as Instances

One perennial problem associated with modeling biological taxonomies using RDF is whether to attempt to model individual species as Classes, or whether to simply model species as instances of a generic Species class. The latter approach is simpler and avoids creating a huge ontology that attempts to model all biological organisms. Existing ontologies have taken different approaches to resolving this issue, some choosing one style, others another. At present there doesn't seem to be a consensus. With this in mind, the Wildlife Ontology adopts the simpler of the two approaches, i.e. modeling species as instances of a Species class, as this maximises interoper-

---

[16] http://www.iucnredlist.org/

[17] See http://simple.wikipedia.org/wiki/Ecozone

ability with many of the existing Linked Data sources, particularly DBpedia, which adopt similar approaches.

4.1.3 Web identifiers - using DBpedia as a controlled vocabulary

As noted above DBpedia provides a controlled vocabulary to help link programme clips and episodes, and news stories to web identifiers within Wildlife Finder. All resources within Wildlife Finder are constructed using the corresponding Wikipedia web identifier slug. A URI slug is the fragment of a URI that uniquely identifies a resource within a domain, for example, in the case of Wikipedia the URI slug for the entry Stoat: `http://en.wikipedia.org/wiki/Stoat` is "Stoat".

By using identifiers that are already widely used across the Web it means that:

1. The BBC can effectively outsource a significant proportion of the effort required to maintain a controlled vocabulary to the Web;
2. It makes it easier for third party developers to integrate with BBC content because of a shared definition of a resource;
3. The BBC can contribute its knowledge to the Web by linking data to those common identifiers and by creating new identifiers where necessary.

The added advantage in using Wikipedia is the addition of a large evidence set. The Wikipedia article text defines the meaning and use of the identifier and hence allows the BBC to confirm which identifier to use in which context.

DBpedia URIs are used to categorise programme episodes and clips and, news stories. The cagorisation is used to assert that the programme, clip or news story is "about" the concept identified by the DBpedia URI i.e. it is about an animal, plant, habitat or adaptation. This categorisation is thus used to identify news stories and programmes before transcluding the relevant information on Wildlife Finder pages. The canonical web identifier for a clip, news story etc. remains with BBC Programmes (see section 2.1), news site etc. The clip is therefore discoverable both in a BBC Programmes context and within a Wildlife Finder context (a clip can be about both a species and an adaptation).

4.2 Web identifiers

As mentioned above, in addition to using DBpedia as a controlled vocabulary to tag content, Wildlife Finder also reuses Wikipedia URI slugs to construct its web identifiers. The high level web identifier scheme is therefore as follows:

For biological taxa:

- `/nature/rank/:wikipedia_slug#:rank` – the actual organism;
- `/nature/rank/:wikipedia_slug` – a document about that organism;
- `/nature/rank/:wikipedia_slug.html` – an XHTML page about that organism;

- `/nature/rank/:wikipedia_slug.rdf` – an RDF/XML document about that organism

For habitats:

- `/nature/habitats/:wikipedia_slug#habitat` – the actual habitat;
- `/nature/habitats/:wikipedia_slug` – a document about that habitat;
- `/nature/habitats/:wikipedia_slug.html` – an XHTML page about that habitat;
- `/nature/habitats/:wikipedia_slug.rdf` – an RDF/XML document about that habitat

For adaptations:

- `/nature/adaptations/:wikipedia_slug#:adaptation` – the actual adaptation;
- `/nature/adaptations/:wikipedia_slug` – a document about that adaptation;
- `/nature/adaptations/:wikipedia_slug.html` – an XHTML page about that adaptation;
- `/nature/adaptations/:wikipedia_slug.rdf` – an RDF/XML document about that adaptation

The only exception to this web identifier scheme is with collections (editorially curated aggregations of BBC content):

- `/nature/collections/:pid#:adaptation` – the actual collection;
- `/nature/collections/:pid` – a document about that collection;
- `/nature/collections/:pid.html` – an XHTML page about that collection;
- `/nature/collections/:pid.rdf` – an RDF/XML document about that collection

Programme identifiers similar to the ones used in BBC Programmes (PIDs) where chosen to identify collections because, like a programme, a collection is an editorially curated entity created by the BBC. The provenance of a collection means that not only will Wikipedia not have an entry but also that its ownership resides with the BBC not with the Web at large, since it is the BBC who chose the clips and edited the introductory video. It is therefore appropriate that the BBC provide the identifier for these objects.

From `/nature/rank/:wikipedia_slug` etc. to one specific representation (e.g. XHTML or RDF/XML), we use content negotiation, exactly as described in section 2.3. The format that is most appropriate for the user agent will be sent back, along with a `Content-Location` HTTP header pointing to the canonical URL for that particular format.

4.3 The Web as a Content Management System

The data that makes up a page on Wildlife Finder is taken from a range of range of sources, both inside and outside the BBC. Some of this data is in effect read-only that is the BBC nor its audience is at liberty to modify it. This includes, for example, the information about the conservation status of a species and is used, as supplied, by the IUCN. Other sources of data notably Wikipedia can be edited by both the BBC and its audience - this has the effect of making Wikipedia part of the BBC's content management 'system'.

The use of Wikipedia on Wildlife Finder means that the BBC and its audience benefits from access to (generally) high quality content about things in the natural world and additional, contextual links to that content. People can continue their journey and discover information elsewhere on the Web. In addition, the rest of the Web also benefits because where the BBC is able to improve the content on Wikipedia, it does so not on bbc.co.uk but on Wikipedia directly and in doing so users of Wikipedia also benefit.

4.4 The importance of curation

It is not always possible nor desirable to automate all aspects of page building. It is sometimes advantageous to curate specific collections of content - for example a collection of David Attenborough's favourite moments from the last 30 years[18], as depicted in Figure 4, or a collection highlighting one of the worlds endangered animals, the tiger[19].

While in theory both these collections could be separately modeled and codified within the ontology it wouldn't be practical to do so - there would be little additional benefit in modeling one off collections. Instead it is sufficient to define a collection as a group of editorially selected and sequenced clips, habitats, adaptations and taxa introduced through a bespoke clip i.e. one edited specifically for the collection.

Collections add a personalised context to the content within Wildlife Finder — they are not simply a set of aggregated clips, they have been selected, sequences and used to tell a specific story. This added layer adds a level of trust to the content and helps guide the users of the site through particular aspects of the site. Without this layer the site would remain largely encyclopedic, providing information to those that know what they are looking for but not introducing people to the content and acting as a guide through that content. With the addition of collections the BBC can guide people through some of that information, to present it in a different light and add a new context to the raw information; and in doing so the collections not only provide the audience with an easier route into the site but can also facilite a conversation by positioning the content within a specific light.

---

[18] see http://www.bbc.co.uk/nature/collections/p0048522
[19] see http://www.bbc.co.uk/nature/collections/p0063wt7

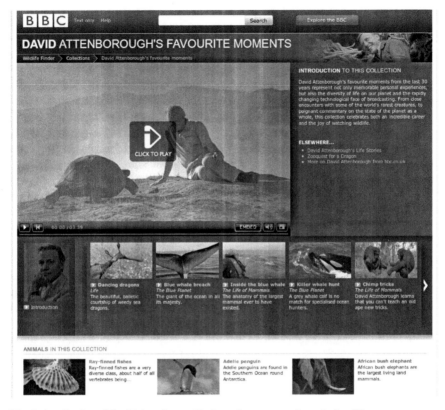

Fig. 4 A collection of David Attenborough's favourite moments from the last 30 years

5 Journalism

BBC Journalism incorporates News, Sport, Travel and the Weather. The majority of this content (News and Sport) consist of stories published out of a content production system. Once published these stories are manually managed on to a small number of topical indexes. For years this has been sufficient but recent business requirements have created an impetus for more sophisticated publishing and navigation strategies. For example:

- Automating the creation of lower profile indexes;
- More sophisticated information architectures with many more topical indexes;
- Merging data (sports statistics for example) with stories to create a more coherent product;
- Linking to other BBC sites and external sites.

The starting point has been sporting events like the Winter Olympics and World Cup. These are easier to model and populate with data because you know when they will happen, who will participate and where the event will happen. For example the model for the Winter Olympics includes athletes, sports disciplines and sports venues. For the 2010 Winter Olympics we published a page for every sports discipline. These pages consisted of stories, statistics, other BBC content and links to external sites.

The process of creating these pages was to first model the event. Working with domain experts we established the key concepts and relationships important to the event. This was then turned into a formal OWL ontology. Where possible bits of existing ontologies were reused and the Winter Olympics model was based largely on the Event Ontology mentioned in section 2.2. This will make it easier for others to query and access the data in the future as well as reducing the number of design decisions required.

5.1 Populating and using the ontology

The modeling of the Winter Olympics was relatively low cost in terms of design time but populating the ontology would involve significant effort. Because of this we looked to consume data freely available on the web. The primary source is Wikipedia but there were gaps that we would need to fill with data the BBC would author. To facilitate the integration of the Wikipedia data and BBC data we are using the Uberblic service[20]. This means live updates from Wikipedia can be combined along with data created in a local MediaWiki[21] instance. The data can then be consolidated in real time and the resulting RDF used by services producing the Winter Olympics site.

The Uberblic service provides DBpedia identifiers for those entities that are in Wikipedia. This ensures Winter Olympics data can interoperate with other BBC systems that work with DBpedia identifiers. For those entities not in Wikipedia new BBC identifiers were created. This means we are not restricted to entities existing in Wikipedia alone. This approach is taken, as opposed to creating new Wikipedia pages, because the concepts are considered to be unlikely to be of significant cultural interest to justify the existence of a page in Wikipedia (for example Canadian Winter Olympics Team at the Winter Olympics 2010).

The populated ontology was primarily used to provide data for an auto-categorisation system. The presence of various entities in a document could be used, once compared to concepts and relationships in the ontology, to help disambiguate the entities extracted. This service suggested concepts to journalists to tag stories with. Once done, tagged stories were then dynamically included on Winter Olympics pages.

---

[20] see http://uberblic.org
[21] see http://www.mediawiki.org

5.2 Future developments

In future projects greater use could be made of the ontology and the common web identifiers. Sharing common identifiers across the BBC ensures the aggregated pages contain as much variety of content as possible. For example the use of DBpedia identifiers by the BBC Programmes service and sporting events like the Winter Olympics allow for the transclusion of BBC programmes in to the sport event pages. In addition if there was a requirement to add a rich navigation structure linking the aggregated pages we have the option of using the relationships in the ontology. For example the relationships in DBpedia could be used to generate links between Winter Olympic athletes and the sports disciplines they participate in.

An easily achieved use of Linked Data for news organisations would be to make their topic aggregation pages available as Linked Data. This is something the New York Times have already done[22] and there are now established design patterns for publishing lists of stories associated with a particular topic. This will offer a clear and simple path for other news organisation to follow the New York Times lead. Once we have a number of organisations publishing stories as Linked Data it will be increasingly easy to link from a BBC topic index to the most recent stories on other news sites. The key here will be the use of common web identifiers. We can already see in the BBC, New York Times and Reuters the use of DBpedia as a way to commonly identify topics and entities. The publishing of established controlled vocabularies (like IPTC) as Linked Data and mapping them to common web identfiers will also be critical to lowering the barrier of entry to those organisations already using these vocabularies.

Going beyond the syndication of lists of stories the next stage for a news organisation would be to take advantage of the data freely available as Linked Data. Data sets like DBpedia, CIA Fact Book and the recently released UK Government data[23] could all be used to add context and navigation to otherwise dry aggregation pages. For example an aggregation page for an MP could be enriched with a personal profile, data about their previous election results and the policies they have voted on. In addition links between an MP aggregation page and a constituency aggregation page could be provided for free from the Linked Data sources. This is a technique already used by Wildlife Finder and BBC Music, as described above, and Linked Data makes this process considerably easier than collecting distributed data sets in different formats (for example CSV files and custom database dumps).

Not only will this improve the user experience but could also significantly improve the process of story creation for the journalists. If common Government identifiers are provider for a politician and we tag our assets with the same identifier then when a journalist is researching a story about a politician it becomes increasingly easy to pull data to them. By identifying the politician a journalist is interested in, it would be trivial to pull together all assets created by their news organisation as well as Linked Data about the politician from trusted web sources. This goes beyond the

---

[22] see http://data.nytimes.com

[23] see http://data.gov.uk

document retrieval of Google as it could merge useful data and documents to provide context regarding the politicians career, popularity with voters and impact on their constituency.

The question of trust regarding Linked Data is very important for journalism. Where sources like Wikipedia may not be acceptable by editorial standards it puts even more emphasis on trusted sources. For this reason the recent publishing of UK Government Linked Data sets is critically important to journalism, providing trusted identifiers, labels and relationships for things like politicians, schools and UK locations.

6 Conclusion

Creating web identifiers for every item the BBC has an interest in, and considering those as aggregations of BBC content about that item, allows us to enable very rich cross-domain user journeys. This means BBC content can be discovered by users in many different ways, and content teams within the organisation have a focal point around which to organise their content.

Reusing data from existing online sources such as Musicbrainz or Wikipedia means that the community at large benefits from our use of the data, as our editorial staff is directly contributing to those sources. It is also more efficient than maintaining an in-house Content Management System, which would require development and integration costs, and which would be very difficult to bootstrap, curate and maintain up-to-date.

The RDF representations of these web identifiers allow developers to use our data to build applications. The two issues, providing cross-domain navigation and machine-readable representations, are tightly interleaved. Giving access to machine-readable representations that hold links to further such representations, crossing domain boundaries, means that much richer applications can be built on top of our data, including new BBC products. In addition the system gives us a flexibility and a maintainability benefit: our web site becomes our API. Considering our feeds as an integral part of building a web site also means that they are very cheap to generate, even when built in a best efforts way: they are just a different view of our data.

The approach has also proved to be an efficient one – allowing different development teams to concentrate on different domains while at the same time benefiting from the activities of the other teams. The small pieces loosely joined approach, which is manifest in any Linked Data project, significantly reduces the need to coordinate teams while at the same time allowing each team to benefit from the activities of others.

References

1. S. Auer, C. Bizer, J. Lehmann, G. Kobilarov, R. Cyganiak, and Z. Ives. DBpedia: A nucleus for a web of open data. In Proceedings of the International Semantic Web Conference, Busan, Korea, November 11-15 2007.
2. Danny Ayers. Review vocabulary. Working draft. http://vocab.org/review/terms.html. Last accessed June 2010.
3. Leigh Dodds and Tom Scott. Wildlife ontology. Online ontology, February 2010. Available at http://purl.org/ontology/wo/. Last accessed April 2010.
4. S. Green, P. Lamere, J. Alexander, and F. Maillet. Generating transparent, steerable recommendations from textual descriptions of items. In Proceedings of the 3rd ACM Conference on Recommender Systems, 2009.
5. I. Horrocks, P. F. Patel-Schneider, and F. van Harmelen. From SHIQ and RDF to OWL: The making of a web ontology language. Journal of Web Semantics, 1:726, 2003.
6. IanJacobsandNormanWalsh.ArchitectureoftheWorldWideWeb,volumeone.W3CRecommendation, December 2004. http://www.w3.org/TR/webarch/. Last accessed July 2008.
7. Georgi Kobilarov, Tom Scott, Yves Raimond, Silver Oliver, Chris Sizemore, Michael Smethurst, Chris Bizer, and Robert Lee. Media meets semantic web - how the BBC uses DBpedia and linked data to make connections. In Proceedings of the European Semantic Web Conference In-Use track, 2009.
8. Alistair Miles and Sean Bechhofer. Skos simple knowledge organization system refer- ence. W3C Recommendation, August 2009. Available at http://www.w3.org/TR/ skos-reference/. Last accessed June 2010.
9. YvesRaimond. A distributed music information system. PhD thesis, Department of Electronic Engineering, Queen Mary, University of London, 2008.
10. Yves Raimond, Samer Abdallah, Mark Sandler, and Frederick Giasson. The music ontology. In Proceedings of the International Conference on Music Information Retrieval, pages 417 422, September 2007.
11. Yves Raimond, Patrick Sinclair, Nicholas J. Humfrey, and Michael Smethurst. Programmes ontology. Online ontology, September 2009. Available at http://purl.org/ ontology/po/. Last accessed April 2010.
12. Leo Sauermann and Richard Cyganiak. Cool uris for the semantic web. W3C Interest Group Note, March 2008. http://www.w3.org/TR/cooluris/. Last accessed June 2008.

Glossary

Readers are encouraged to also see the acronym list located in the front matter.

Abox One of two types of statements in an ontology (the other being Tbox). Abox statements represent facts (or "assertions", hence the "A"), e.g. John is a Person (where Person is a defined class).

backward chaining A method of reasoning that begins with a conclusion being sought and works backward to determine if any data supports that conclusion. Backward chaining is the reverse of forward chaining.

Big O notation A definition of the worst case performance of a mathematical function, often a computer algorithm.

closed world The presumption that what is not known to be true must be false. The assumption underlying relational databases, most forms of logical programming, OWL DL and OWL Lite.

controlled vocabularies Carefully selected sets of terms that are used to describe units of information; used to create thesauri, taxonomies and ontologies.

data warehouse A storage and retrieval system for enterprise information designed to centralize information from other stores to facilitate cross-system querying and reporting.

DBPedia An RDF representation of the metadata held in Wikipedia and made available for SPARQL query on the World Wide Web.

directed graph A graph in which the links between nodes are directional (they only go from one node to another). RDF represents things (nouns) and the relationships between them (verbs) in a directed graph. In RDF, the links are differentiated by being assigned URIs.

enterprise For the purposes of this book, any human organization that uses computer systems to store, retrieve and analyze information.

forward chaining A method of reasoning that begins with statements of all the relevant facts and infers new facts based on a set of rules. Equivalent to the logical operation *modus ponens*. The reverse of forward chaining is backward chaining.

graph A collection of objects (represented by "nodes") any of which may be connected by links between them. See directed graph.

Jena An Open Source Software implementation of a Semantic Web development framework. Supports the storage, retrieval and analysis of RDF information. See http://openjena.org and compare to Mulgara and Sesame.

linked data A pattern for hyperlinking machine-readable data sets to each other using Semantic Web techniques, especially via the use of RDF and URIs. Enables distributed SPARQL queries of the data sets and a "browsing" or "discovery" approach to finding information (as compared to a search strategy).

metadata Information used to administer, describe, preserve, present, use or link other information held in resources, especially knowledge resources, be they physical or virtual.

Mulgara An Open Source Software implementation of an RDF database. Supports the storage, retrieval and analysis of RDF information. See http://mulgara.org and compare to Jena and Sesame.

ontology A formal representation of relationships between items in a directed graph structure. See taxonomy.

open world The presumption that what is not known to be true may yet be true if additional information is later obtained. The assumption underlying RDF and OWL Full.

pattern A general reusable approach to solving a commonly occurring type of problem.

protocol A set of instructions for transferring data from one computer to another over a network. A protocol standard defines both message formats and the rules for sending and receiving those messages.

quad store A colloquial phrase for an RDF database that stores RDF triples plus an additional element of information, often used to collect statements into groups.

RDF database A type of database designed specifically to store and retrieve RDF information.

schema A data model that represents the relationships between a set of concepts. Some types of schemas include relational database schemas (which define how data is stored and retrieved), taxonomies and ontologies.

semantic technologies The broad set of technologies that relate to the extraction, representation, storage, retrieval and analysis of machine-readable information. The Semantic Web standards are a subset of semantic technologies and techniques.

Semantic Web An evolution or part of the World Wide Web that consists of machine-readable data in RDF and an ability to query that information in standard ways (e.g. via SPARQL).

Semantic Web standards Standards of the World Wide Web Consortium (W3C) relating to the Semantic Web, including RDF, RDFa, SKOS and OWL.

Sesame An Open Source Software implementation of a Semantic Web development framework. Supports the storage, retrieval and analysis of RDF information. See http://www.openrdf.org and compare to Jena and Mulgara.

taxonomy A formal representation of relationships between items in a hierarchical structure. See ontology.

Tbox One of two types of statements in an ontology (the other being Abox). Tbox statements describe a knowledge system in terms of controlled vocabularies (or "terminology", hence the "T"), e.g. A Person is a Mammal.

term For the purposes of this book, an entry in a controlled vocabulary, schema, taxonomy or ontology.

triple An RDF statement, consisting of two things (a "subject" and an "object") and a relationship between them (a verb, or "predicate"). This subject-predicate-object triple forms the smallest possible RDF graph (although most RDF graphs consist of many statements).

triple store A colloquial phrase for an RDF database that stores RDF triples.

tuple An ordered list of elements. RDF statements are 3-tuples; an ordered list of three elements.

Turtle An RDF serialization format, designed to be easier to read than others such as RDF/XML. A subset of N3.

Web 2.0 A colloquial description of the part of the World Wide Web that implements social networking, blogs, user comments and ratings and related human-centered activities.

Web 3.0 A colloquial description of the part of the World Wide Web that implements machine-readable data and the ability to perform distributed queries and analysis on that data. Considered synonymous with the phrases "Semantic Web" and "The Web of Data".

Index

Breinigsville, PA USA
28 November 2010
250090BV00002B/21/P